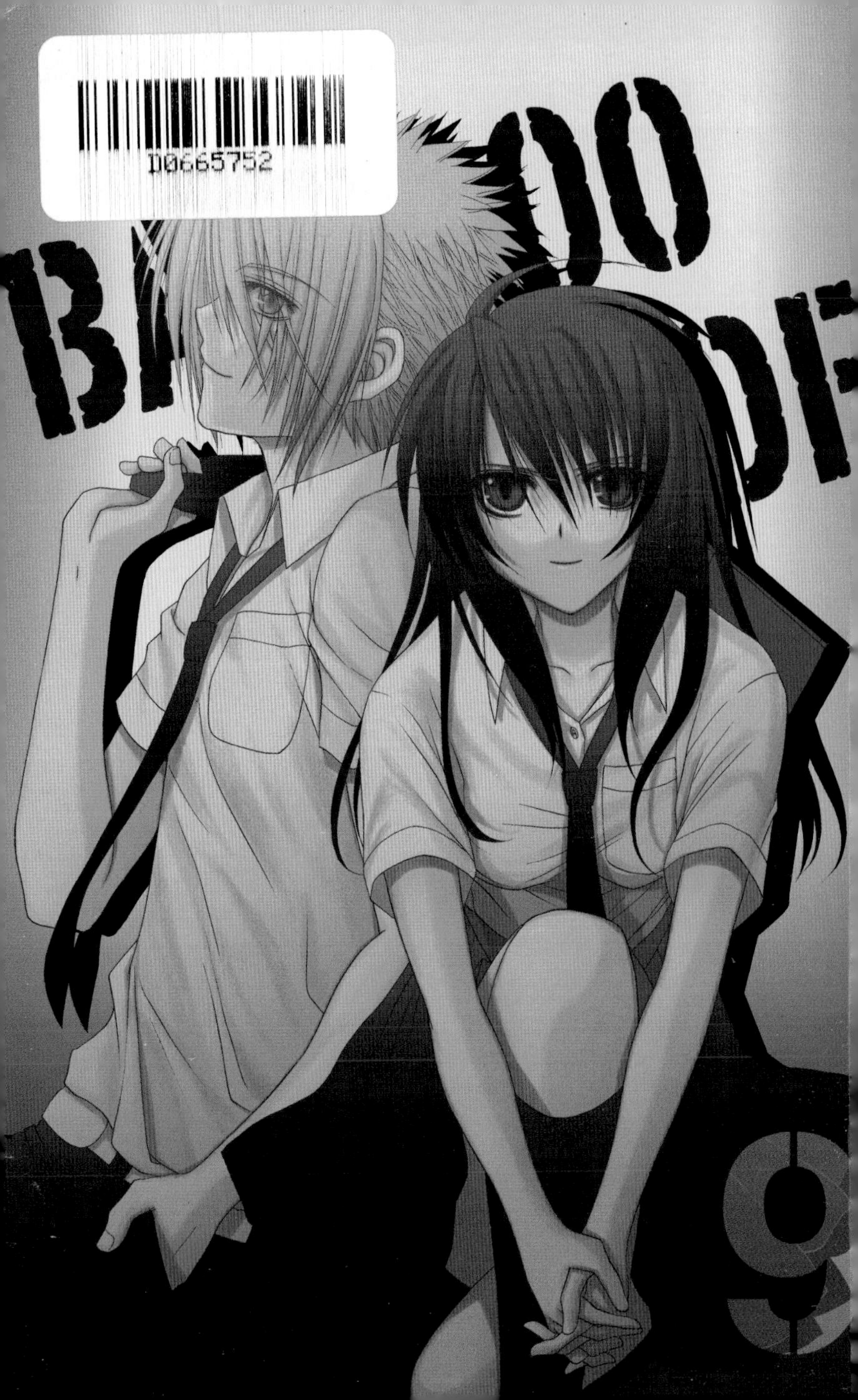
9

BAMBOO BLADE 9
CONTENTS

Story: Masahiro Totsuka / Art: Aguri Igarashi

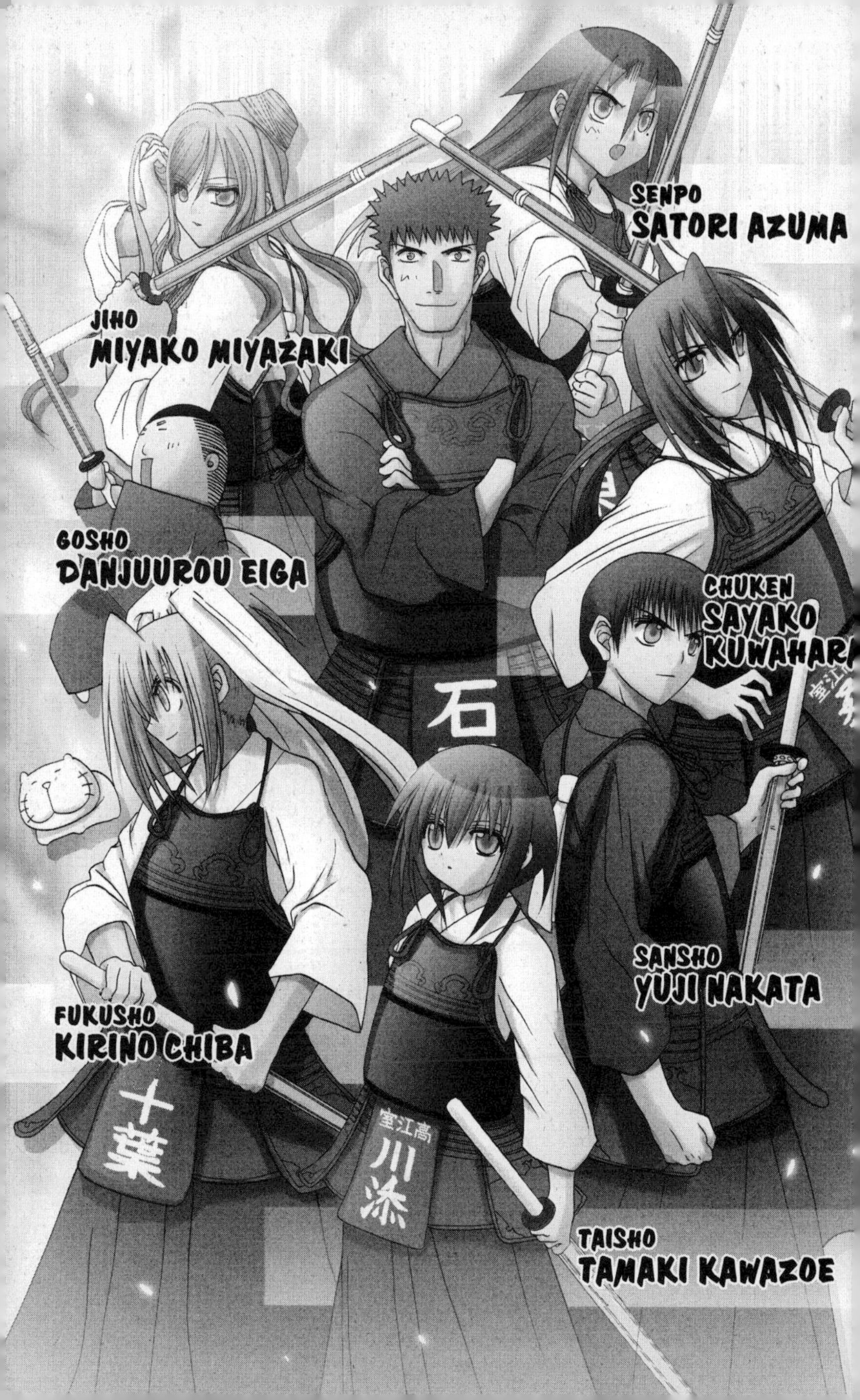
SENPO
SATORI AZUMA
JIHO
MIYAKO MIYAZAKI
GOSHO
DANJUUROU EIGA
CHUKEN
SAYAKO KUWAHARA
石
SANSHO
YUJI NAKATA
FUKUSHO
KIRINO CHIBA
室江高
川添
TAISHO
TAMAKI KAWAZOE

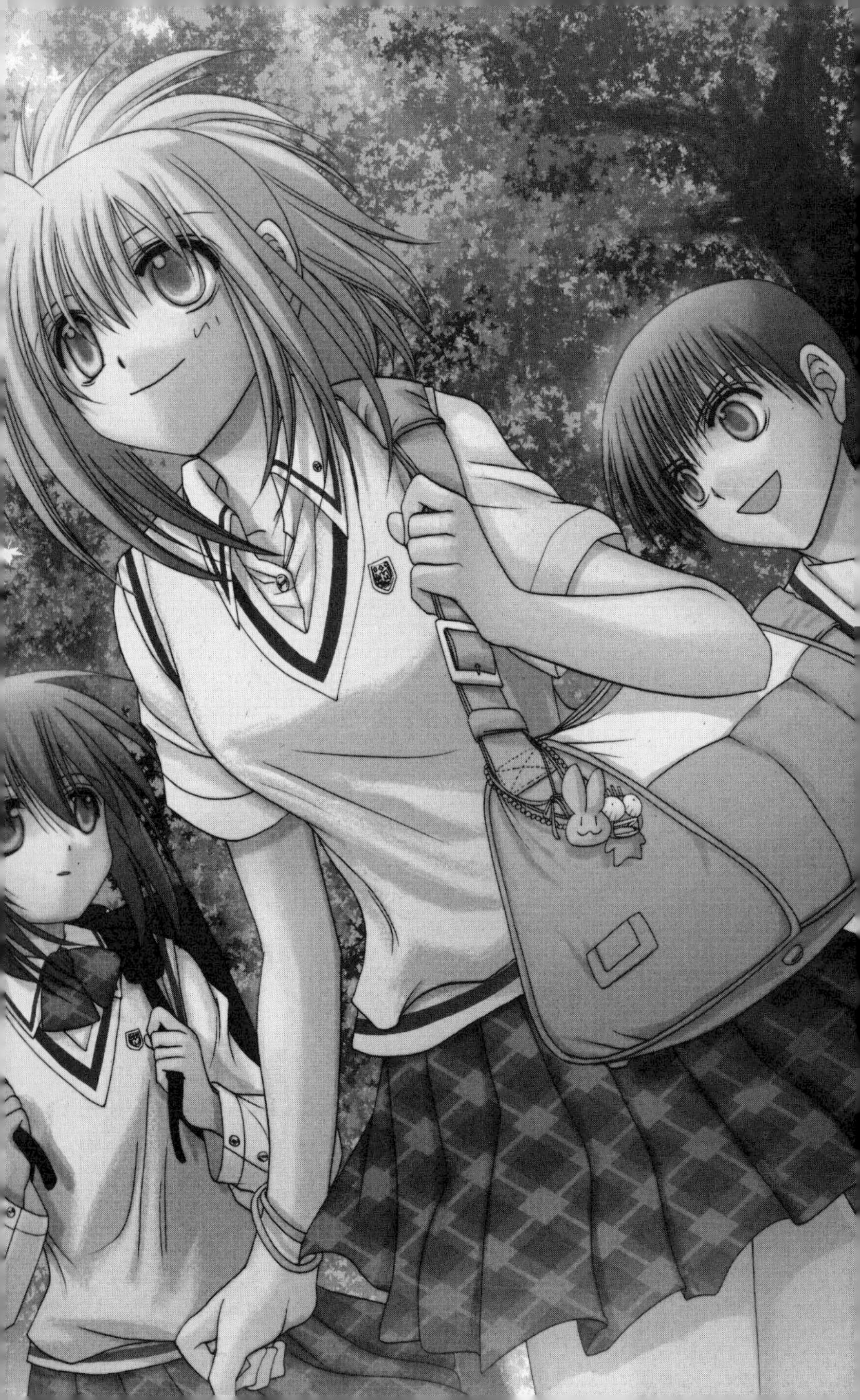

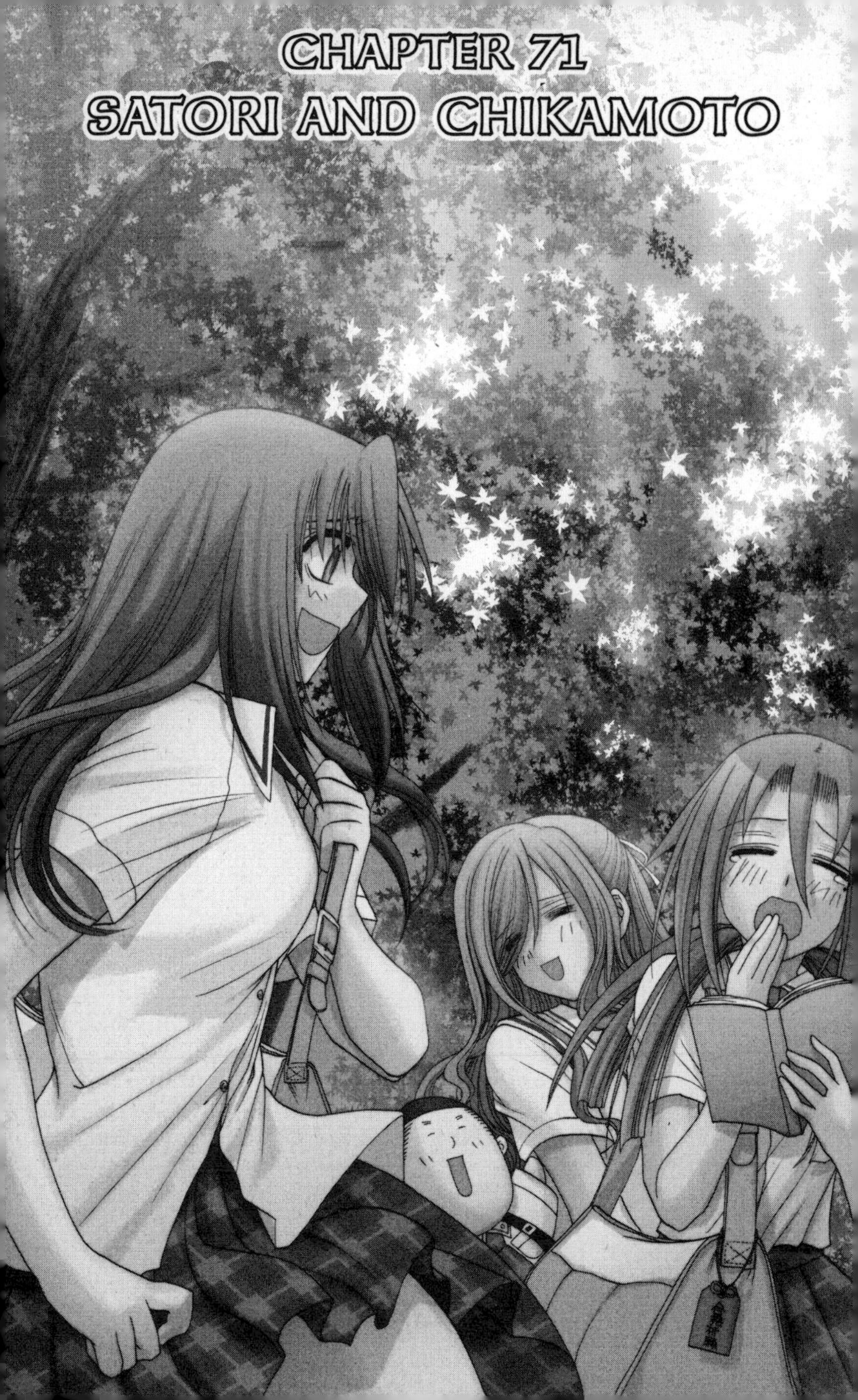
CHAPTER 71
SATORI AND CHIKAMOTO

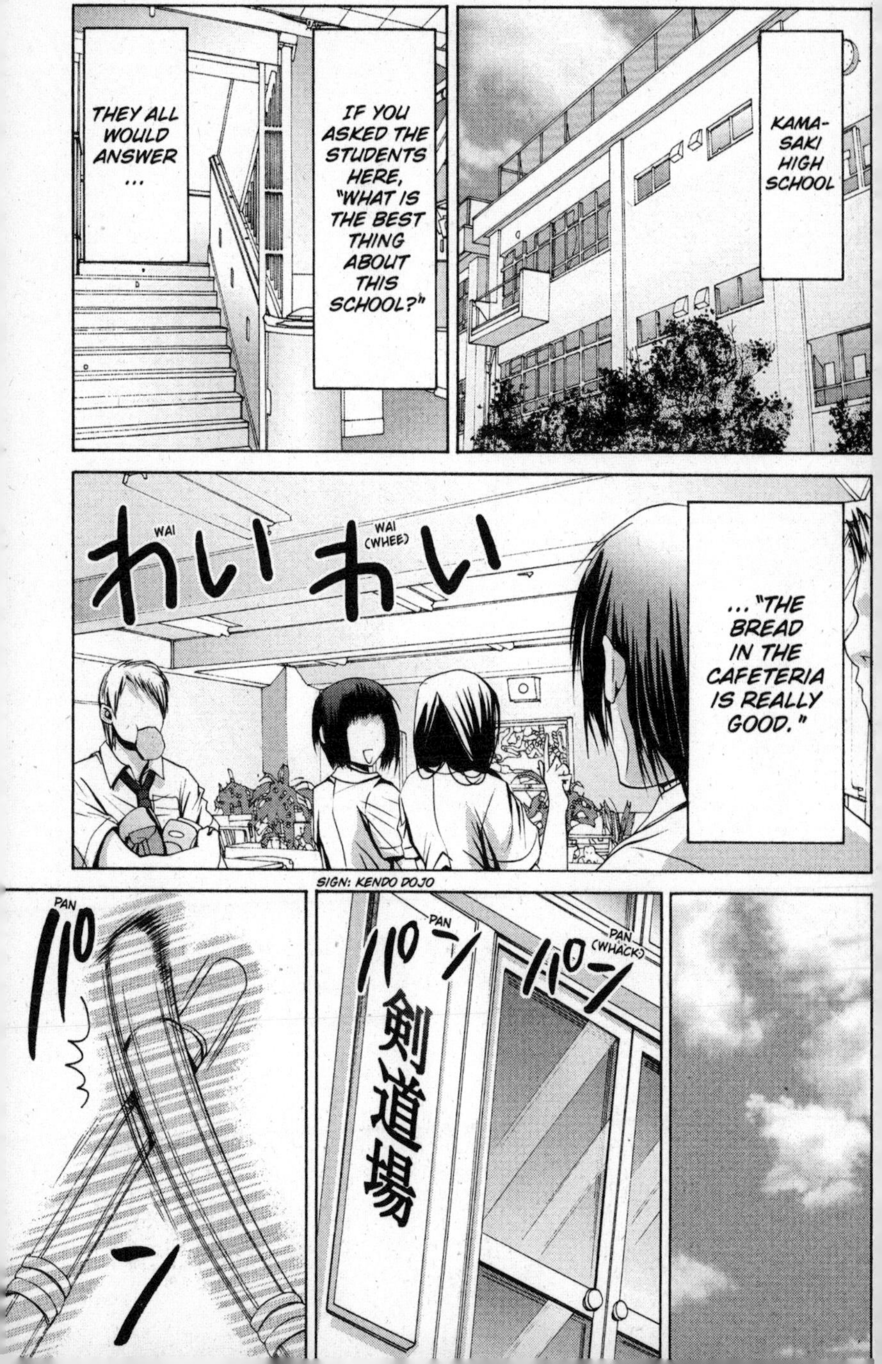
KAMA-SAKI HIGH SCHOOL
IF YOU ASKED THE STUDENTS HERE, "WHAT IS THE BEST THING ABOUT THIS SCHOOL?"
THEY ALL WOULD ANSWER ...
... "THE BREAD IN THE CAFETERIA IS REALLY GOOD."
わい
WAI (WHEE)
わい
WAI
SIGN: KENDO DOJO
パーン
PAN (WHACK)
パーン
PAN
剣道場
パーン
PAN

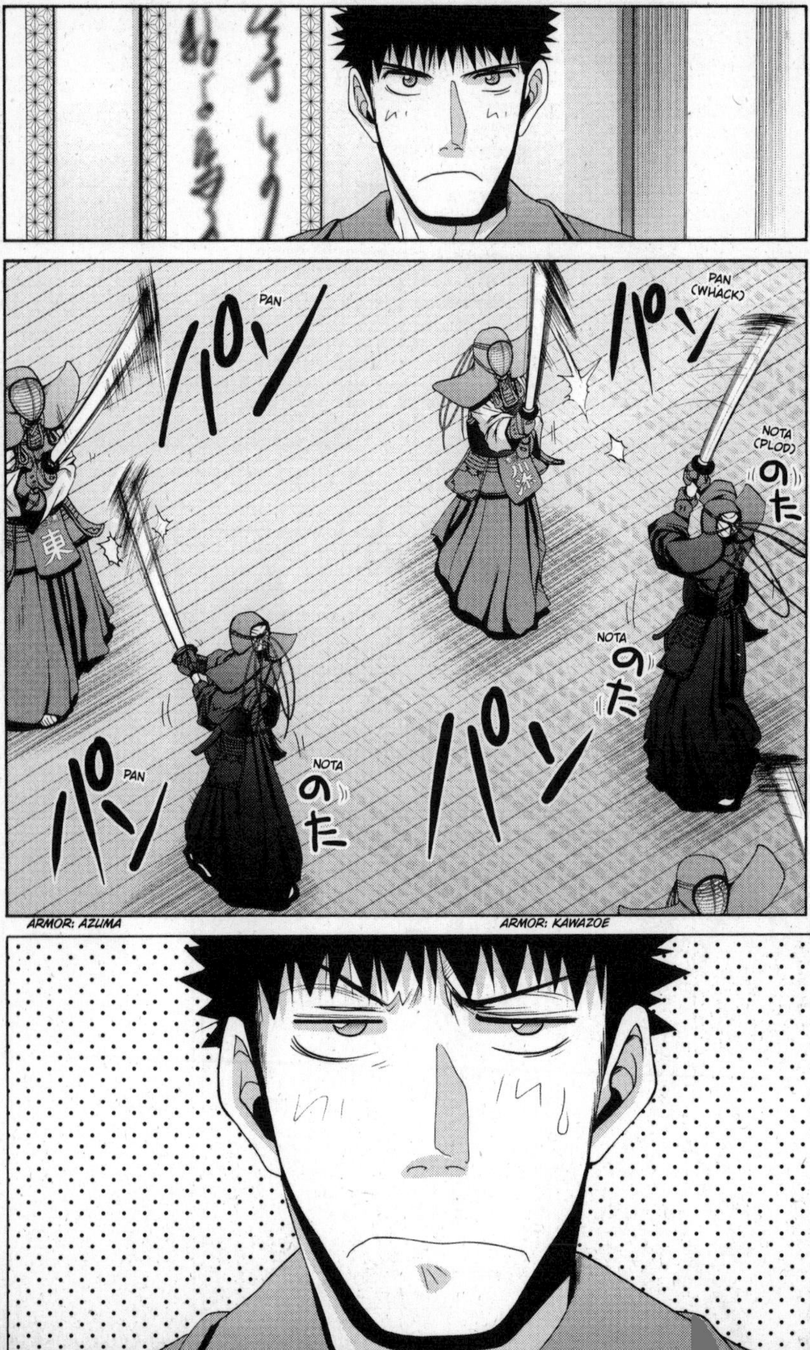

パン
PAN (WHACK)
のた
NOTA (PLOD)
のた
NOTA
パン
パン
PAN
のた
NOTA
パン
PAN
ARMOR: KAWAZOE
ARMOR: AZUMA

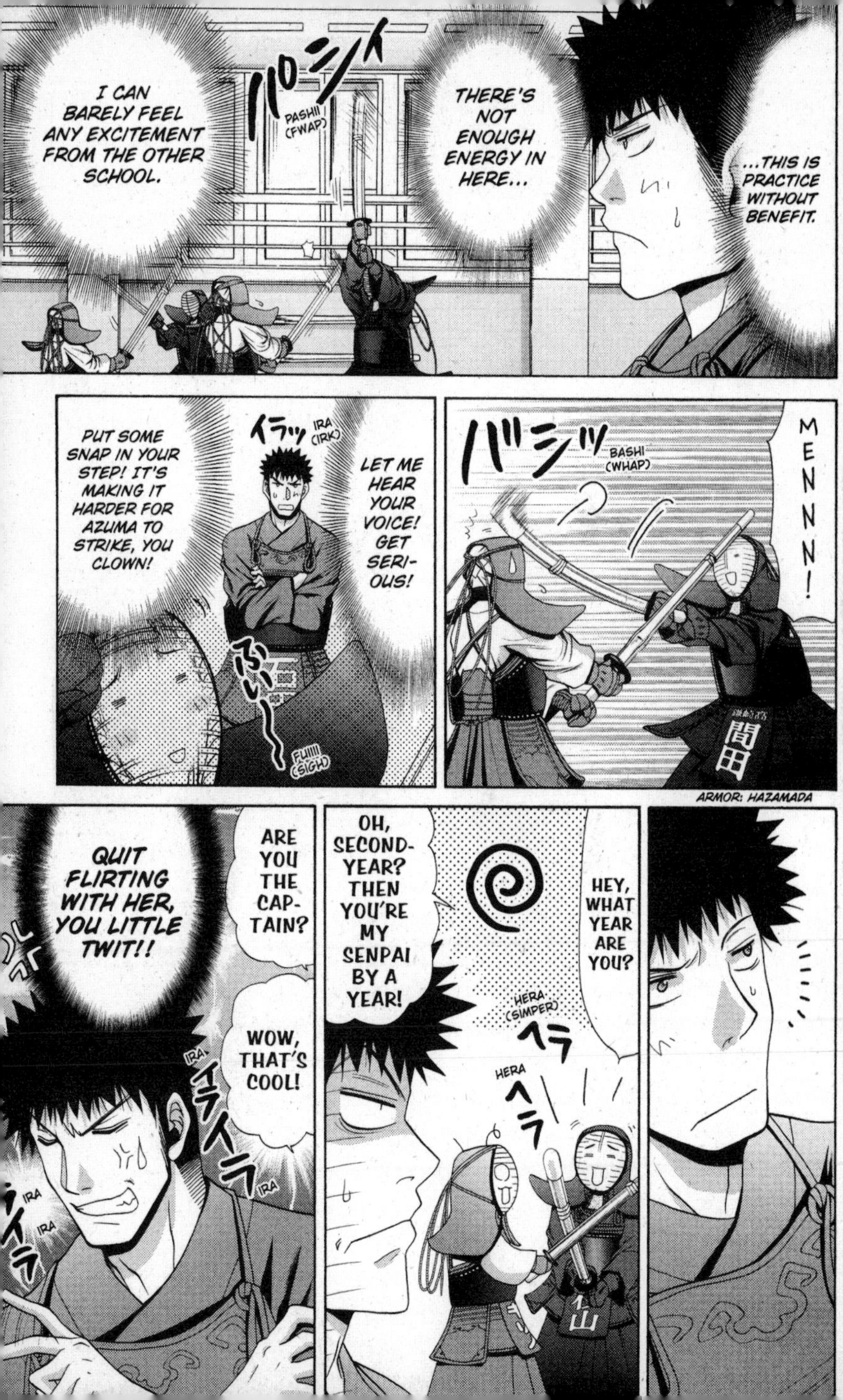
THERE'S NOT ENOUGH ENERGY IN HERE...
...THIS IS PRACTICE WITHOUT BENEFIT.
PASHII (FWAP)
I CAN BARELY FEEL ANY EXCITEMENT FROM THE OTHER SCHOOL.
MENNNN!
BASHI (WHAP)
ARMOR: HAZAMADA
LET ME HEAR YOUR VOICE! GET SERI-OUS!
IRA (IRK)
PUT SOME SNAP IN YOUR STEP! IT'S MAKING IT HARDER FOR AZUMA TO STRIKE, YOU CLOWN!
FUIII (SIGH)
HEY, WHAT YEAR ARE YOU?
OH, SECOND-YEAR? THEN YOU'RE MY SENPAI BY A YEAR!
HERA (SIMPER)
HERA
ARE YOU THE CAP-TAIN?
WOW, THAT'S COOL!
QUIT FLIRTING WITH HER, YOU LITTLE TWIT!!
IRA
IRA
IRA
IRA

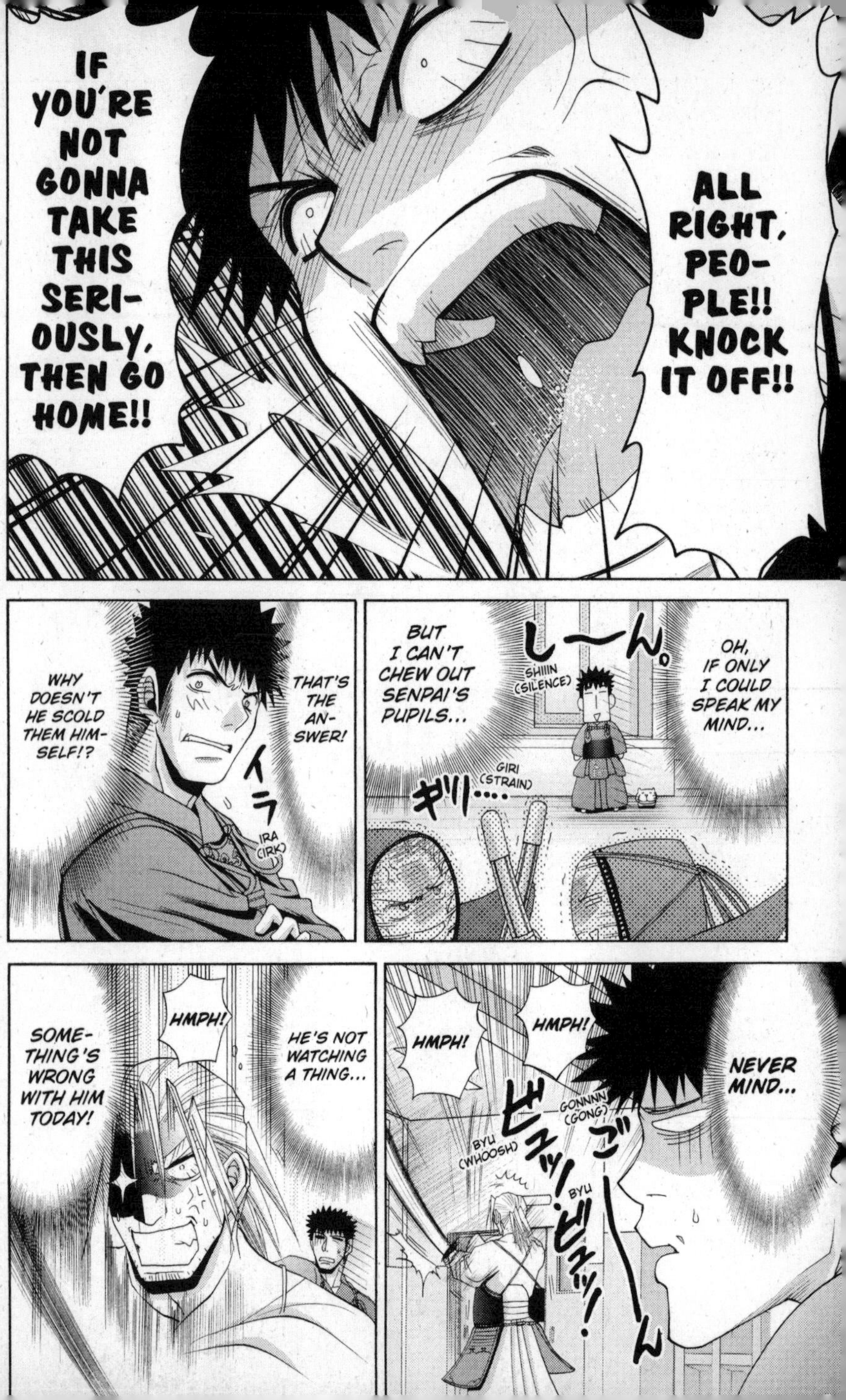
ALL RIGHT, PEOPLE!! KNOCK IT OFF!!
IF YOU'RE NOT GONNA TAKE THIS SERIOUSLY, THEN GO HOME!!
OH, IF ONLY I COULD SPEAK MY MIND...
しーん。
SHIIIN (SILENCE)
BUT I CAN'T CHEW OUT SENPAI'S PUPILS...
GIRI (STRAIN)
ギリ....
THAT'S THE ANSWER!
WHY DOESN'T HE SCOLD THEM HIMSELF!?
イラ
IRA (IRK)
NEVER MIND...
HMPH!
HMPH!
GONNNN (GONG)
BYU (WHOOSH)
BYU
HMPH!
HE'S NOT WATCHING A THING...
SOMETHING'S WRONG WITH HIM TODAY!

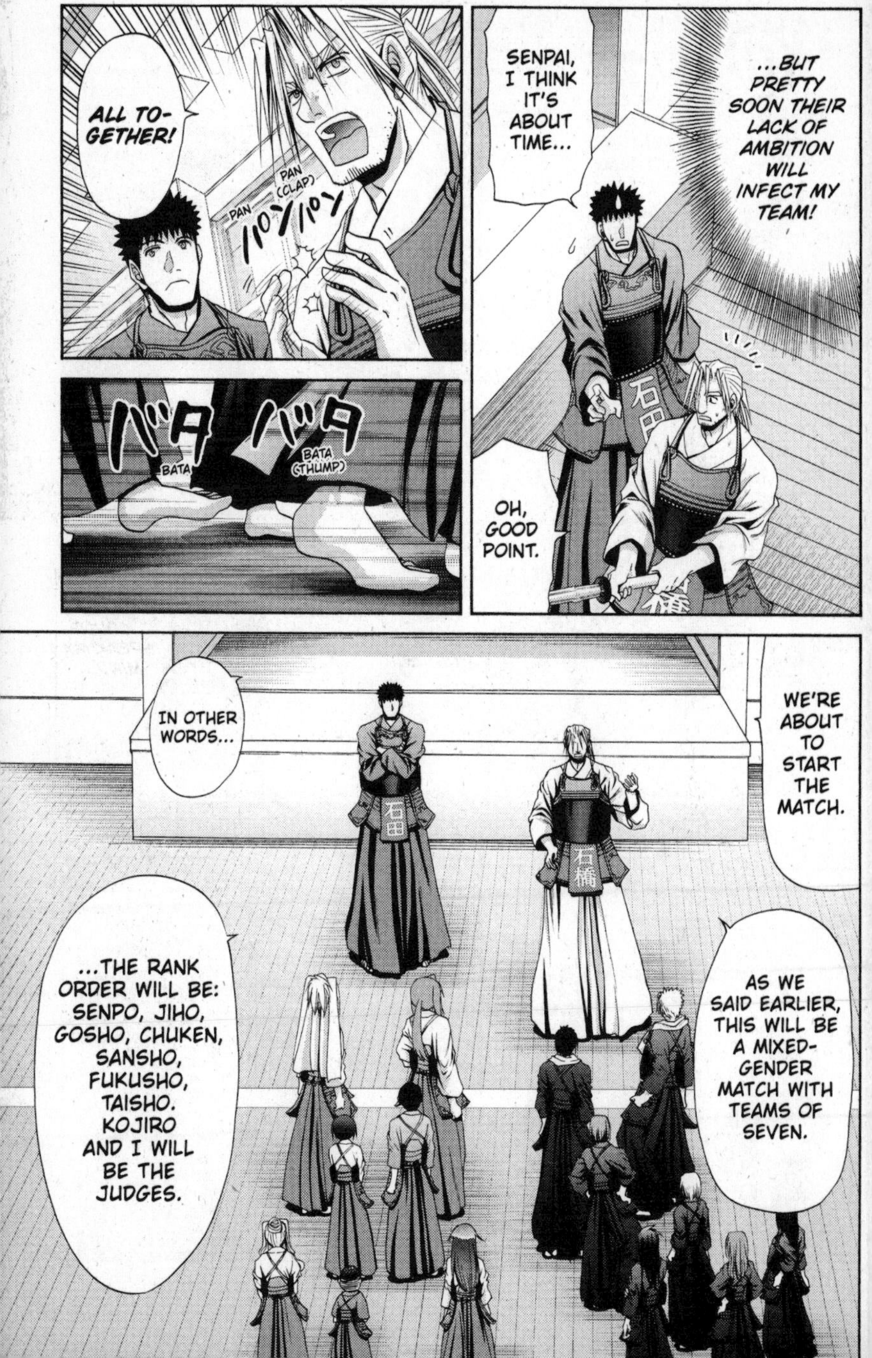
...BUT PRETTY SOON THEIR LACK OF AMBITION WILL INFECT MY TEAM!
SENPAI, I THINK IT'S ABOUT TIME...
石田
OH, GOOD POINT.
ALL TO-GETHER!
パンパン
PAN PAN (CLAP)
バタ バタ
BATA BATA (THUMP)
WE'RE ABOUT TO START THE MATCH.
IN OTHER WORDS...
石田
石橋
AS WE SAID EARLIER, THIS WILL BE A MIXED-GENDER MATCH WITH TEAMS OF SEVEN.
...THE RANK ORDER WILL BE: SENPO, JIHO, GOSHO, CHUKEN, SANSHO, FUKUSHO, TAISHO. KOJIRO AND I WILL BE THE JUDGES.

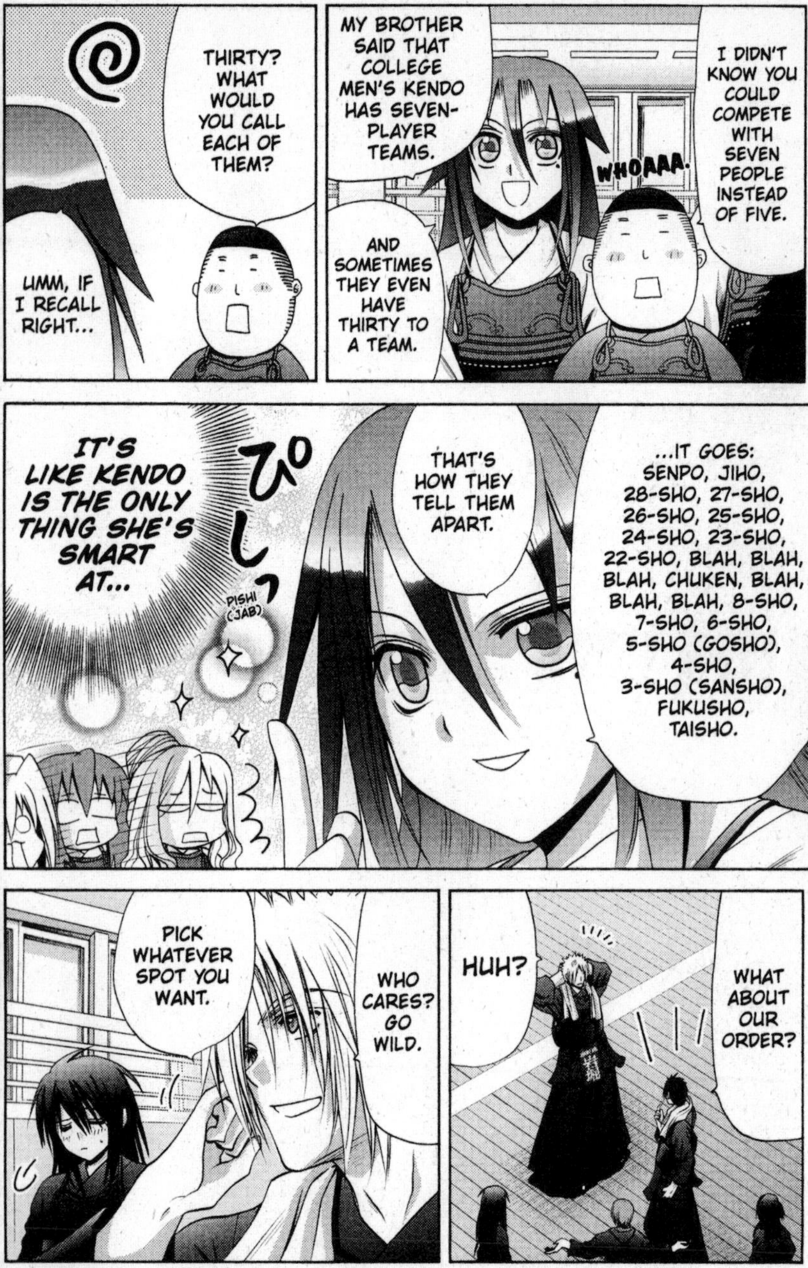
I DIDN'T KNOW YOU COULD COMPETE WITH SEVEN PEOPLE INSTEAD OF FIVE.
WHOAAA.
MY BROTHER SAID THAT COLLEGE MEN'S KENDO HAS SEVEN-PLAYER TEAMS.
AND SOMETIMES THEY EVEN HAVE THIRTY TO A TEAM.
THIRTY? WHAT WOULD YOU CALL EACH OF THEM?
UMM, IF I RECALL RIGHT...
...IT GOES: SENPO, JIHO, 28-SHO, 27-SHO, 26-SHO, 25-SHO, 24-SHO, 23-SHO, 22-SHO, BLAH, BLAH, BLAH, CHUKEN, BLAH, BLAH, BLAH, 8-SHO, 7-SHO, 6-SHO, 5-SHO (GOSHO), 4-SHO, 3-SHO (SANSHO), FUKUSHO, TAISHO.
THAT'S HOW THEY TELL THEM APART.
PISHI (JAB)
IT'S LIKE KENDO IS THE ONLY THING SHE'S SMART AT...
WHAT ABOUT OUR ORDER?
HUH?
WHO CARES? GO WILD.
PICK WHATEVER SPOT YOU WANT.

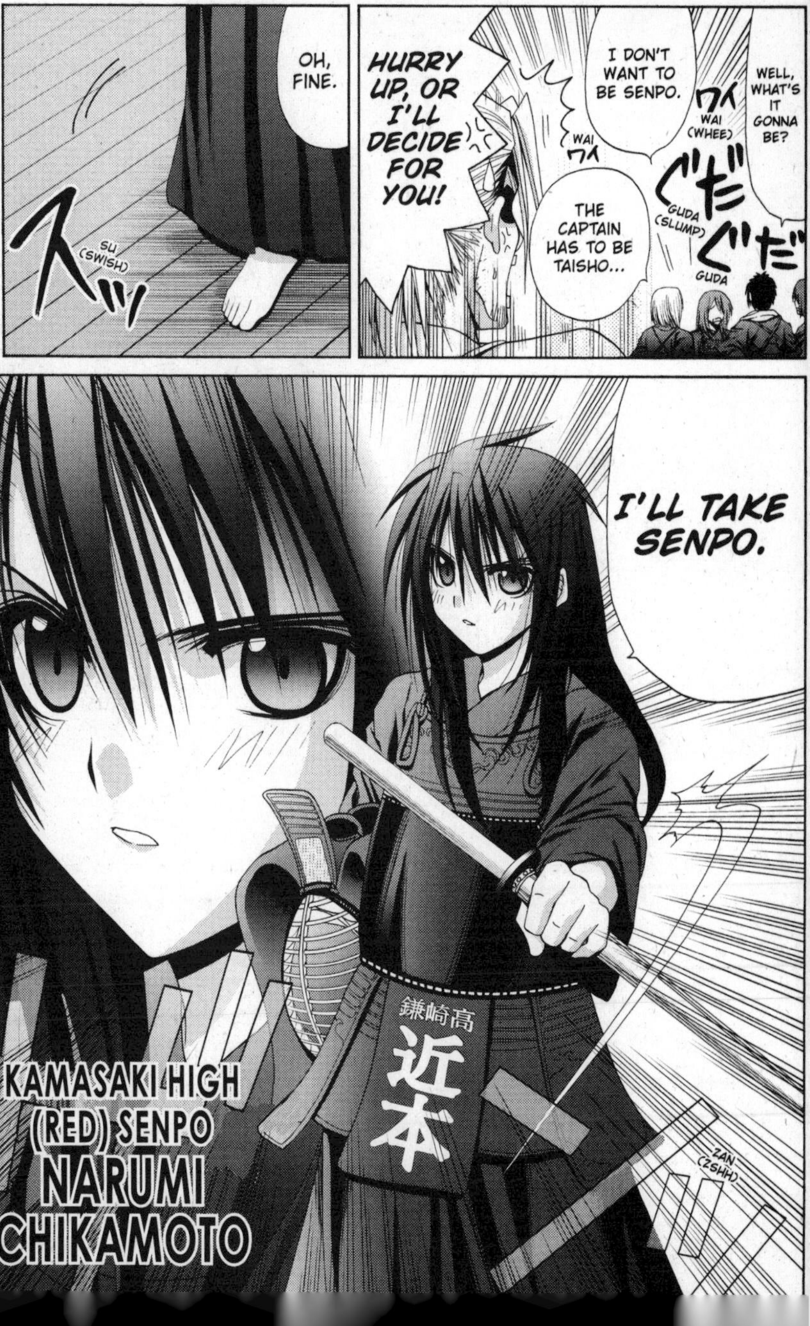
WELL, WHAT'S IT GONNA BE?
I DON'T WANT TO BE SENPO.
WAI (WHEE)
GUDA (SLUMP)
GUDA
THE CAPTAIN HAS TO BE TAISHO...
WAI
HURRY UP, OR I'LL DECIDE FOR YOU!
OH, FINE.
SU (SWISH)
I'LL TAKE SENPO.
ZAN (ZSHH)
鎌崎高
近本
KAMASAKI HIGH (RED) SENPO
NARUMI CHIKAMOTO

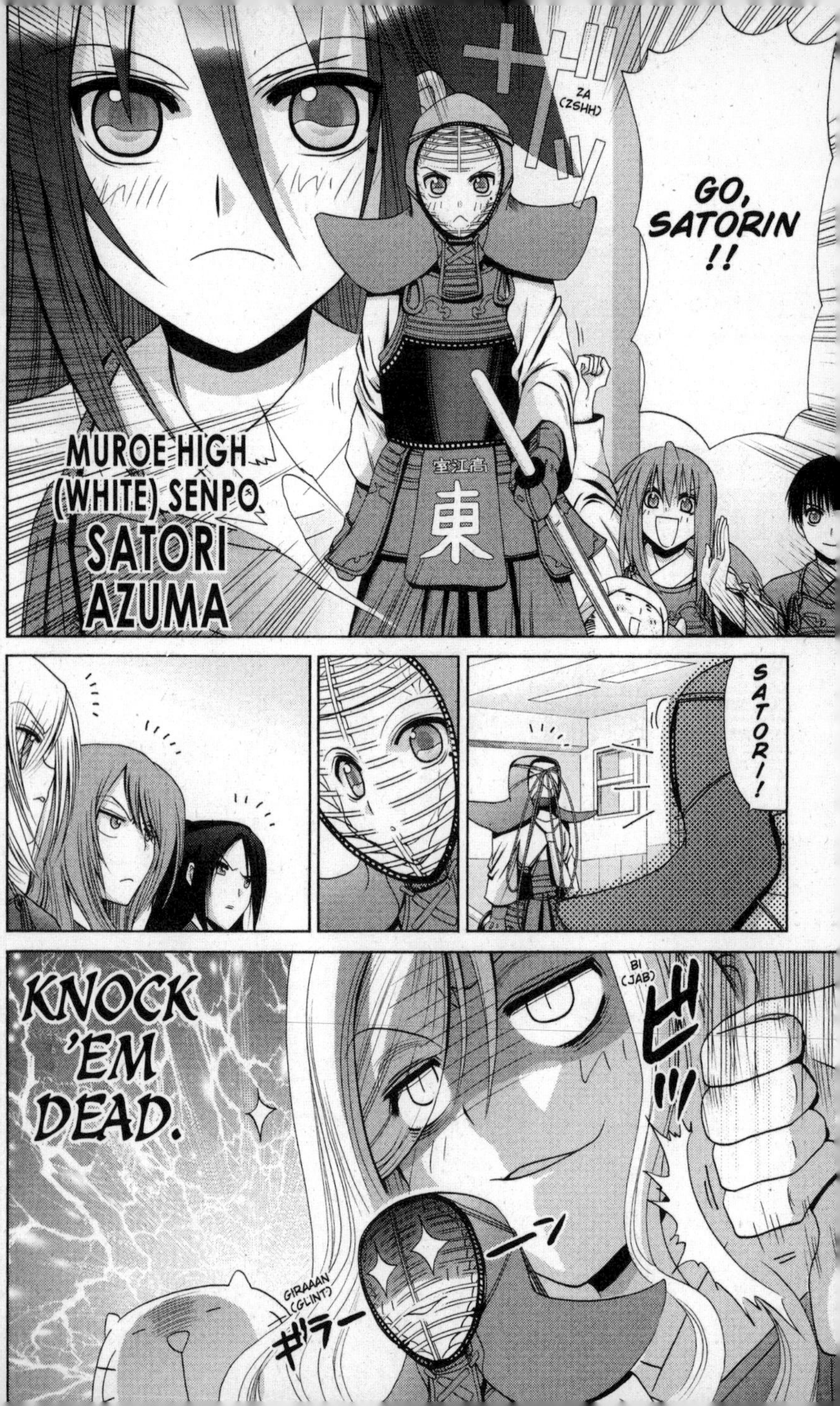
GO, SATORIN !!
ZA (ZSHH)
MUROE HIGH (WHITE) SENPO, SATORI AZUMA
SATORI!
BI (JAB)
KNOCK 'EM DEAD.
GIRAAAN (GLINT)

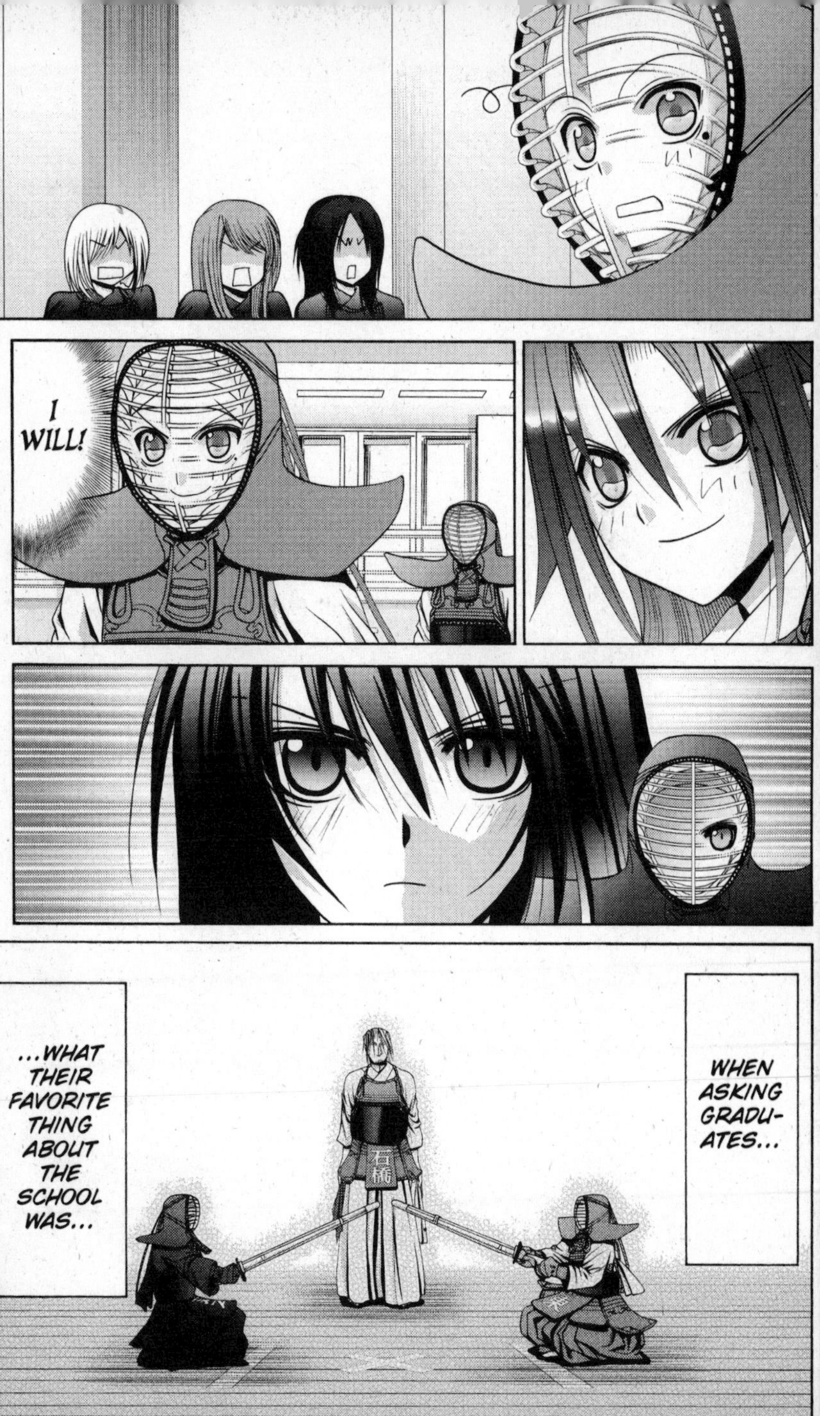
I WILL!
WHEN ASKING GRADU-ATES...
...WHAT THEIR FAVORITE THING ABOUT THE SCHOOL WAS...

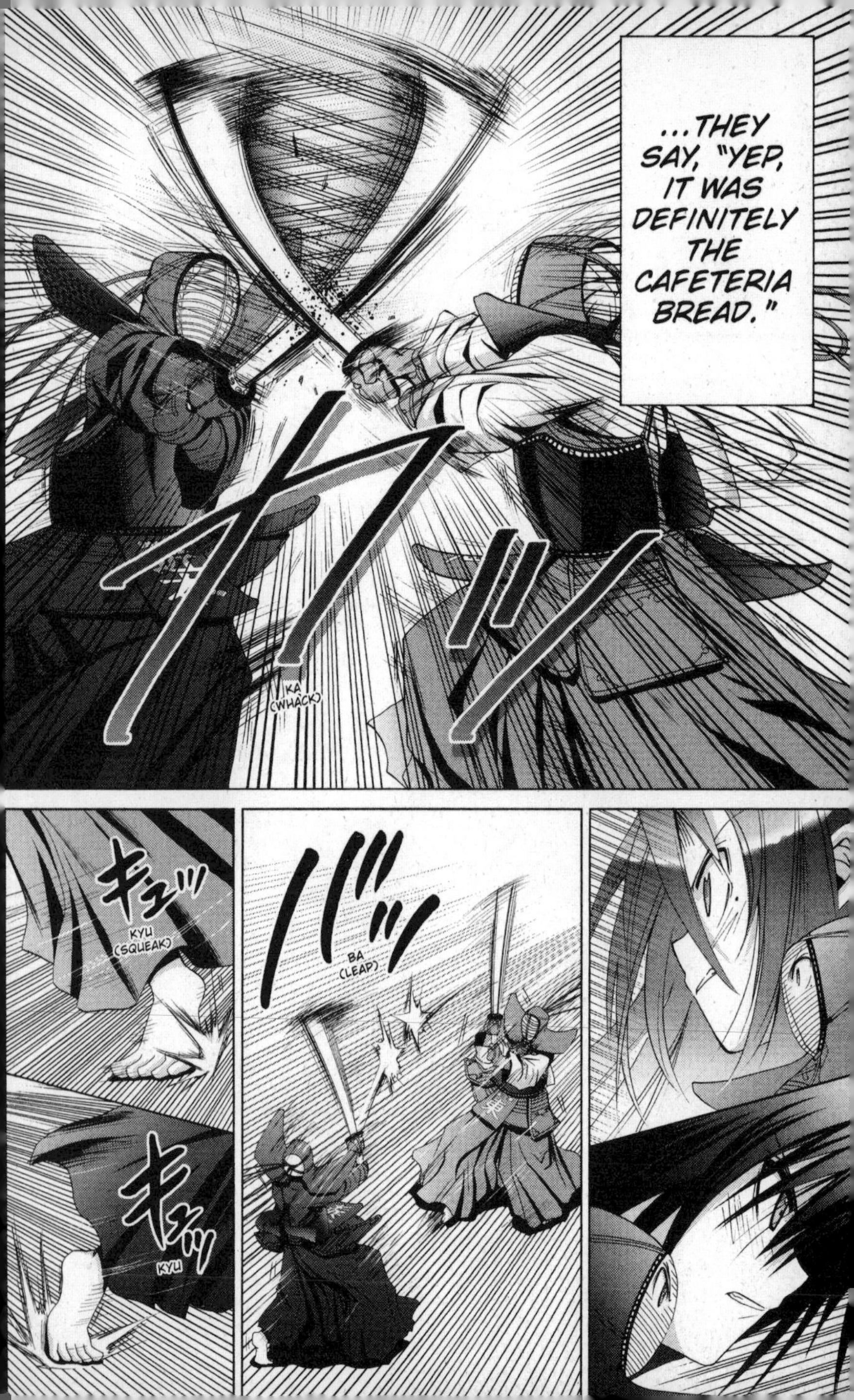
...THEY SAY, "YEP, IT WAS DEFINITELY THE CAFETERIA BREAD."
KA (WHACK)
BA (LEAP)
KYU (SQUEAK)
KYU

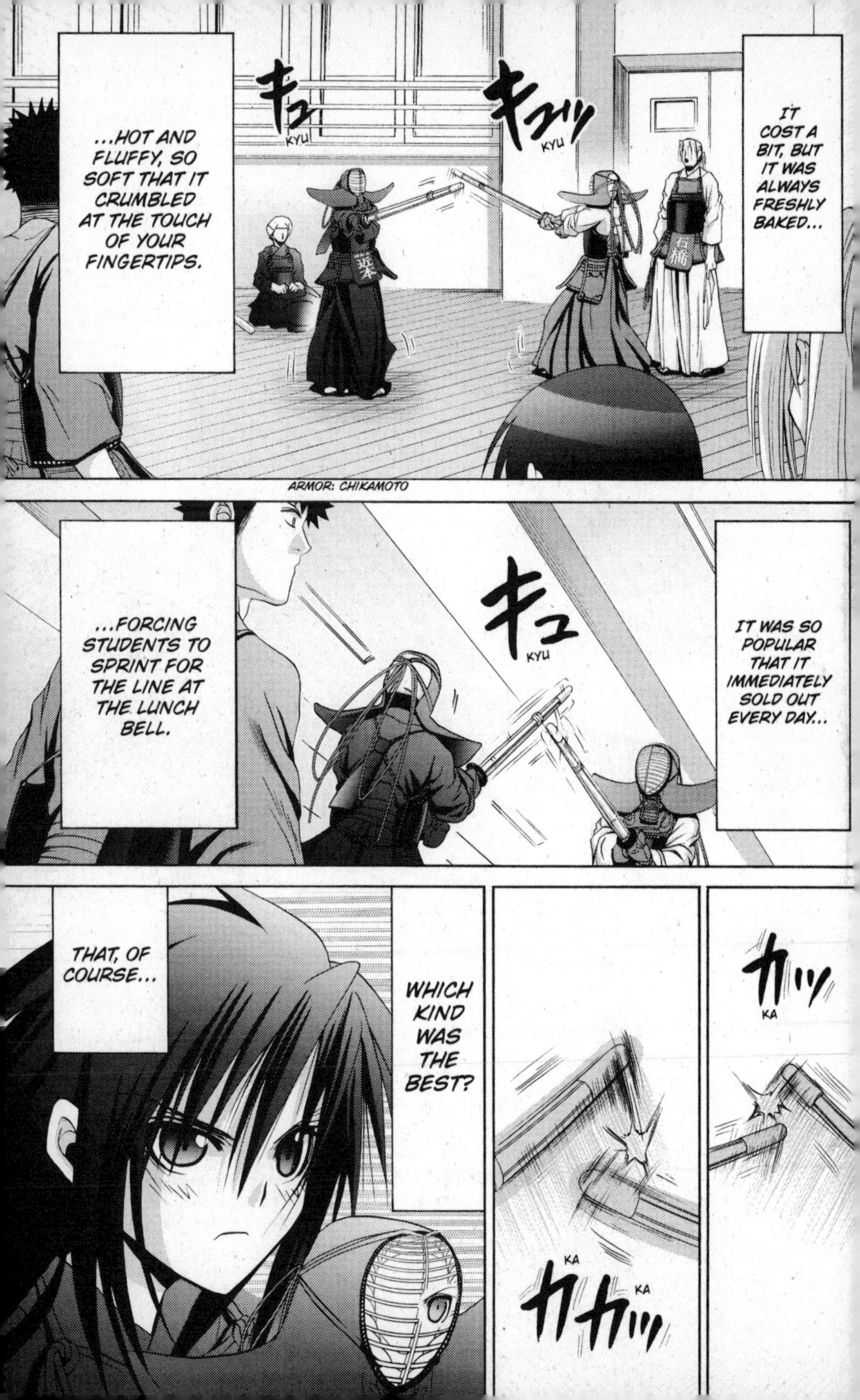
IT COST A BIT, BUT IT WAS ALWAYS FRESHLY BAKED...
KYU
KYU
...HOT AND FLUFFY, SO SOFT THAT IT CRUMBLED AT THE TOUCH OF YOUR FINGERTIPS.
ARMOR: CHIKAMOTO
IT WAS SO POPULAR THAT IT IMMEDIATELY SOLD OUT EVERY DAY...
KYU
...FORCING STUDENTS TO SPRINT FOR THE LINE AT THE LUNCH BELL.
KA
KA
KA
WHICH KIND WAS THE BEST?
THAT, OF COURSE...

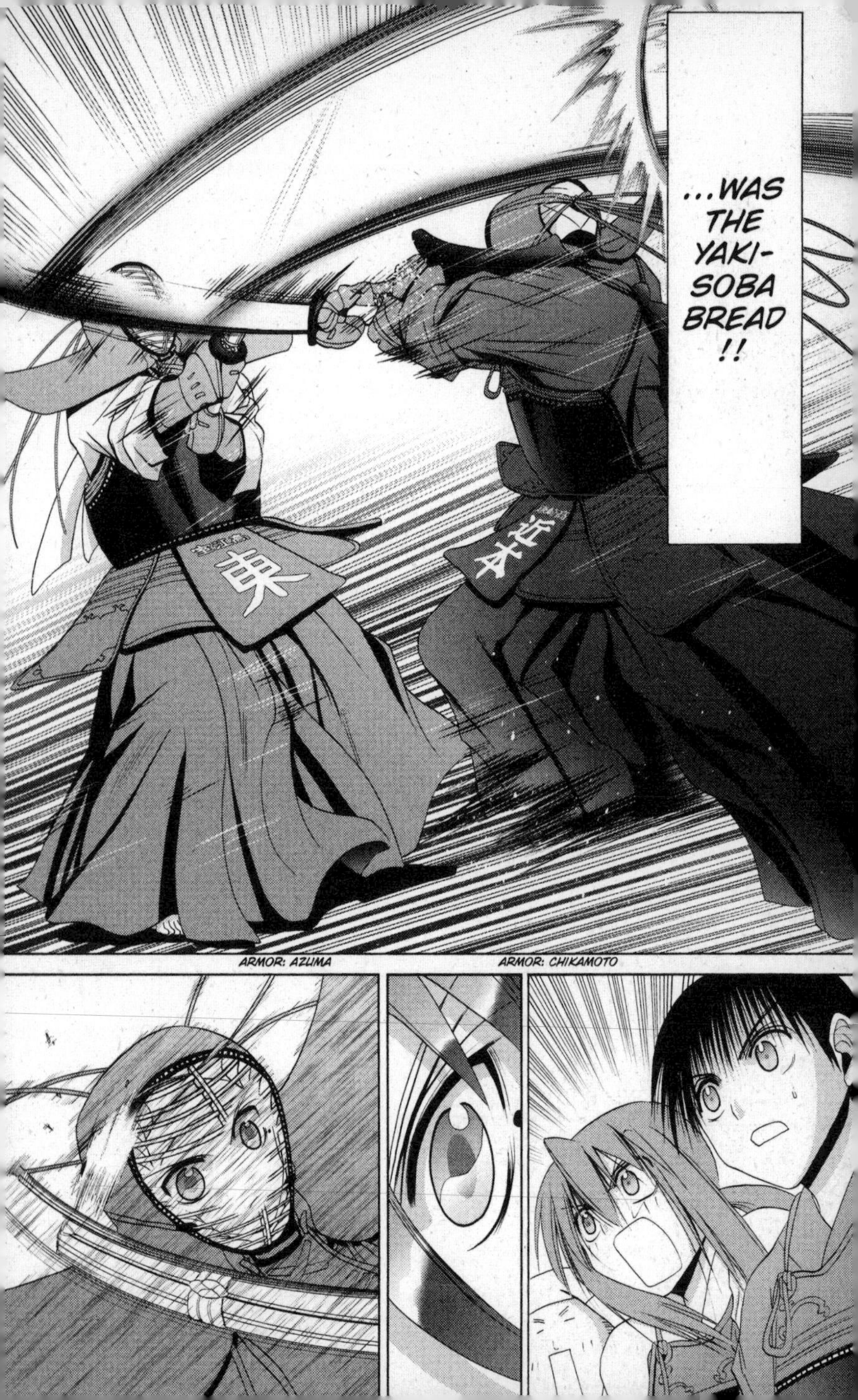
...WAS THE YAKI-SOBA BREAD !!
近本
東
ARMOR: CHIKAMOTO
ARMOR: AZUMA

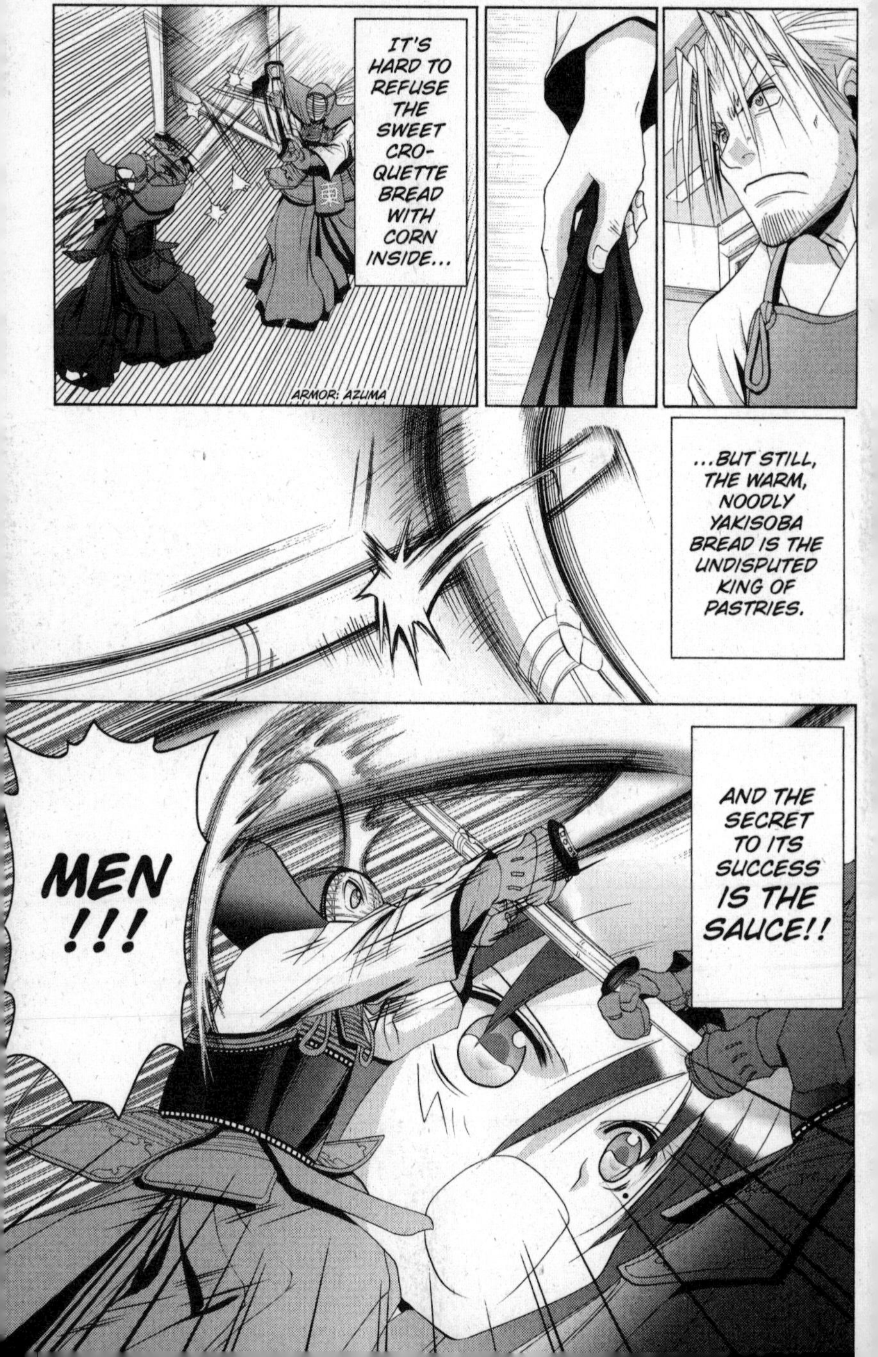
IT'S HARD TO REFUSE THE SWEET CRO-QUETTE BREAD WITH CORN INSIDE...
ARMOR: AZUMA
...BUT STILL, THE WARM, NOODLY YAKISOBA BREAD IS THE UNDISPUTED KING OF PASTRIES.
AND THE SECRET TO ITS SUCCESS IS THE SAUCE!!
MEN !!!

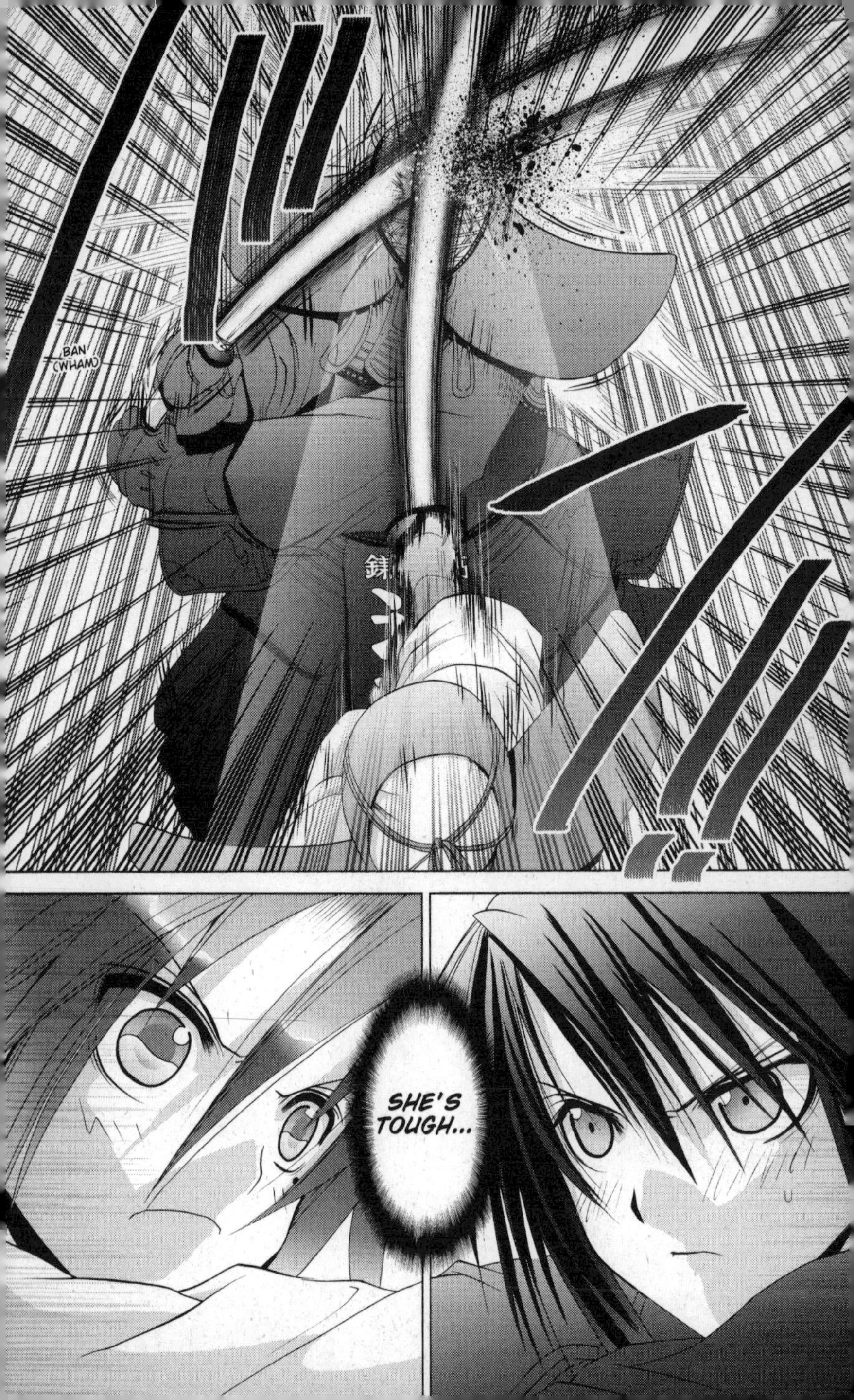
BAN (WHAM)
SHE'S TOUGH...

BAMBOO BLADE
バンブーブレード

BAMBOO BLADE
バンブーブレード

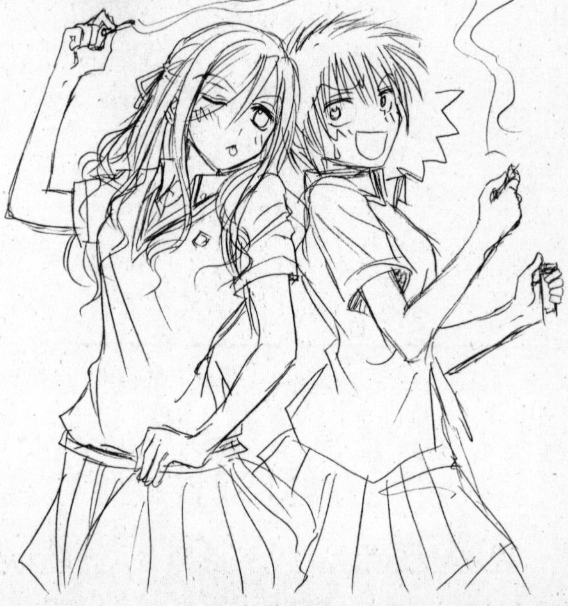

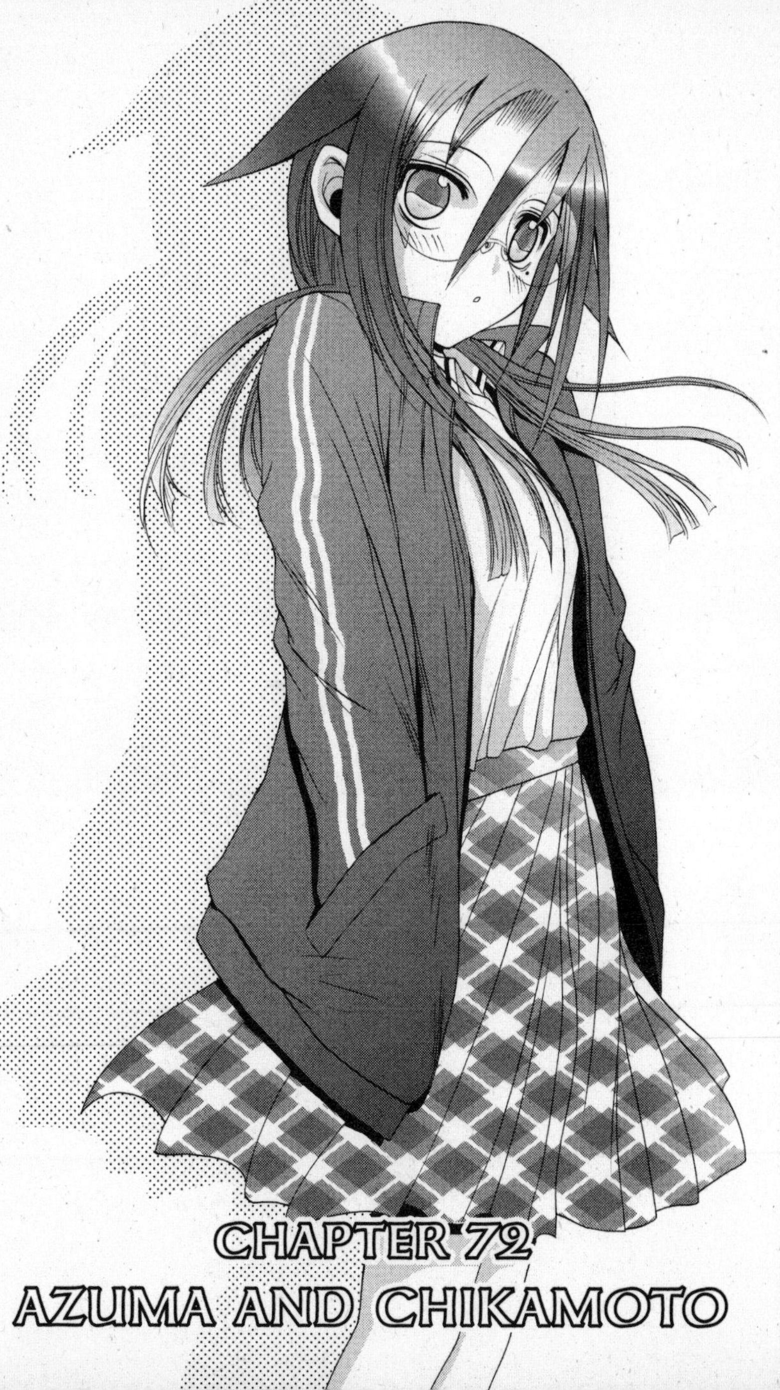

CHAPTER 72
AZUMA AND CHIKAMOTO

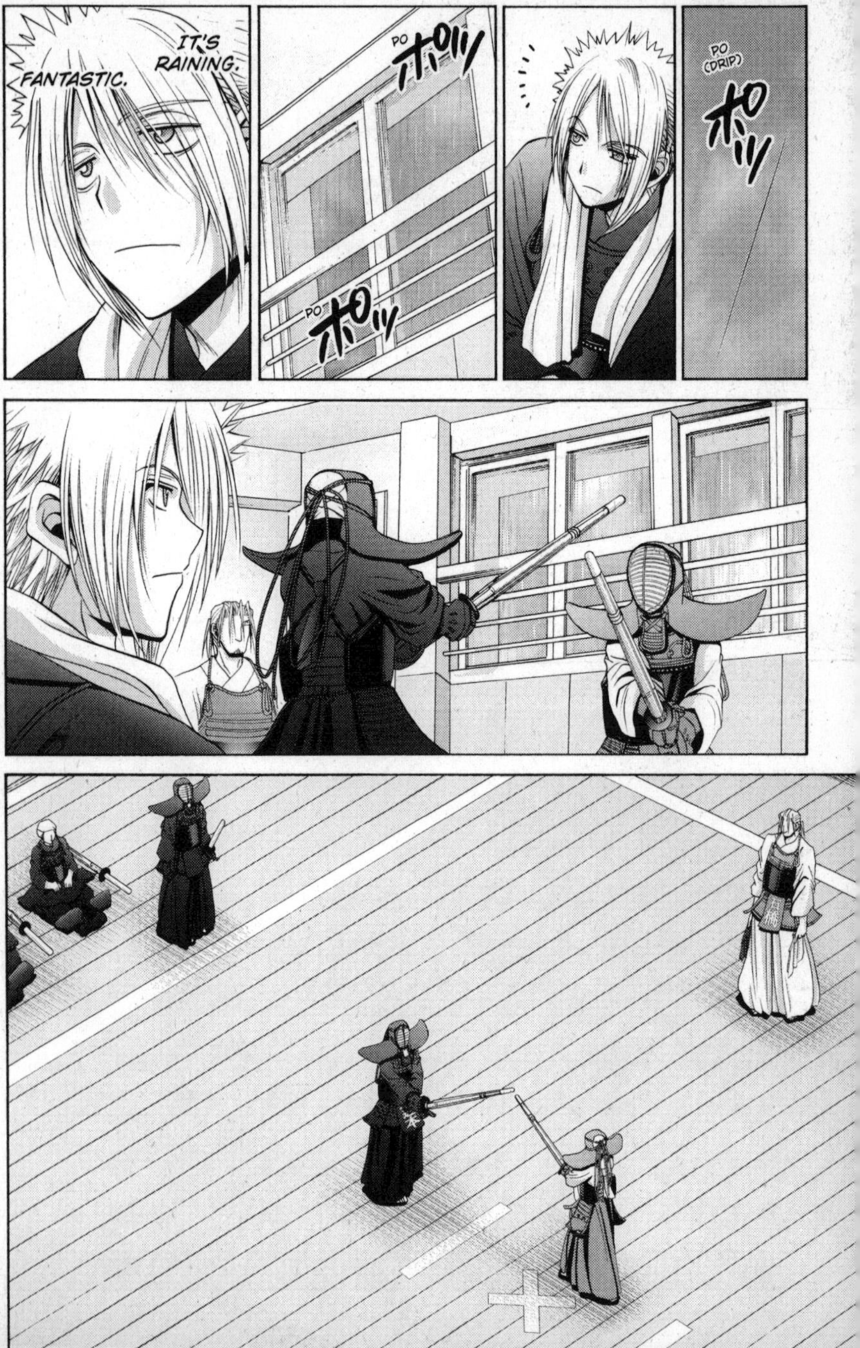
PO (DRIP)
PO
PO
IT'S RAINING.
FANTASTIC.

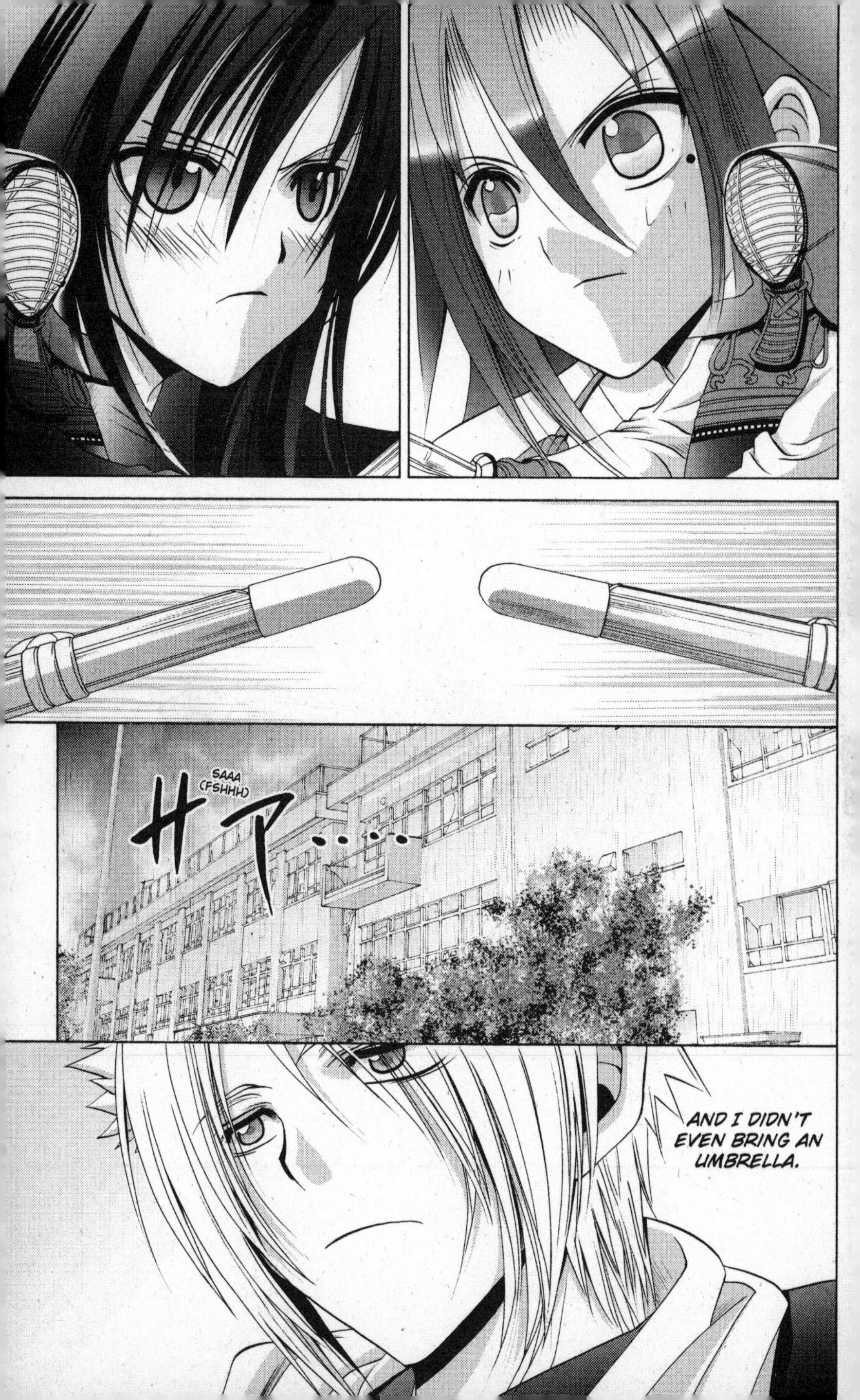
SAAA
(FSHHH)
サァ・・・
AND I DIDN'T EVEN BRING AN UMBRELLA.

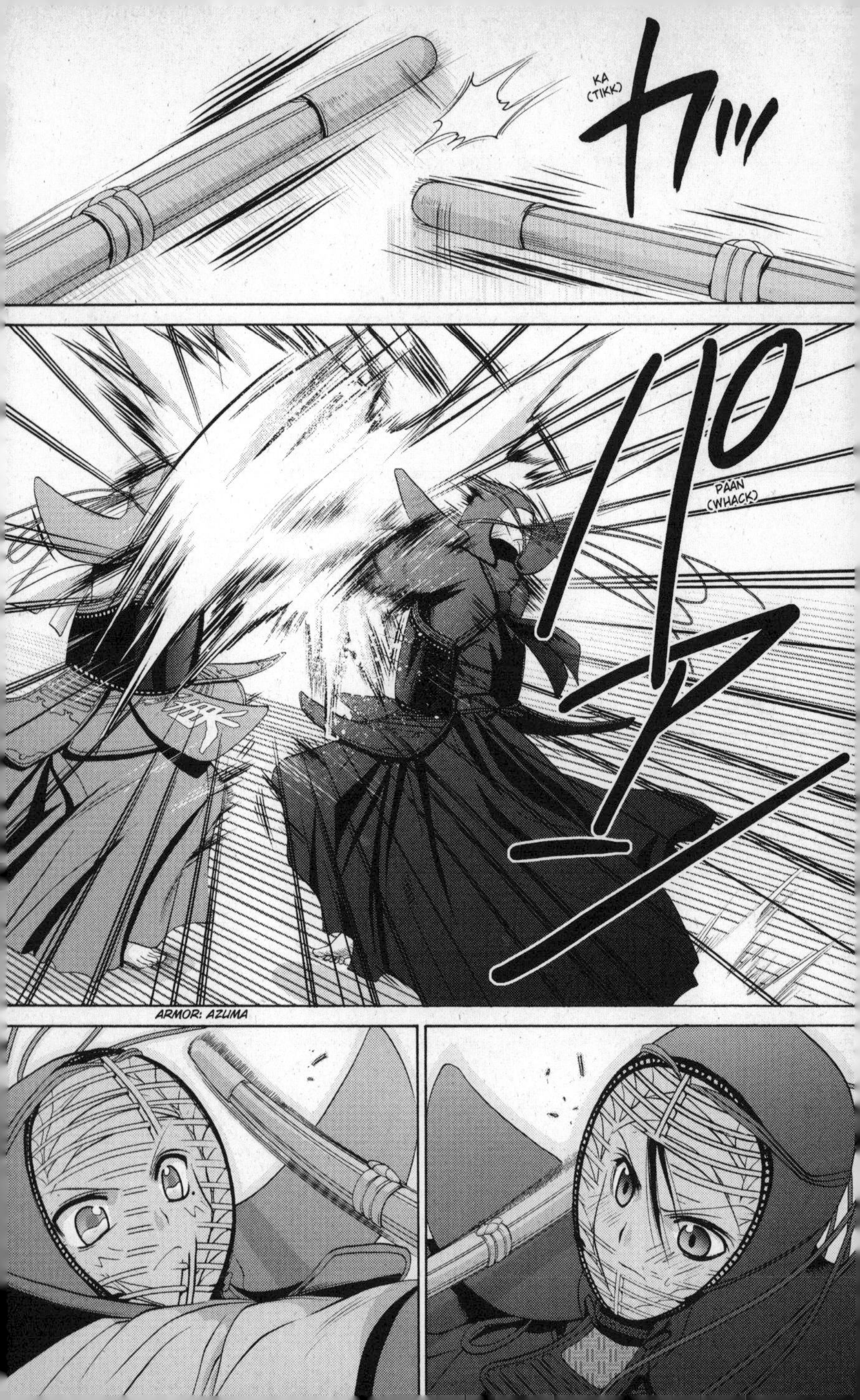
カッ
KA
(TIKK)
パァーン
PAAN
(WHACK)
ARMOR: AZUMA

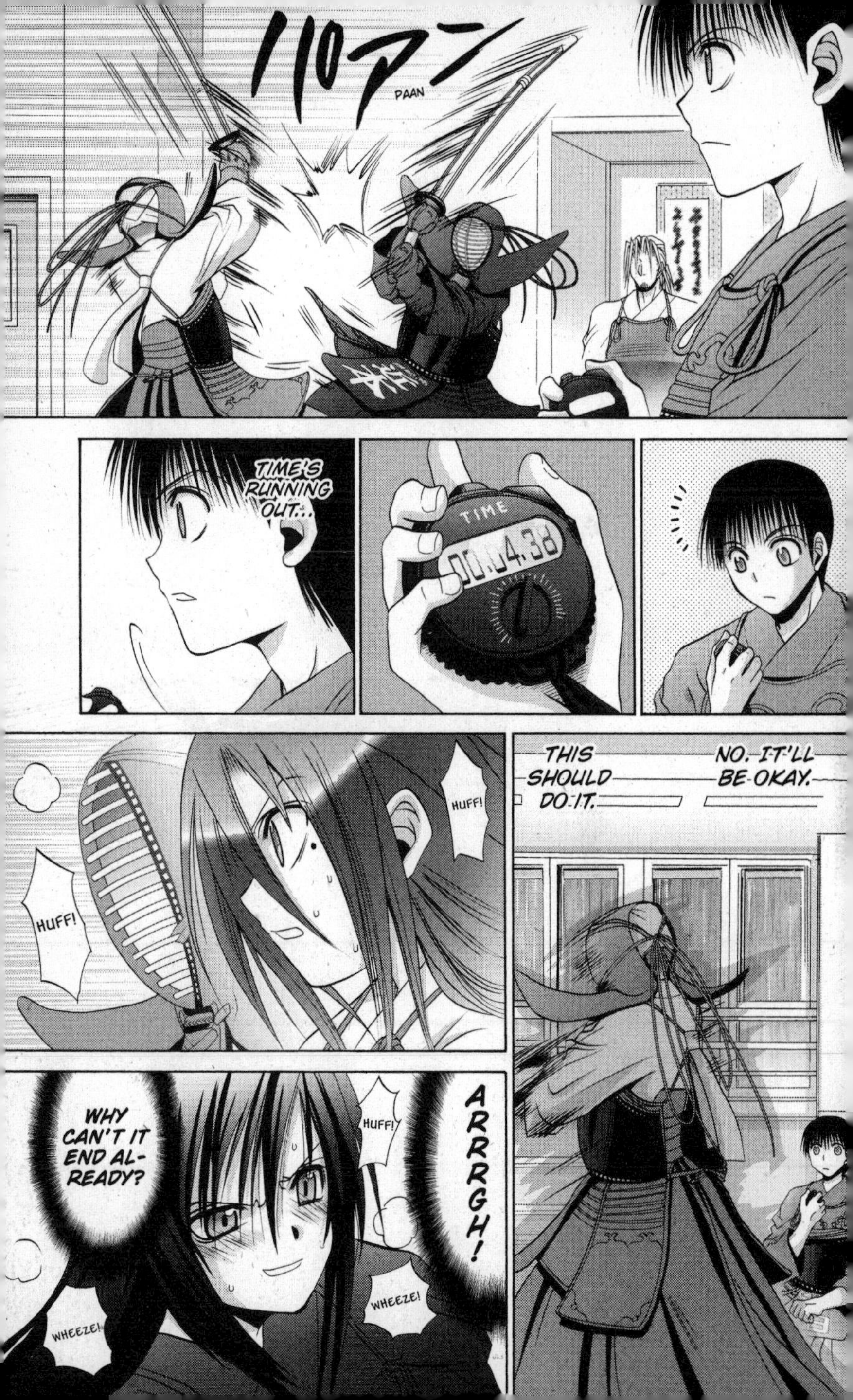
PAAN
TIME
TIME'S RUNNING OUT...
NO. IT'LL BE OKAY.
THIS SHOULD DO IT.
HUFF!
HUFF!
ARRRGH!
HUFF!
WHY CAN'T IT END AL-READY?
WHEEZE!
WHEEZE!

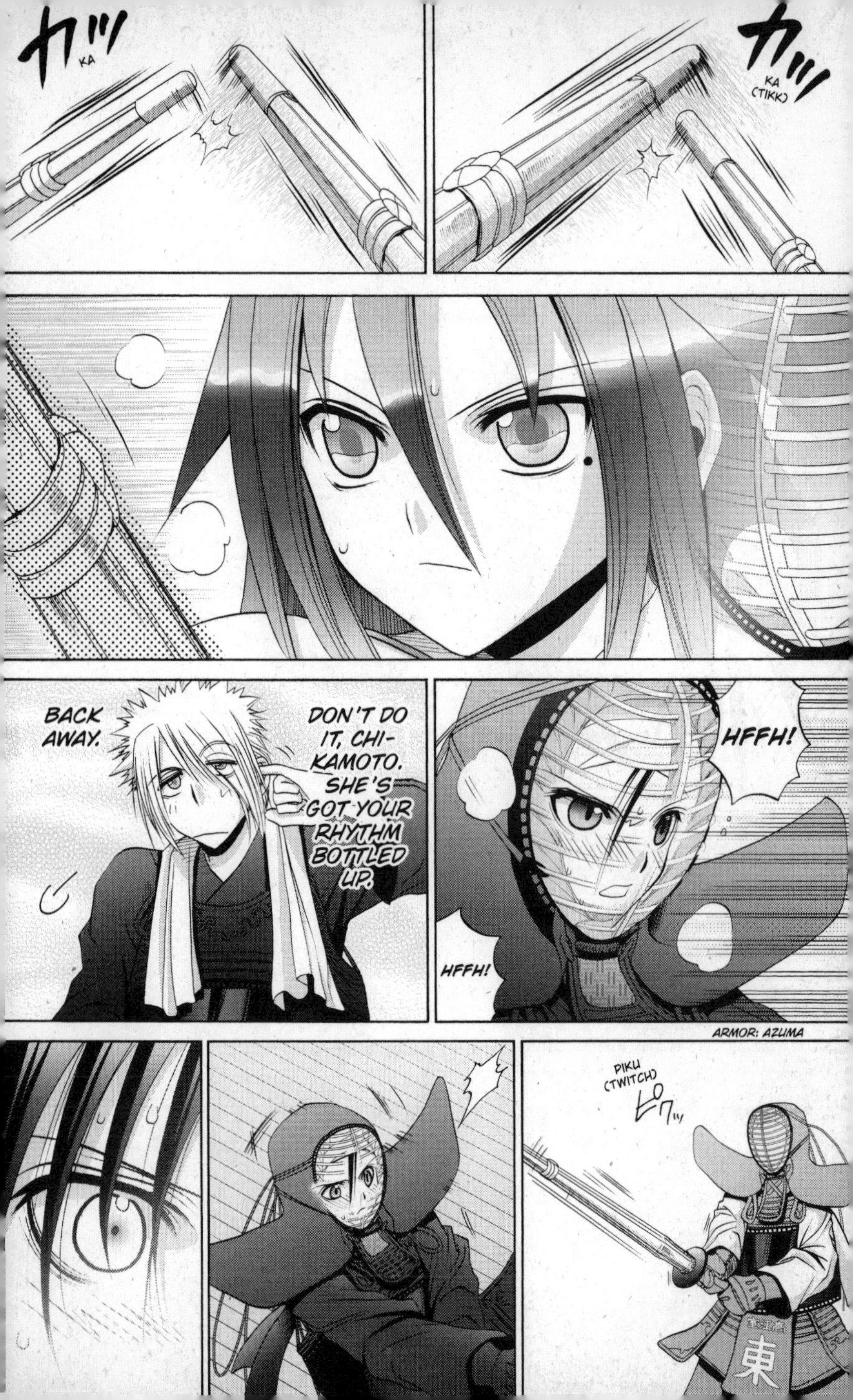
カッ
KA (TIKK)
カッ
KA
HFFH!
HFFH!
ARMOR: AZUMA
DON'T DO IT, CHI-KAMOTO. SHE'S GOT YOUR RHYTHM BOTTLED UP.
BACK AWAY.
PIKU (TWITCH)
ピクッ

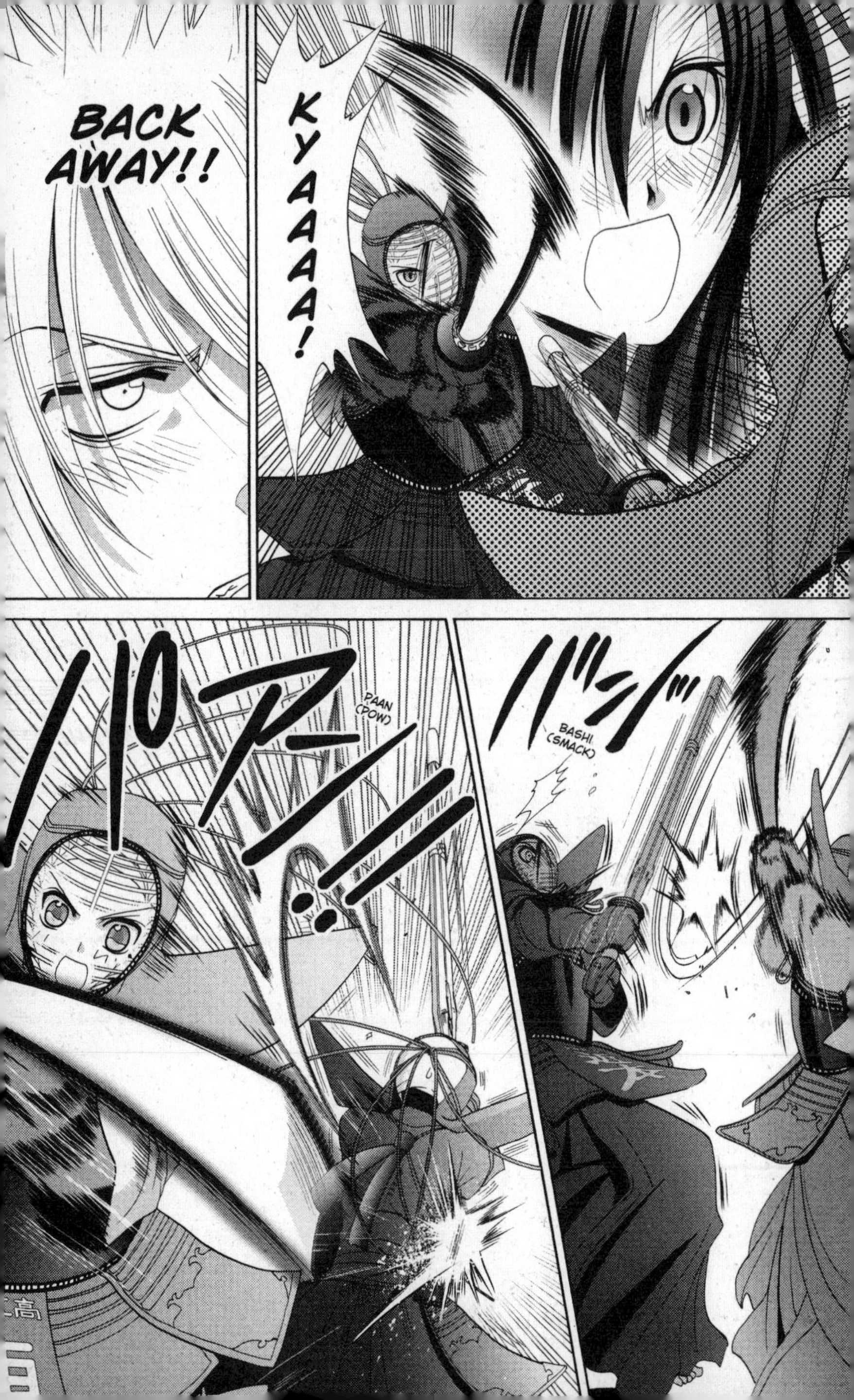
KYAAAAA!
BACK AWAY!!
BASHI (SMACK)
PAAN (POW)

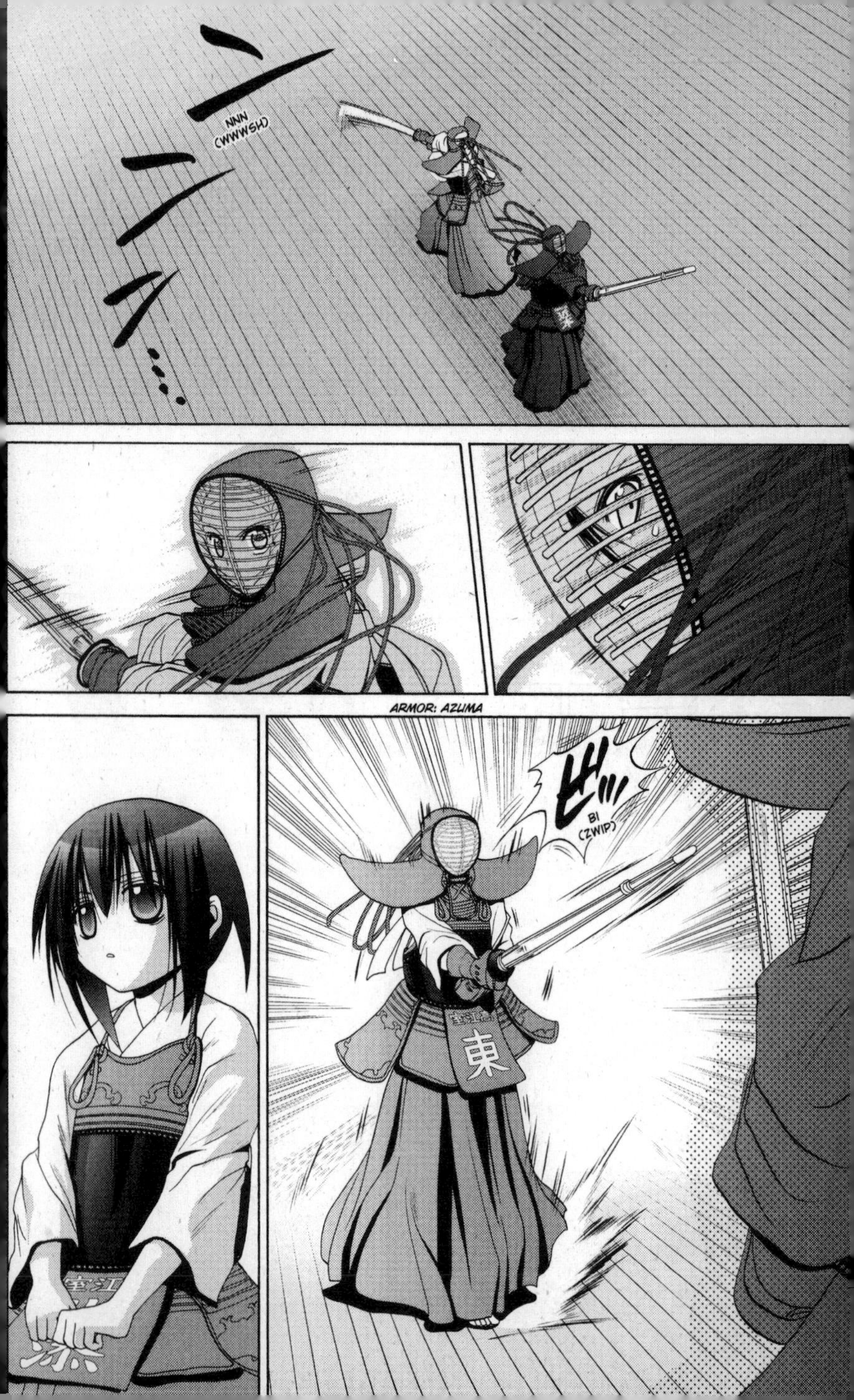
NNN (WWWSH)
ARMOR: AZUMA
BI (ZWIP)

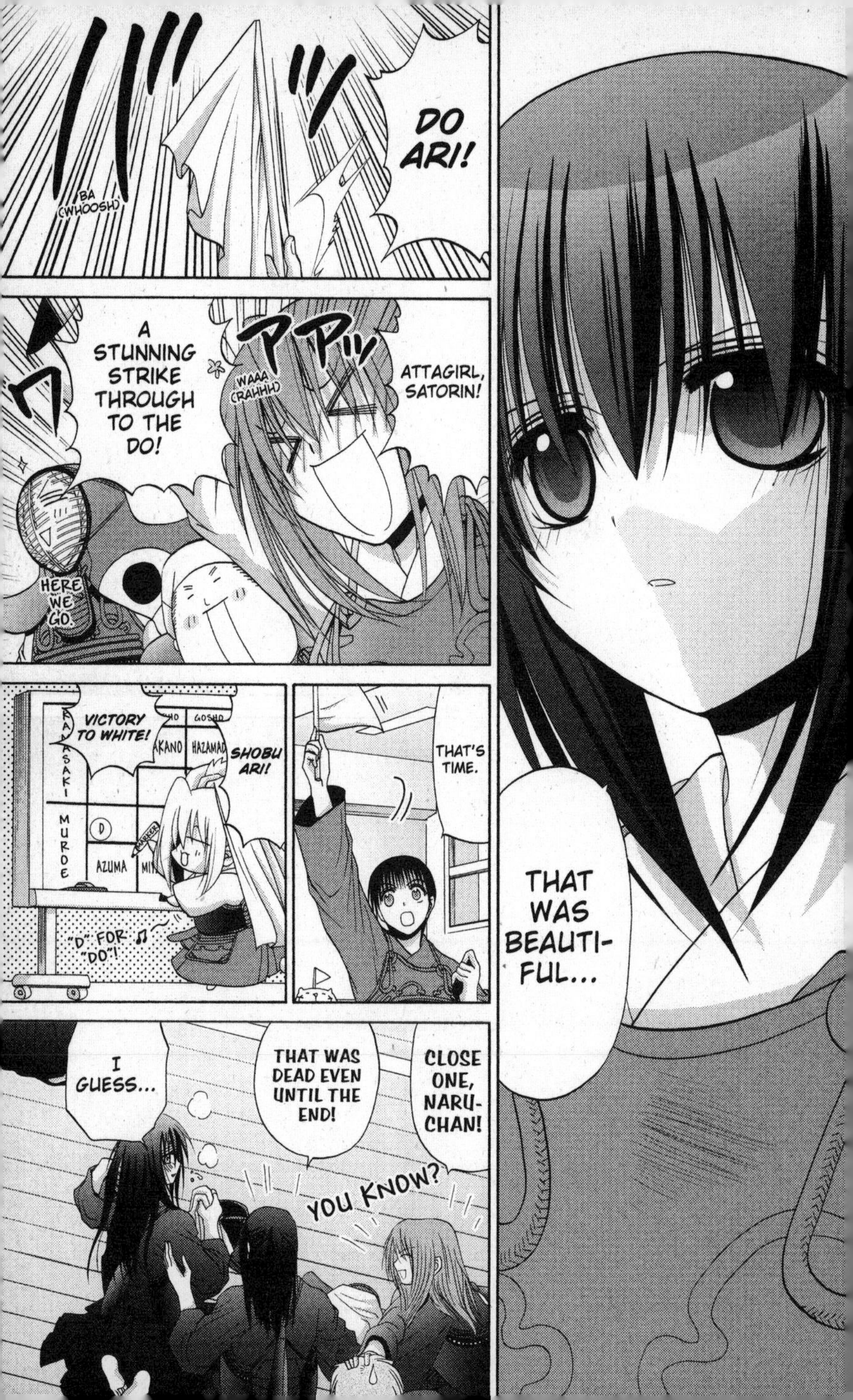

THAT WAS BEAUTI-FUL...
DO ARI!
BA (WHOOSH)
ATTAGIRL, SATORIN!
WAAA (RAHHH)
A STUNNING STRIKE THROUGH TO THE DO!
HERE WE GO.
THAT'S TIME.
SHOBU ARI!
VICTORY TO WHITE!
GOSHO
HAZAMADA
AKANO
KAWASAKI
MURODE
D
AZUMA
MARKER
"D" FOR "DO"! ♫
CLOSE ONE, NARU-CHAN!
THAT WAS DEAD EVEN UNTIL THE END!
I GUESS...
YOU KNOW?

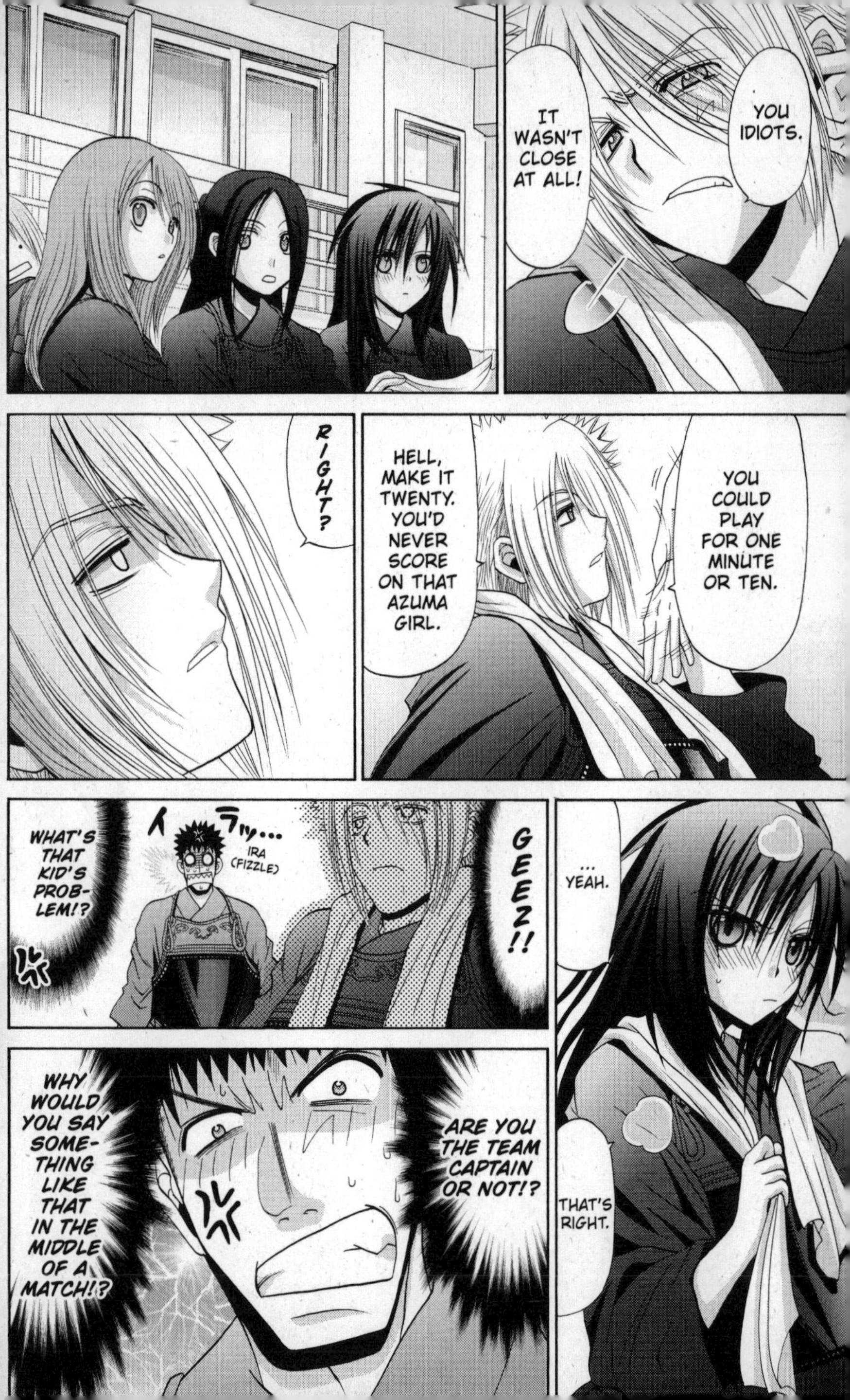
YOU IDIOTS.
IT WASN'T CLOSE AT ALL!
YOU COULD PLAY FOR ONE MINUTE OR TEN.
HELL, MAKE IT TWENTY. YOU'D NEVER SCORE ON THAT AZUMA GIRL.
RIGHT?
... YEAH.
THAT'S RIGHT.
GEEZ!!
イラッ...
IRA (FIZZLE)
WHAT'S THAT KID'S PROBLEM!?
ARE YOU THE TEAM CAPTAIN OR NOT!?
WHY WOULD YOU SAY SOMETHING LIKE THAT IN THE MIDDLE OF A MATCH!?

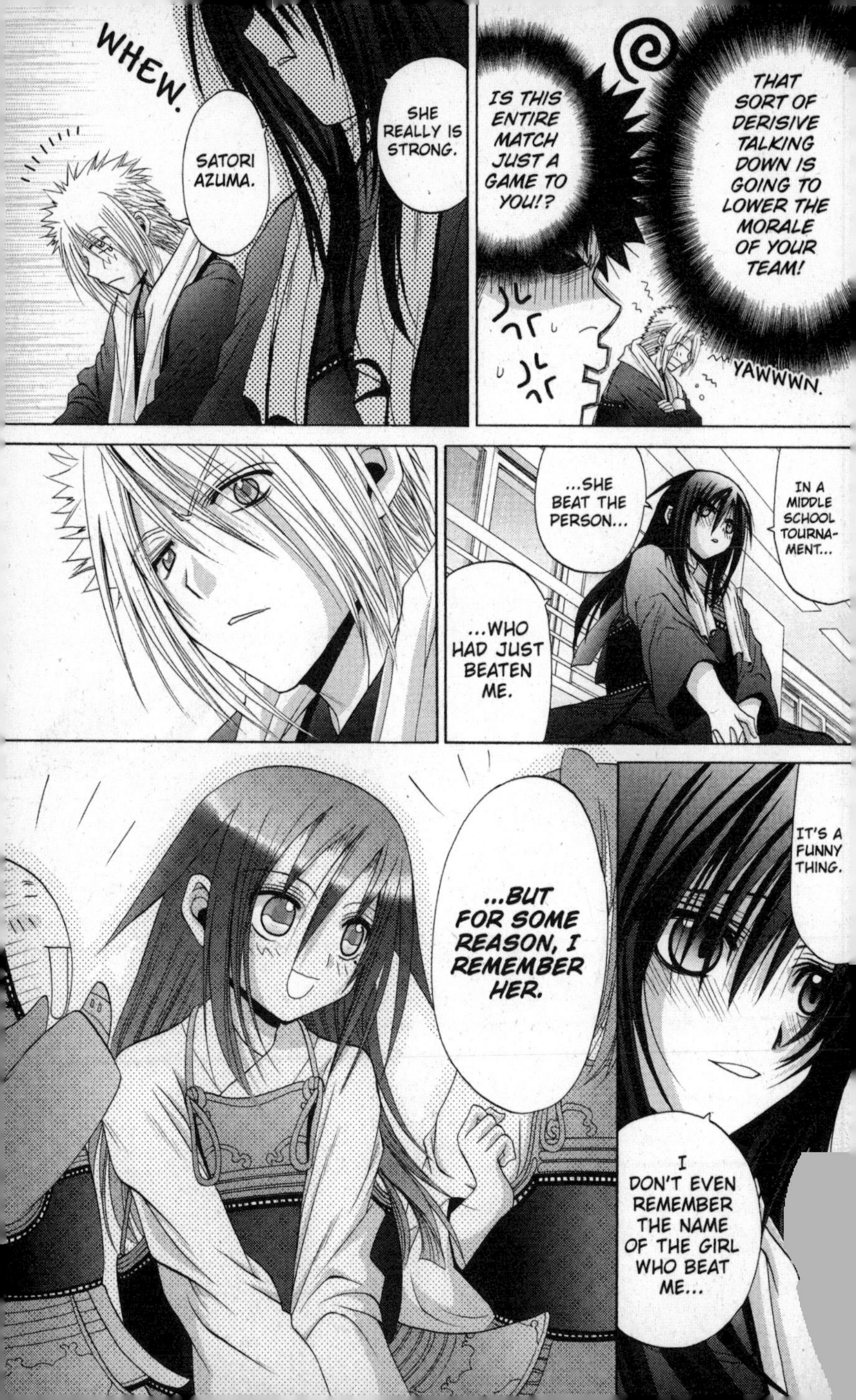
THAT SORT OF DERISIVE TALKING DOWN IS GOING TO LOWER THE MORALE OF YOUR TEAM!
IS THIS ENTIRE MATCH JUST A GAME TO YOU!?
YAWWWN.
SHE REALLY IS STRONG.
SATORI AZUMA.
WHEW.
IN A MIDDLE SCHOOL TOURNA-MENT...
...SHE BEAT THE PERSON...
...WHO HAD JUST BEATEN ME.
IT'S A FUNNY THING.
I DON'T EVEN REMEMBER THE NAME OF THE GIRL WHO BEAT ME...
...BUT FOR SOME REASON, I REMEMBER HER.

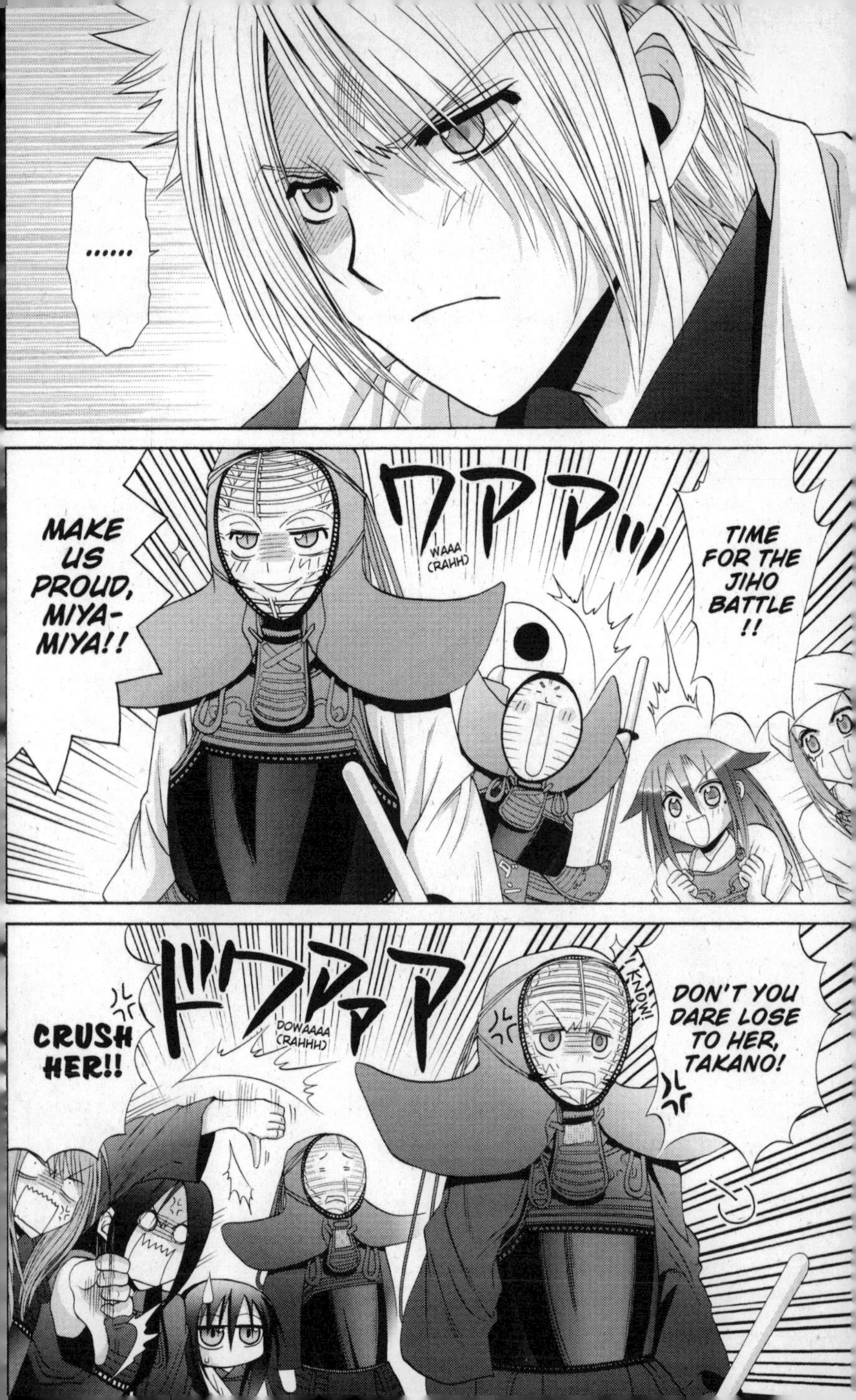
......
TIME FOR THE JIHO BATTLE!!
ワァァッ
WAAA (RAHHH)
MAKE US PROUD, MIYA-MIYA!!
DON'T YOU DARE LOSE TO HER, TAKANO!
I KNOW!
ドワァァア
DOWAAAA (RAHHH)
CRUSH HER!!

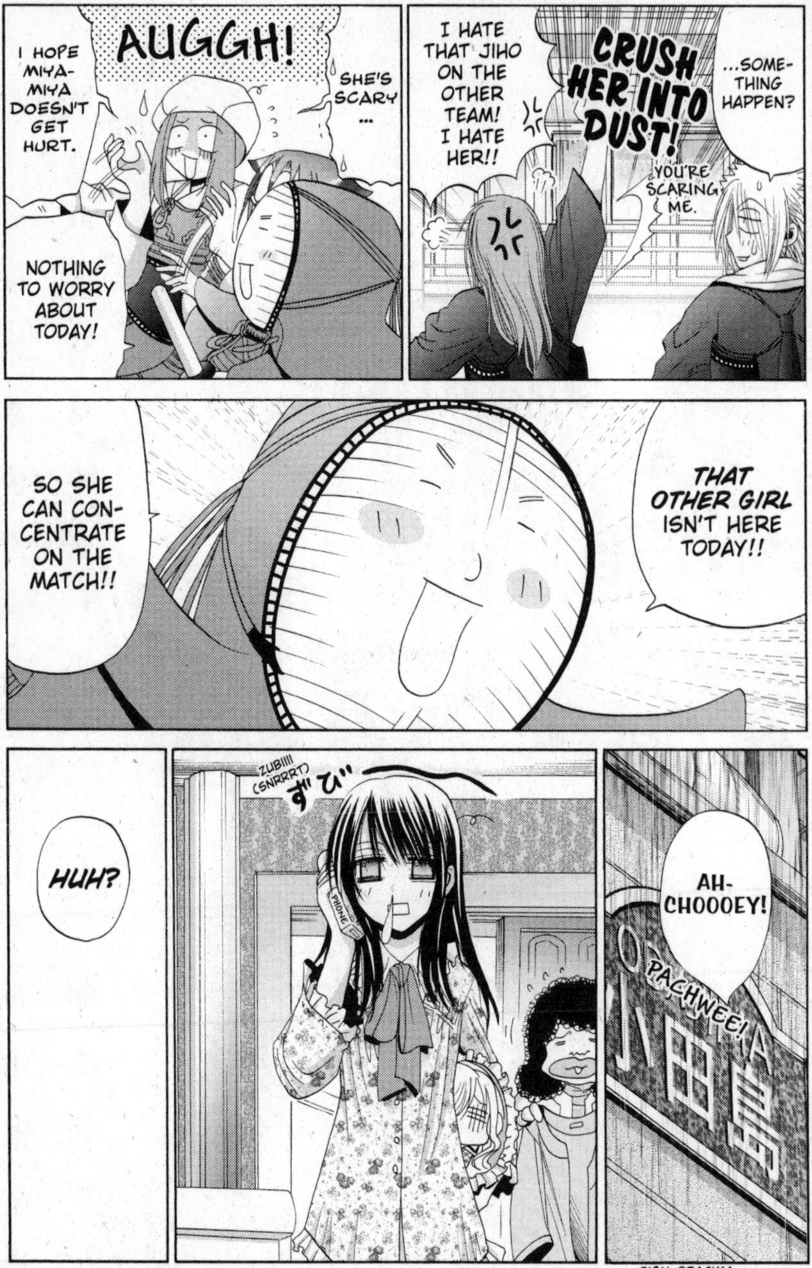
...SOME-THING HAPPEN?
CRUSH HER INTO DUST!
I HATE THAT JIHO ON THE OTHER TEAM! I HATE HER!!
YOU'RE SCARING ME.
SHE'S SCARY...
AUGGH!
I HOPE MIYA-MIYA DOESN'T GET HURT.
NOTHING TO WORRY ABOUT TODAY!
THAT OTHER GIRL ISN'T HERE TODAY!!
SO SHE CAN CONCENTRATE ON THE MATCH!!
AH-CHOOOEY!
PACHWEE!
小田島
ZUBIIII (SNRRRT)
ずび
PHONE
HUH?

SIGN: ODAJIMA

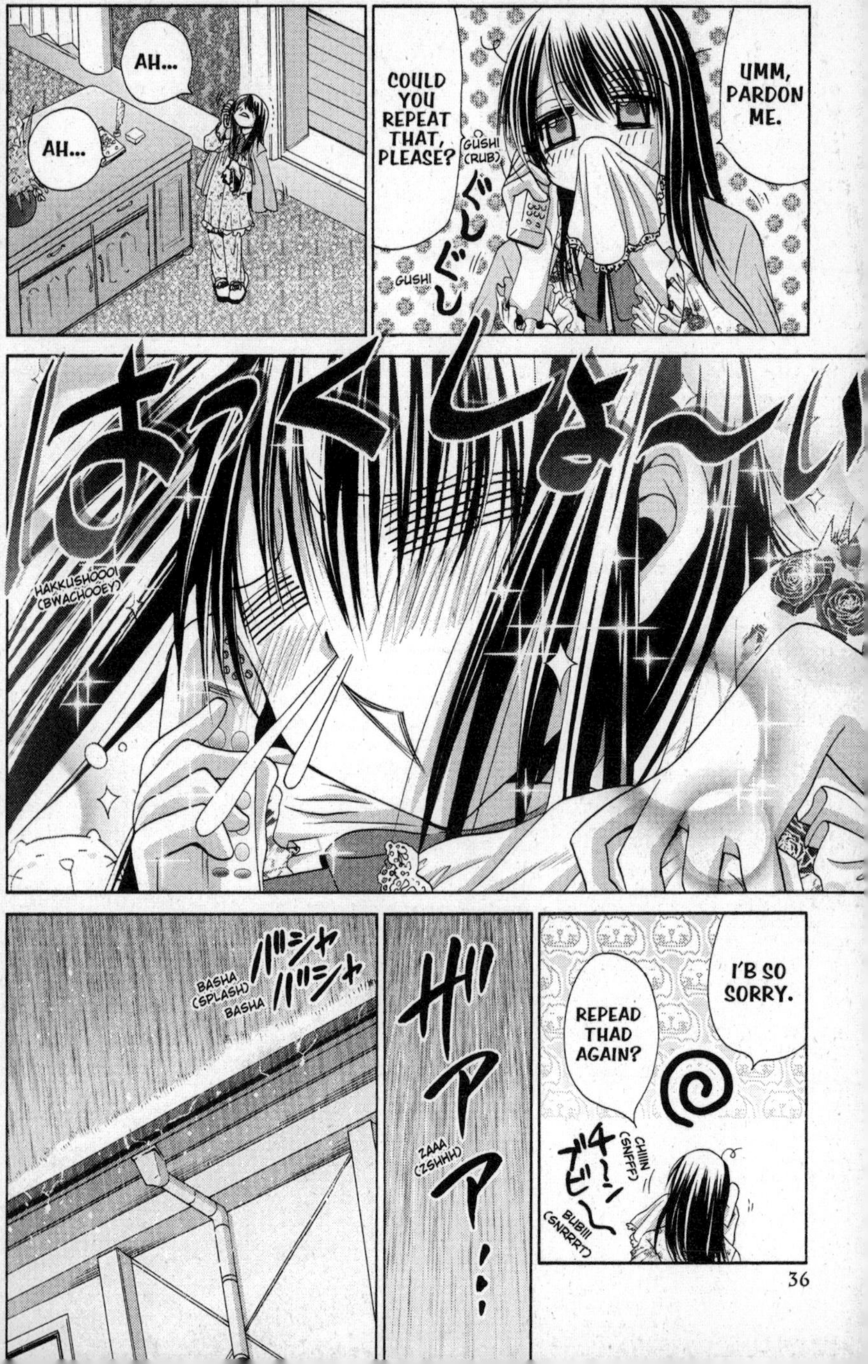
UMM, PARDON ME.
COULD YOU REPEAT THAT, PLEASE?
ぐしぐし
GUSHI (RUB)
GUSHI
AH...
AH...
はっくしょ〜い
HAKKUSHOOOI (BWACHOOEY)
I'B SO SORRY.
REPEAD THAD AGAIN?
チ〜ン
CHIIIN (SNFFF)
ブビ〜
BUBIII (SNRRRT)
ザァァ…
ZAAA (ZSHHH)
バシャバシャ
BASHA (SPLASH) BASHA

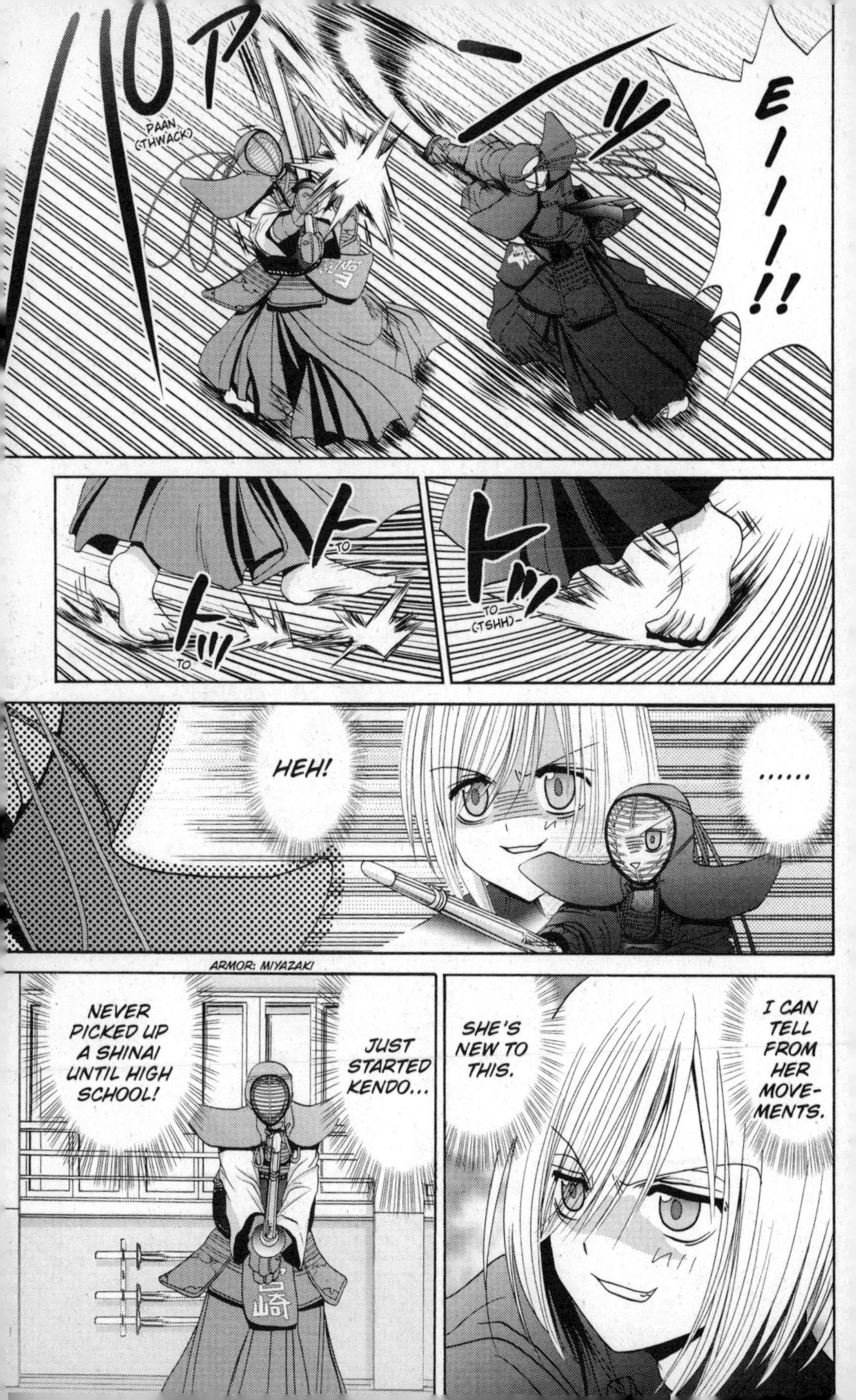
PAAN (THWACK)
E—!!
TO (TSHH)
TO
TO
......
HEH!
I CAN TELL FROM HER MOVEMENTS.
SHE'S NEW TO THIS.
JUST STARTED KENDO...
NEVER PICKED UP A SHINAI UNTIL HIGH SCHOOL!
ARMOR: MIYAZAKI

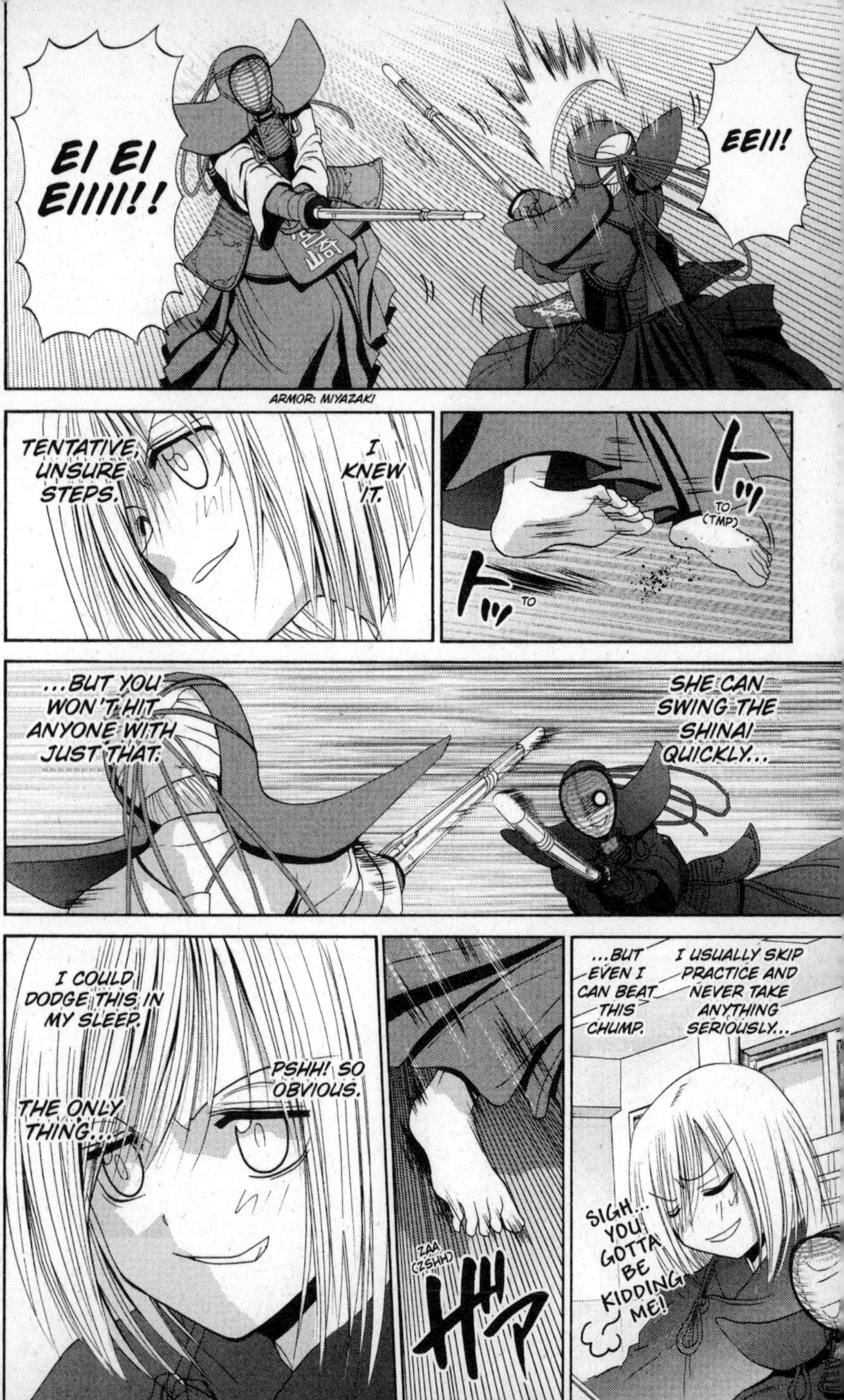

EEII!
EI EI EIIII!!
ARMOR: MIYAZAKI
トッ TO (TMP)
トッ TO
I KNEW IT.
TENTATIVE, UNSURE STEPS.
SHE CAN SWING THE SHINAI QUICKLY...
...BUT YOU WON'T HIT ANYONE WITH JUST THAT.
I USUALLY SKIP PRACTICE AND NEVER TAKE ANYTHING SERIOUSLY...
...BUT EVEN I CAN BEAT THIS CHUMP.
SIGH... YOU GOTTA BE KIDDING ME!
ザァ ZAA (ZSHH)
I COULD DODGE THIS IN MY SLEEP.
PSHH! SO OBVIOUS.
THE ONLY THING...

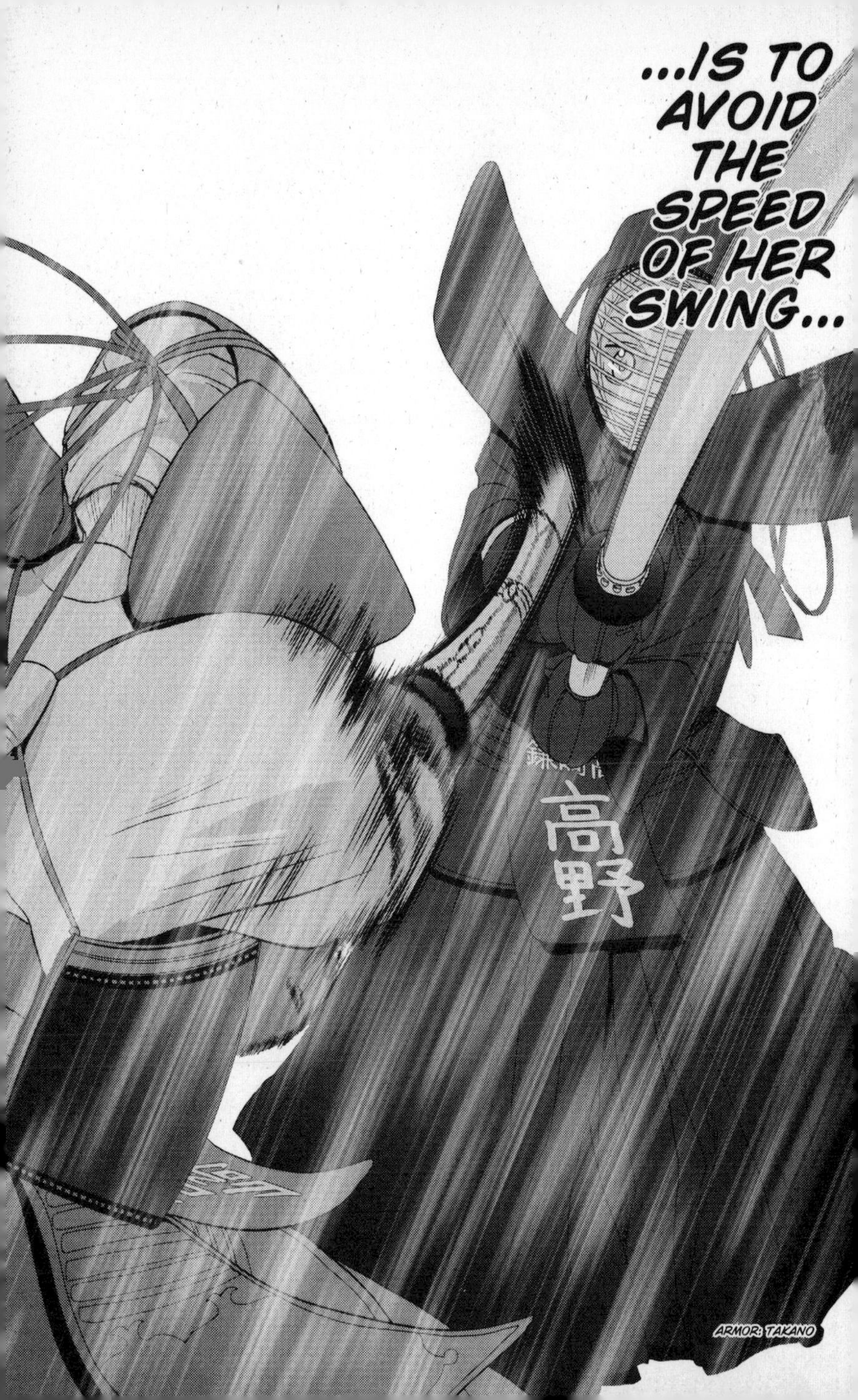
...IS TO AVOID THE SPEED OF HER SWING...
高野
ARMOR: TAKANO

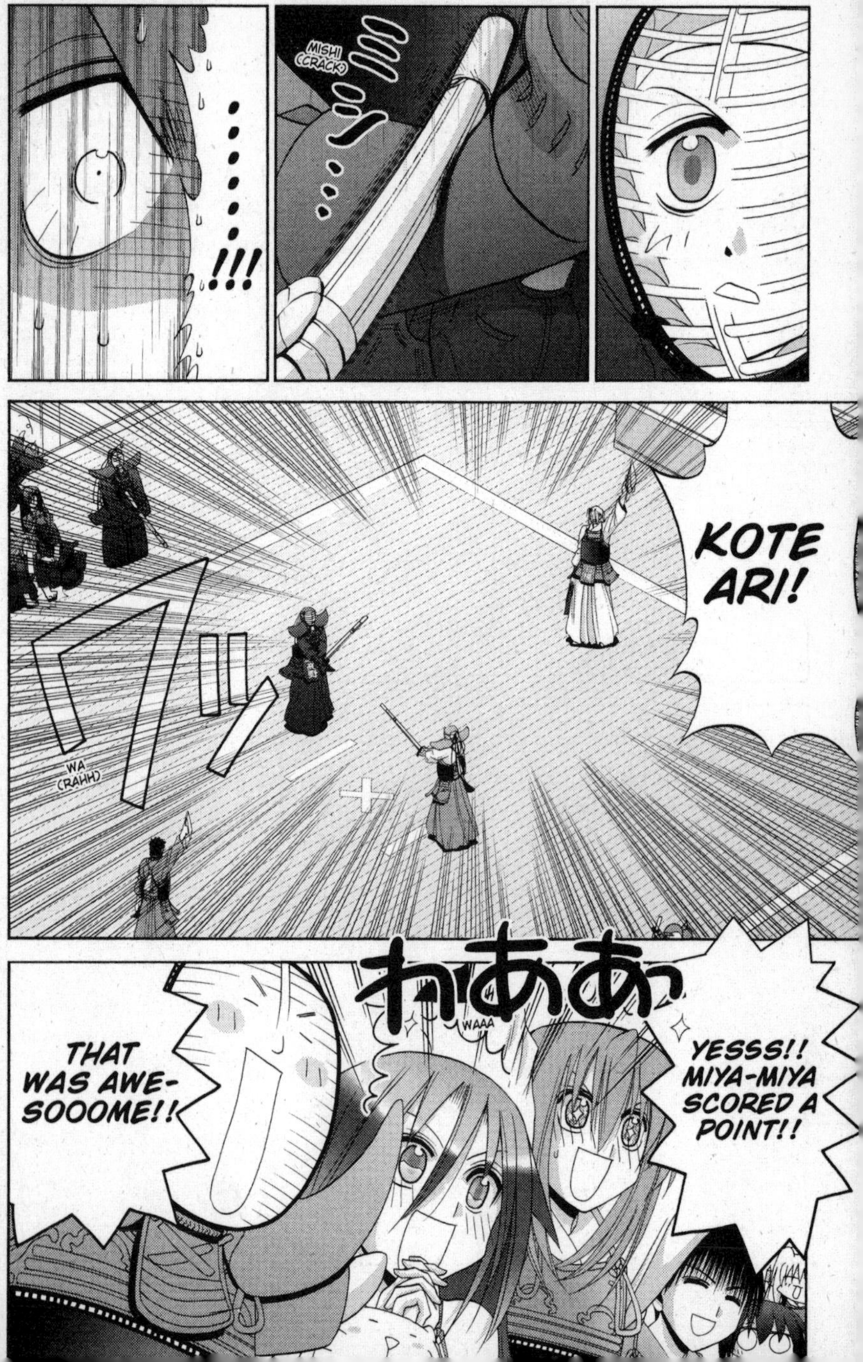

MISHI (CRACK)
......!!!
KOTE ARI!
WA (RAHH)
わあああ
WAAA
YESSS!! MIYA-MIYA SCORED A POINT!!
THAT WAS AWE-SOOOME!!

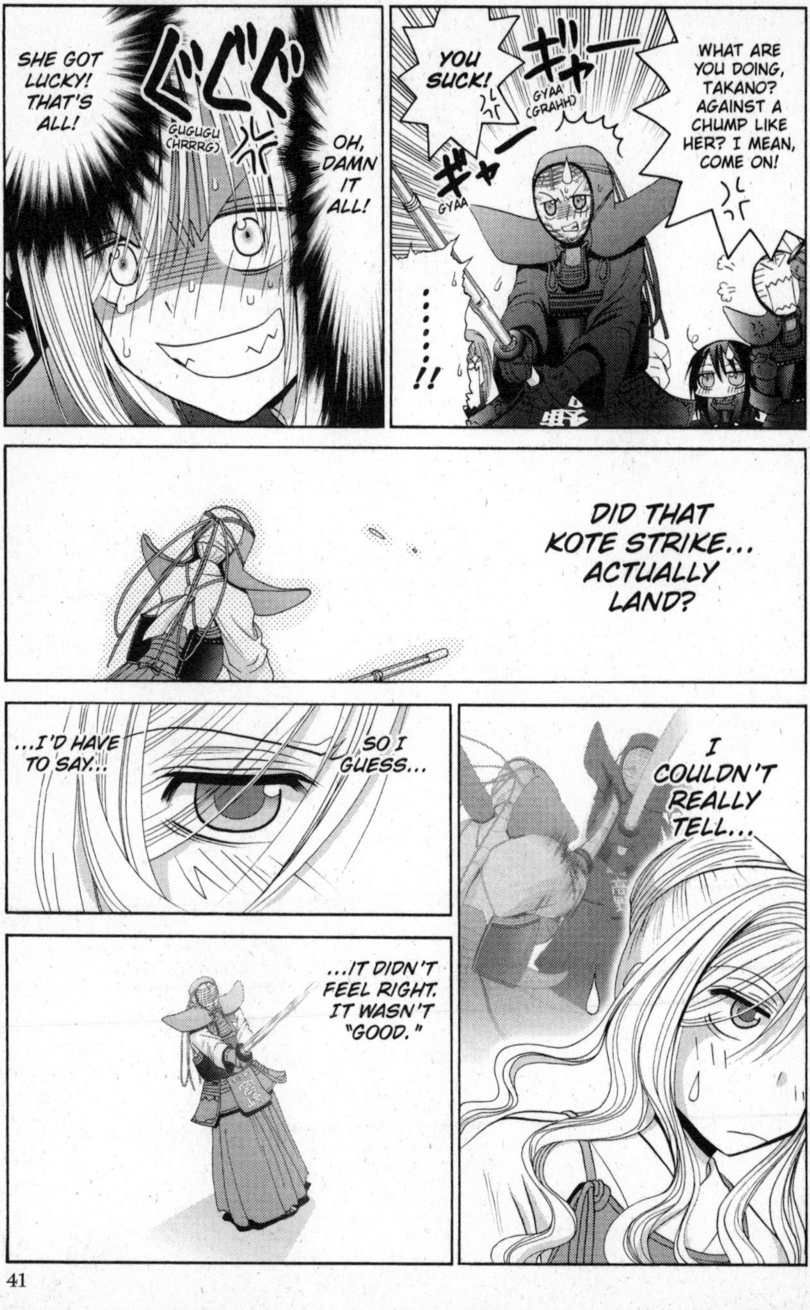
WHAT ARE YOU DOING, TAKANO? AGAINST A CHUMP LIKE HER? I MEAN, COME ON!
ギャー
GYAA (GRAHH)
YOU SUCK!
ギャー
GYAA
......!!
OH, DAMN IT ALL!
ぐぐぐ
GUGUGU (HRRRG)
SHE GOT LUCKY! THAT'S ALL!
DID THAT KOTE STRIKE... ACTUALLY LAND?
I COULDN'T REALLY TELL...
SO I GUESS...
...I'D HAVE TO SAY...
...IT DIDN'T FEEL RIGHT. IT WASN'T "GOOD."

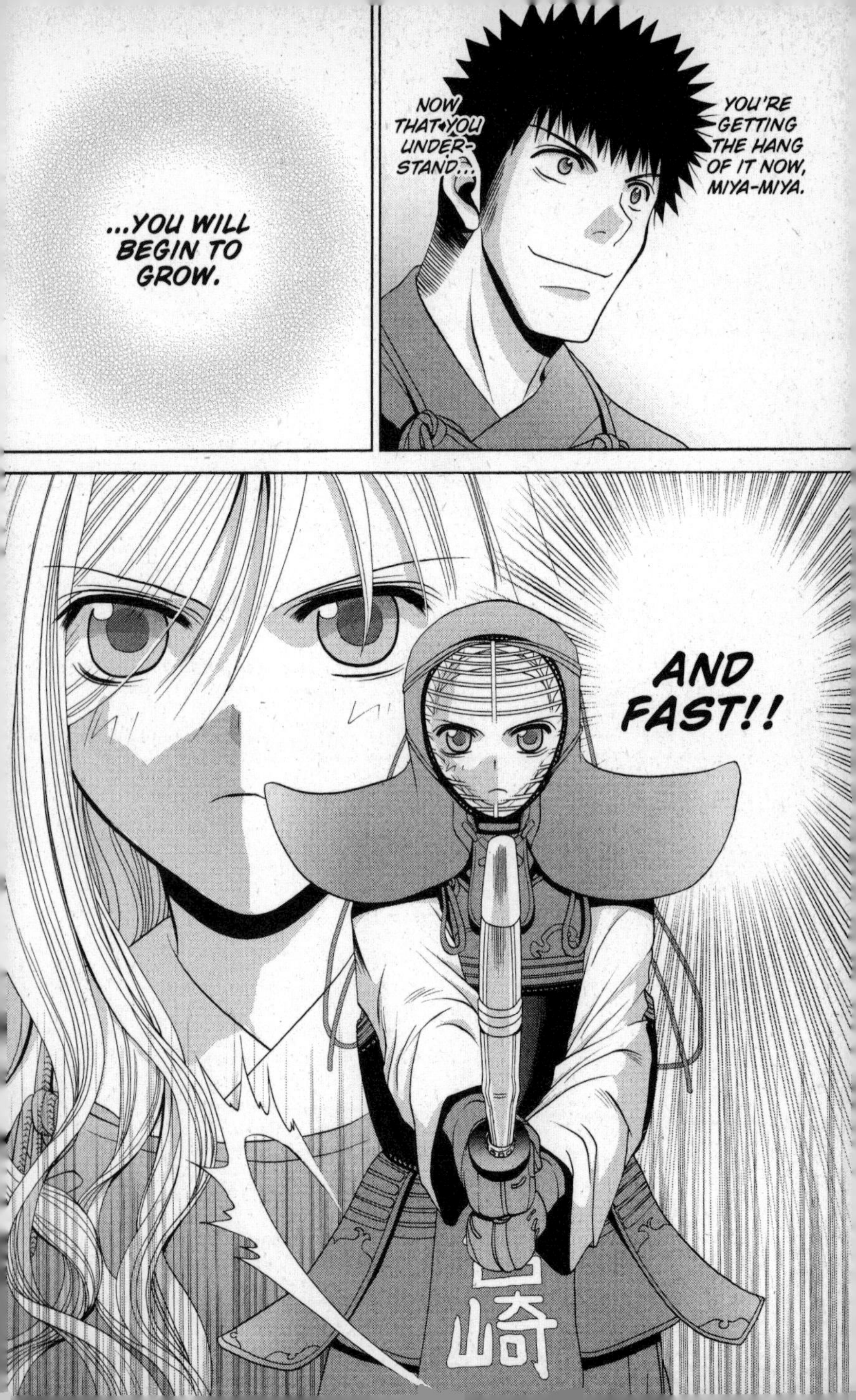
YOU'RE GETTING THE HANG OF IT NOW, MIYA-MIYA.
NOW THAT YOU UNDER-STAND...
...YOU WILL BEGIN TO GROW.
AND FAST!!
山崎

BAMBOO BLADE
バンブーブレード

BAMBOO BLADE

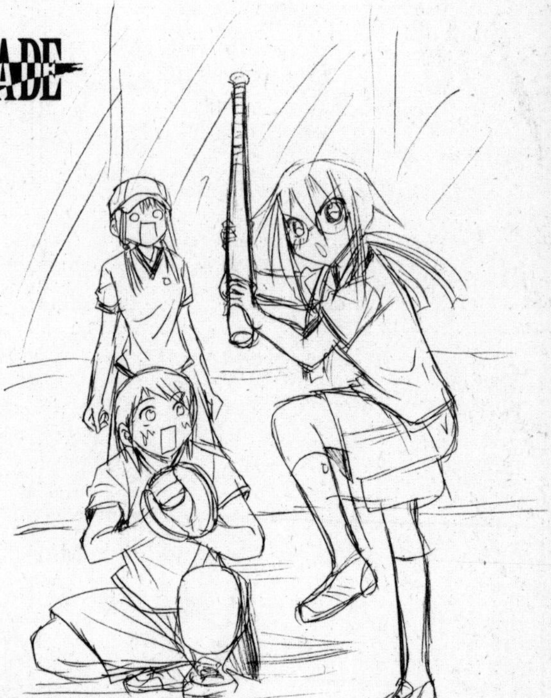

パン
PAN
(THWACK)

ザァァァ
ZAAA

剣道場
SIGN: KENDO DOJO

パ ンッ
PAN

ザァァァ
ZAAAA

ザァァァァ
ZAAAAA
(FSHHH)

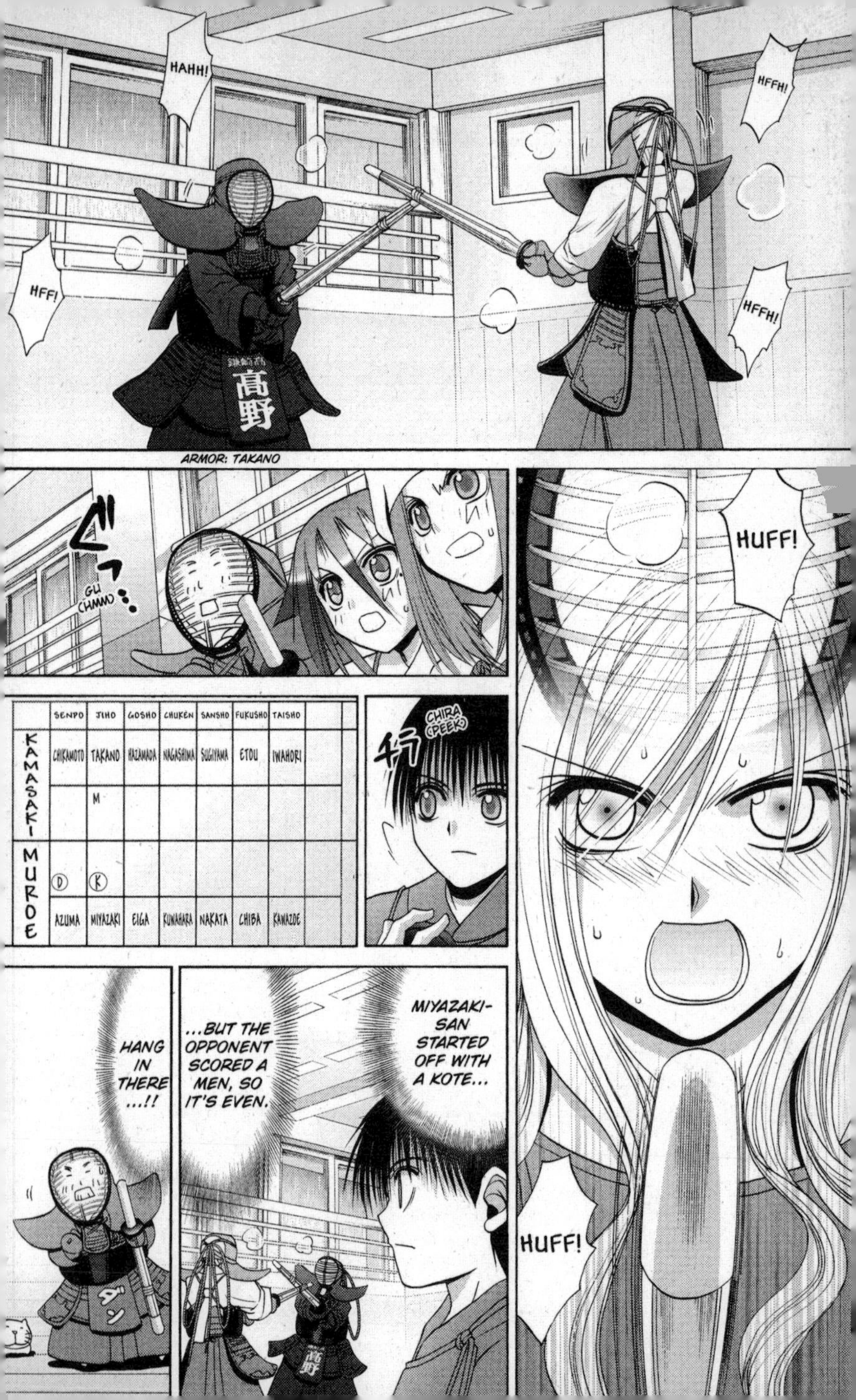
HFFH!
HAHH!
HFFH!
HFF!
ARMOR: TAKANO
HUFF!
HUFF!
GU (CHMM)...
CHIRA (PEEK)
SENPO JIHO GOSHO CHUKEN SANSHO FUKUSHO TAISHO
KAMASAKI
CHIKAMOTO TAKANO HAZAMADA NAGASHIMA SUGIYAMA ETOU IWAHORI
M
D K
MUROE
AZUMA MIYAZAKI EIGA KUWAHARA NAKATA CHIBA KAWAZOE
MIYAZAKI-SAN STARTED OFF WITH A KOTE...
...BUT THE OPPONENT SCORED A MEN, SO IT'S EVEN.
HANG IN THERE ...!!

MIYA-MIYA!!!

YOU CAN DO IT!!!

HUFF!

HUFF!

WHAT'S HER DEAL?

WHAT?

I DON'T GET IT!

WHY IS SHE TAKING THIS STUPID PRACTICE MEET SO SERIOUSLY!? IT DOESN'T MEAN ANYTHING!

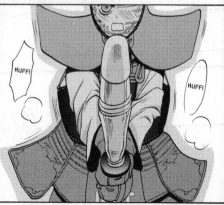

HUFF!

HUFF!

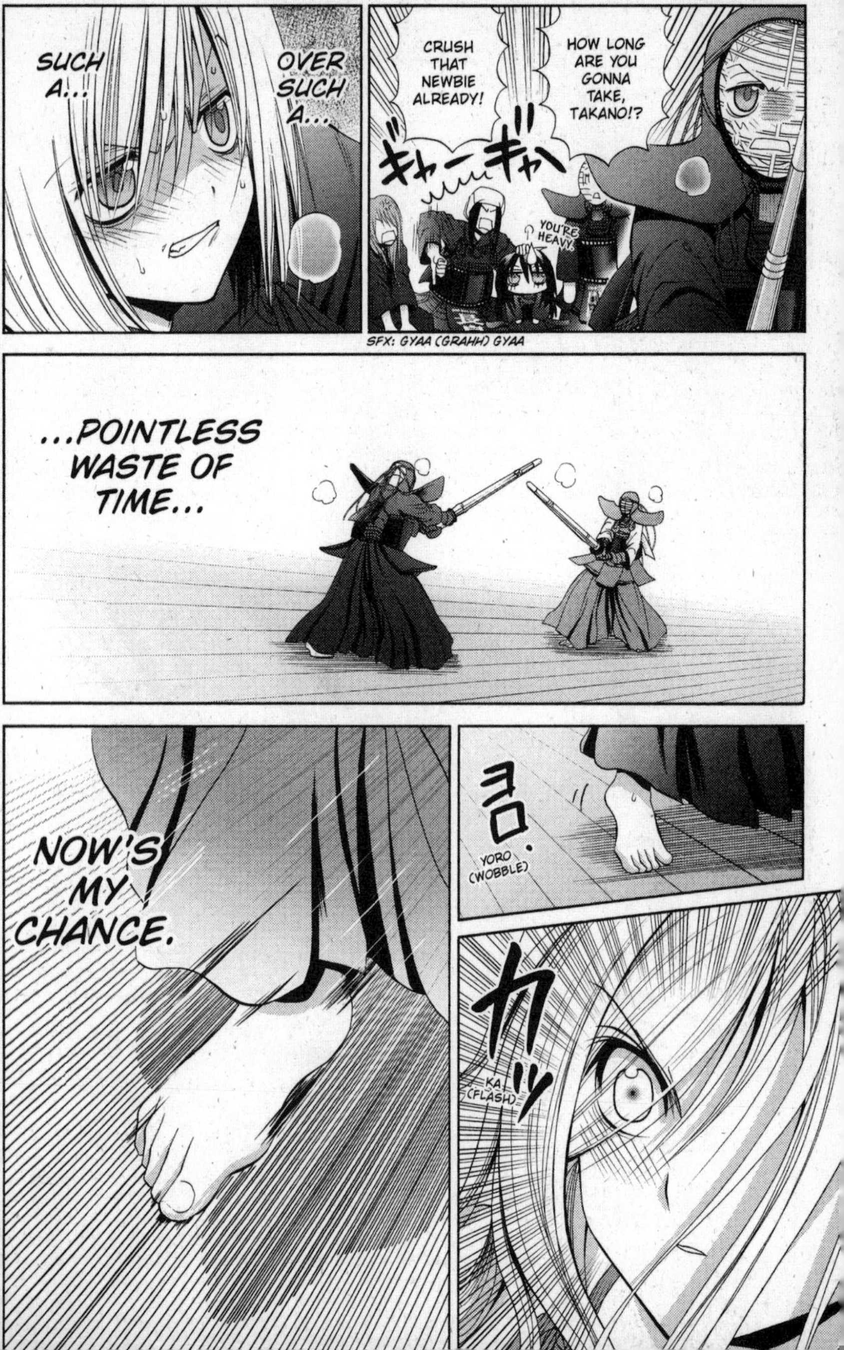
HOW LONG ARE YOU GONNA TAKE, TAKANO!?
CRUSH THAT NEWBIE ALREADY!
ギャーギャ
YOU'RE HEAVY.
OVER SUCH A...
SUCH A...
SFX: GYAA (GRAHH) GYAA
...POINTLESS WASTE OF TIME...
ヨロ.
YORO (WOBBLE)
カッ
KA (FLASH)
NOW'S MY CHANCE.

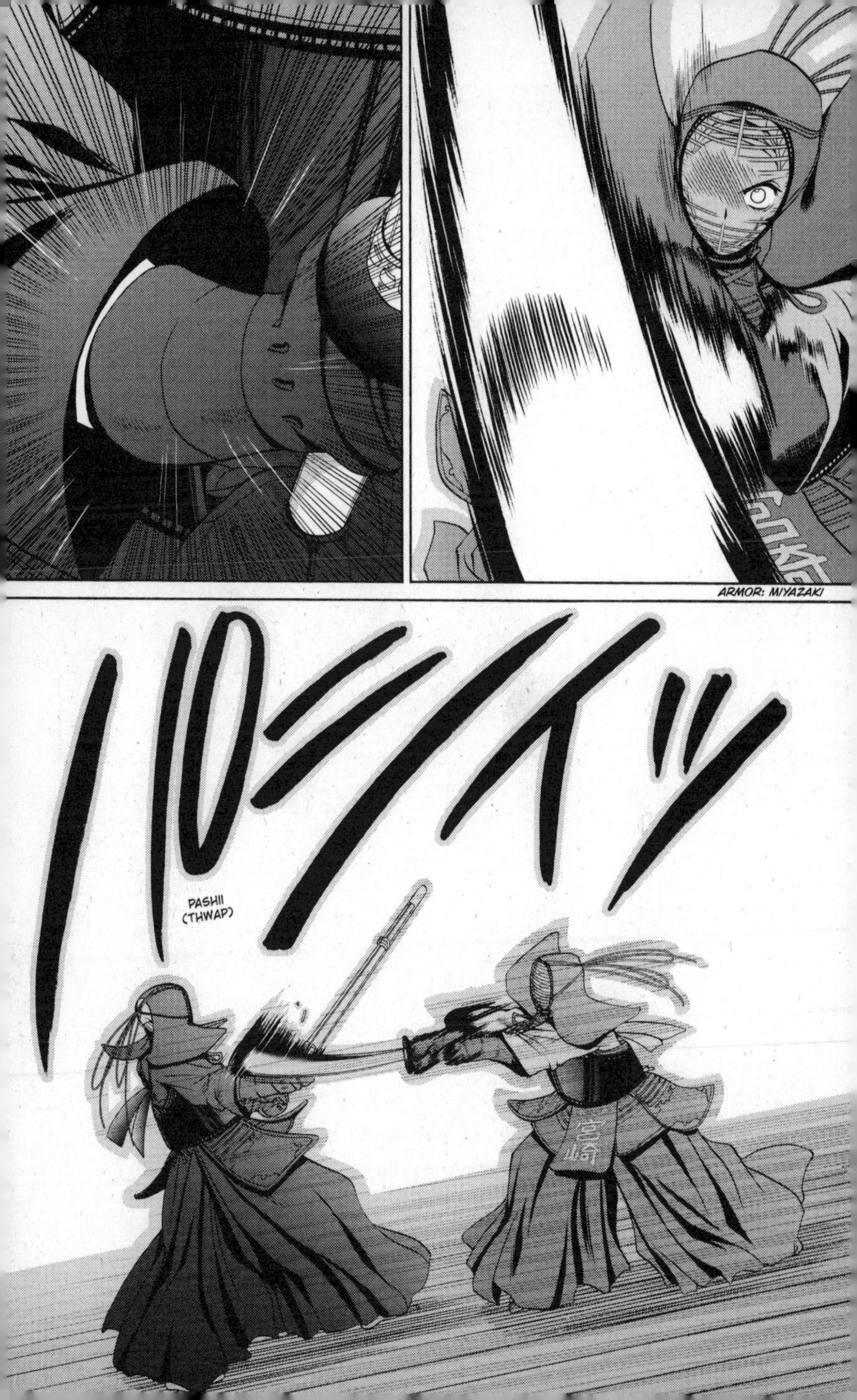

ARMOR: MIYAZAKI
宮崎
PASHII
(THWAP)
パシイッ
宮崎

CHAPTER 73
MIYA-MIYA AND THE SENSATION OF VICTORY

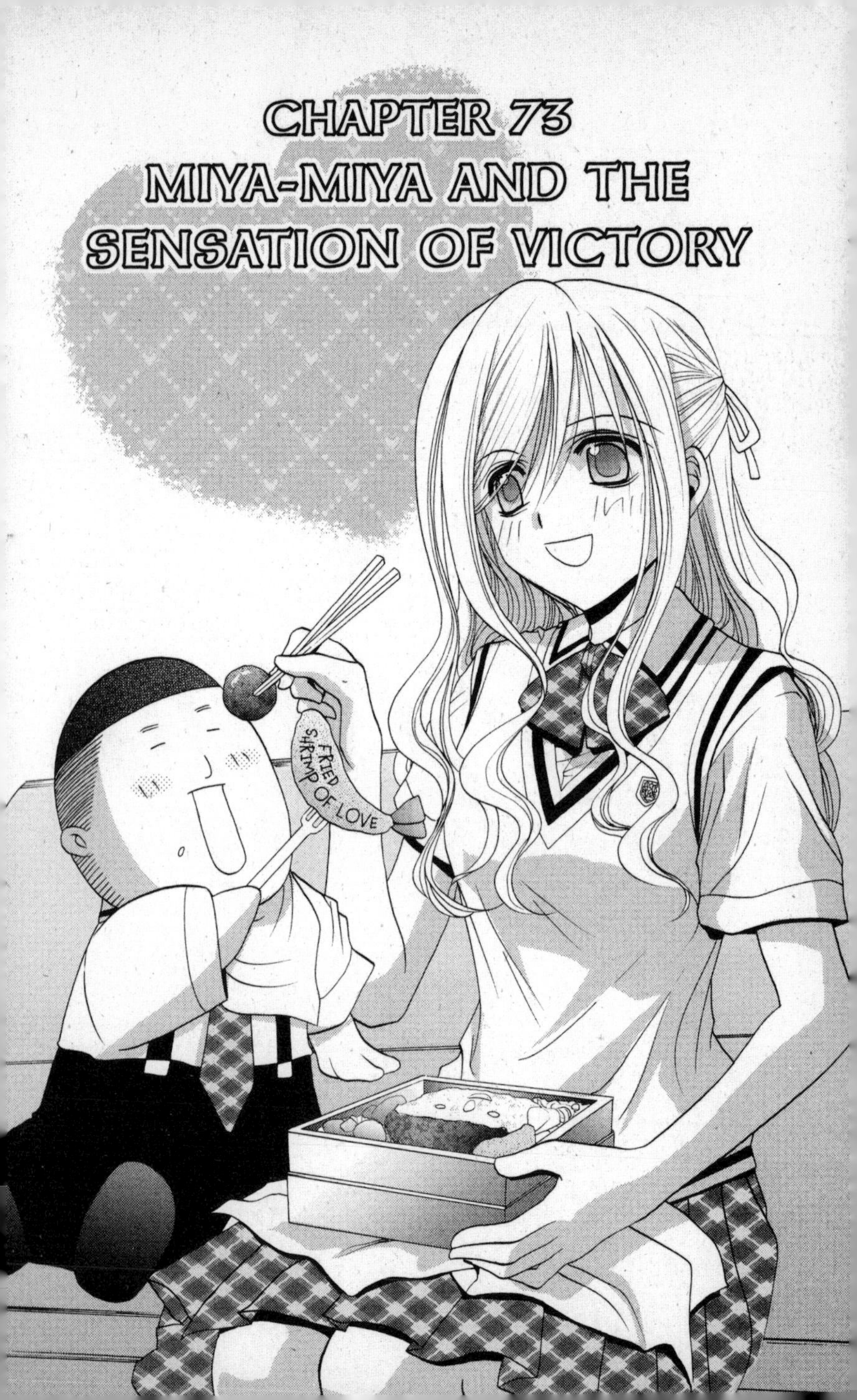
FRIED SHRIMP OF LOVE

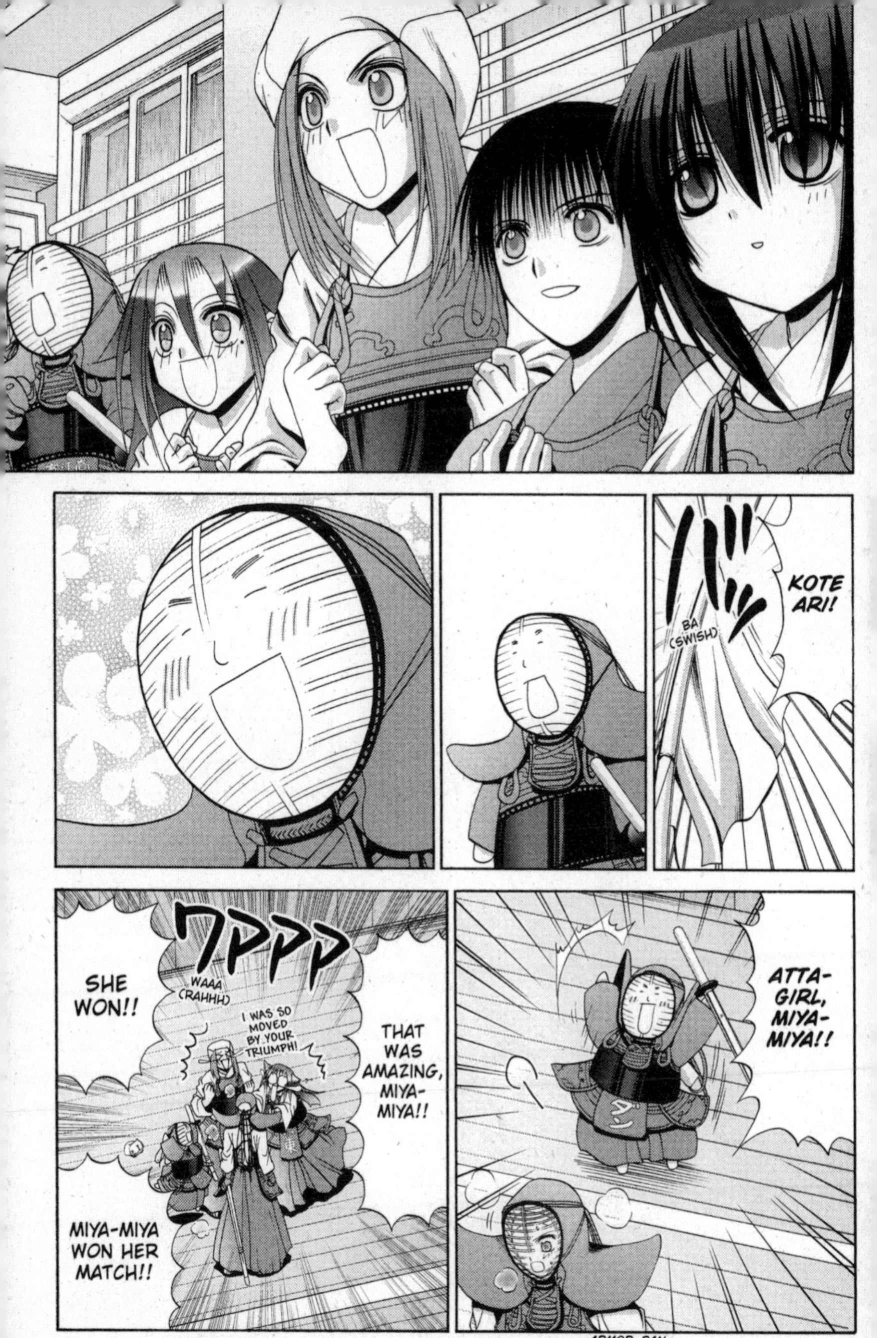
BA (SWISH)
KOTE ARI!
ATTA-GIRL, MIYA-MIYA!!
WAAA (RAHHH)
THAT WAS AMAZING, MIYA-MIYA!!
I WAS SO MOVED BY YOUR TRIUMPH!
SHE WON!!
MIYA-MIYA WON HER MATCH!!

ARMOR: DAN

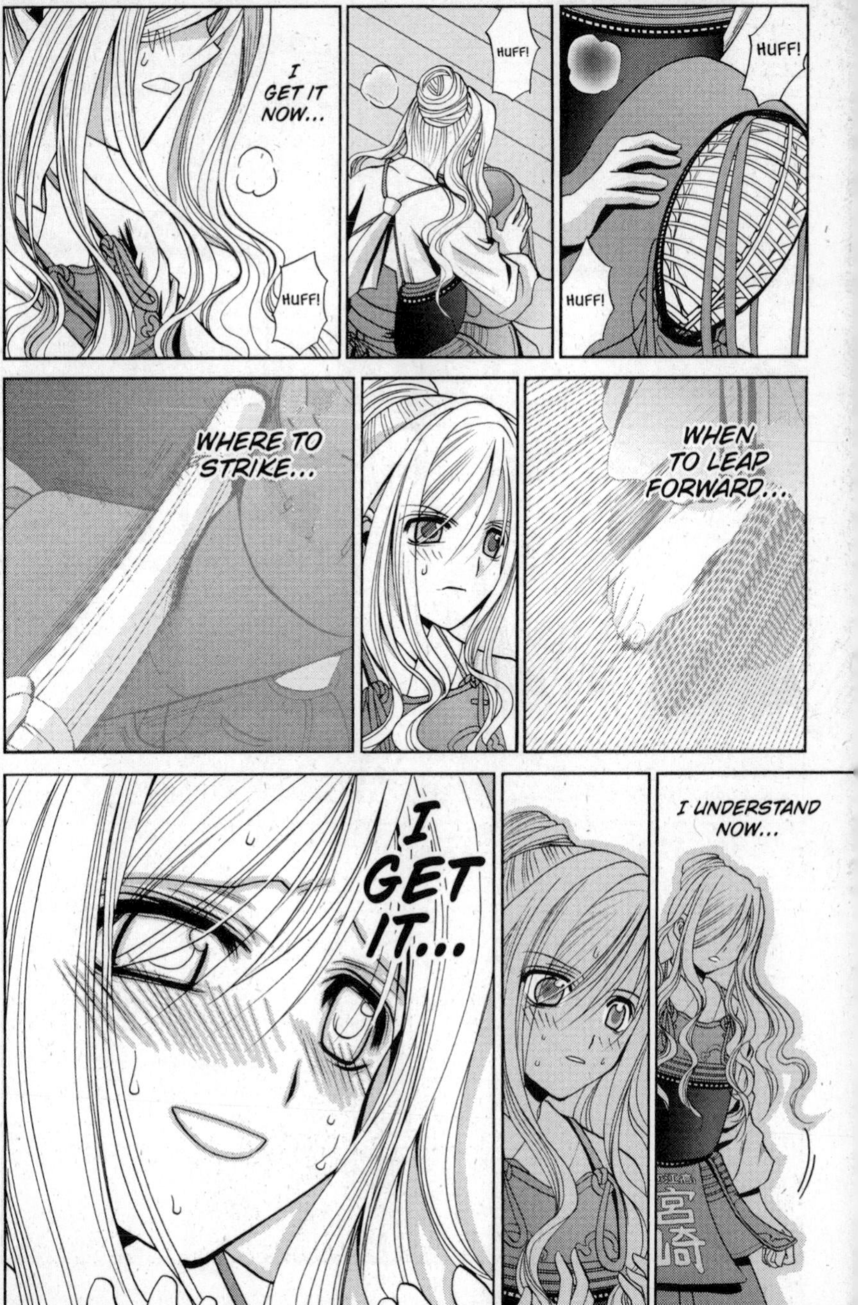
HUFF!
HUFF!
HUFF!
I GET IT NOW...
HUFF!
WHEN TO LEAP FORWARD...
WHERE TO STRIKE...
I UNDERSTAND NOW...
宮崎
I GET IT...

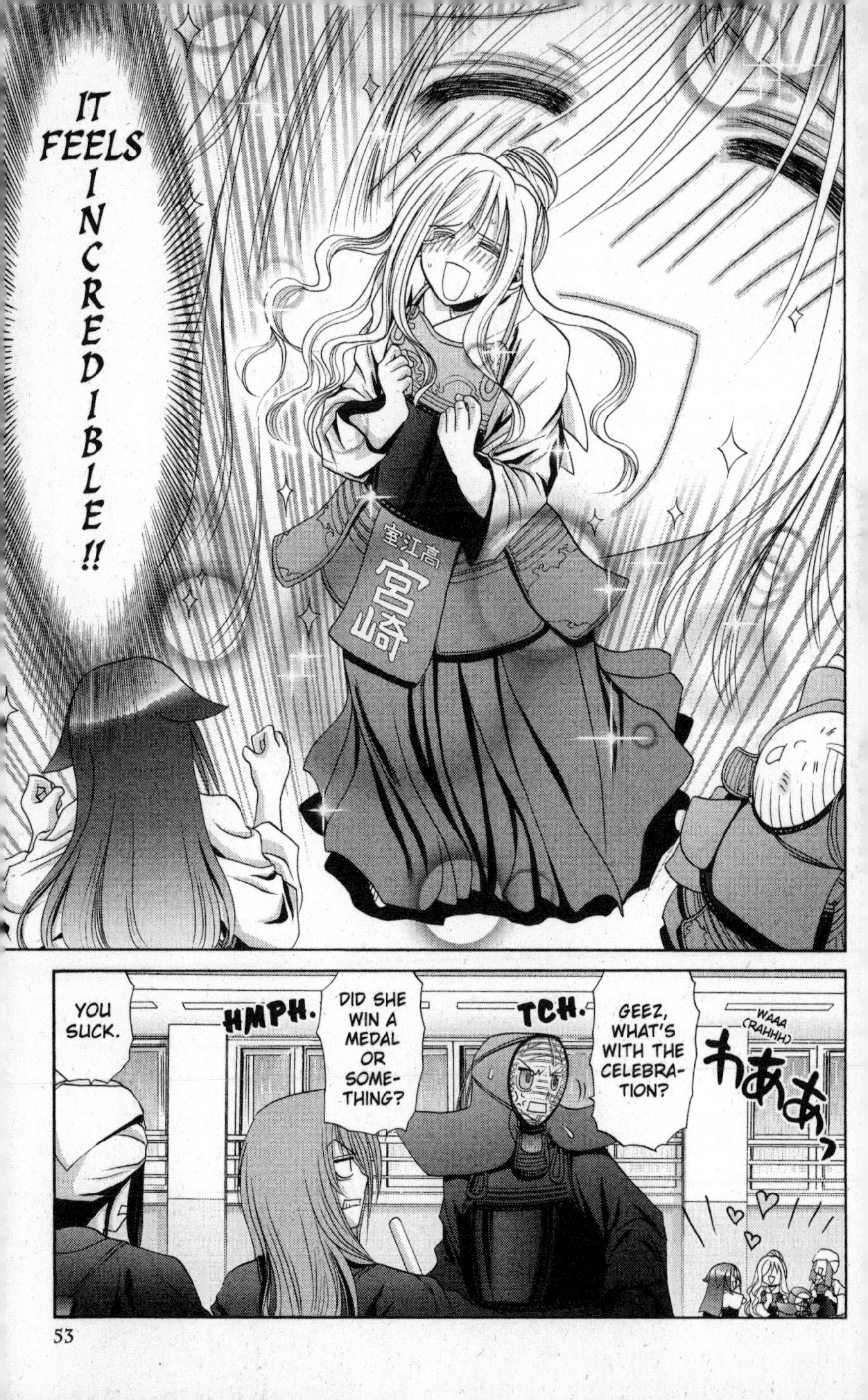
IT FEELS INCREDIBLE!!
室江高
宮崎
わあぁっ
WAAA (RAHHH)
GEEZ, WHAT'S WITH THE CELEBRA-TION?
TCH.
DID SHE WIN A MEDAL OR SOME-THING?
HMPH.
YOU SUCK.

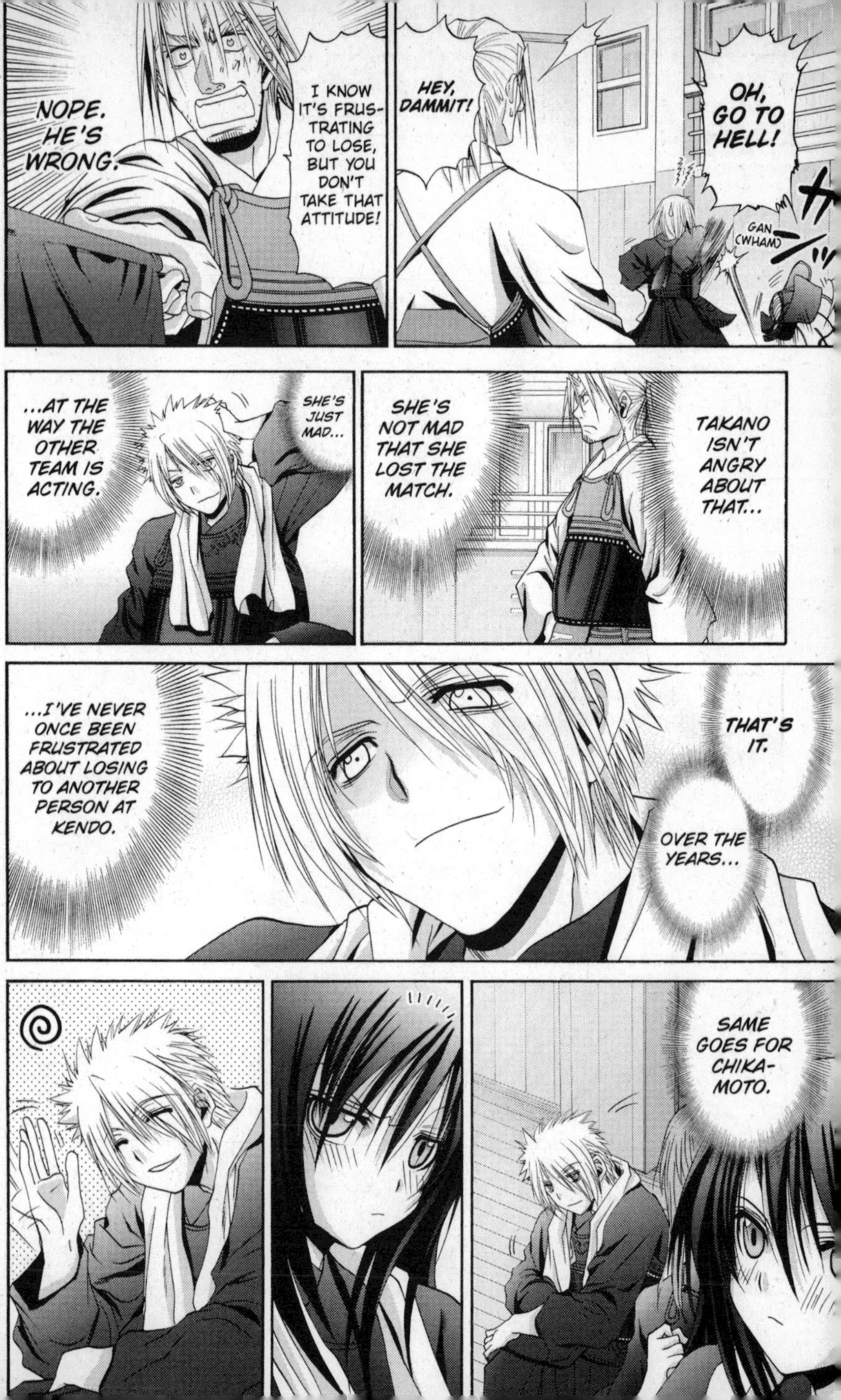

HEY, DAMMIT!
OH, GO TO HELL!
GAN (WHAM)
I KNOW IT'S FRUS-TRATING TO LOSE, BUT YOU DON'T TAKE THAT ATTITUDE!
NOPE. HE'S WRONG.
TAKANO ISN'T ANGRY ABOUT THAT...
SHE'S NOT MAD THAT SHE LOST THE MATCH.
SHE'S JUST MAD...
...AT THE WAY THE OTHER TEAM IS ACTING.
THAT'S IT.
OVER THE YEARS...
...I'VE NEVER ONCE BEEN FRUSTRATED ABOUT LOSING TO ANOTHER PERSON AT KENDO.
SAME GOES FOR CHIKA-MOTO.

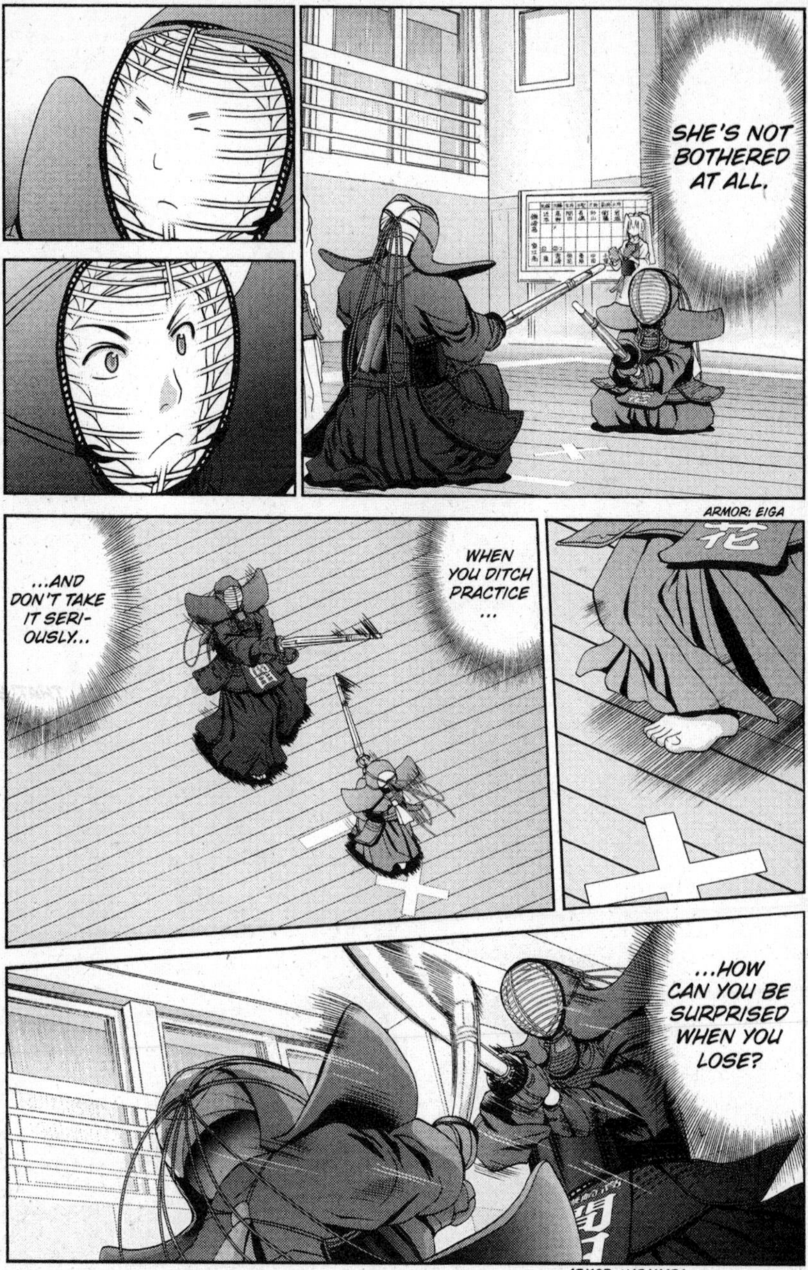
SHE'S NOT BOTHERED AT ALL.
ARMOR: EIGA
花
WHEN YOU DITCH PRACTICE ...
...AND DON'T TAKE IT SERIOUSLY...
...HOW CAN YOU BE SURPRISED WHEN YOU LOSE?
ARMOR: HAZAMADA

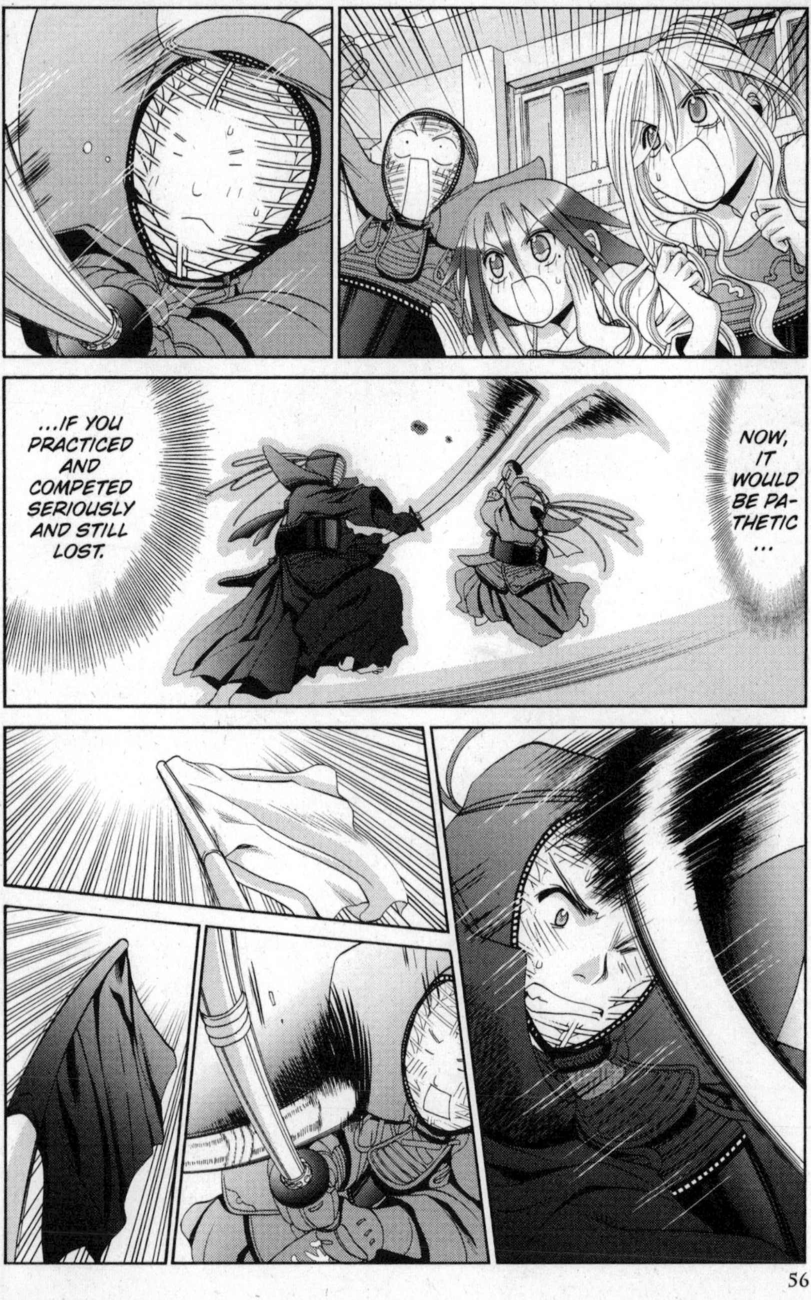
NOW, IT WOULD BE PA-THETIC...
...IF YOU PRACTICED AND COMPETED SERIOUSLY AND STILL LOST.

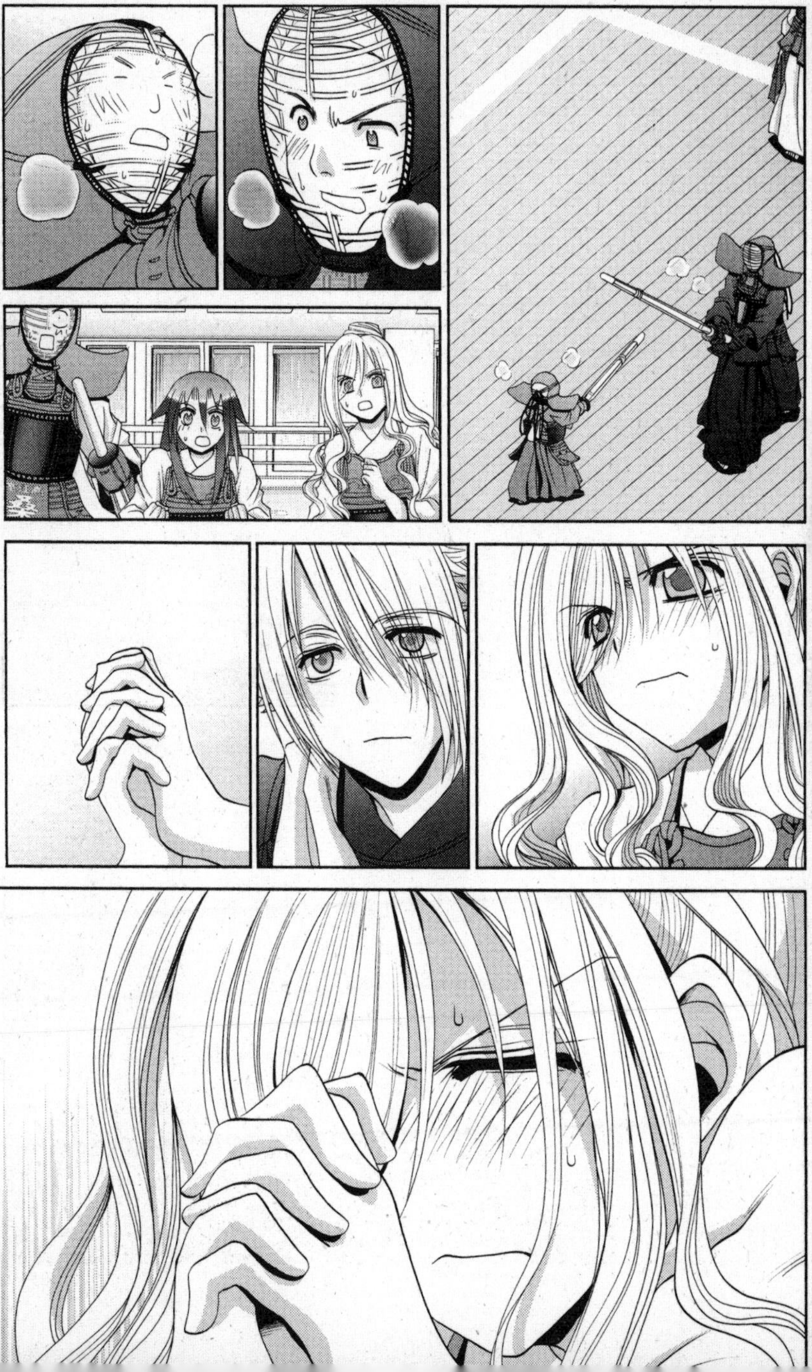

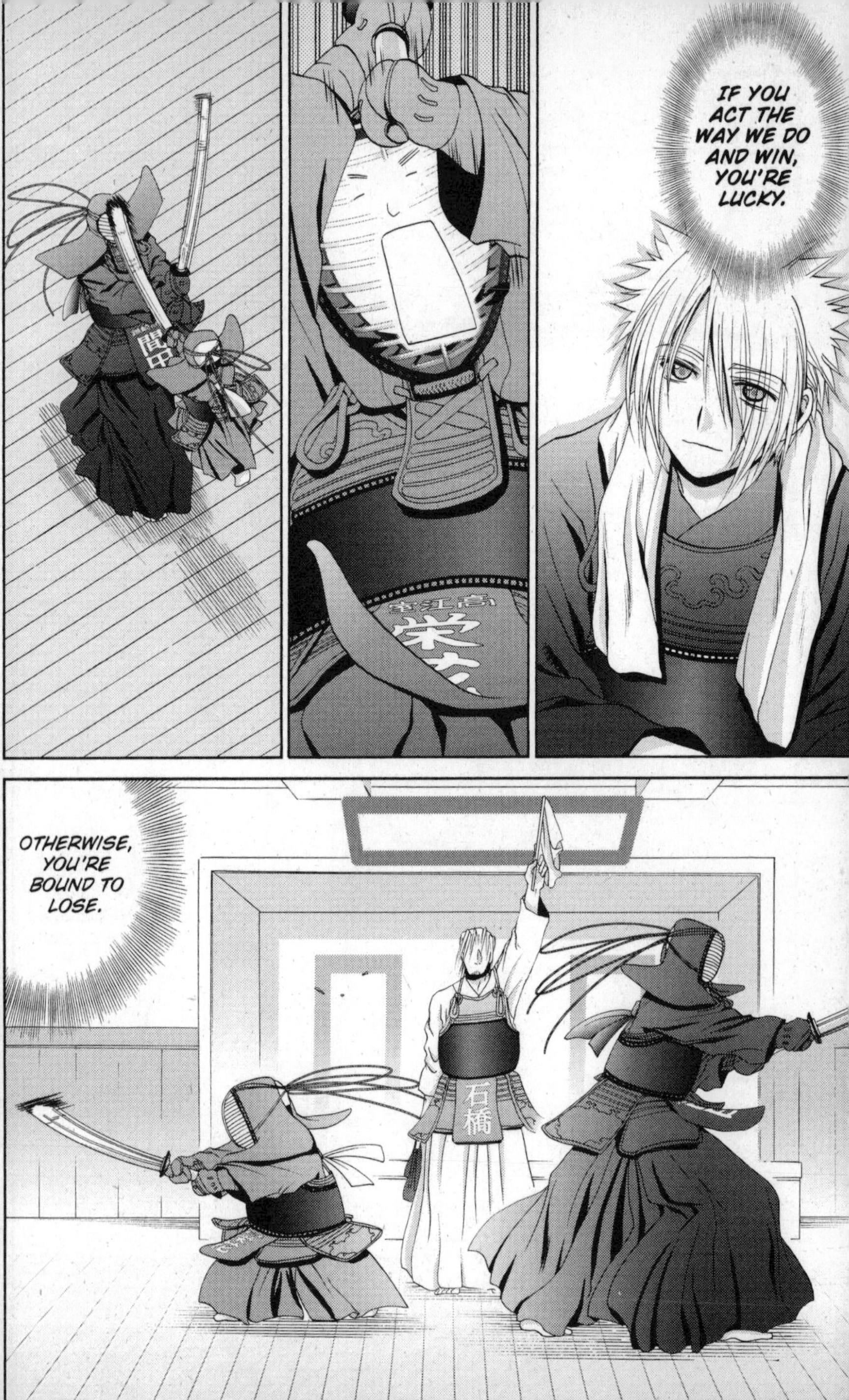
IF YOU ACT THE WAY WE DO AND WIN, YOU'RE LUCKY.
OTHERWISE, YOU'RE BOUND TO LOSE.

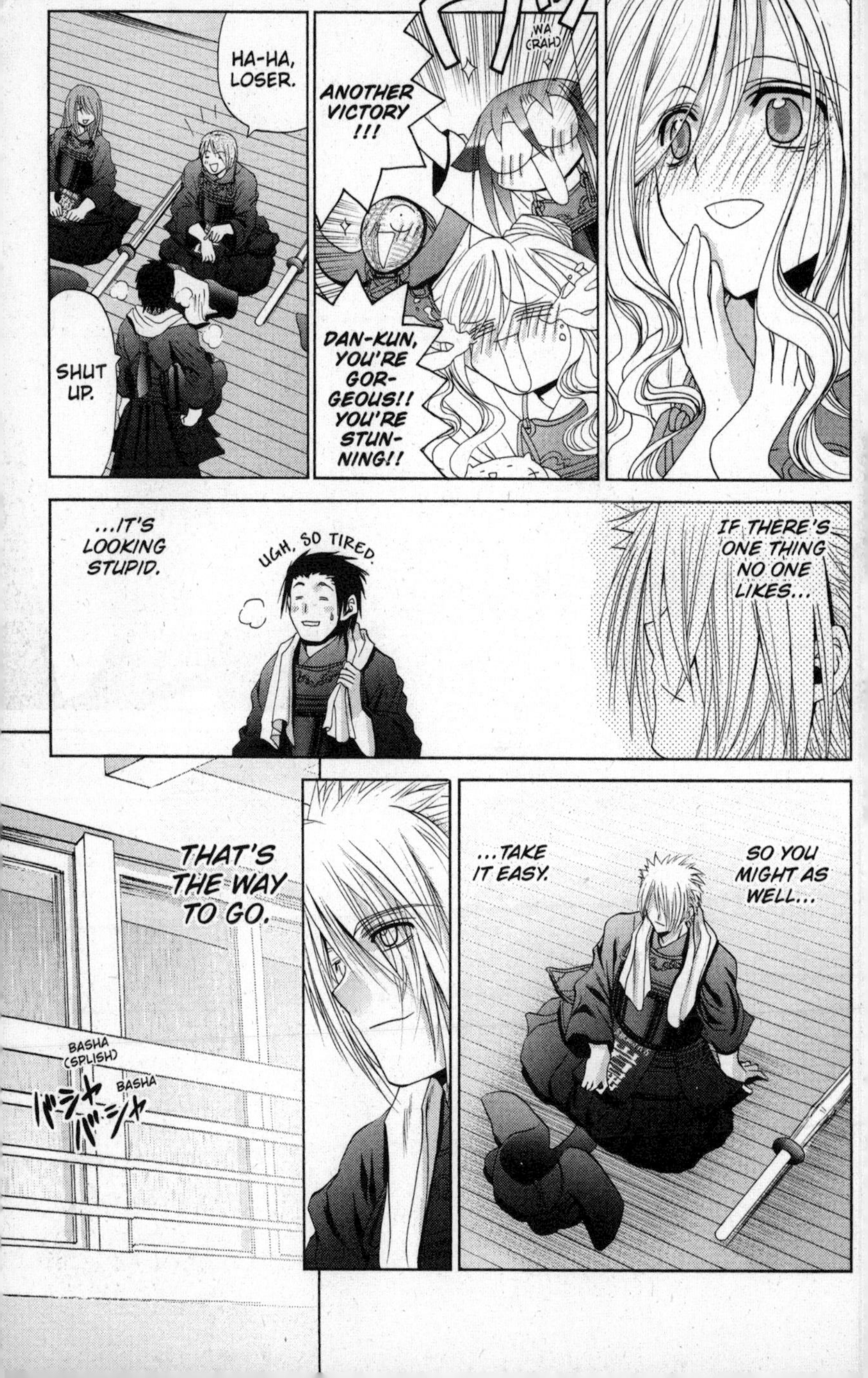
WA (RAH)
ANOTHER VICTORY !!!
DAN-KUN, YOU'RE GOR-GEOUS!! YOU'RE STUN-NING!!
HA-HA, LOSER.
SHUT UP.
IF THERE'S ONE THING NO ONE LIKES...
UGH, SO TIRED.
...IT'S LOOKING STUPID.
SO YOU MIGHT AS WELL...
...TAKE IT EASY.
THAT'S THE WAY TO GO.
BASHA (SPLISH)
BASHA

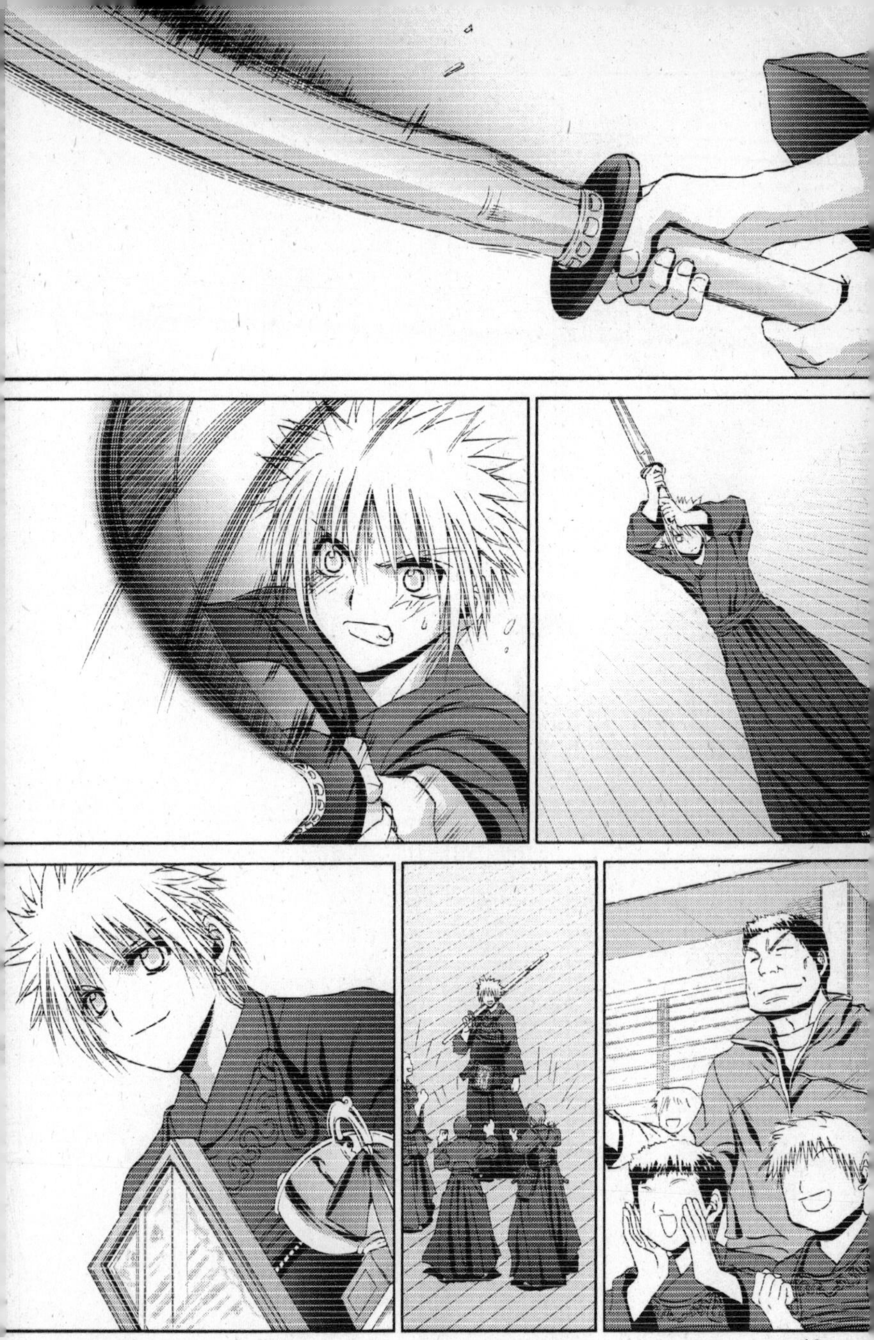

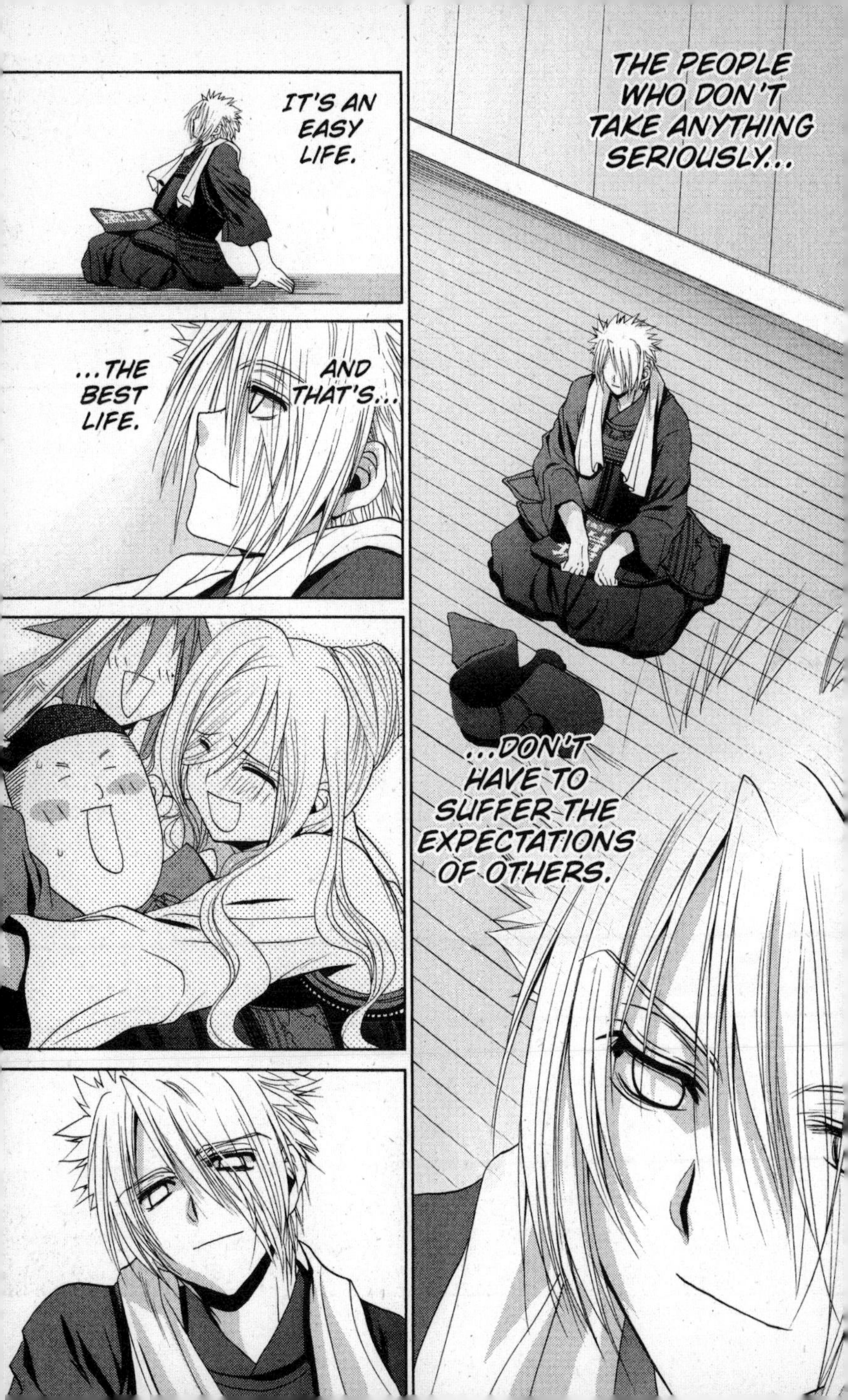
THE PEOPLE WHO DON'T TAKE ANYTHING SERIOUSLY...
...DON'T HAVE TO SUFFER THE EXPECTATIONS OF OTHERS.
IT'S AN EASY LIFE.
AND THAT'S...
...THE BEST LIFE.

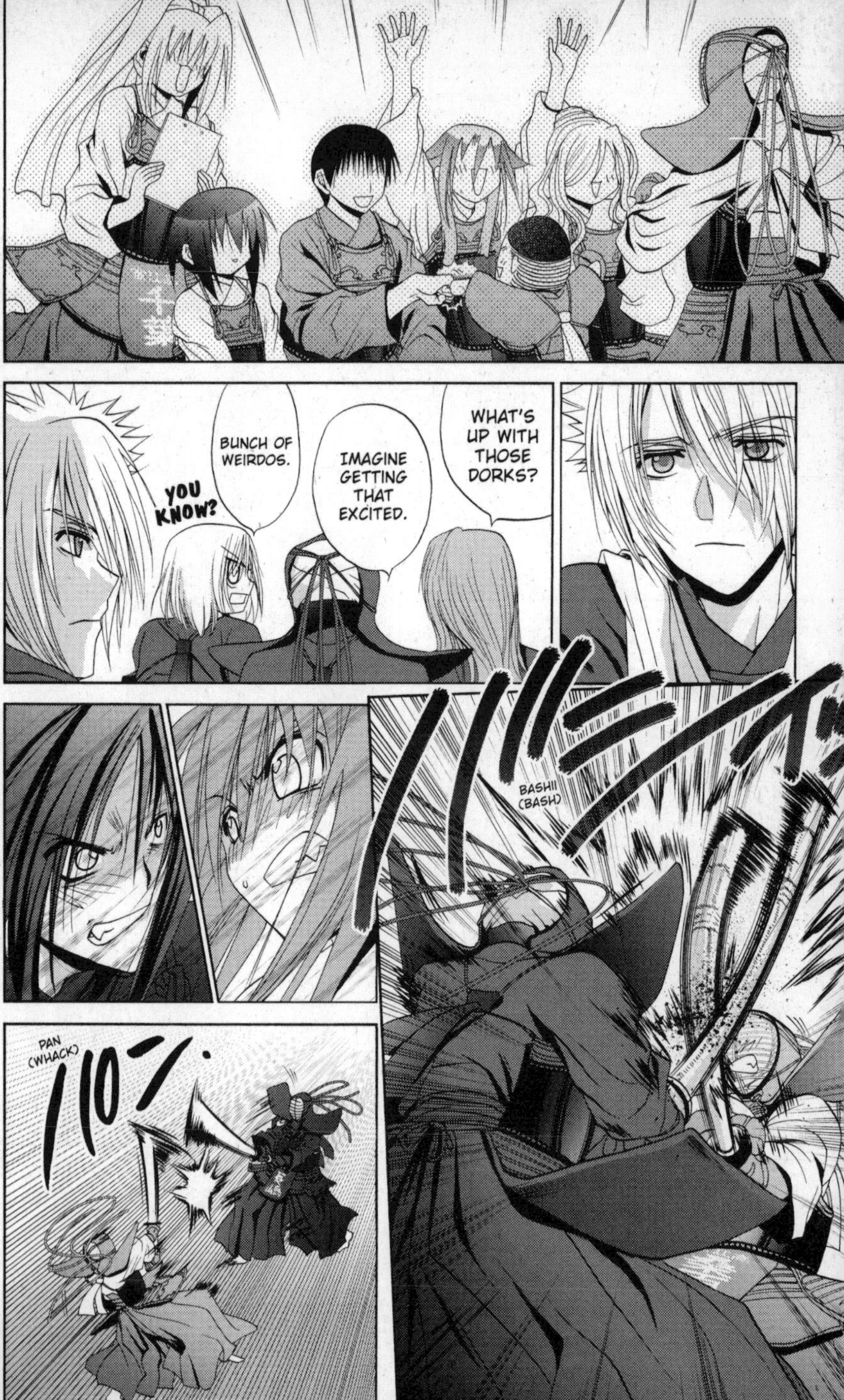
WHAT'S UP WITH THOSE DORKS?
IMAGINE GETTING THAT EXCITED.
BUNCH OF WEIRDOS.
YOU KNOW?
BASHI (BASH)
PAN (WHACK)

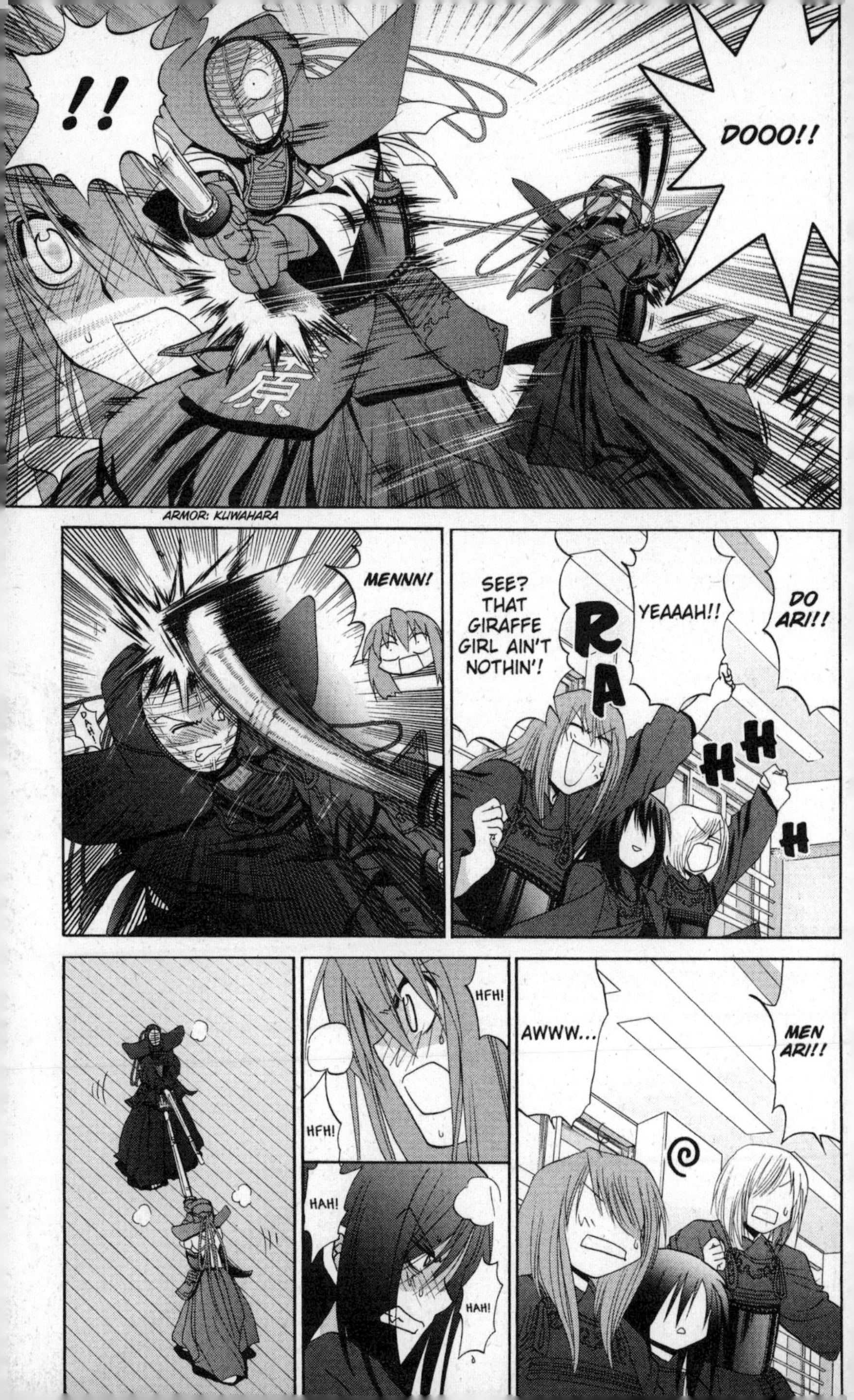
DOOO!!
!!
ARMOR: KUWAHARA
DO ARI!!
YEAAAH!!
RAHHHH
SEE? THAT GIRAFFE GIRL AIN'T NOTHIN'!
MENNN!
DAH!
MEN ARI!!
AWWW...
HFH!
HFH!
HAH!
HAH!

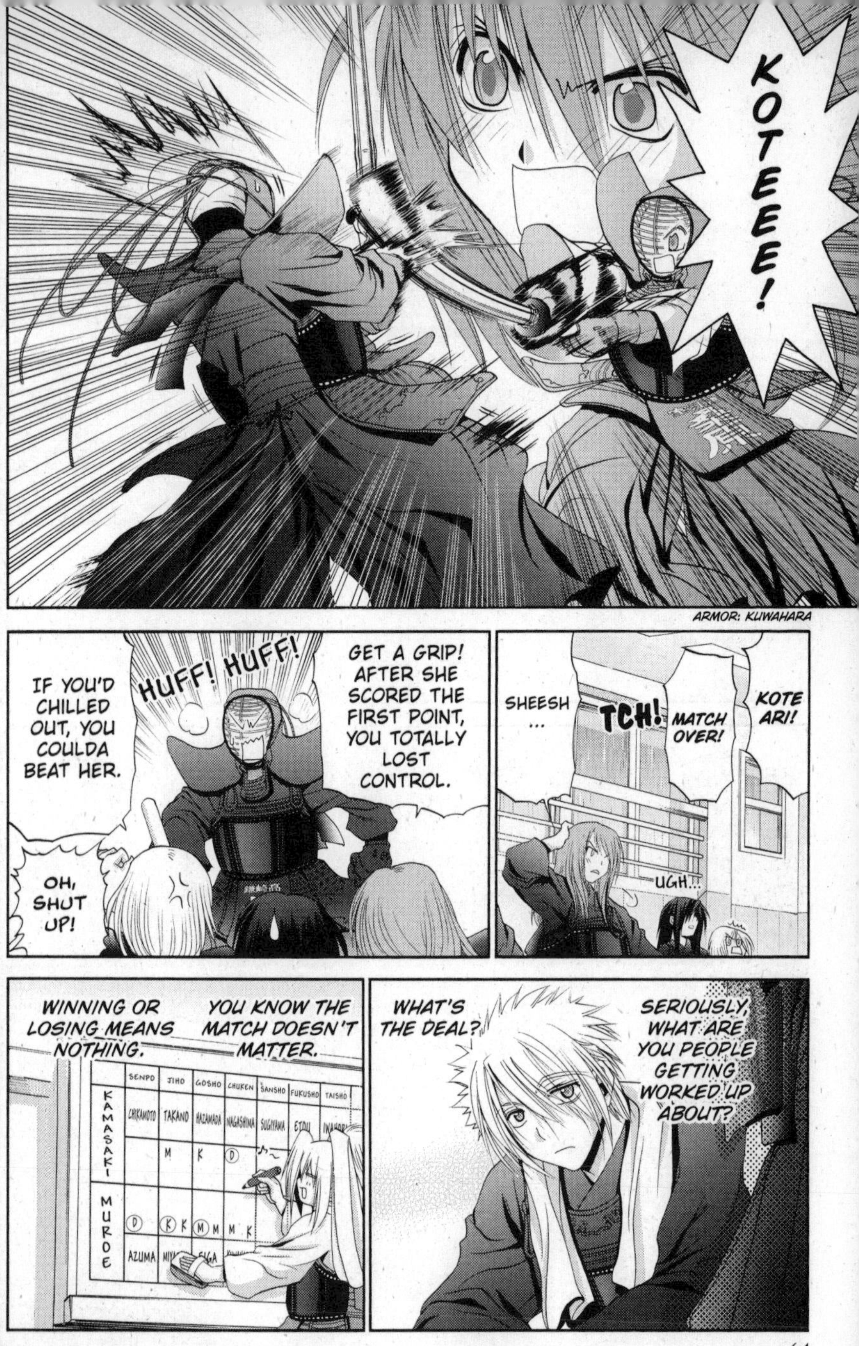
KOTEEE!
ARMOR: KUWAHARA
KOTE ARI!
MATCH OVER!
TCH!
SHEESH ...
UGH...
GET A GRIP! AFTER SHE SCORED THE FIRST POINT, YOU TOTALLY LOST CONTROL.
HUFF! HUFF!
IF YOU'D CHILLED OUT, YOU COULDA BEAT HER.
OH, SHUT UP!
SERIOUSLY, WHAT ARE YOU PEOPLE GETTING WORKED UP ABOUT?
WHAT'S THE DEAL?
YOU KNOW THE MATCH DOESN'T MATTER.
WINNING OR LOSING MEANS NOTHING.
SENPO JIHO GOSHO CHUKEN SANSHO FUKUSHO TAISHO
KAMASAKI
CHIKAMOTO TAKANO HAZAMADA NAGASHIMA SUGIYAMA ETOU
M K D
MUROE
D K K M M M K
AZUMA

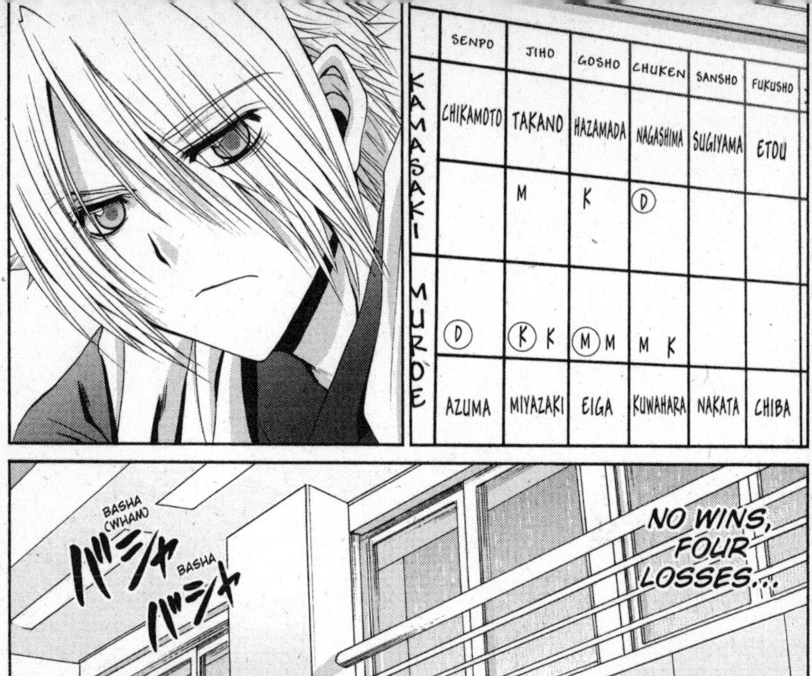

SENPO
JIHO
GOSHO
CHUKEN
SANSHO
FUKUSHO
KAMASAKI
CHIKAMOTO
TAKANO
HAZAMADA
NAGASHIMA
SUGIYAMA
ETOU
M
K
D
D
K K
M M
M K
MUROE
AZUMA
MIYAZAKI
EIGA
KUWAHARA
NAKATA
CHIBA
NO WINS, FOUR LOSSES...
BASHA (WHAM)
BASHA
THAT WAS TOO BAD.
SHE JUST NEEDED ONE MORE BLOW TO WIN.
EXCUSE ME!
CAN YOU TAKE OVER THE SCORING FOR ME?
IT'S MY TURN TO COMPETE SOON.
SURE.
GIVE IT HERE.
ERASER
IT'S LOOKING LIKE A CLEAN SWEEP...
WHAT DO YOU THINK, KAMASAKI HIGH?
ARMOR: ISHIDA

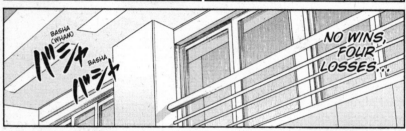

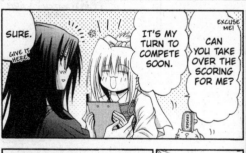

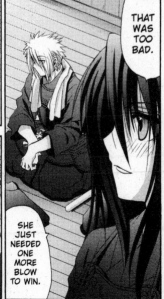

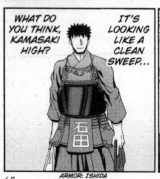

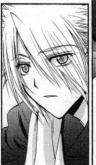

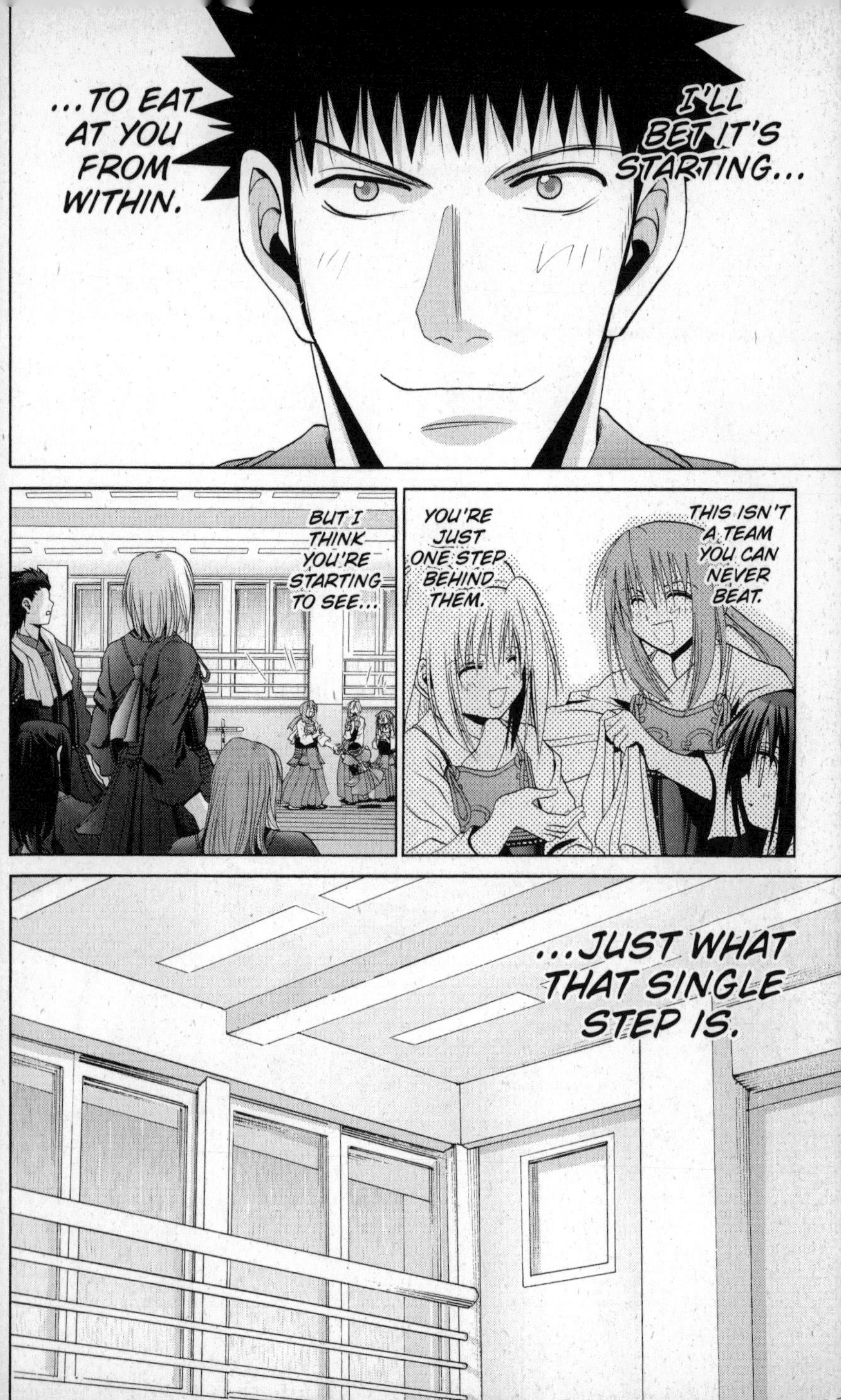
I'LL BET IT'S STARTING...
...TO EAT AT YOU FROM WITHIN.
THIS ISN'T A TEAM YOU CAN NEVER BEAT.
YOU'RE JUST ONE STEP BEHIND THEM.
BUT I THINK YOU'RE STARTING TO SEE...
...JUST WHAT THAT SINGLE STEP IS.

BAMBOO BLADE

バンブーブレード

BAMBOO BLADE

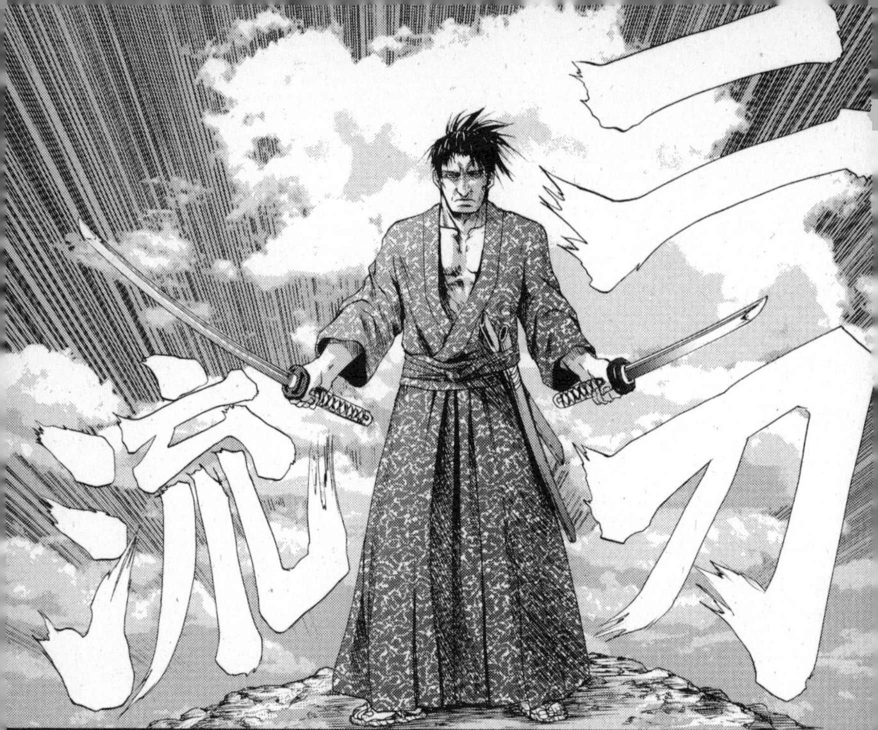
二刀流

BACKGROUND: TWO-SWORD STYLE

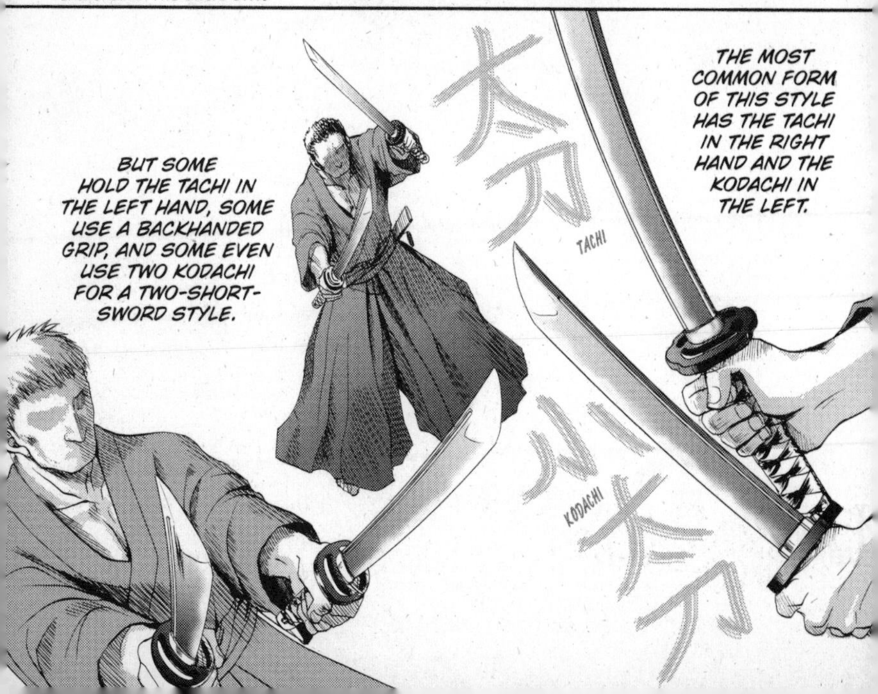
THE MOST COMMON FORM OF THIS STYLE HAS THE TACHI IN THE RIGHT HAND AND THE KODACHI IN THE LEFT.
太刀
TACHI
小太刀
KODACHI
BUT SOME HOLD THE TACHI IN THE LEFT HAND, SOME USE A BACKHANDED GRIP, AND SOME EVEN USE TWO KODACHI FOR A TWO-SHORT-SWORD STYLE.

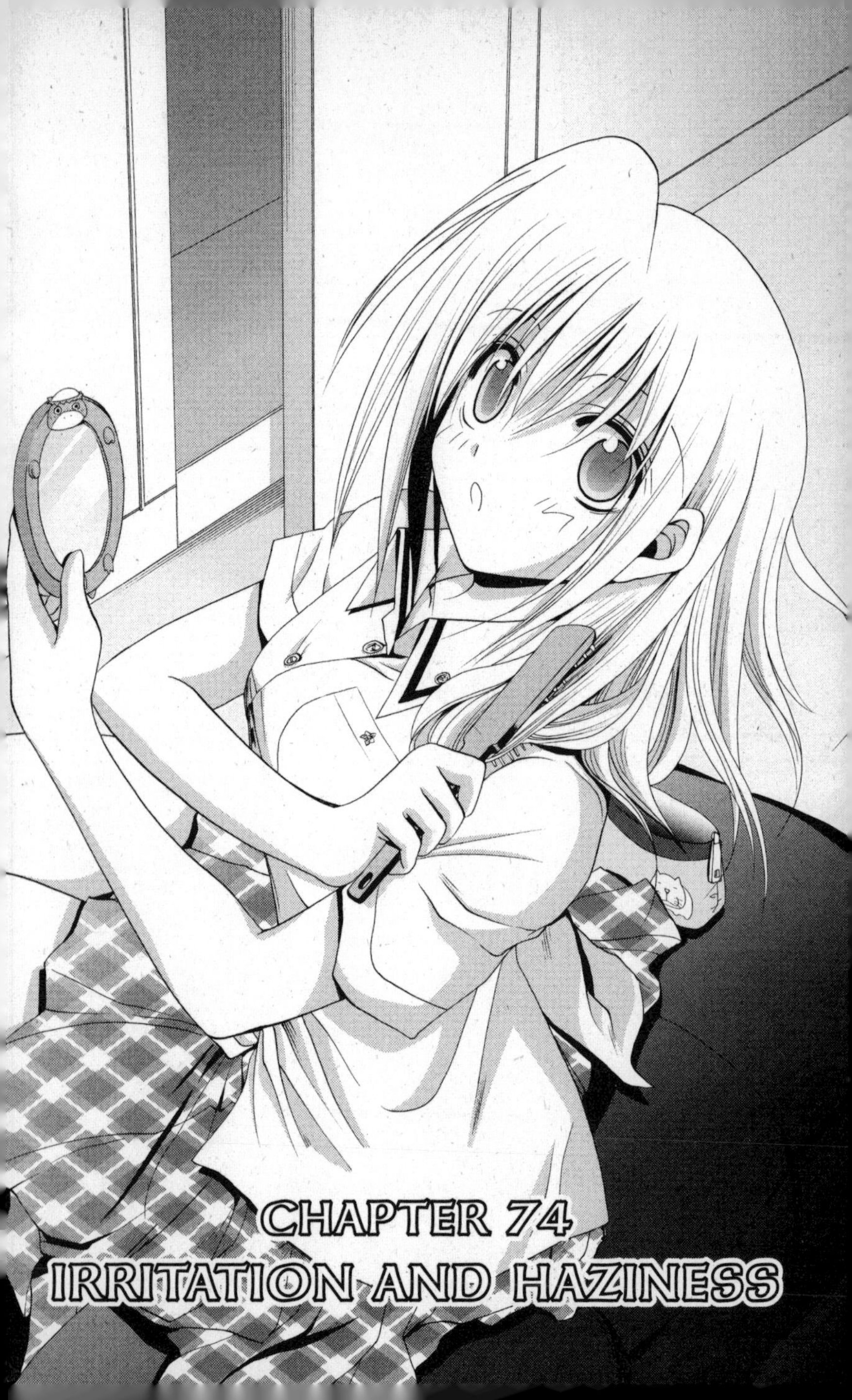
CHAPTER 74
IRRITATION AND HAZINESS

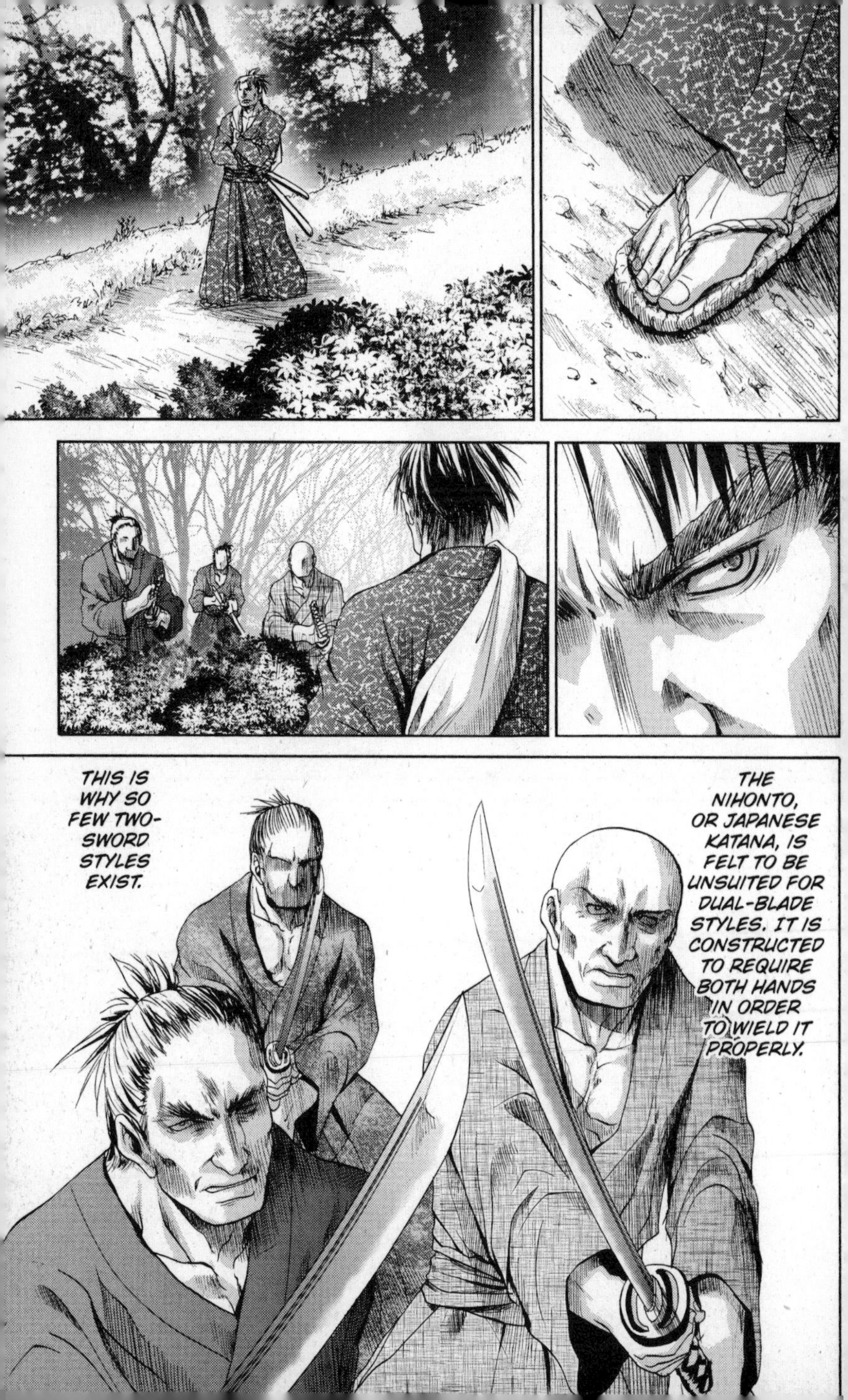
THE NIHONTO, OR JAPANESE KATANA, IS FELT TO BE UNSUITED FOR DUAL-BLADE STYLES. IT IS CONSTRUCTED TO REQUIRE BOTH HANDS IN ORDER TO WIELD IT PROPERLY.
THIS IS WHY SO FEW TWO-SWORD STYLES EXIST.

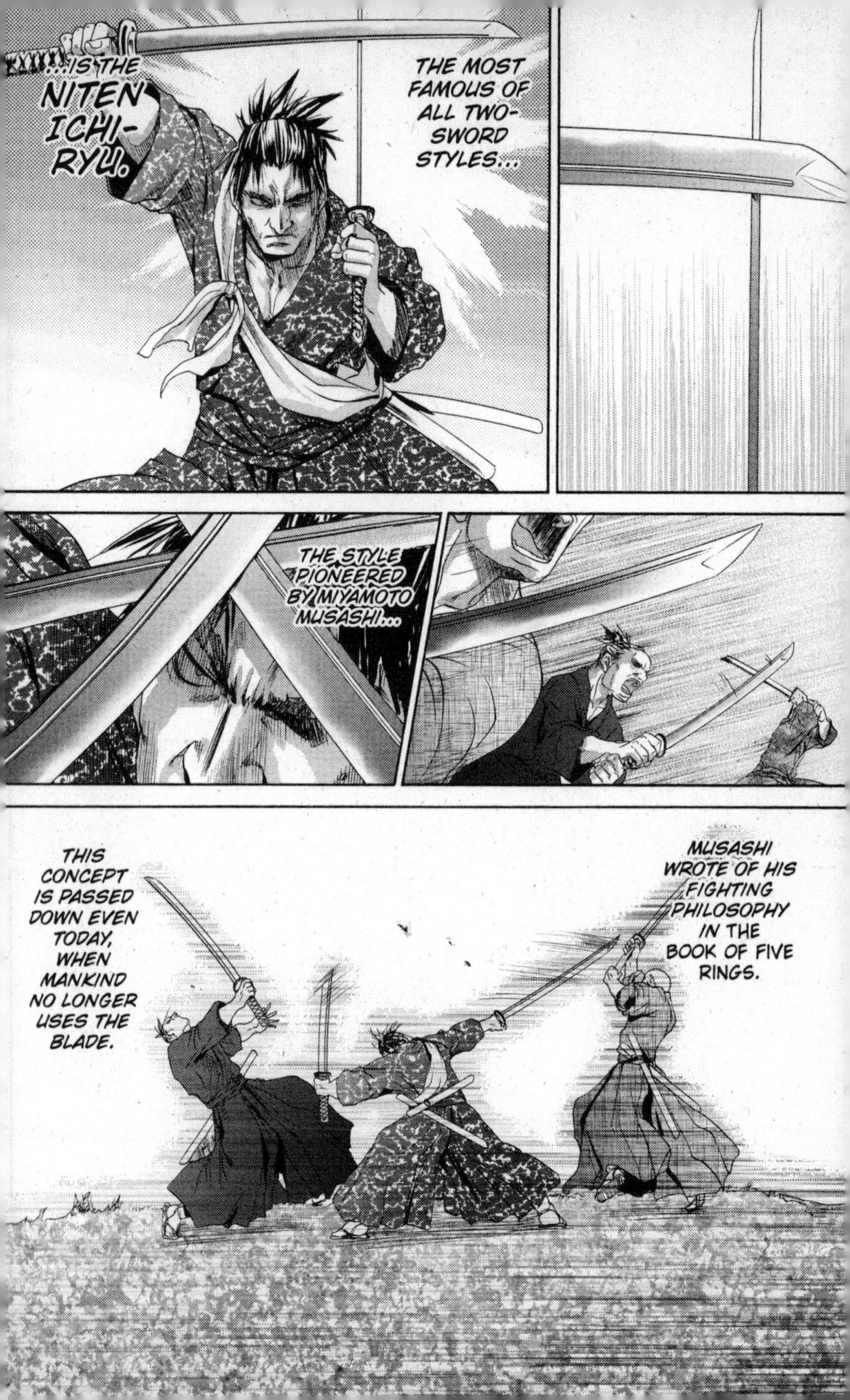
THE MOST FAMOUS OF ALL TWO-SWORD STYLES...
...IS THE NITEN ICHI-RYU.
THE STYLE PIONEERED BY MIYAMOTO MUSASHI...
MUSASHI WROTE OF HIS FIGHTING PHILOSOPHY IN THE BOOK OF FIVE RINGS.
THIS CONCEPT IS PASSED DOWN EVEN TODAY, WHEN MANKIND NO LONGER USES THE BLADE.

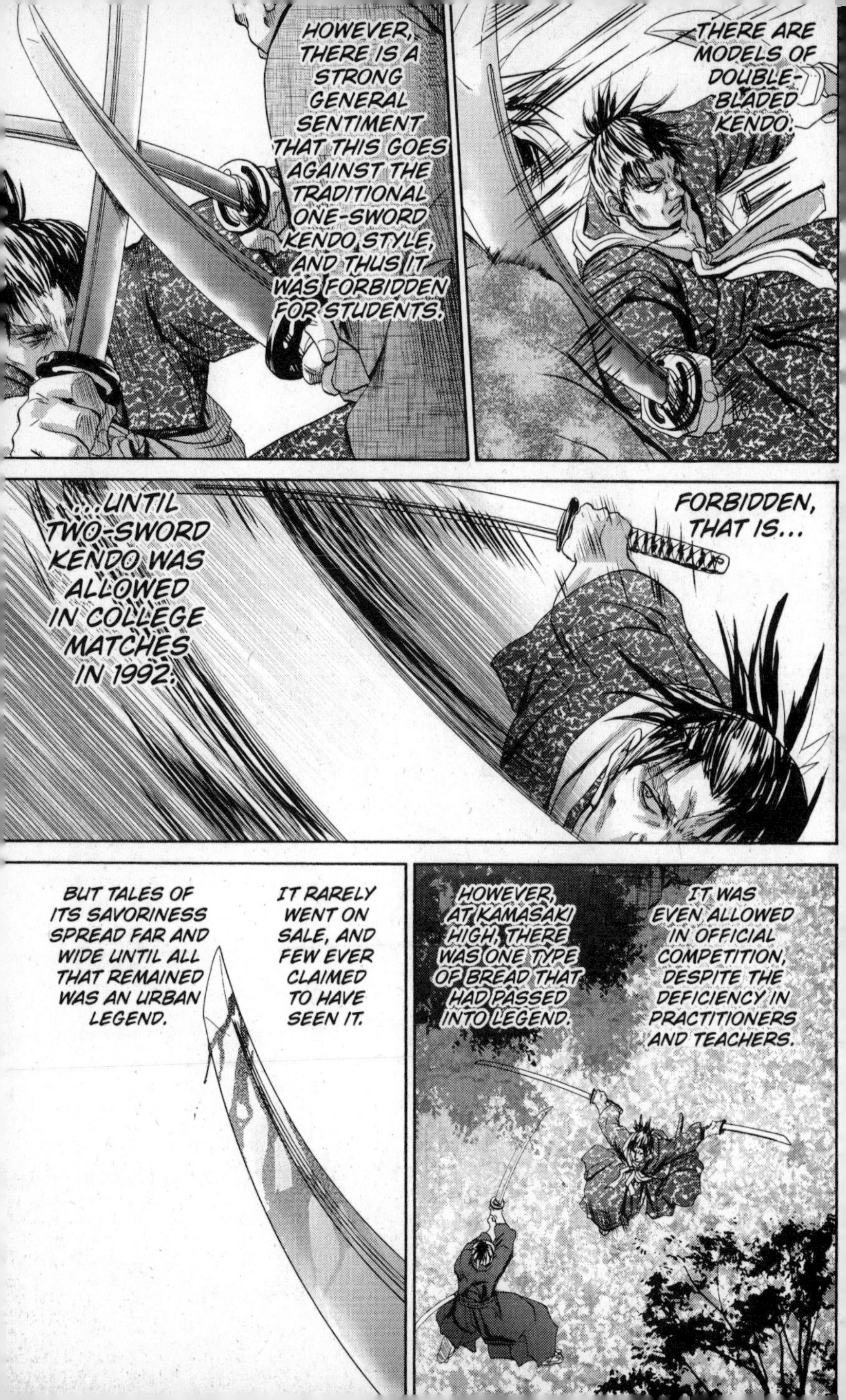
THERE ARE MODELS OF DOUBLE-BLADED KENDO.
HOWEVER, THERE IS A STRONG GENERAL SENTIMENT THAT THIS GOES AGAINST THE TRADITIONAL ONE-SWORD KENDO STYLE, AND THUS IT WAS FORBIDDEN FOR STUDENTS.
FORBIDDEN, THAT IS...
...UNTIL TWO-SWORD KENDO WAS ALLOWED IN COLLEGE MATCHES IN 1992.
IT WAS EVEN ALLOWED IN OFFICIAL COMPETITION, DESPITE THE DEFICIENCY IN PRACTITIONERS AND TEACHERS.
HOWEVER, AT KAMASAKI HIGH, THERE WAS ONE TYPE OF BREAD THAT HAD PASSED INTO LEGEND.
IT RARELY WENT ON SALE, AND FEW EVER CLAIMED TO HAVE SEEN IT.
BUT TALES OF ITS SAVORINESS SPREAD FAR AND WIDE UNTIL ALL THAT REMAINED WAS AN URBAN LEGEND.

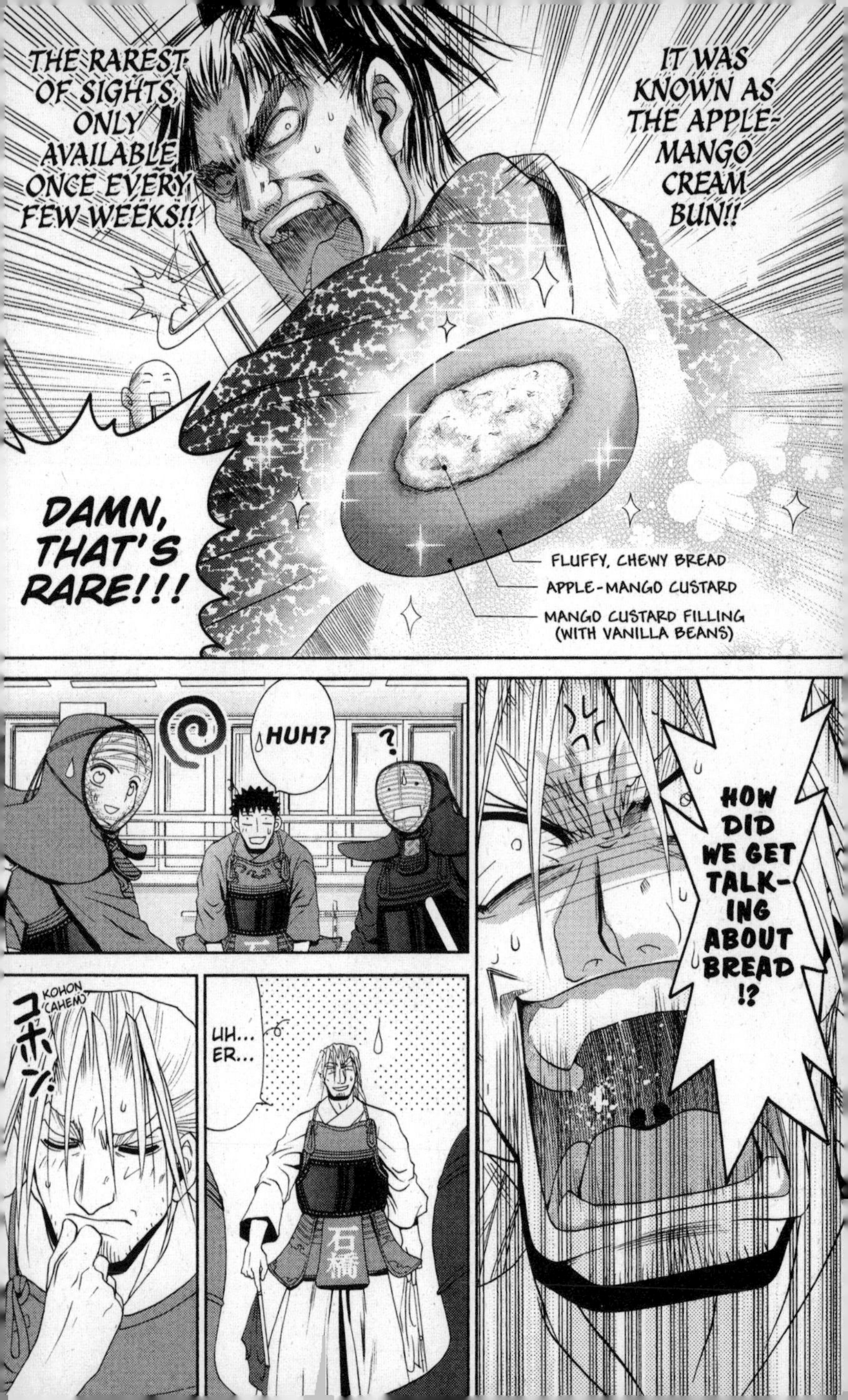
IT WAS KNOWN AS THE APPLE-MANGO CREAM BUN!!
THE RAREST OF SIGHTS, ONLY AVAILABLE ONCE EVERY FEW WEEKS!!
DAMN, THAT'S RARE!!!
FLUFFY, CHEWY BREAD
APPLE-MANGO CUSTARD
MANGO CUSTARD FILLING (WITH VANILLA BEANS)
HOW DID WE GET TALK-ING ABOUT BREAD!?
HUH?
?
UH... ER...
KOHON 'CAHEM'

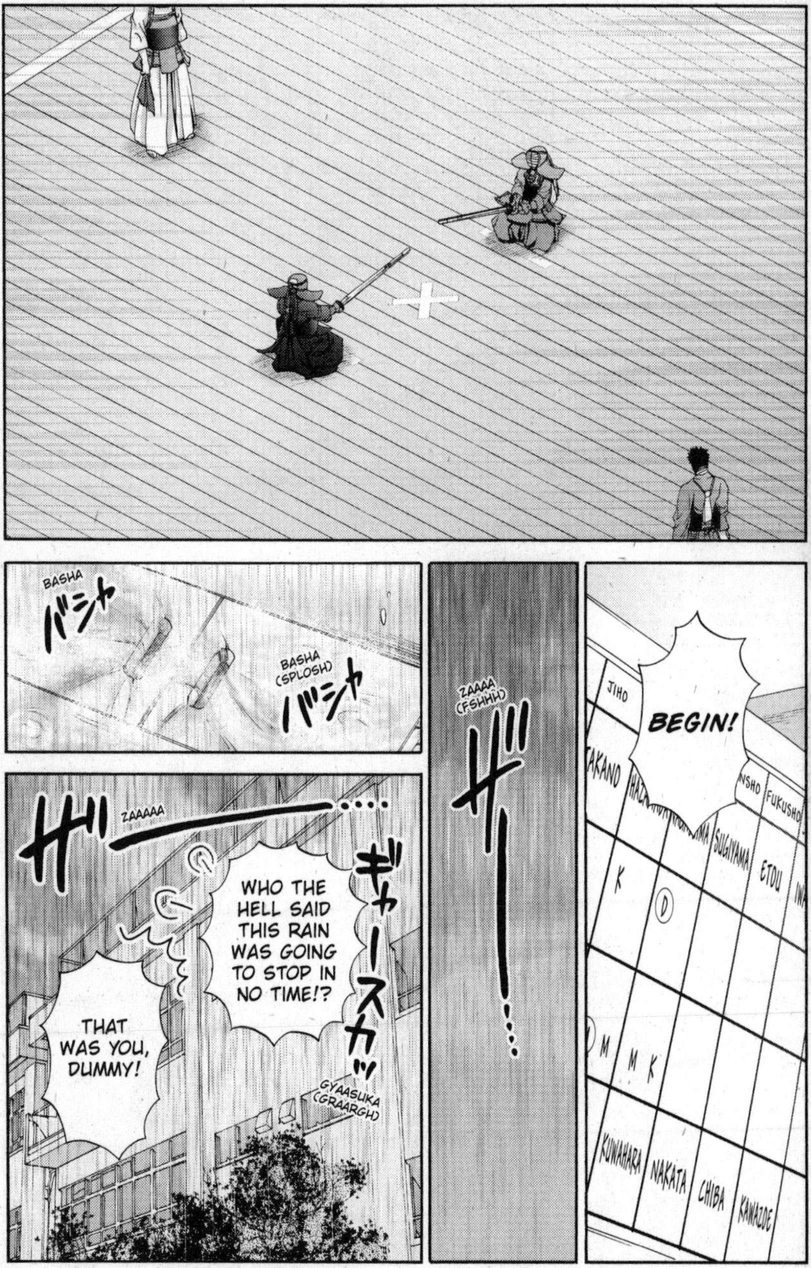
BEGIN!
JIHO
TAKANO
FUKUSHO
SUGIYAMA
ETOU
KUWAHARA
NAKATA
CHIBA
KAWAZOE
ZAAAA (FSHHH)
ザー…
BASHA
バシャ
BASHA (SPLOSH)
バシャ
ZAAAAA
ザー…
WHO THE HELL SAID THIS RAIN WAS GOING TO STOP IN NO TIME!?
ギャースカッ
GYAASUKA (GRAARGH)
THAT WAS YOU, DUMMY!

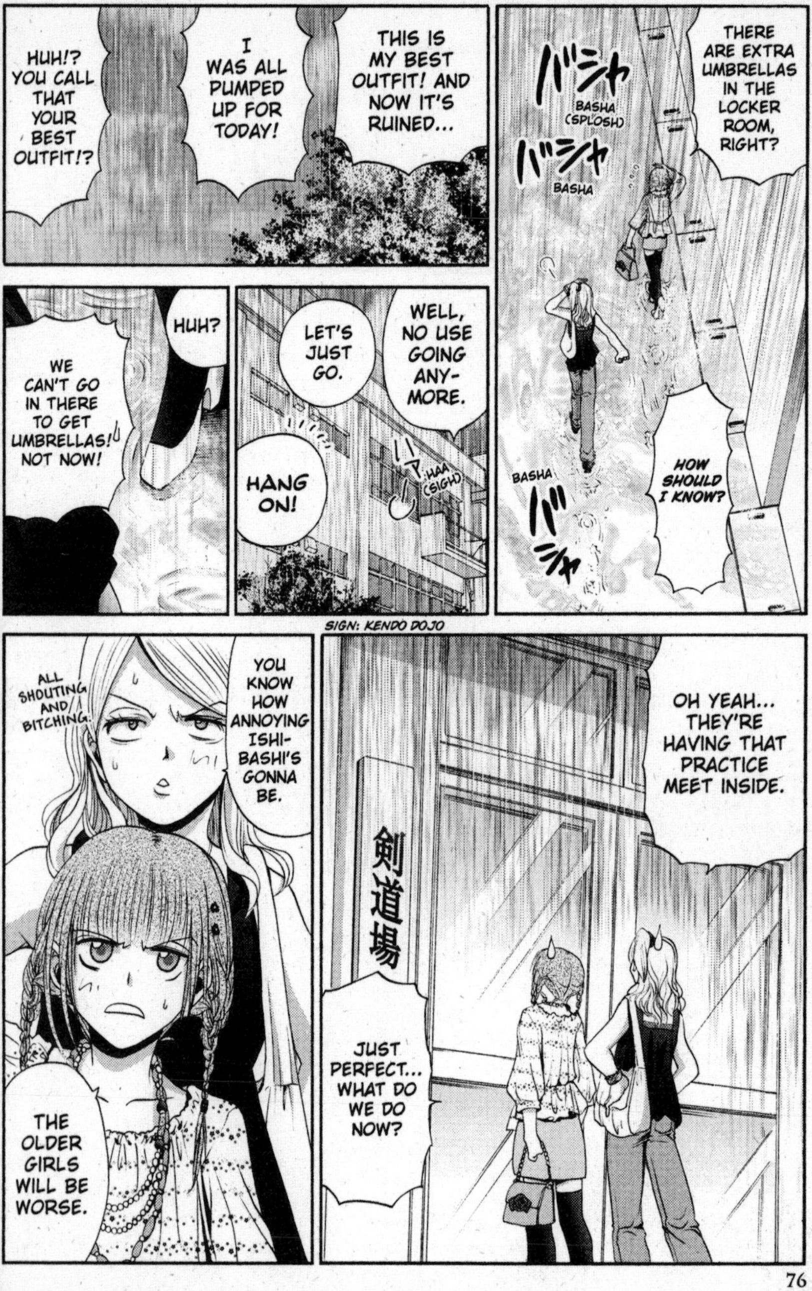
THERE ARE EXTRA UMBRELLAS IN THE LOCKER ROOM, RIGHT?
バシャ
BASHA (SPLOSH)
バシャ
BASHA
HOW SHOULD I KNOW?
BASHA
バシャ
THIS IS MY BEST OUTFIT! AND NOW IT'S RUINED...
I WAS ALL PUMPED UP FOR TODAY!
HUH!? YOU CALL THAT YOUR BEST OUTFIT!?
WELL, NO USE GOING ANY-MORE.
LET'S JUST GO.
ハア
HAA (SIGH)
HANG ON!
HUH?
WE CAN'T GO IN THERE TO GET UMBRELLAS! NOT NOW!
SIGN: KENDO DOJO
OH YEAH... THEY'RE HAVING THAT PRACTICE MEET INSIDE.
剣道場
JUST PERFECT... WHAT DO WE DO NOW?
YOU KNOW HOW ANNOYING ISHI-BASHI'S GONNA BE.
ALL SHOUTING AND BITCHING.
THE OLDER GIRLS WILL BE WORSE.

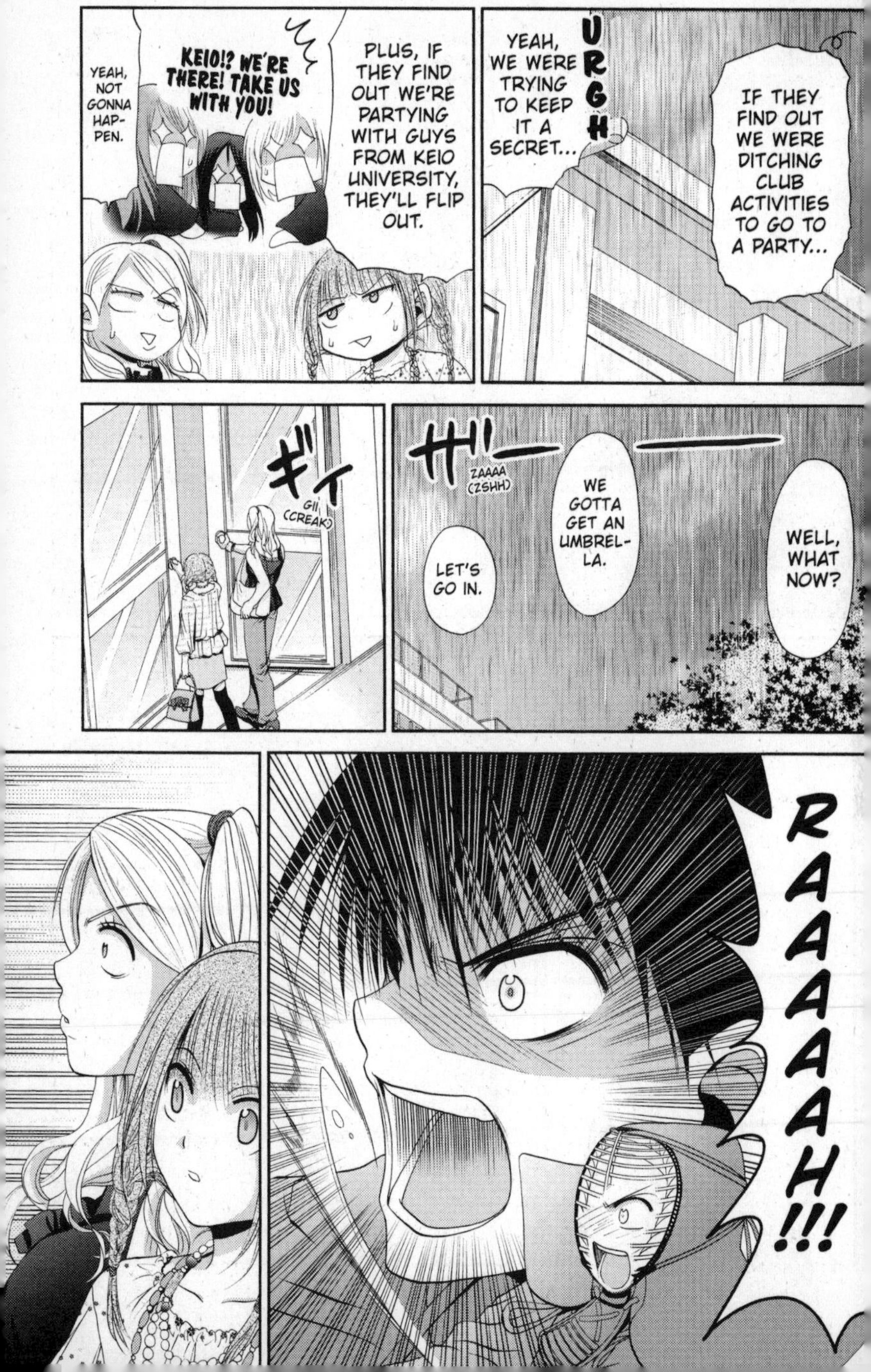
IF THEY FIND OUT WE WERE DITCHING CLUB ACTIVITIES TO GO TO A PARTY...
URGH
YEAH, WE WERE TRYING TO KEEP IT A SECRET...
PLUS, IF THEY FIND OUT WE'RE PARTYING WITH GUYS FROM KEIO UNIVERSITY, THEY'LL FLIP OUT.
KEIO!? WE'RE THERE! TAKE US WITH YOU!
YEAH, NOT GONNA HAP-PEN.
ザー
ZAAAA (ZSHH)
WELL, WHAT NOW?
WE GOTTA GET AN UMBREL-LA.
LET'S GO IN.
ギイ
GII (CREAK)
RAAAAAAH!!!

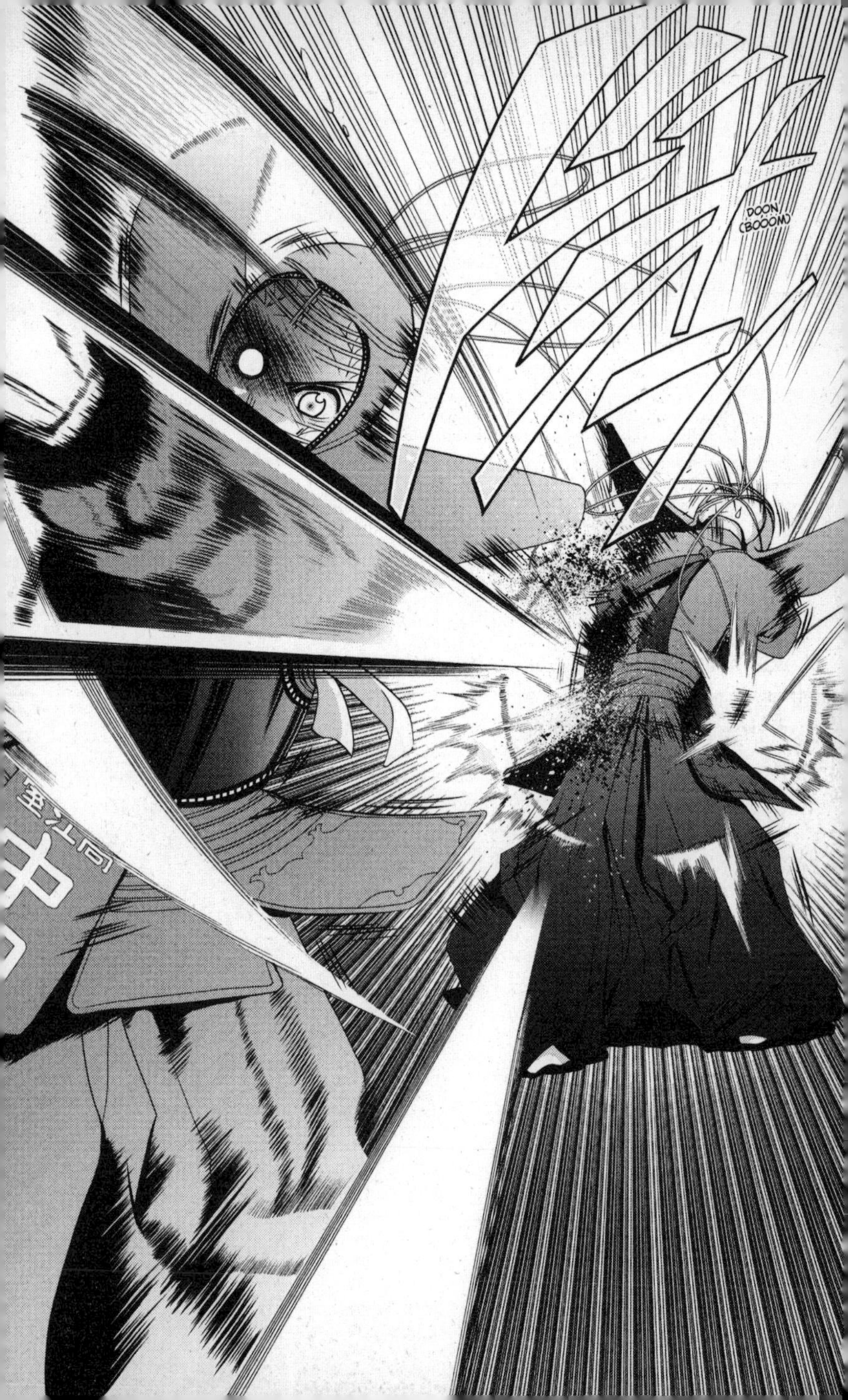
DOON
(BOOOM)

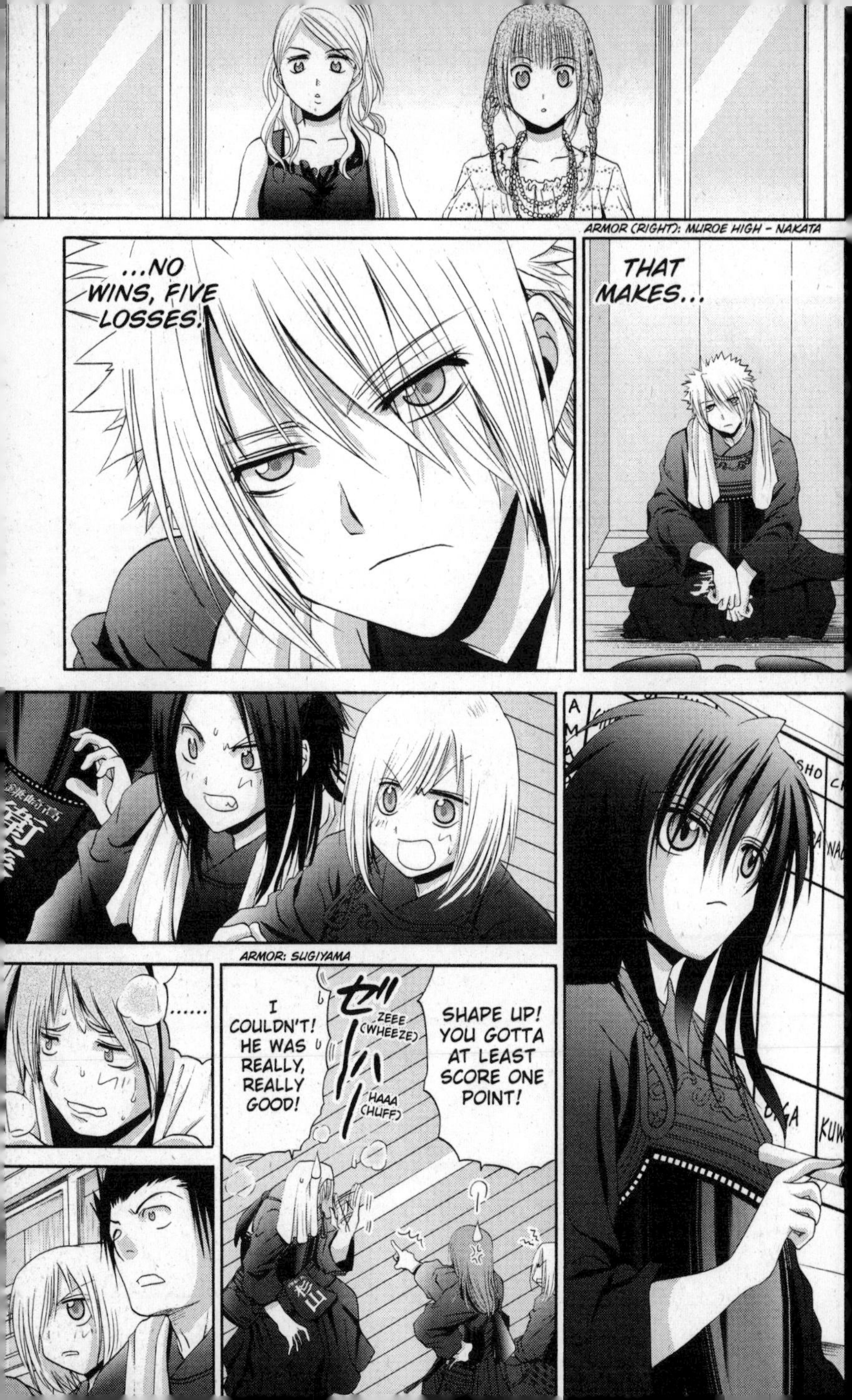
ARMOR (RIGHT): MUROE HIGH - NAKATA
THAT MAKES...
...NO WINS, FIVE LOSSES!
ARMOR: SUGIYAMA
SHAPE UP! YOU GOTTA AT LEAST SCORE ONE POINT!
ZEEE (WHEEZE)
HAAA (HUFF)
I COULDN'T! HE WAS REALLY, REALLY GOOD!
......

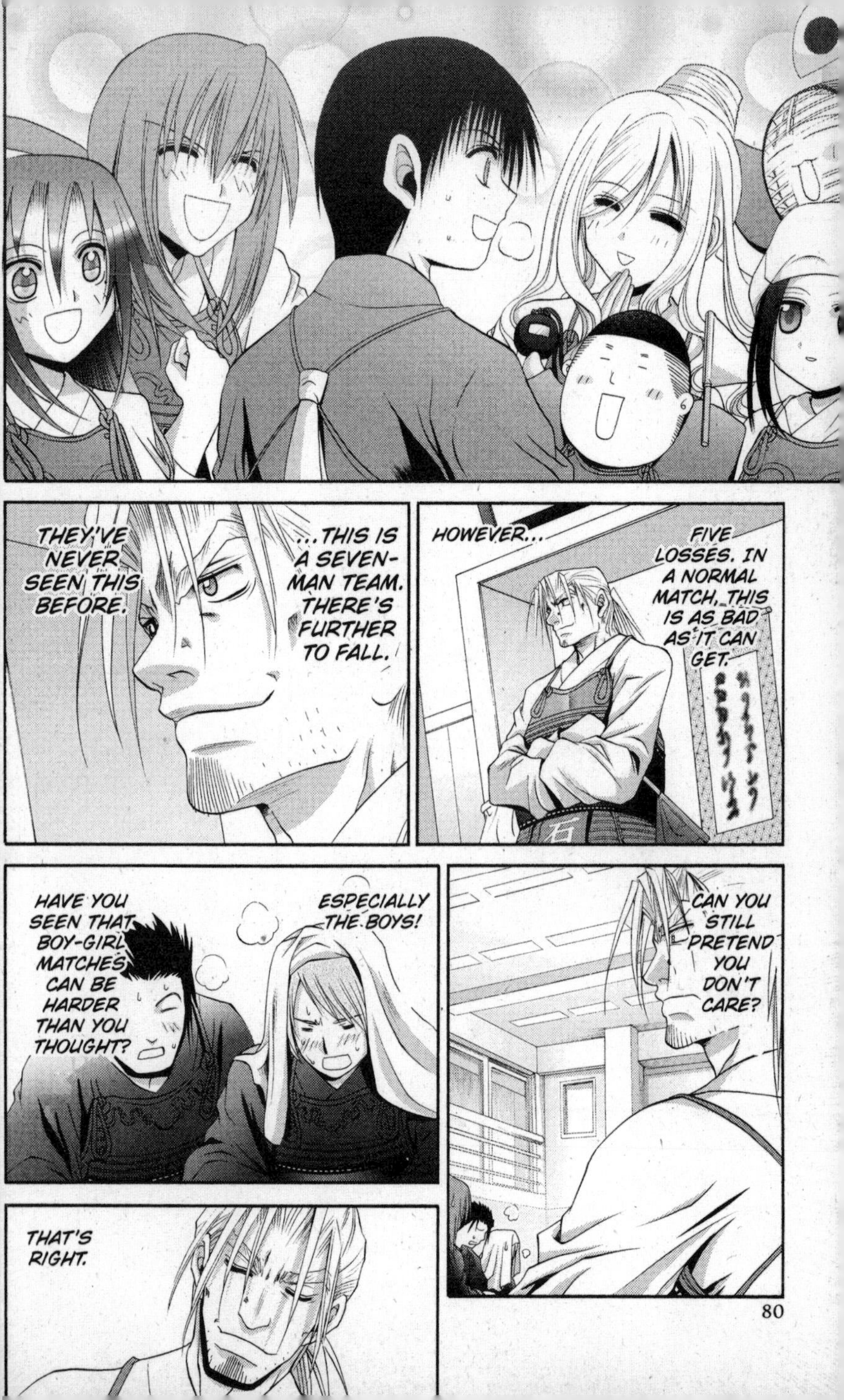
HOWEVER...
FIVE LOSSES. IN A NORMAL MATCH, THIS IS AS BAD AS IT CAN GET.
...THIS IS A SEVEN-MAN TEAM. THERE'S FURTHER TO FALL.
THEY'VE NEVER SEEN THIS BEFORE.
CAN YOU STILL PRETEND YOU DON'T CARE?
ESPECIALLY THE BOYS!
HAVE YOU SEEN THAT BOY-GIRL MATCHES CAN BE HARDER THAN YOU THOUGHT?
THAT'S RIGHT.

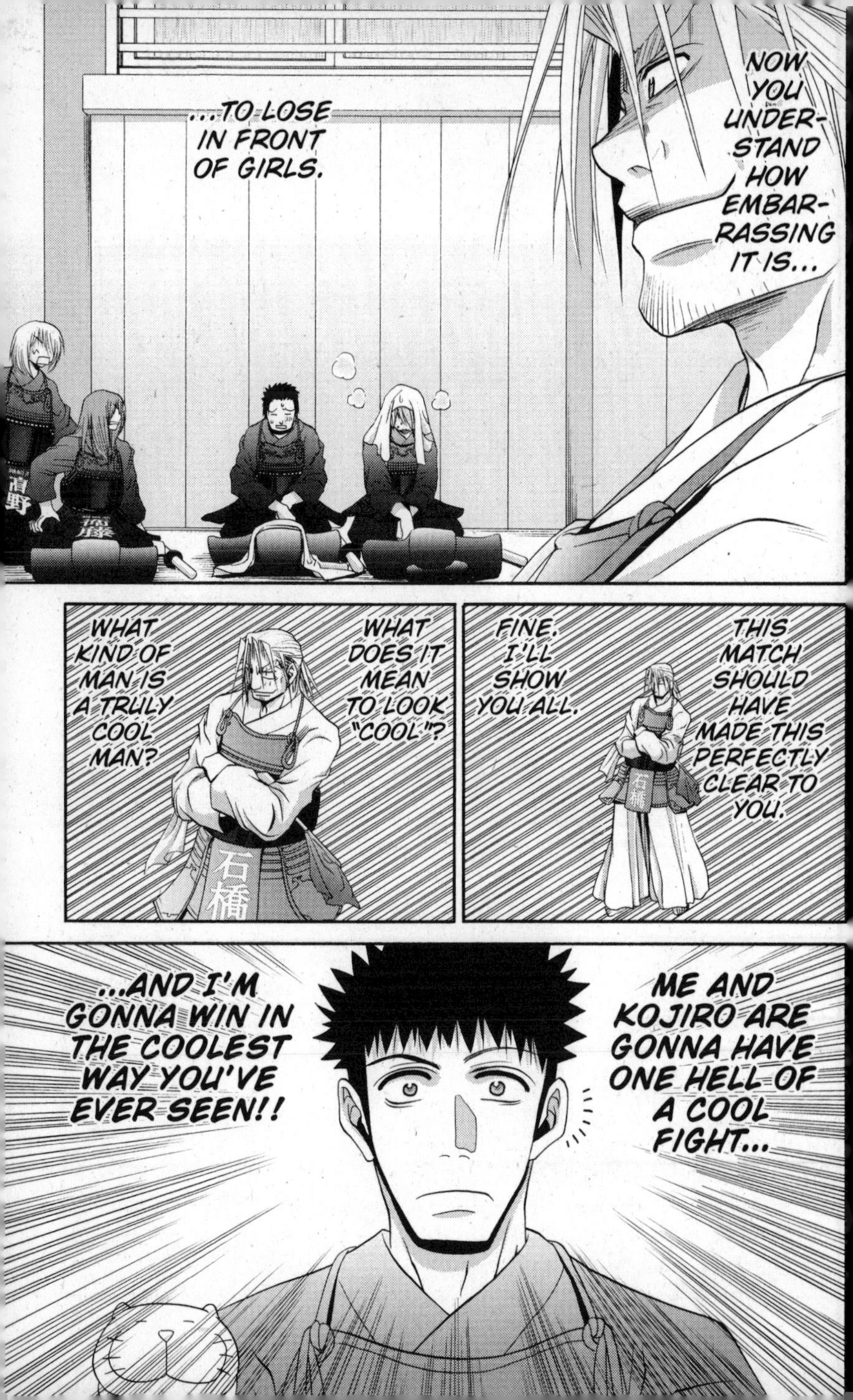
NOW YOU UNDERSTAND HOW EMBARRASSING IT IS...
...TO LOSE IN FRONT OF GIRLS.
THIS MATCH SHOULD HAVE MADE THIS PERFECTLY CLEAR TO YOU.
FINE. I'LL SHOW YOU ALL.
WHAT DOES IT MEAN TO LOOK "COOL"?
WHAT KIND OF MAN IS A TRULY COOL MAN?
ME AND KOJIRO ARE GONNA HAVE ONE HELL OF A COOL FIGHT...
...AND I'M GONNA WIN IN THE COOLEST WAY YOU'VE EVER SEEN!!

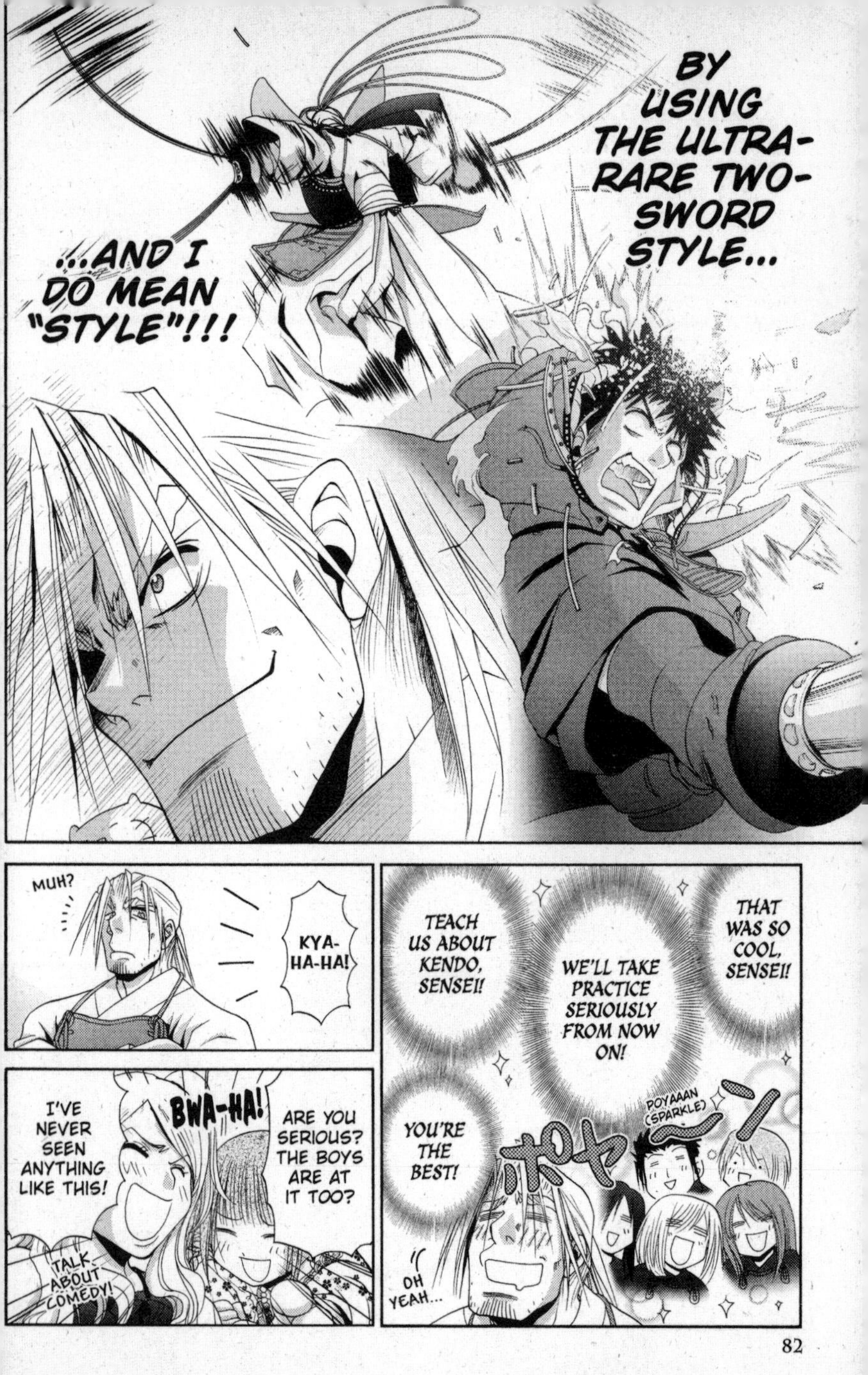
BY USING THE ULTRA-RARE TWO-SWORD STYLE...
...AND I DO MEAN "STYLE"!!!
THAT WAS SO COOL, SENSEI!
WE'LL TAKE PRACTICE SERIOUSLY FROM NOW ON!
TEACH US ABOUT KENDO, SENSEI!
POYAAAN (SPARKLE)
YOU'RE THE BEST!
OH YEAH...
KYA-HA-HA!
MUH?
ARE YOU SERIOUS? THE BOYS ARE AT IT TOO?
BWA-HA!
I'VE NEVER SEEN ANYTHING LIKE THIS!
TALK ABOUT COMEDY!

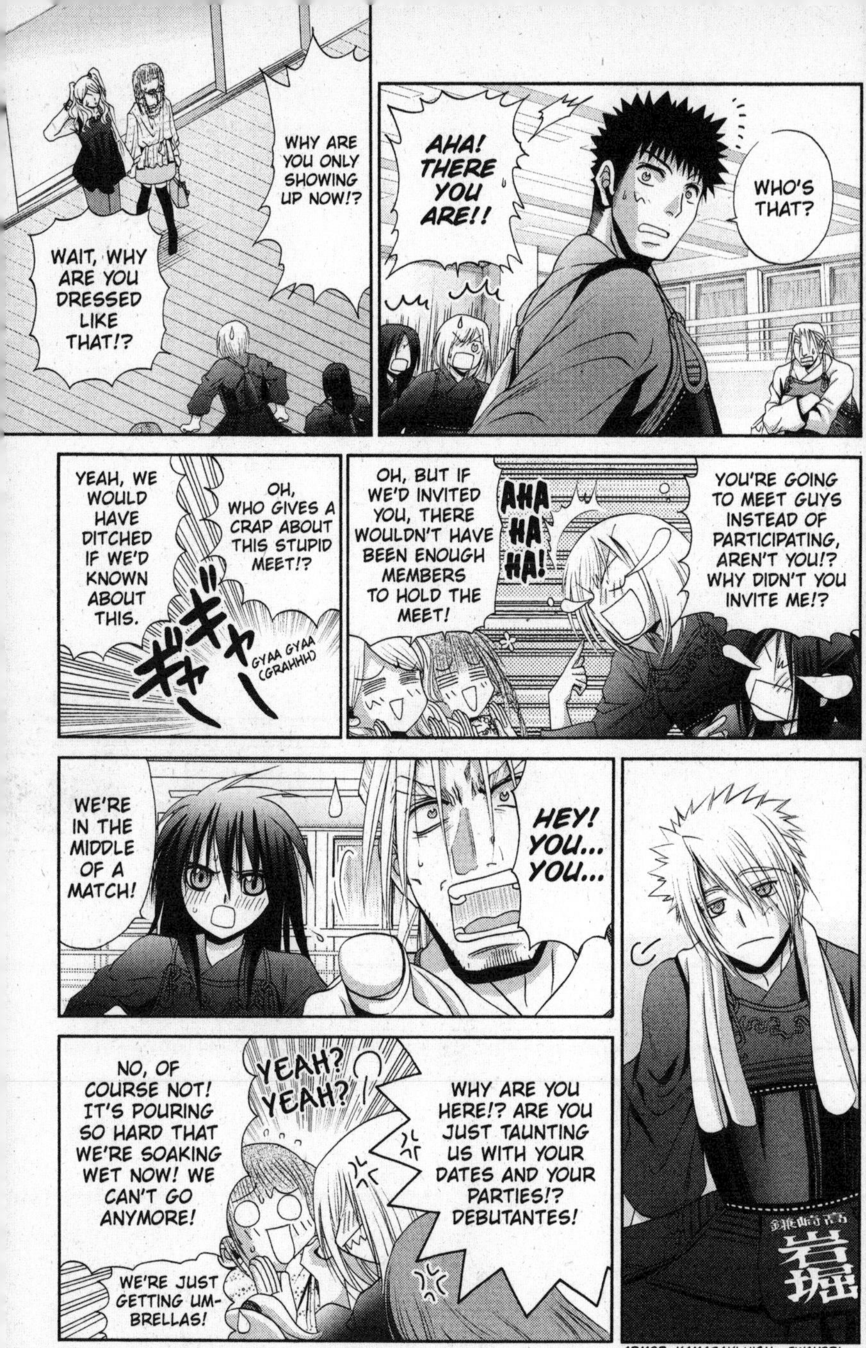

WHO'S THAT?
AHA! THERE YOU ARE!!
WHY ARE YOU ONLY SHOWING UP NOW!?
WAIT, WHY ARE YOU DRESSED LIKE THAT!?
YOU'RE GOING TO MEET GUYS INSTEAD OF PARTICIPATING, AREN'T YOU!? WHY DIDN'T YOU INVITE ME!?
AHAHAHA!
OH, BUT IF WE'D INVITED YOU, THERE WOULDN'T HAVE BEEN ENOUGH MEMBERS TO HOLD THE MEET!
OH, WHO GIVES A CRAP ABOUT THIS STUPID MEET!?
YEAH, WE WOULD HAVE DITCHED IF WE'D KNOWN ABOUT THIS.
ギャーギャー
GYAA GYAA (GRAHHH)
鎌崎高
岩堀
HEY! YOU... YOU...
WE'RE IN THE MIDDLE OF A MATCH!
WHY ARE YOU HERE!? ARE YOU JUST TAUNTING US WITH YOUR DATES AND YOUR PARTIES!? DEBUTANTES!
YEAH? YEAH?
NO, OF COURSE NOT! IT'S POURING SO HARD THAT WE'RE SOAKING WET NOW! WE CAN'T GO ANYMORE!
WE'RE JUST GETTING UMBRELLAS!

ARMOR: KAMASAKI HIGH - IWAHORI

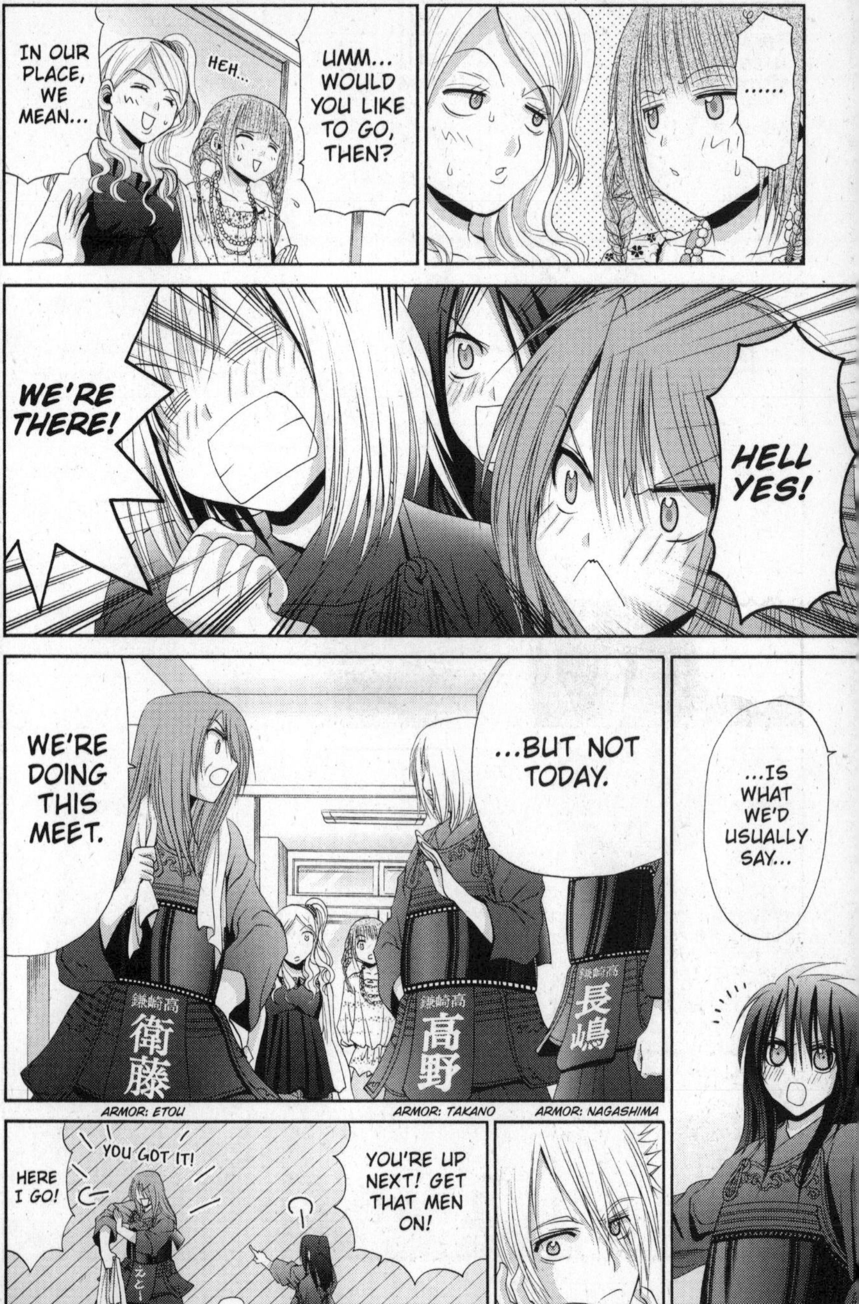
......
UMM... WOULD YOU LIKE TO GO, THEN?
HEH...
IN OUR PLACE, WE MEAN...
HELL YES!
WE'RE THERE!
...IS WHAT WE'D USUALLY SAY...
...BUT NOT TODAY.
WE'RE DOING THIS MEET.
鎌崎高 長嶋
鎌崎高 高野
鎌崎高 衛藤
ARMOR: NAGASHIMA
ARMOR: TAKANO
ARMOR: ETOU
YOU'RE UP NEXT! GET THAT MEN ON!
YOU GOT IT!
HERE I GO!

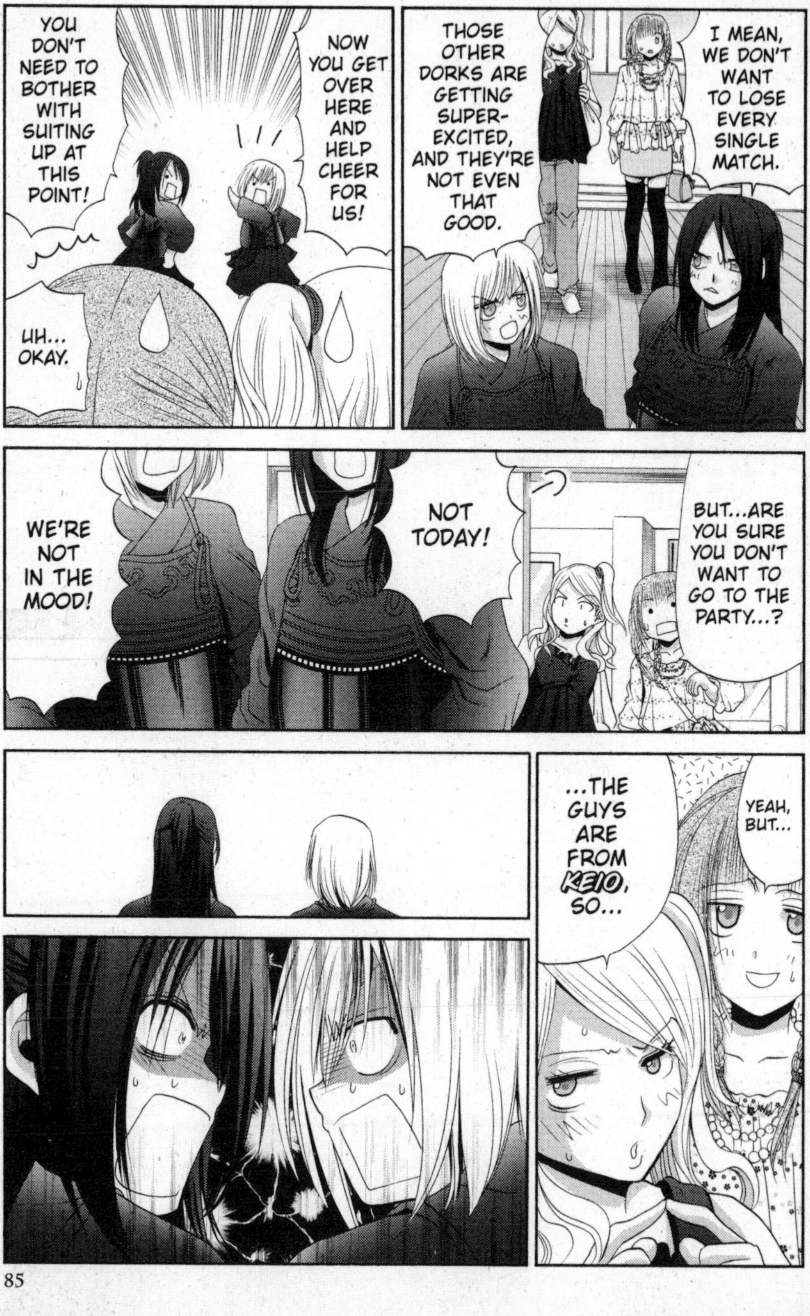
I MEAN, WE DON'T WANT TO LOSE EVERY SINGLE MATCH.
THOSE OTHER DORKS ARE GETTING SUPER-EXCITED, AND THEY'RE NOT EVEN THAT GOOD.
NOW YOU GET OVER HERE AND HELP CHEER FOR US!
YOU DON'T NEED TO BOTHER WITH SUITING UP AT THIS POINT!
UH... OKAY.
BUT...ARE YOU SURE YOU DON'T WANT TO GO TO THE PARTY...?
NOT TODAY!
WE'RE NOT IN THE MOOD!
YEAH, BUT...
...THE GUYS ARE FROM KEIO, SO...

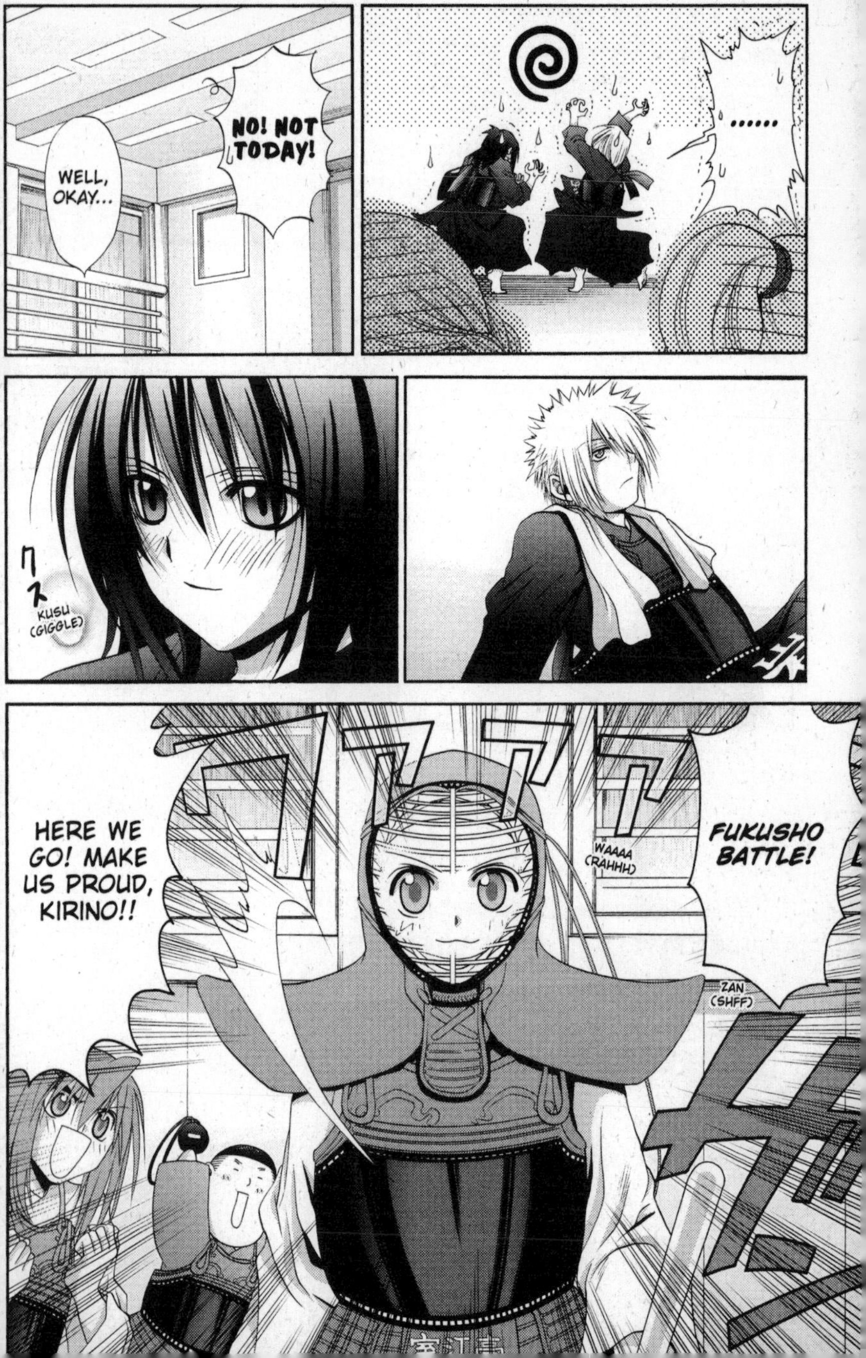
......
NO! NOT TODAY!
WELL, OKAY...
クス
KUSU (GIGGLE)
FUKUSHO BATTLE!
WAAAA (RAHHH)
HERE WE GO! MAKE US PROUD, KIRINO!!
ZAN (SHFF)

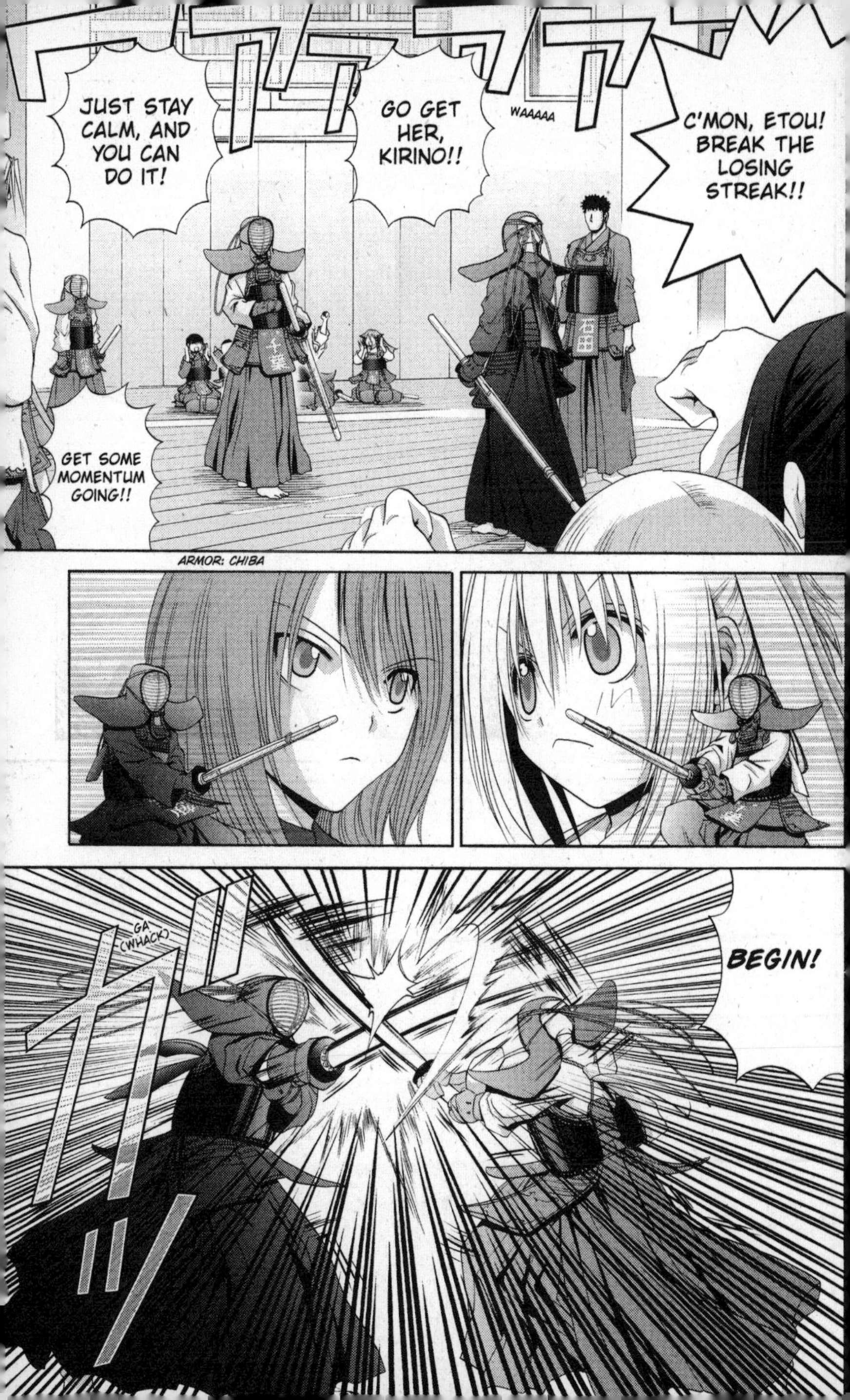
C'MON, ETOU! BREAK THE LOSING STREAK!!
WAAAAA
GO GET HER, KIRINO!!
JUST STAY CALM, AND YOU CAN DO IT!
GET SOME MOMENTUM GOING!!
ARMOR: CHIBA
BEGIN!
GA (WHACK)

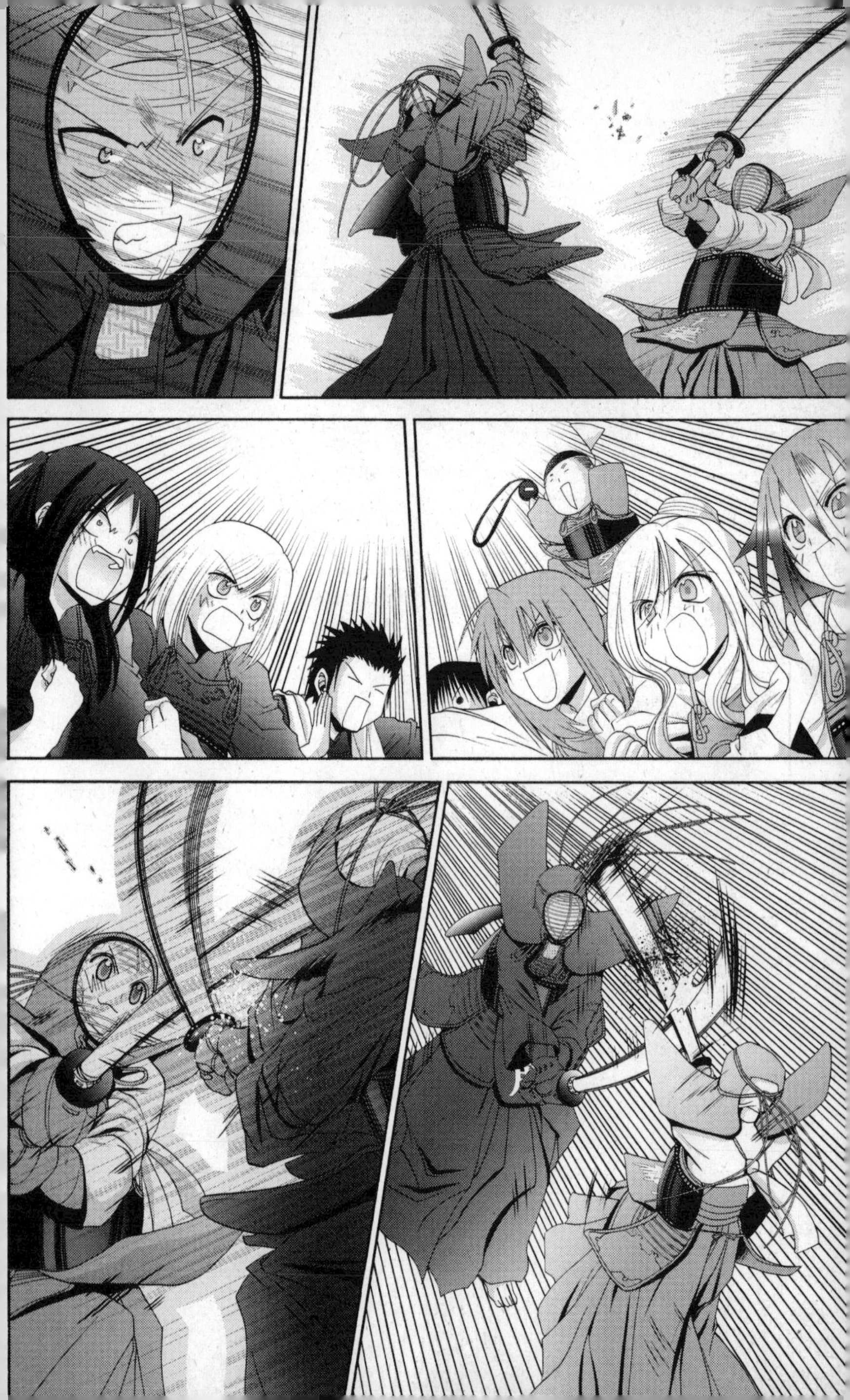

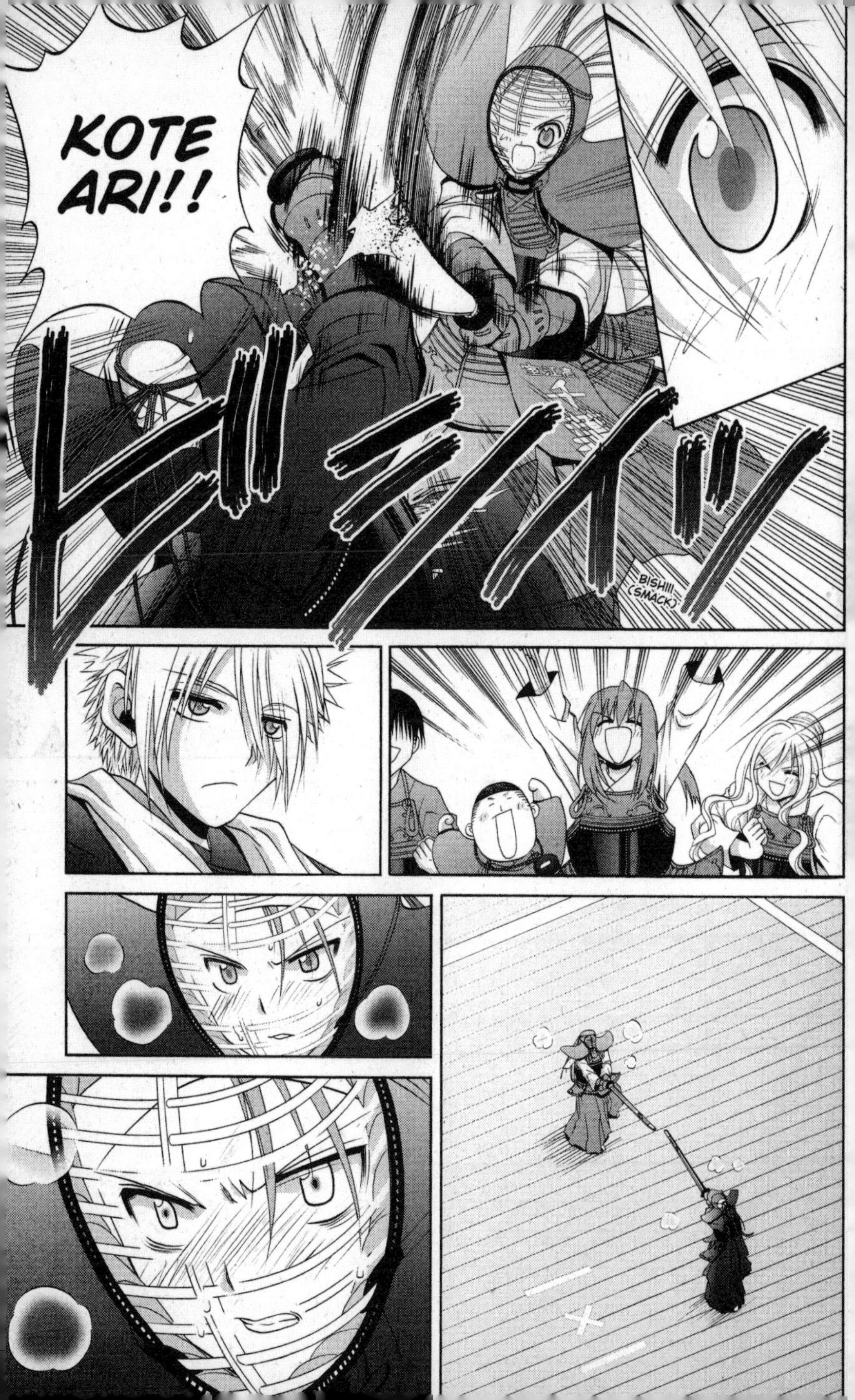
KOTE ARI!!
ビシイイッ
BISHIII (SMACK)

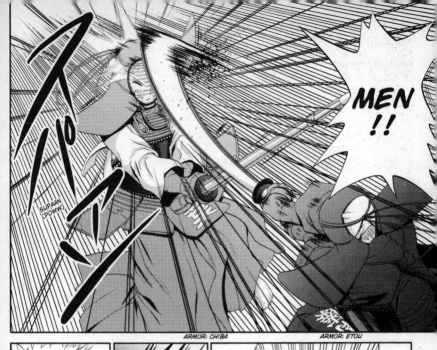

MEN
!!

SUPAAN
(POWW)

ARMOR: CHIBA   ARMOR: ETOU

ATTA-
GIRL!!!

MEN
ARI!

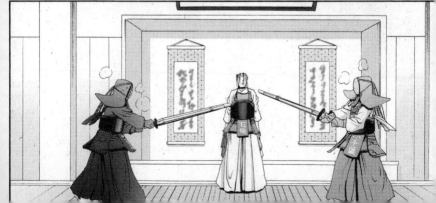

DOKUN
(BADUM)

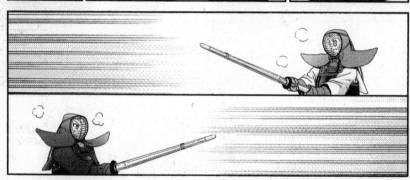

FURA...
FURA
(SWAY)

HUFF!

HUFF!

91

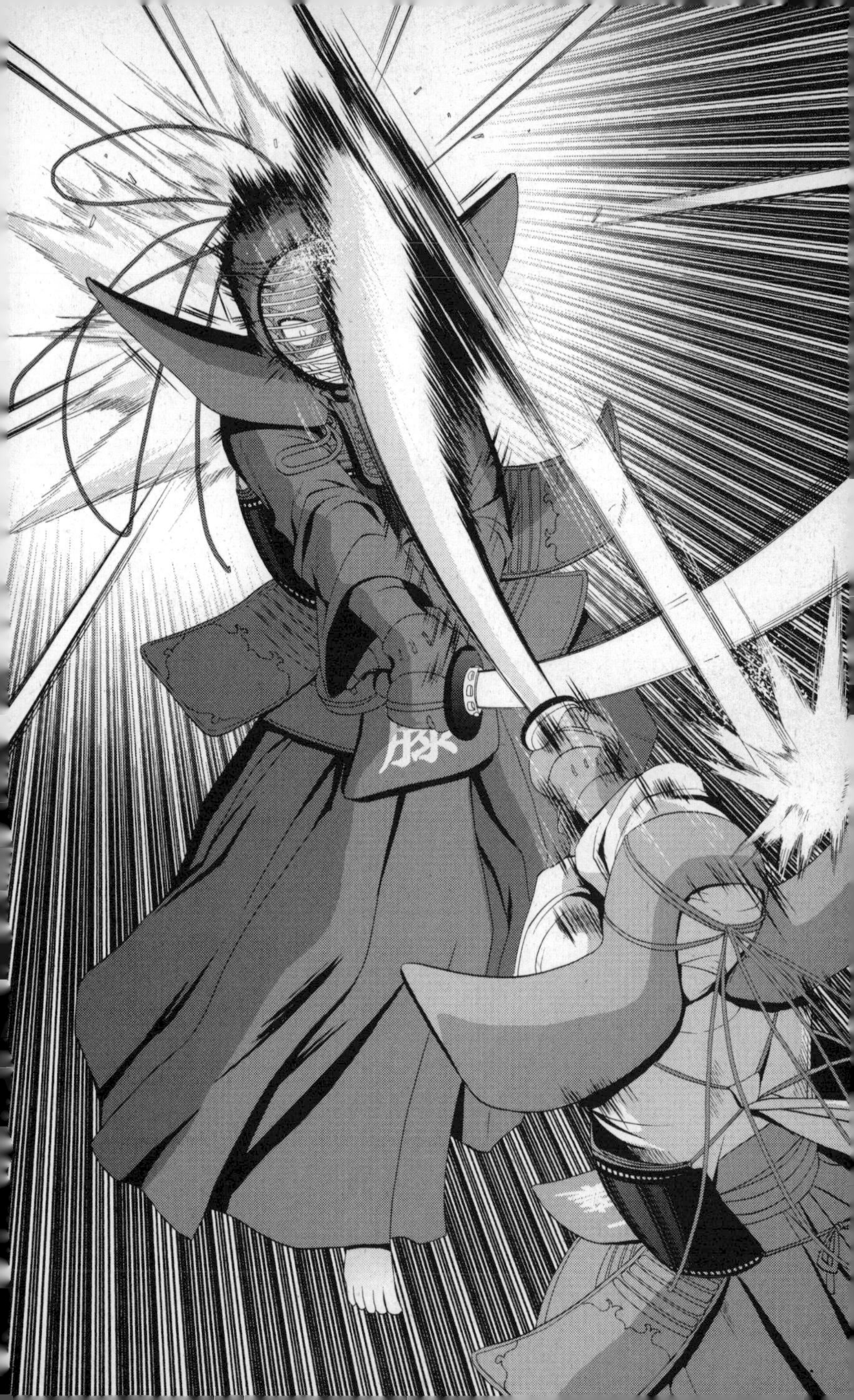

BAMBOO BLADE
バンブーブレード

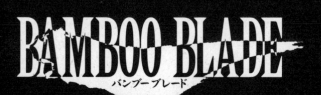

BAMBOO BLADE
バンブーブレード

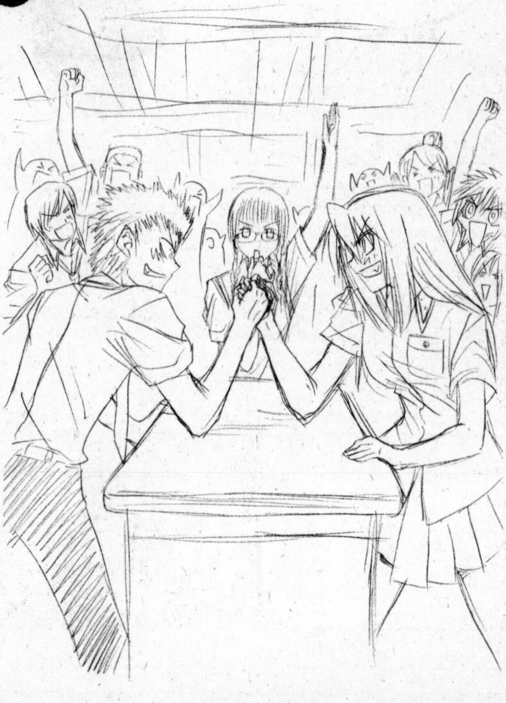

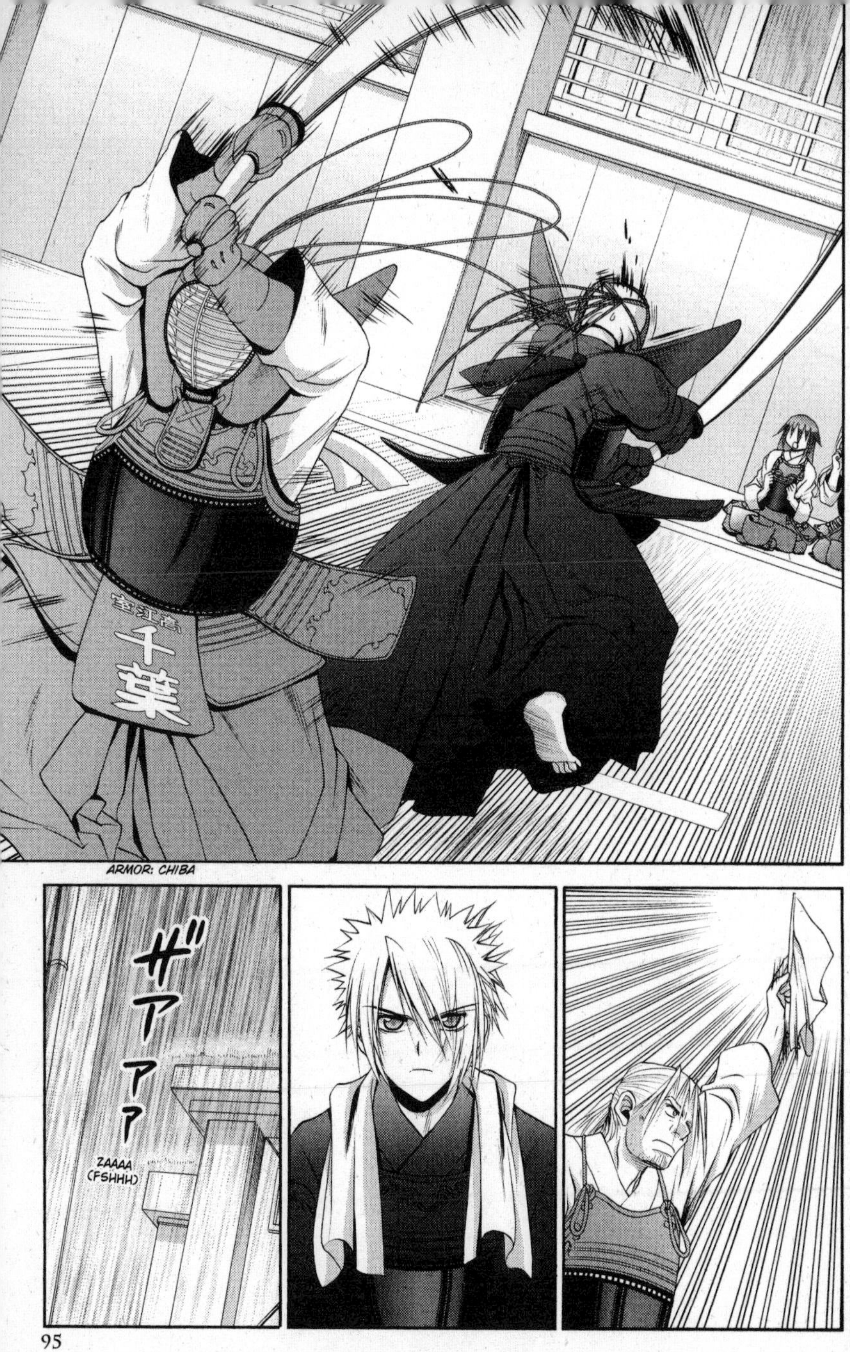
室江高
千葉
ARMOR: CHIBA
ザァァァ
ZAAAA
(FSHHH)

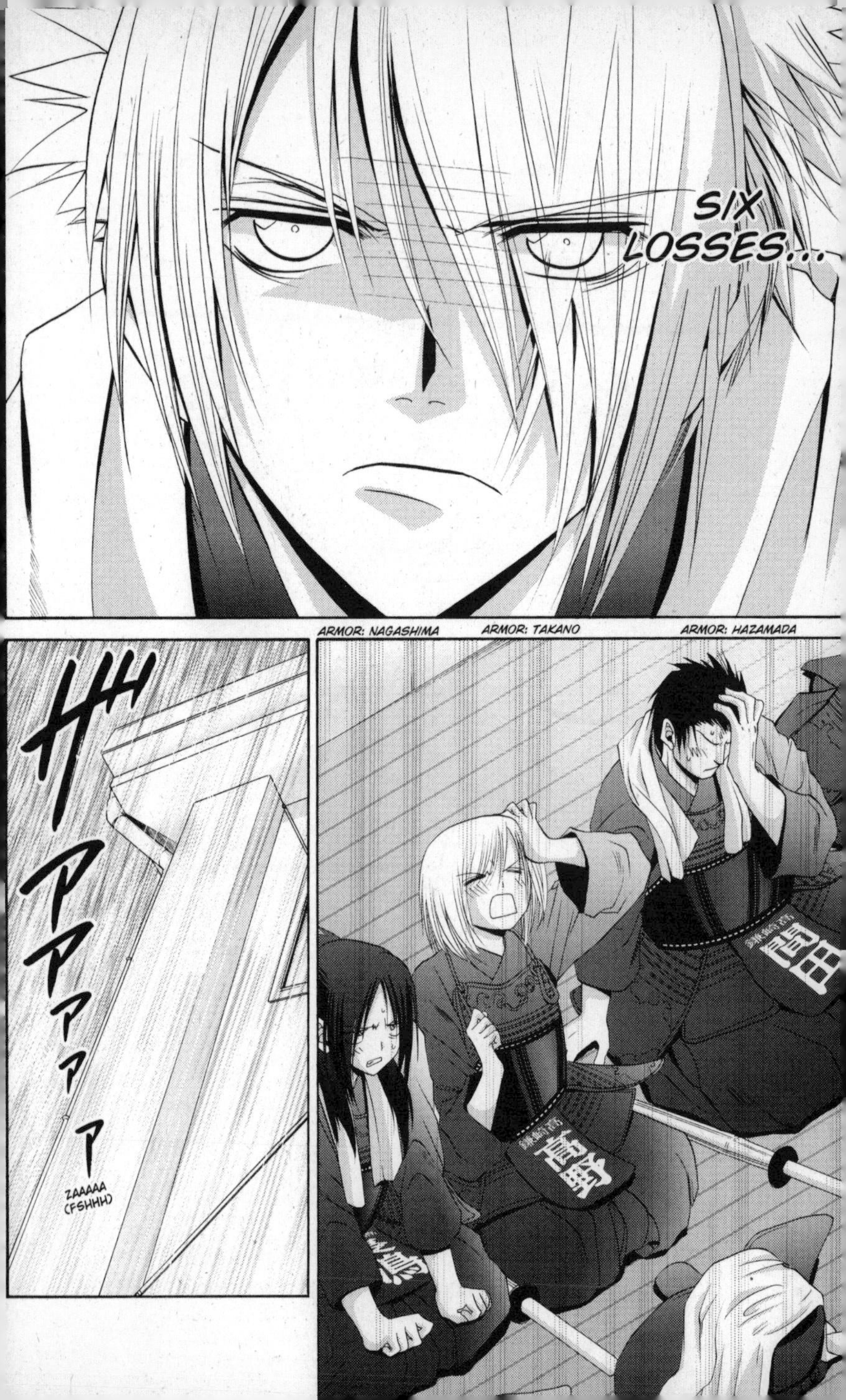
SIX LOSSES...
ARMOR: NAGASHIMA
ARMOR: TAKANO
ARMOR: HAZAMADA
ザァァァァァ
ZAAAAA (FSHHH)

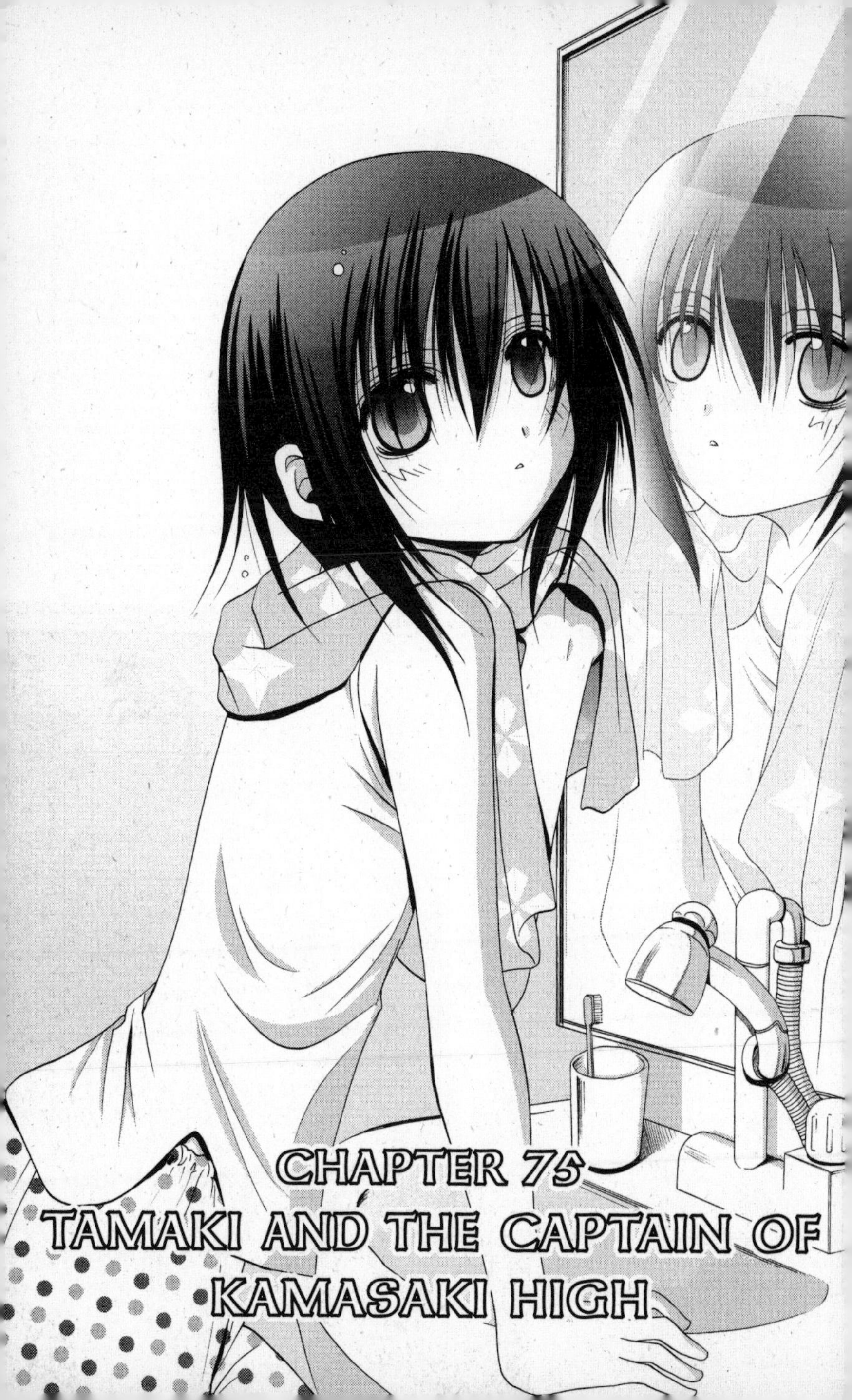
CHAPTER 75
TAMAKI AND THE CAPTAIN OF KAMASAKI HIGH

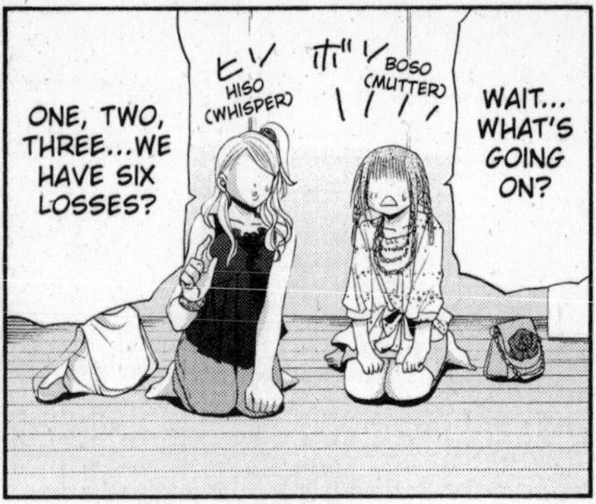
WAIT... WHAT'S GOING ON?
ヒソ HISO (WHISPER)
ボソ BOSO (MUTTER)
ONE, TWO, THREE...WE HAVE SIX LOSSES?
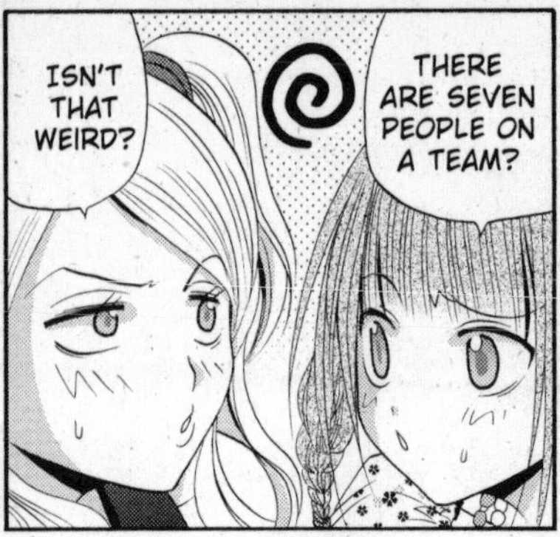
THERE ARE SEVEN PEOPLE ON A TEAM?
ISN'T THAT WEIRD?
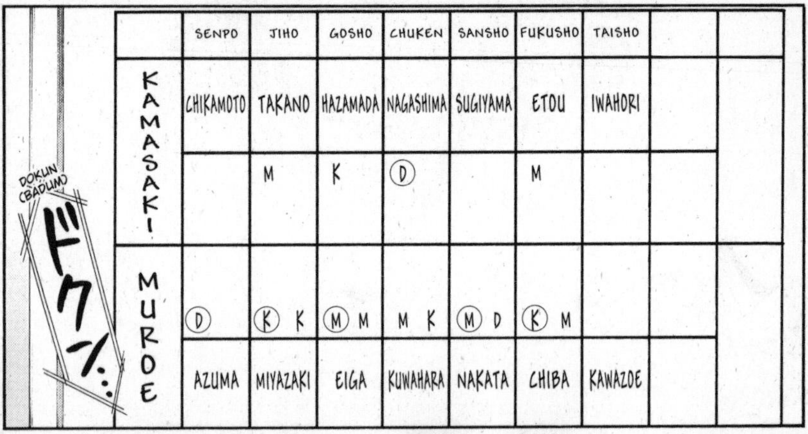
ドクン… DOKUN (BADUM)

	SENPO	JIHO	GOSHO	CHUKEN	SANSHO	FUKUSHO	TAISHO		
KAMASAKI	CHIKAMOTO	TAKANO	HAZAMADA	NAGASHIMA	SUGIYAMA	ETOU	IWAHORI		
		M	K	(D)		M			
MUROE	(D)	(K) K	(M) M	M K	(M) D	(K) M			
	AZUMA	MIYAZAKI	EIGA	KUWAHARA	NAKATA	CHIBA	KAWAZOE		

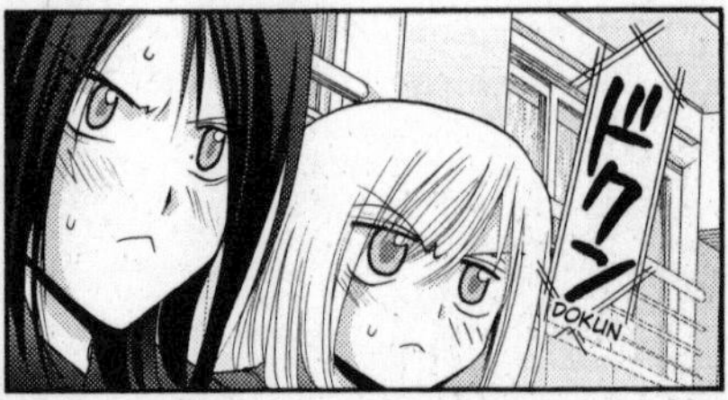
ドクン DOKUN
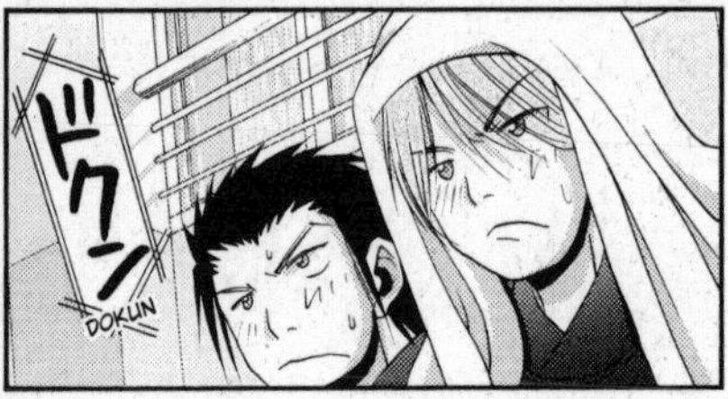
ドクン DOKUN
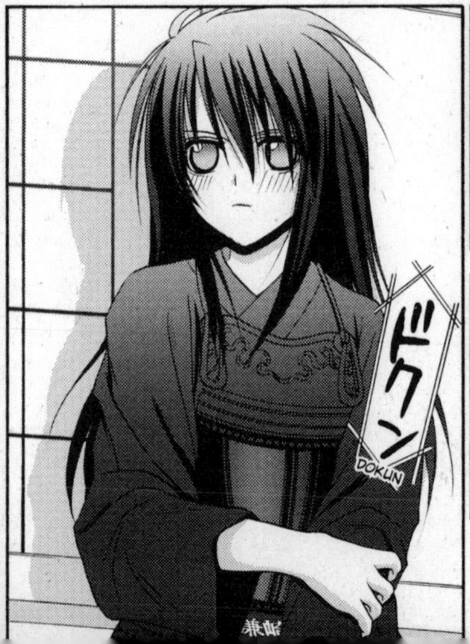
ドクン DOKUN

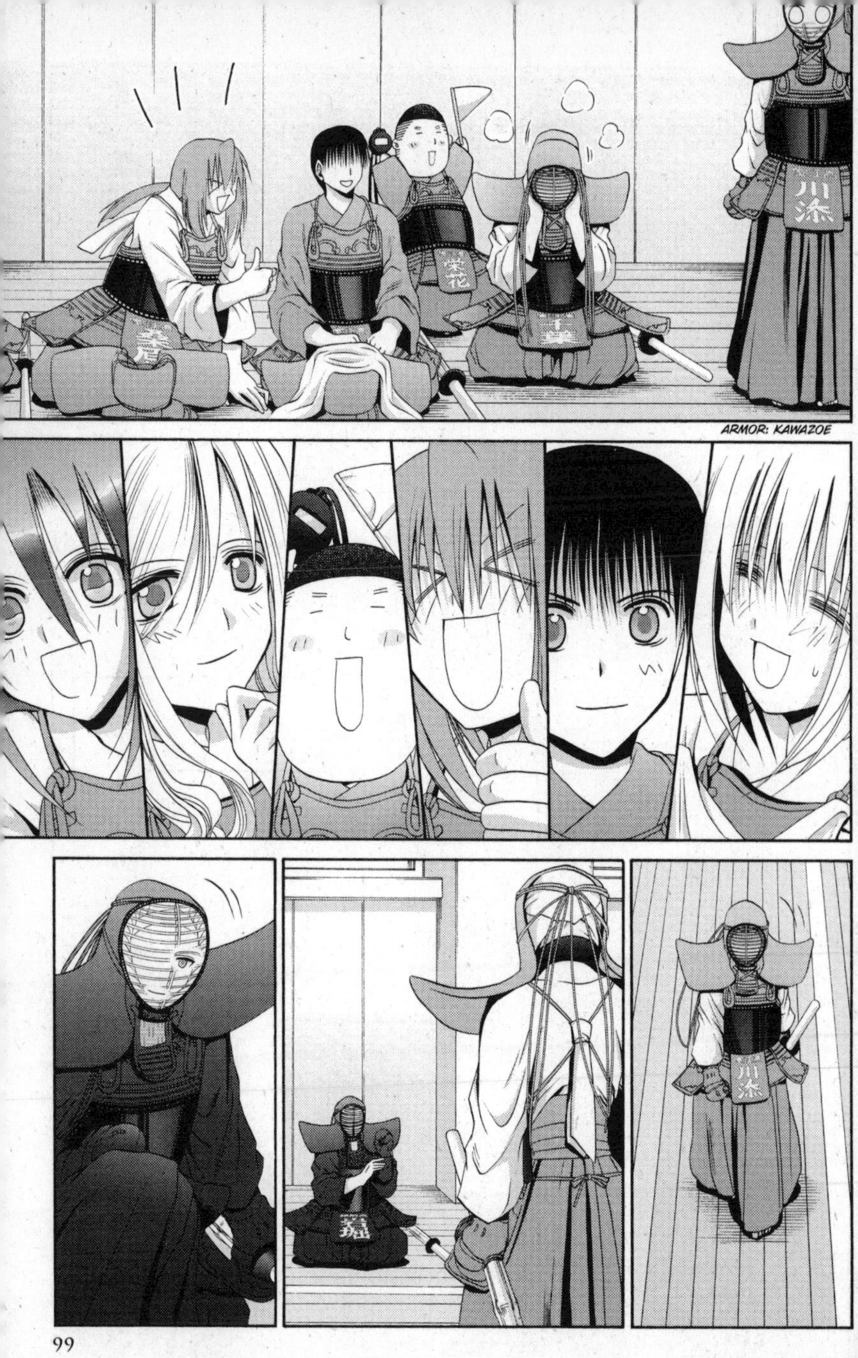
川添
ARMOR: KAWAZOE
川添

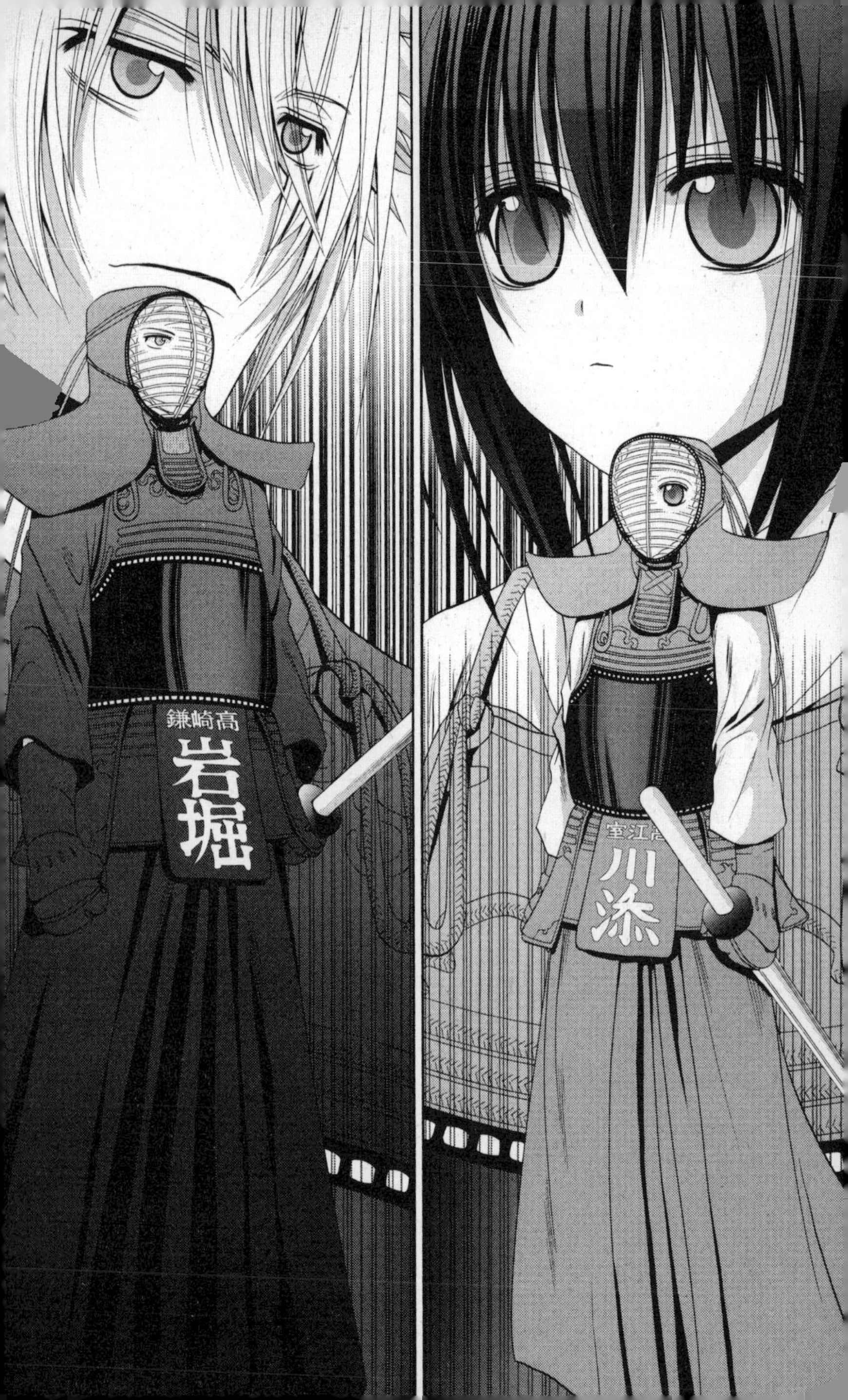

室江高
川添
鎌崎高
岩堀

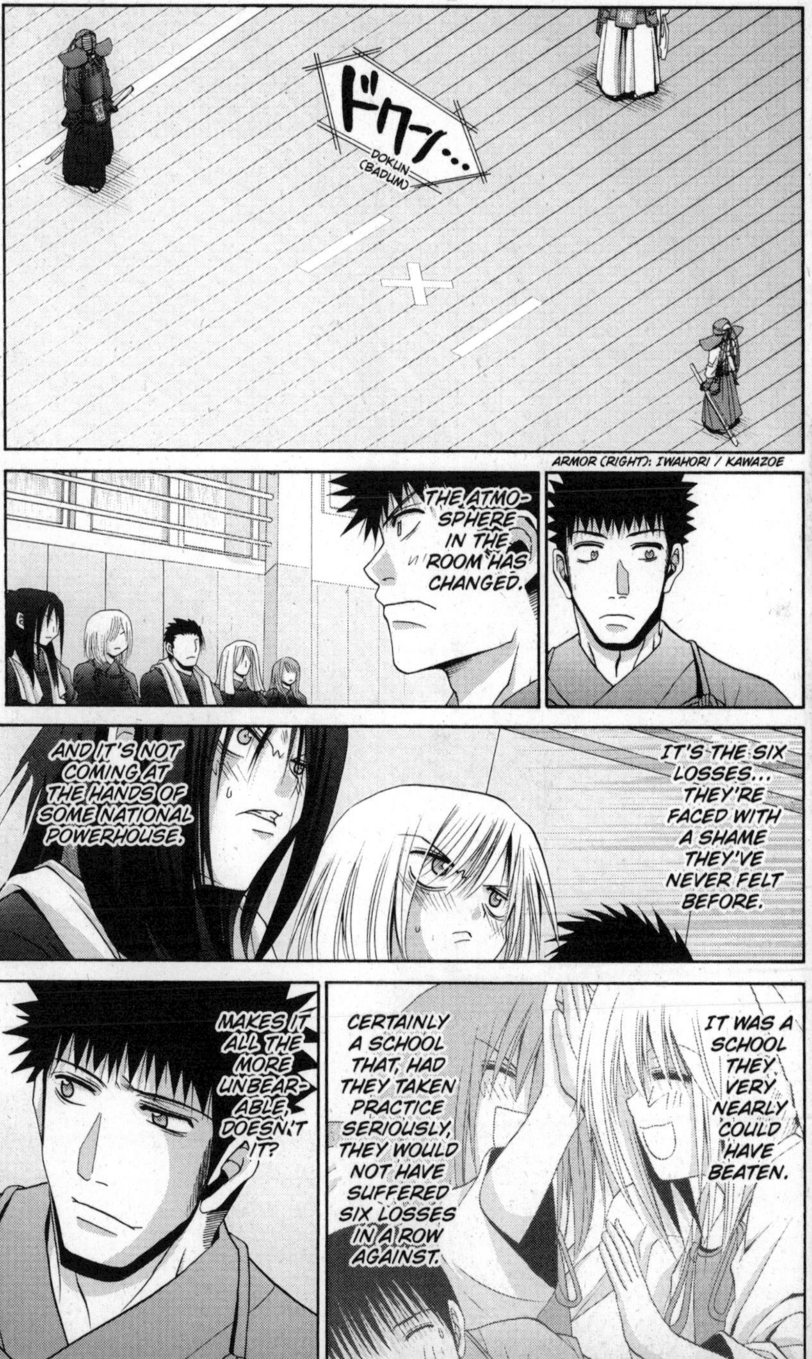
ドクーン…
DOKUN (BADUM)
ARMOR (RIGHT): IWAHORI / KAWAZOE
THE ATMOSPHERE IN THE ROOM HAS CHANGED.
IT'S THE SIX LOSSES... THEY'RE FACED WITH A SHAME THEY'VE NEVER FELT BEFORE.
AND IT'S NOT COMING AT THE HANDS OF SOME NATIONAL POWERHOUSE.
IT WAS A SCHOOL THEY VERY NEARLY COULD HAVE BEATEN.
CERTAINLY A SCHOOL THAT, HAD THEY TAKEN PRACTICE SERIOUSLY, THEY WOULD NOT HAVE SUFFERED SIX LOSSES IN A ROW AGAINST.
MAKES IT ALL THE MORE UNBEARABLE, DOESN'T IT?

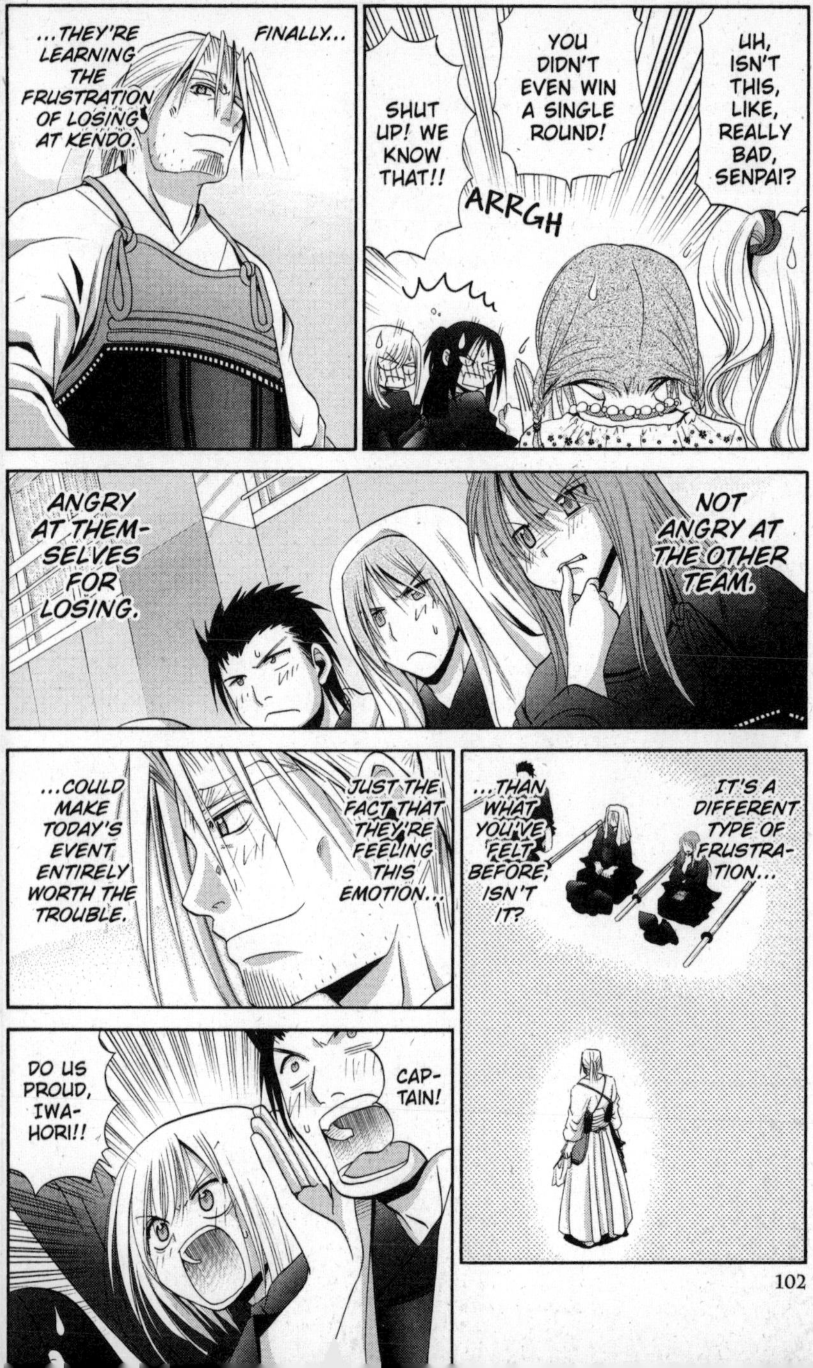
UH, ISN'T THIS, LIKE, REALLY BAD, SENPAI?
YOU DIDN'T EVEN WIN A SINGLE ROUND!
SHUT UP! WE KNOW THAT!!
ARRGH
FINALLY...
...THEY'RE LEARNING THE FRUSTRATION OF LOSING AT KENDO.
NOT ANGRY AT THE OTHER TEAM.
ANGRY AT THEMSELVES FOR LOSING.
IT'S A DIFFERENT TYPE OF FRUSTRATION...
...THAN WHAT YOU'VE FELT BEFORE, ISN'T IT?
JUST THE FACT THAT THEY'RE FEELING THIS EMOTION...
...COULD MAKE TODAY'S EVENT ENTIRELY WORTH THE TROUBLE.
CAPTAIN!
DO US PROUD, IWAHORI!!

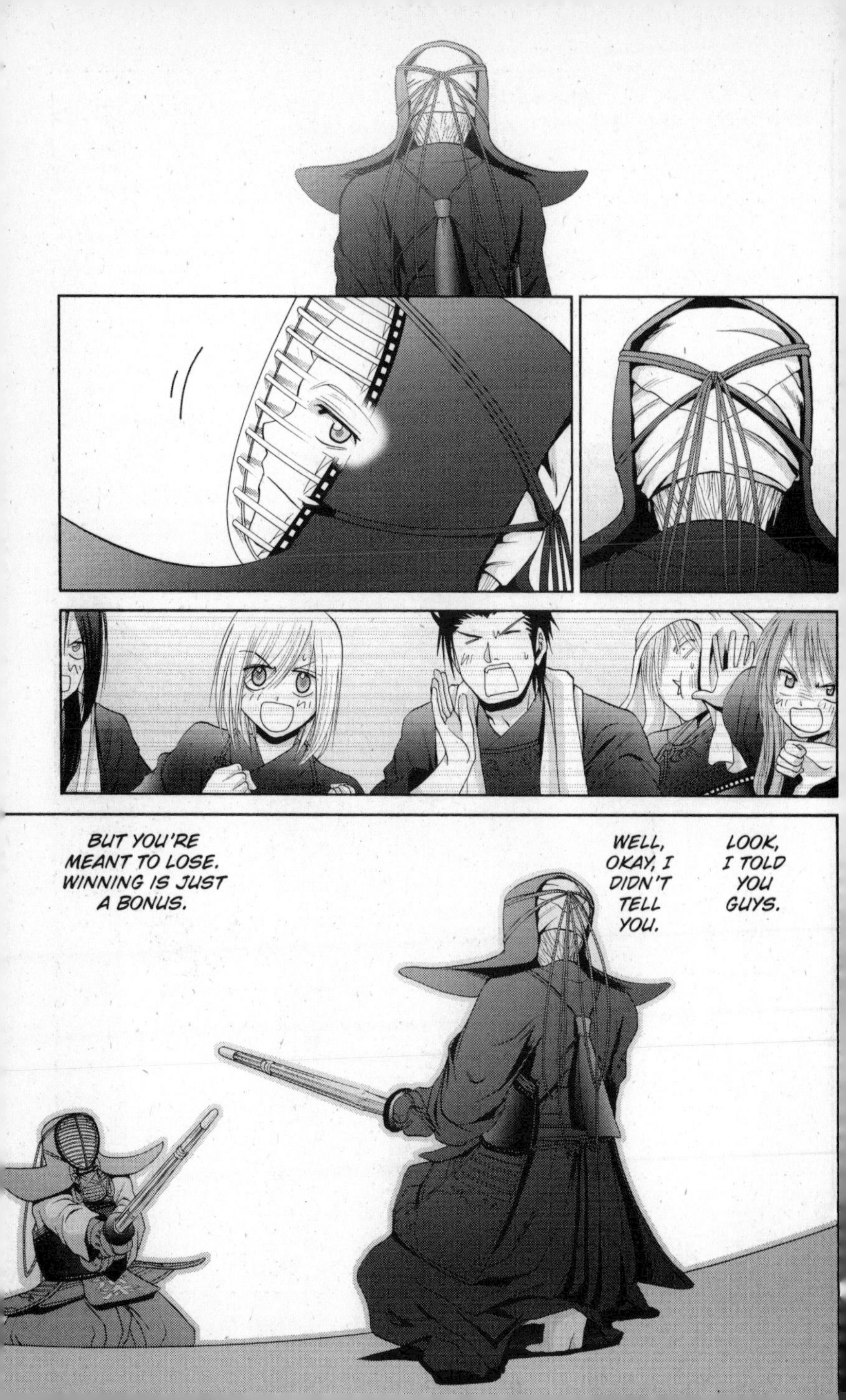
LOOK, I TOLD YOU GUYS.
WELL, OKAY, I DIDN'T TELL YOU.
BUT YOU'RE MEANT TO LOSE. WINNING IS JUST A BONUS.

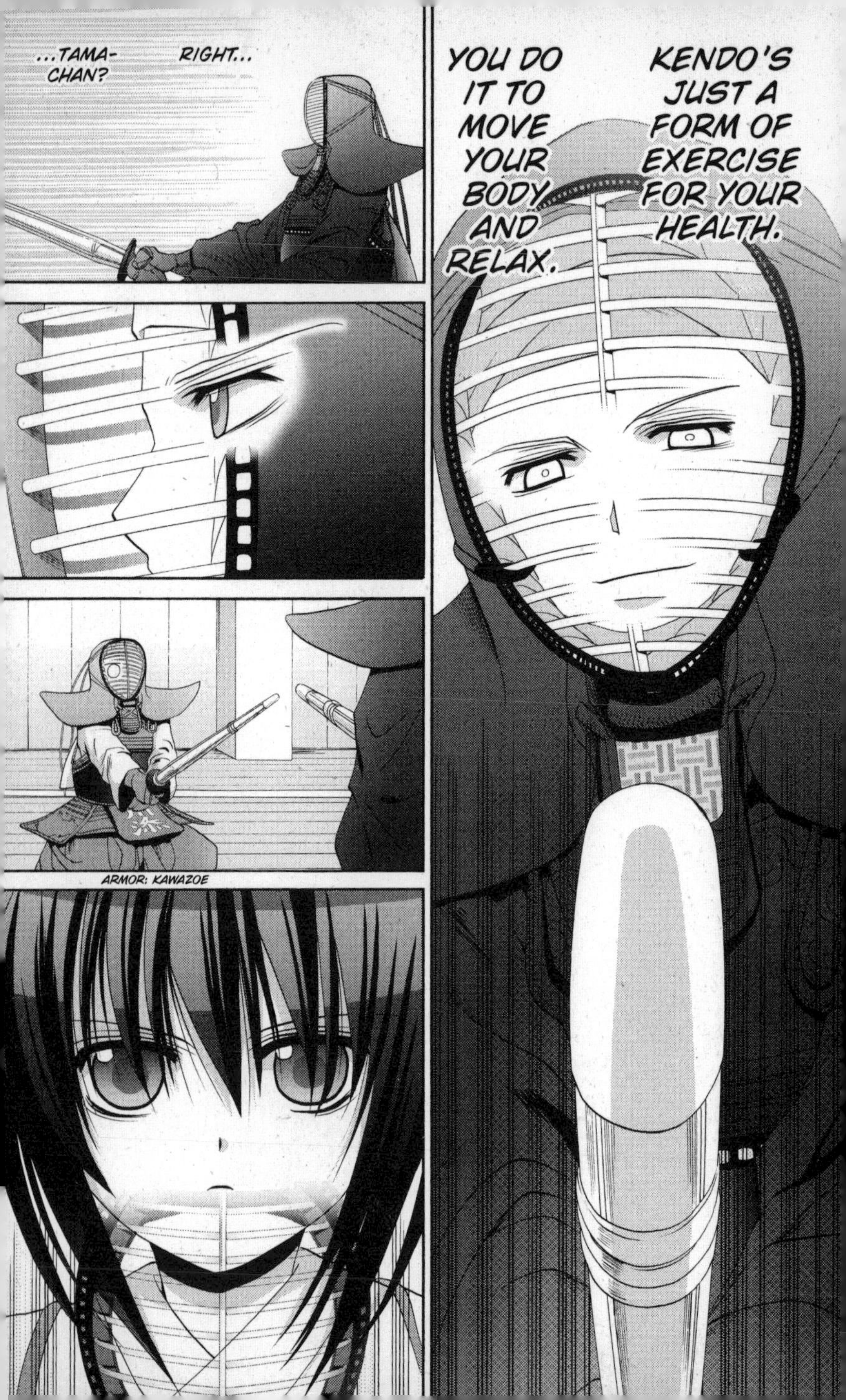
KENDO'S JUST A FORM OF EXERCISE FOR YOUR HEALTH.
YOU DO IT TO MOVE YOUR BODY AND RELAX.
RIGHT...
...TAMA-CHAN?
ARMOR: KAWAZOE

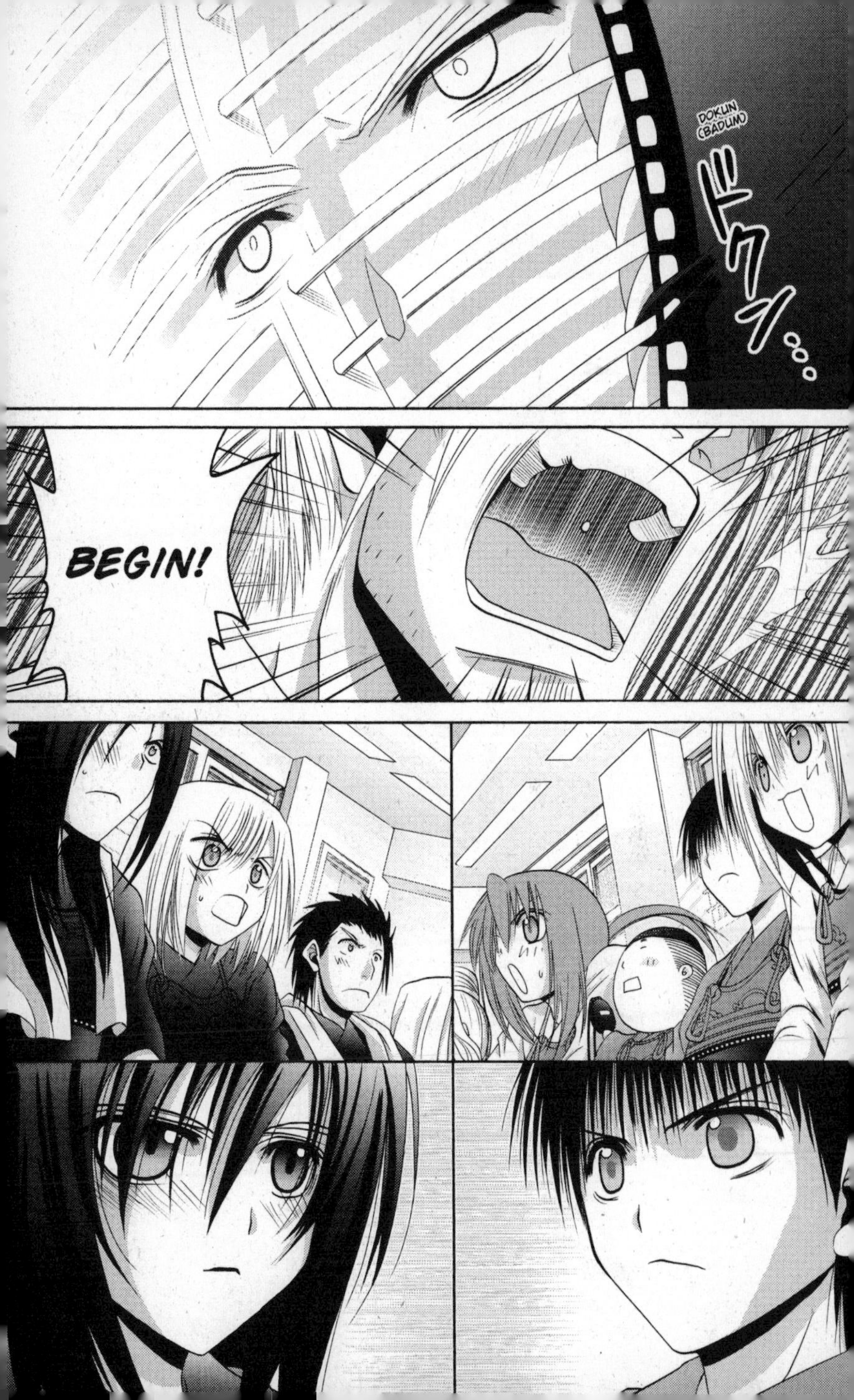
DOKUN (BADUM)
ドクン…
BEGIN!

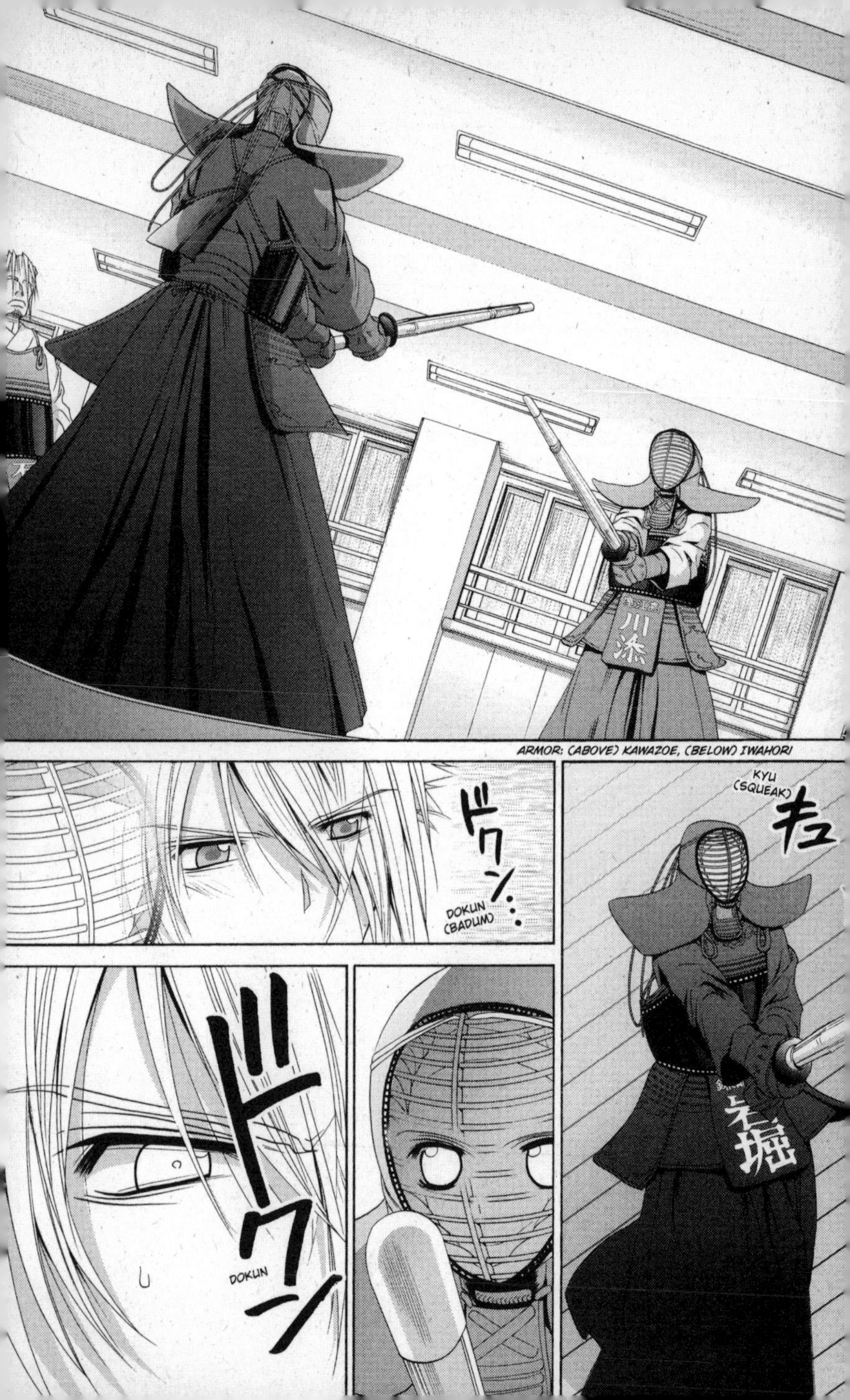
川添
ARMOR: (ABOVE) KAWAZOE, (BELOW) IWAHORI
キュ
KYU (SQUEAK)
ドクン…
DOKUN (BADUM)
ドクン
DOKUN

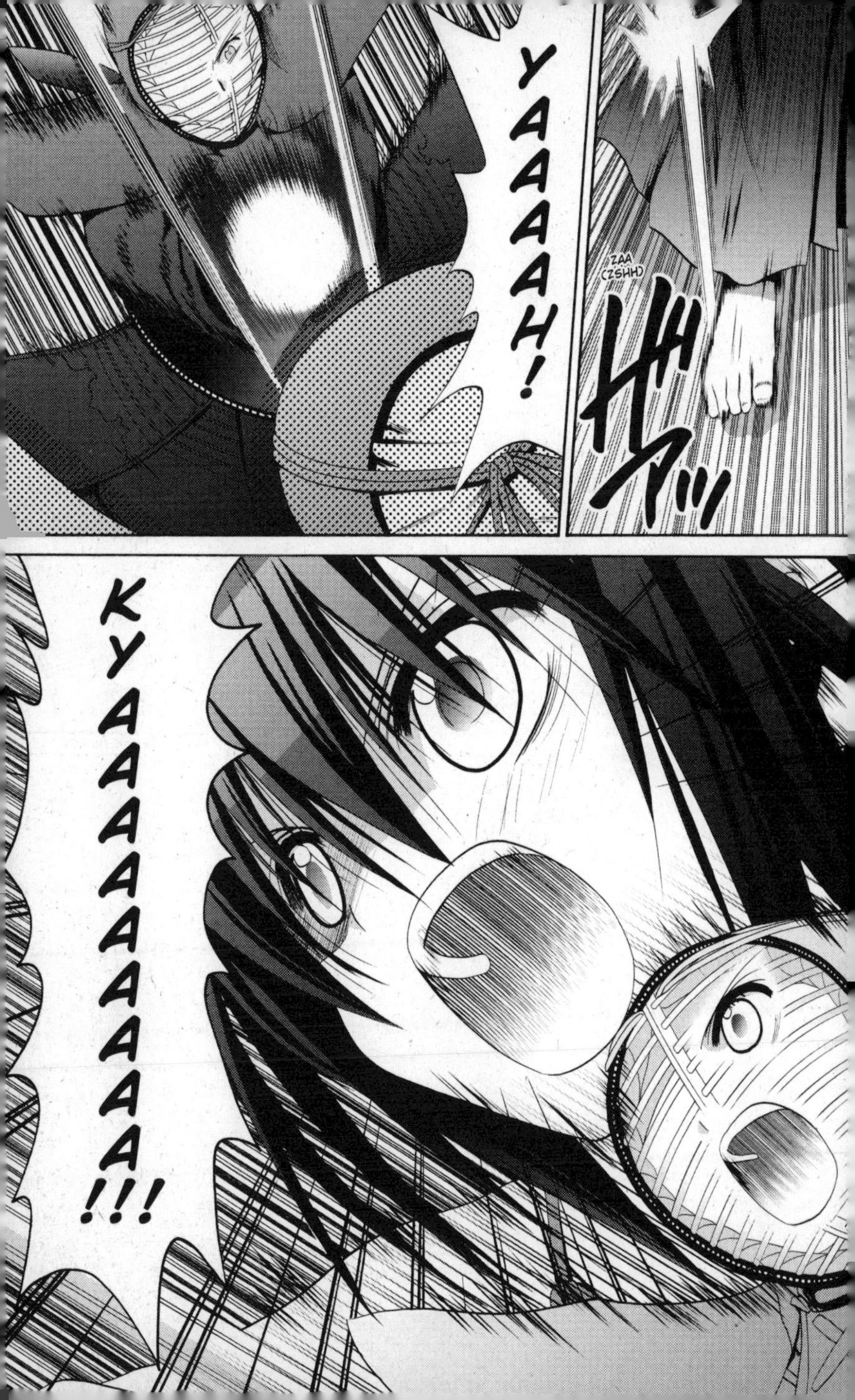
ZAA
(ZSHH)
YAAAAH!
KYAAAAAAAAAA!!!

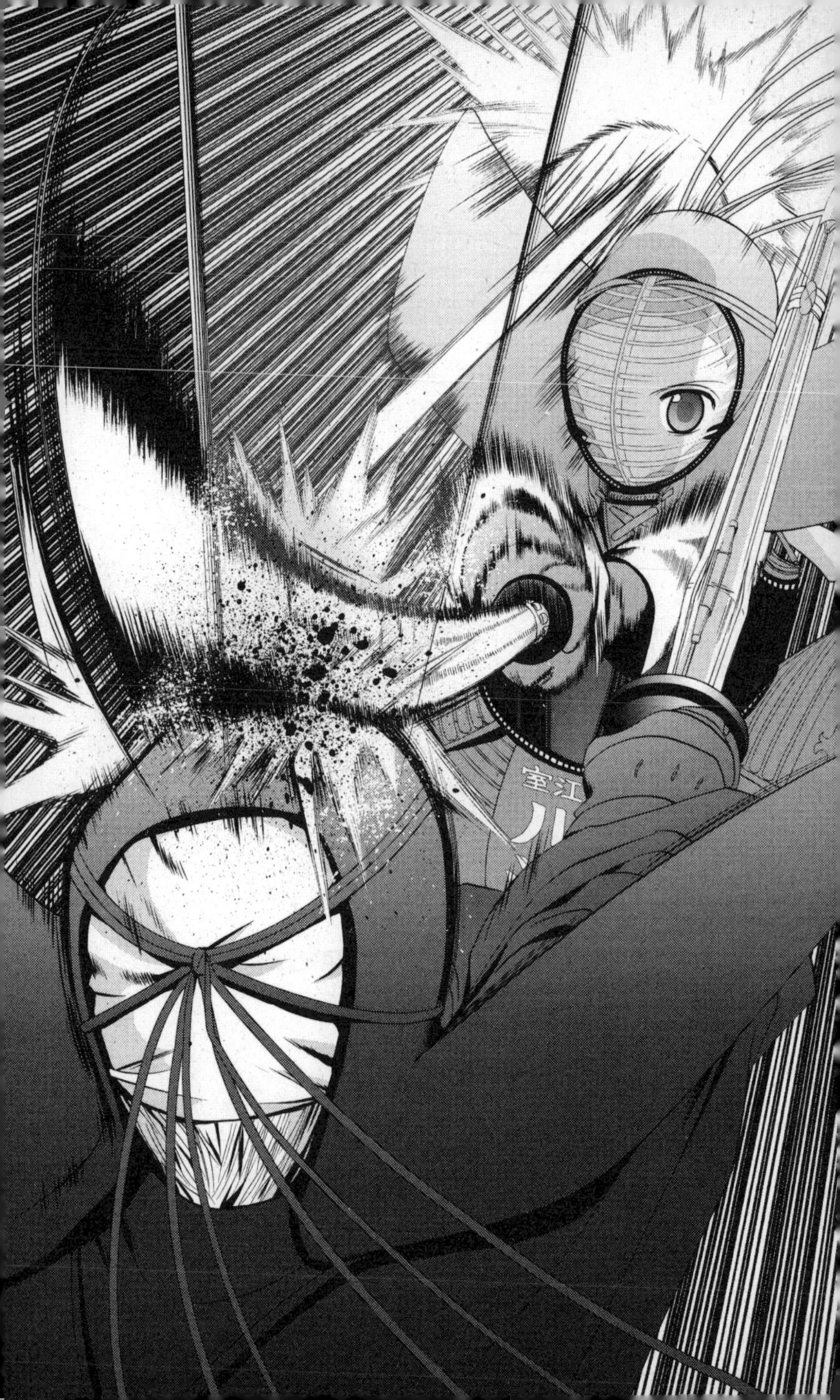
室江

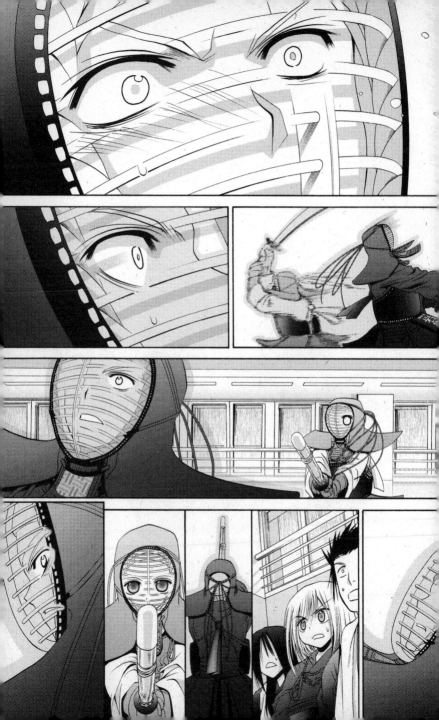

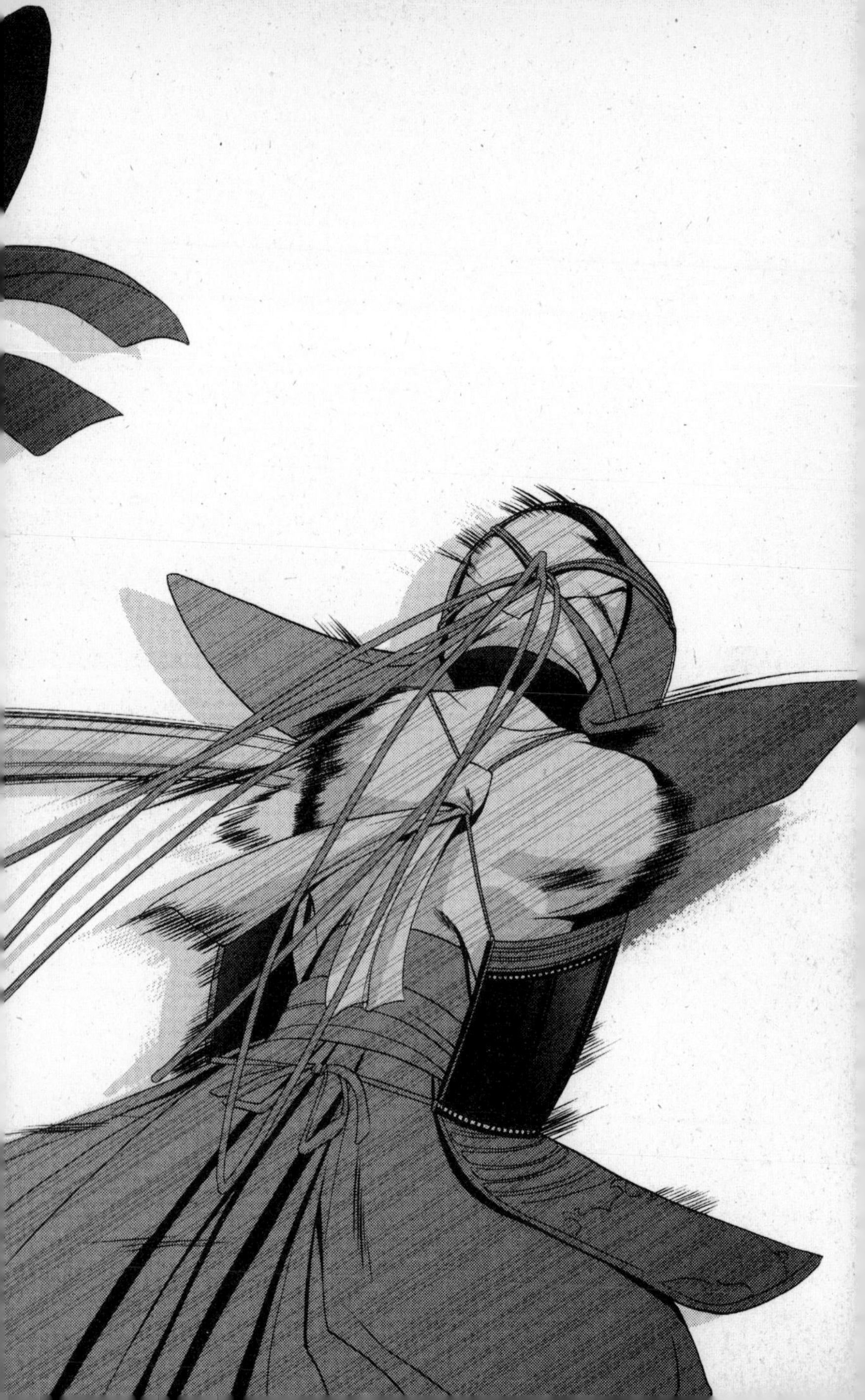

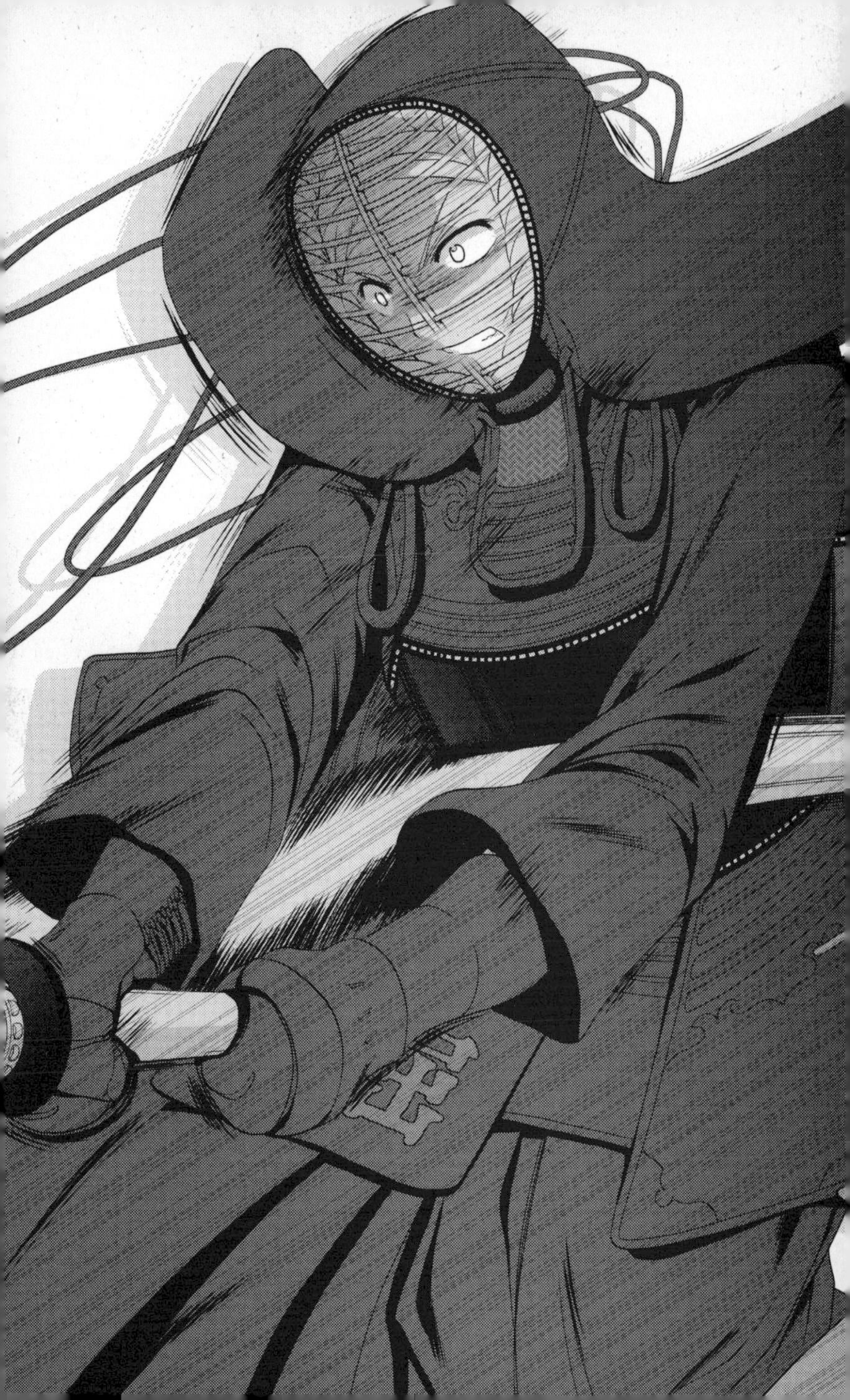

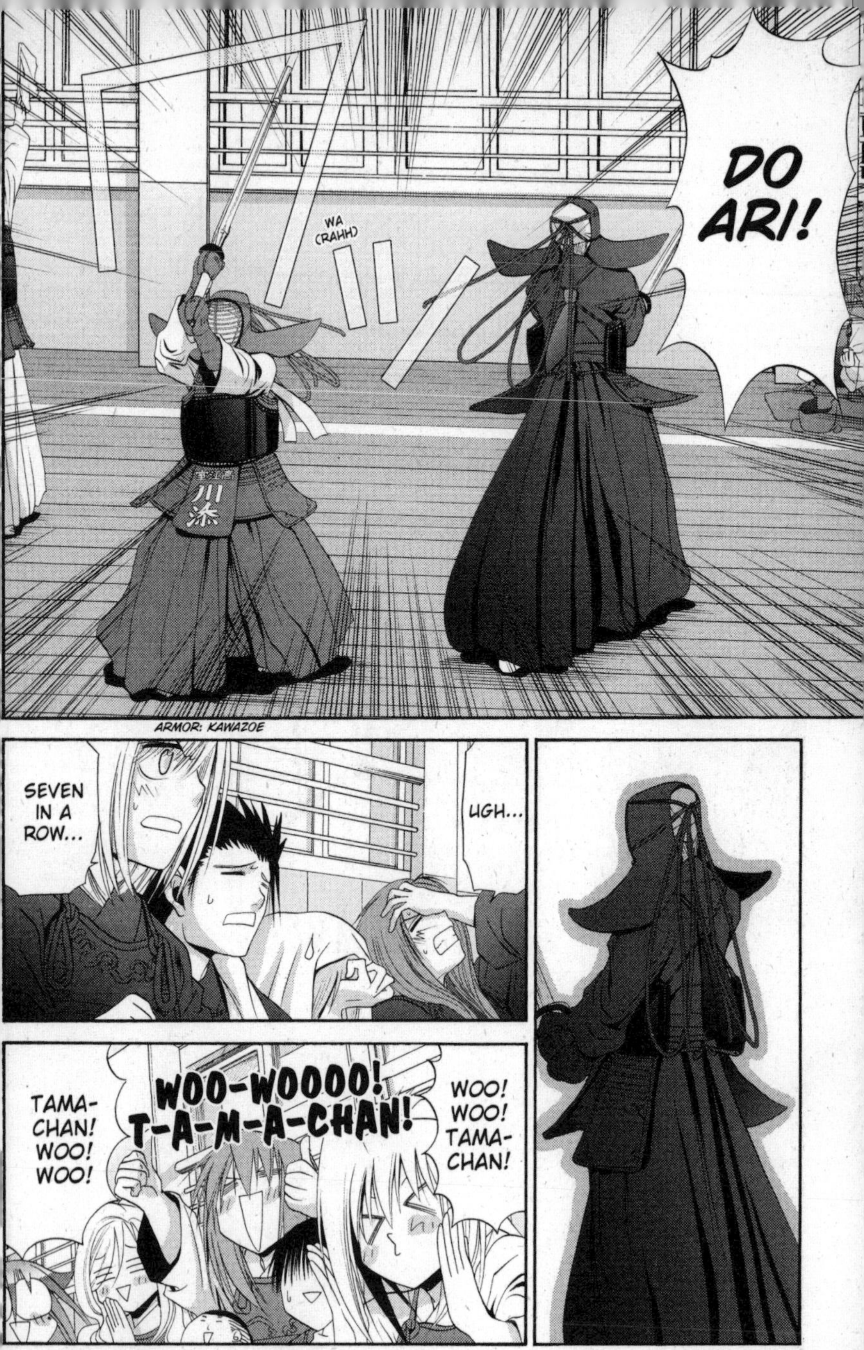
DO ARI!
WA (RAHH)
川添
ARMOR: KAWAZOE
UGH...
SEVEN IN A ROW...
WOO! WOO! TAMA-CHAN!
WOO-WOOOO! T-A-M-A-CHAN!
TAMA-CHAN! WOO! WOO!

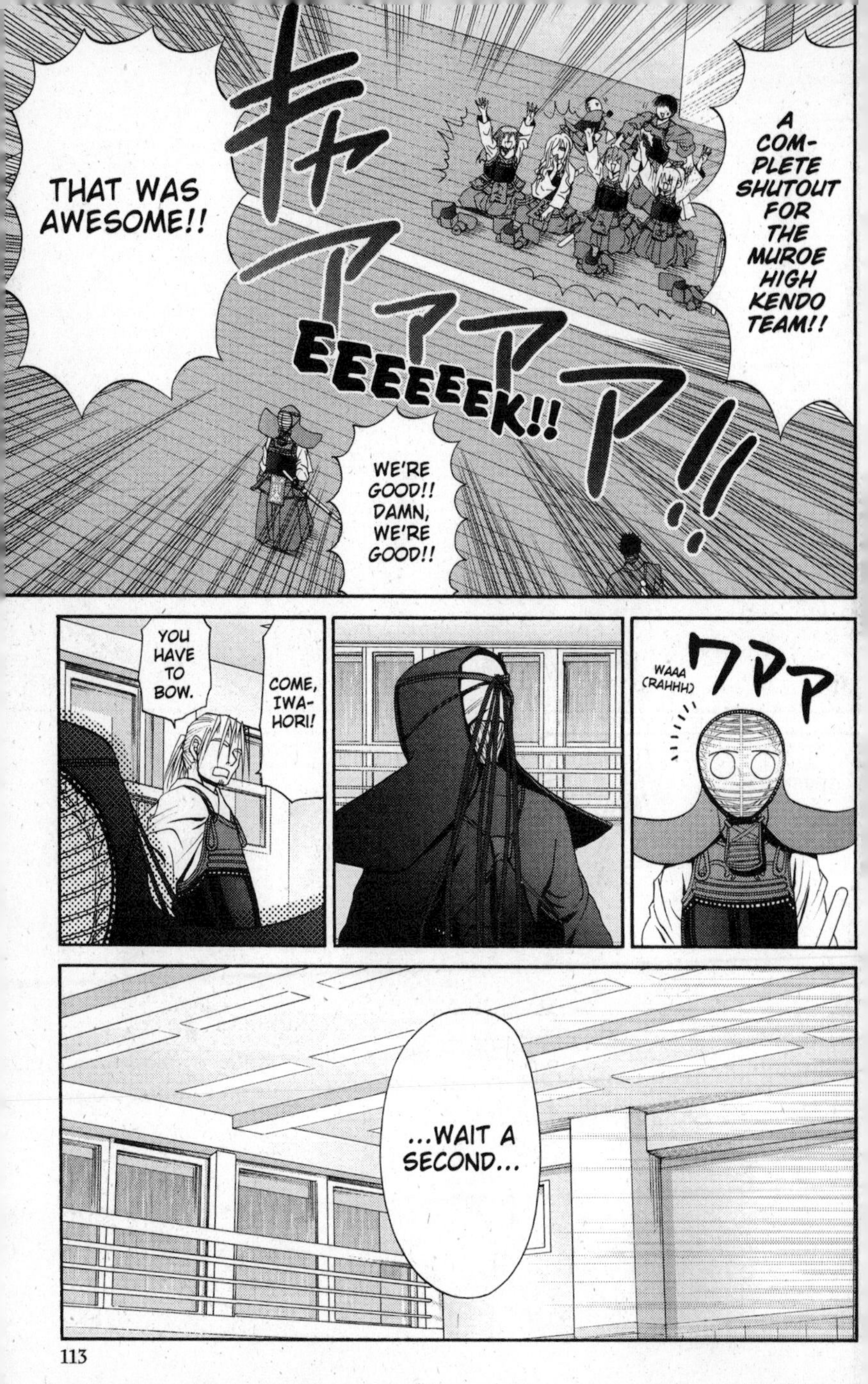
A COMPLETE SHUTOUT FOR THE MUROE HIGH KENDO TEAM!!
キャアアアア!!
EEEEEEK!!
THAT WAS AWESOME!!
WE'RE GOOD!! DAMN, WE'RE GOOD!!
ワアア
WAAA (RAHHH)
COME, IWAHORI!
YOU HAVE TO BOW.
...WAIT A SECOND...

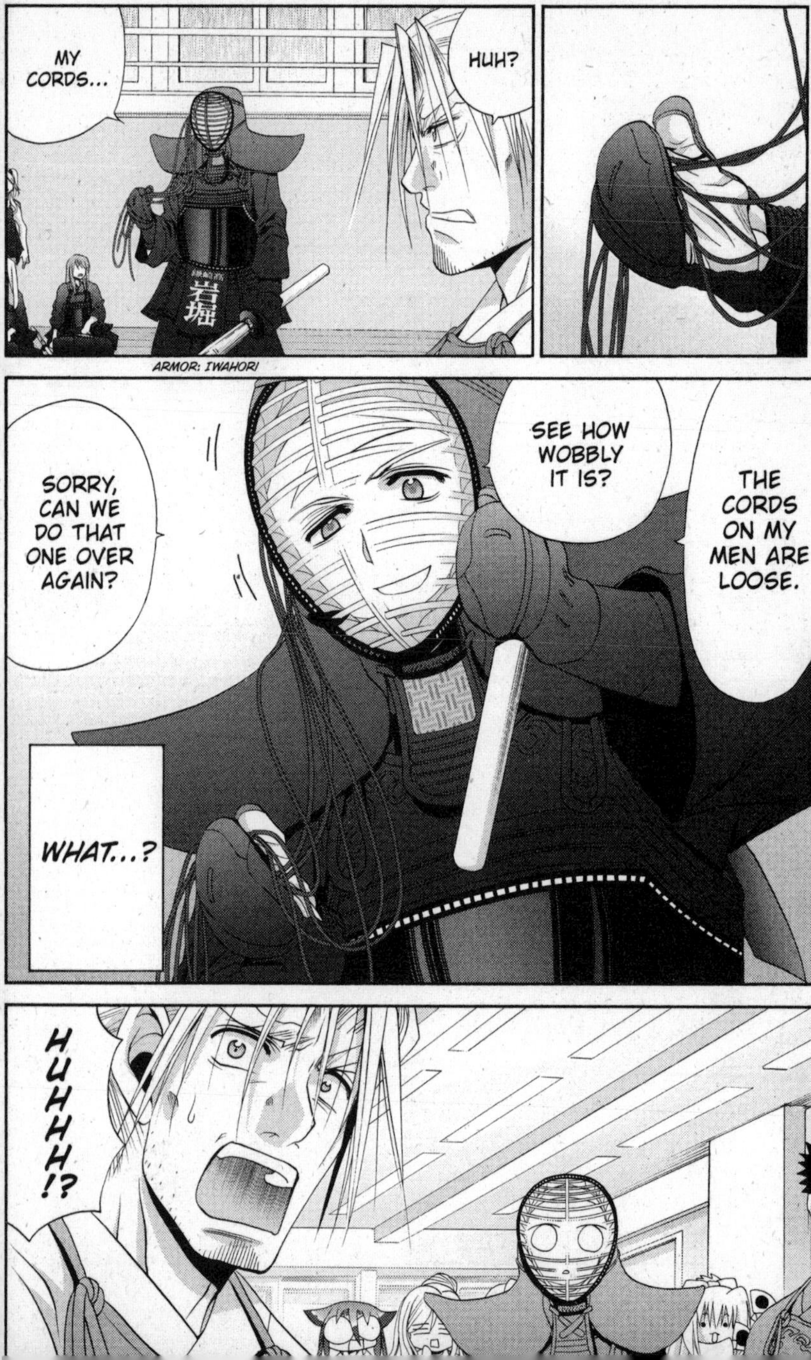
HUH?
MY CORDS...
岩堀
ARMOR: IWAHORI
THE CORDS ON MY MEN ARE LOOSE.
SEE HOW WOBBLY IT IS?
SORRY, CAN WE DO THAT ONE OVER AGAIN?
WHAT...?
HUHHHH!?

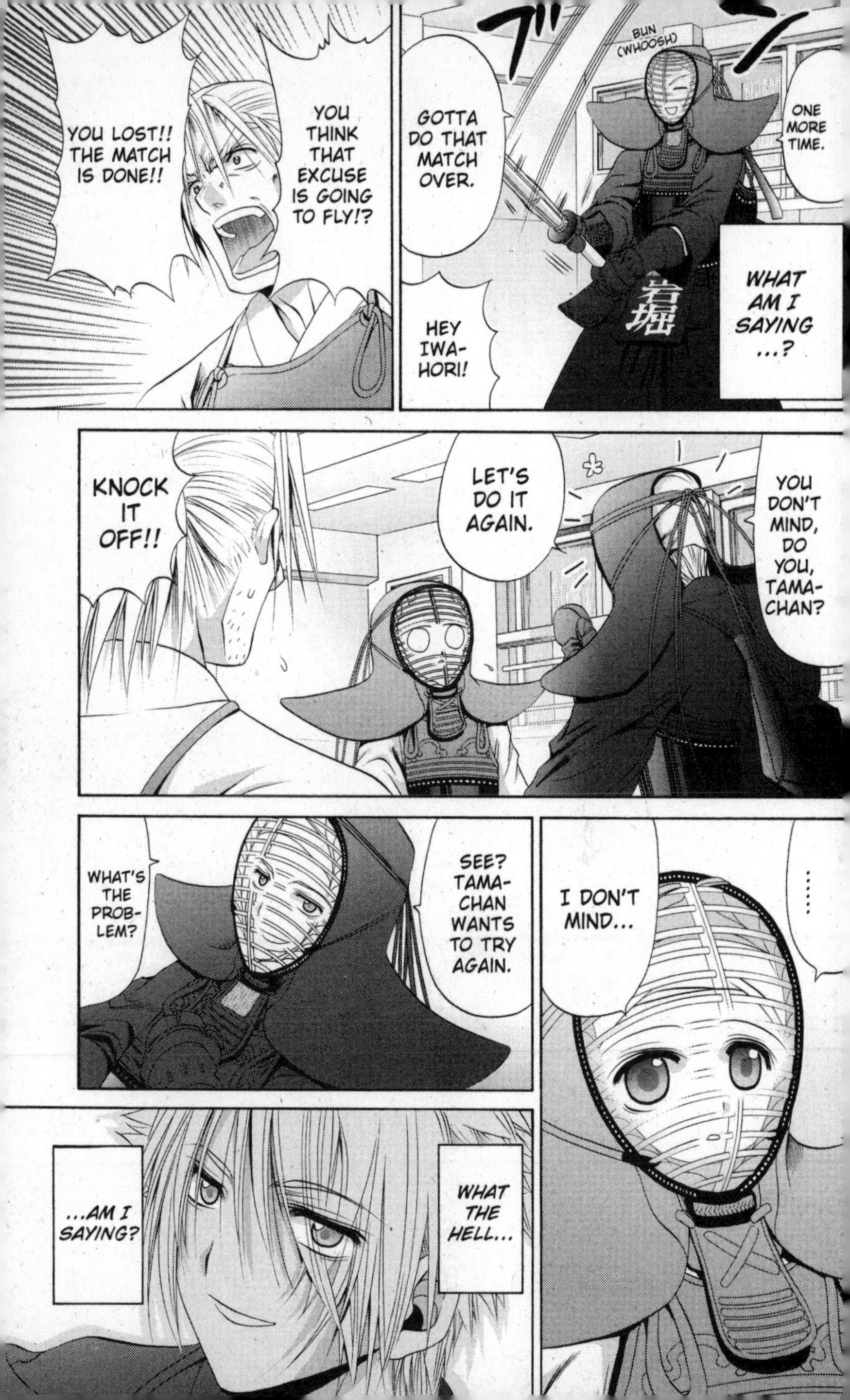
BUN (WHOOSH)
ONE MORE TIME.
GOTTA DO THAT MATCH OVER.
WHAT AM I SAYING...?
岩堀
HEY IWA-HORI!
YOU THINK THAT EXCUSE IS GOING TO FLY!?
YOU LOST!! THE MATCH IS DONE!!
YOU DON'T MIND, DO YOU, TAMA-CHAN?
LET'S DO IT AGAIN.
KNOCK IT OFF!!
......
I DON'T MIND...
SEE? TAMA-CHAN WANTS TO TRY AGAIN.
WHAT'S THE PROBLEM?
WHAT THE HELL...
...AM I SAYING?

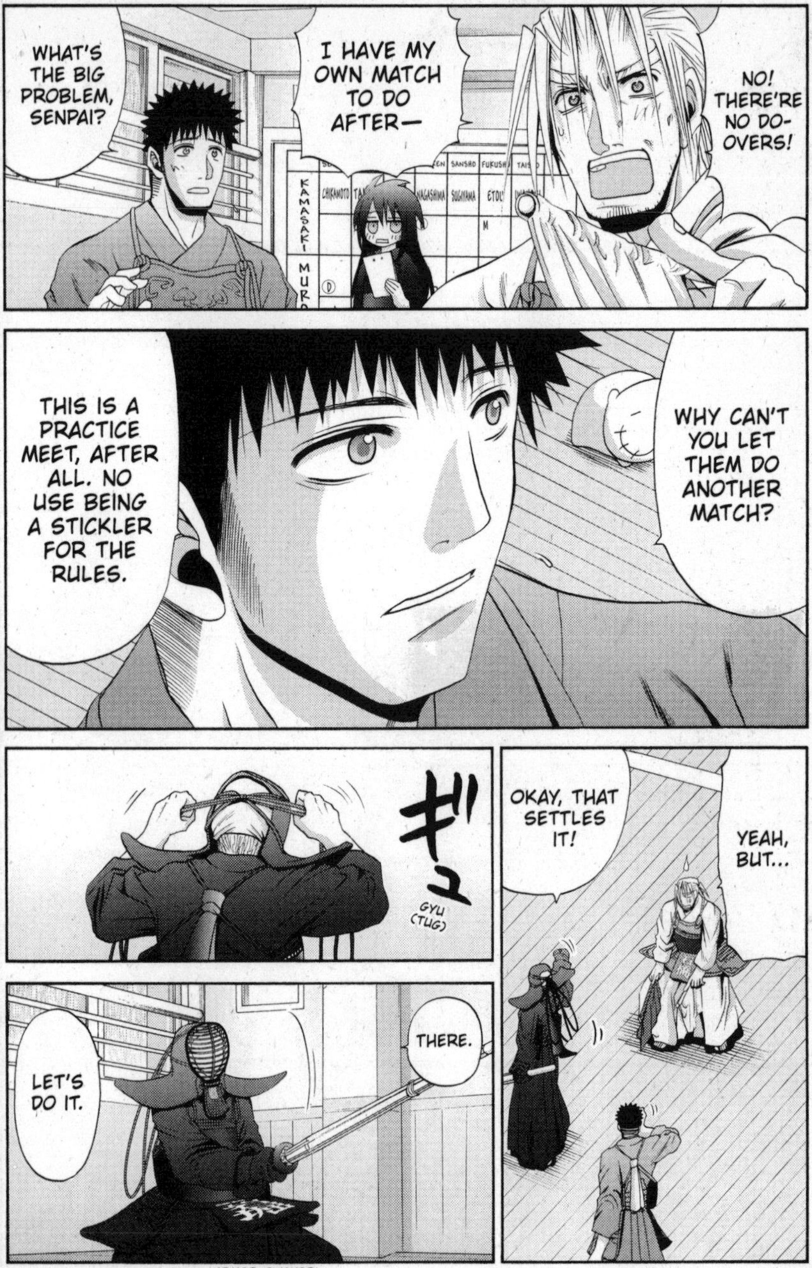
NO! THERE'RE NO DO-OVERS!
I HAVE MY OWN MATCH TO DO AFTER—
WHAT'S THE BIG PROBLEM, SENPAI?
WHY CAN'T YOU LET THEM DO ANOTHER MATCH?
THIS IS A PRACTICE MEET, AFTER ALL. NO USE BEING A STICKLER FOR THE RULES.
YEAH, BUT...
OKAY, THAT SETTLES IT!
ギュ
GYU (TUG)
THERE.
LET'S DO IT.

ARMOR: IWAHORI

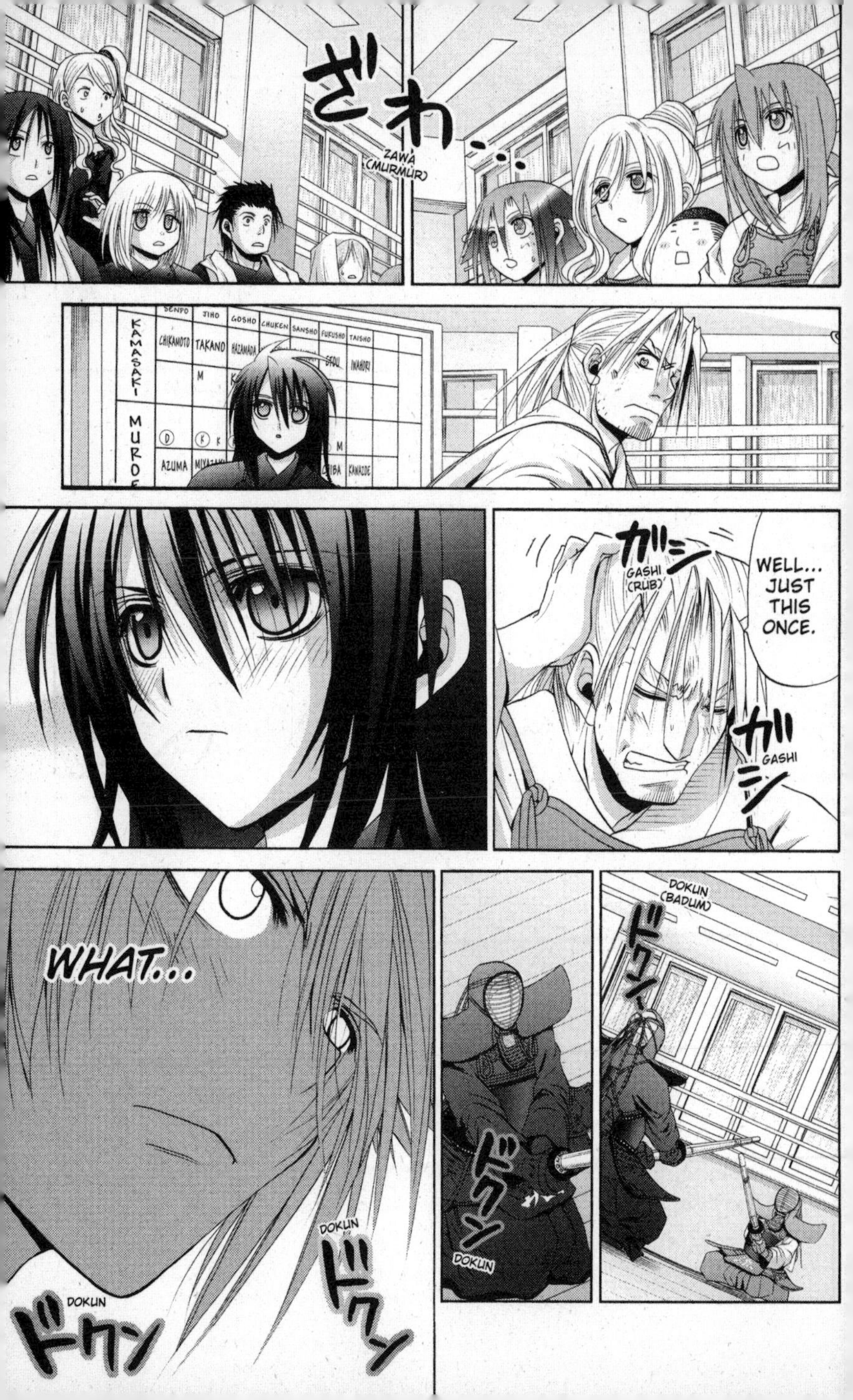
ざわ…
ZAWA (MURMUR)
SENPO JIHO GOSHO CHUKEN SANSHO FUKUSHO TAISHO
KAMASAKI
CHIKAMOTO TAKANO HAZAMADA SATOU IWAHORI
AZUMA CHIBA KANAZOE
ガシ
GASHI (RUB)
WELL... JUST THIS ONCE.
ガシ
GASHI
ドクン
DOKUN (BADUM)
ドクン
DOKUN
WHAT...
ドクン
DOKUN
ドクン
DOKUN

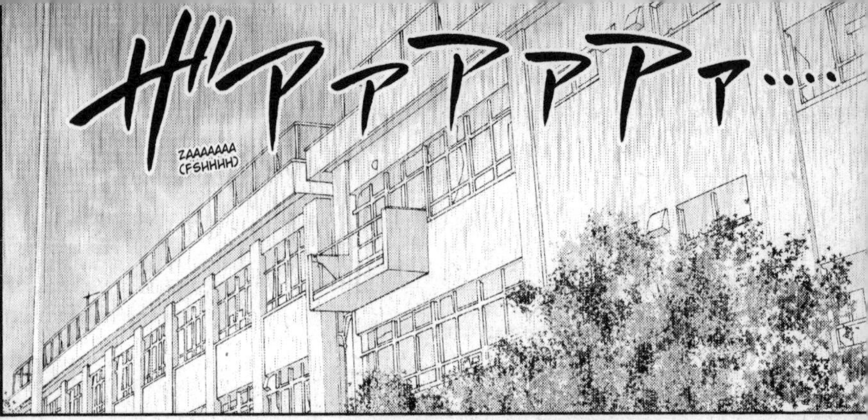
ZAAAAAAA
(FSHHHH)

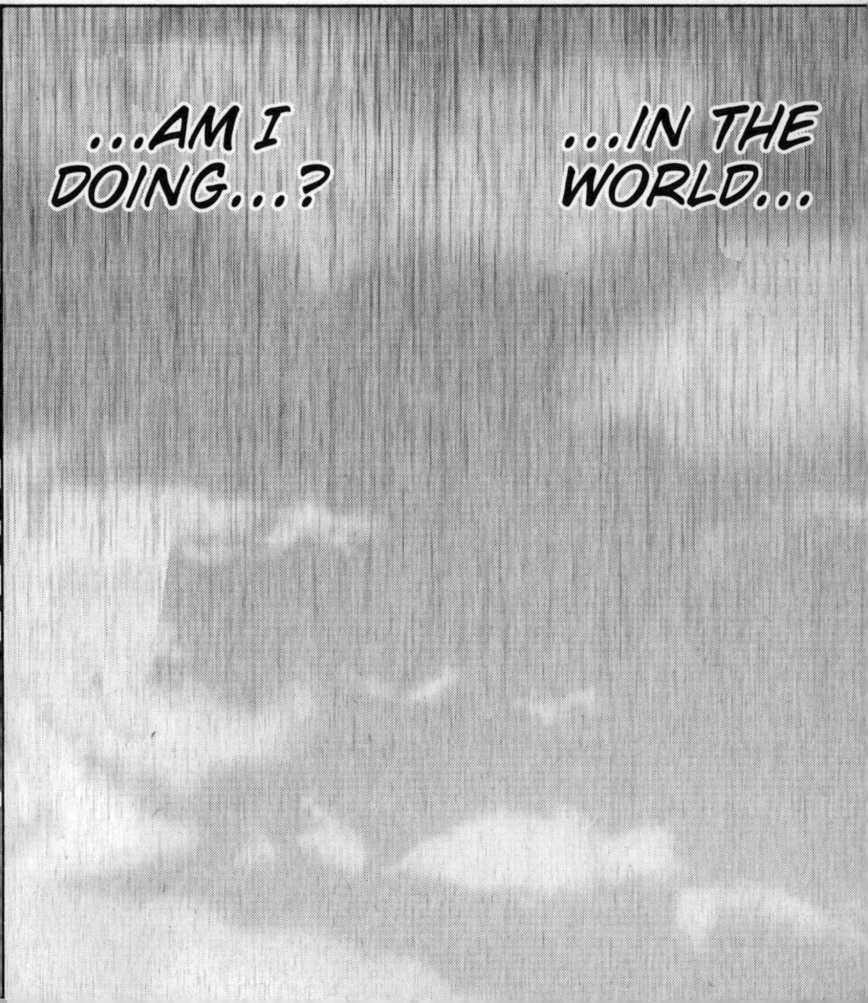
...IN THE WORLD...
...AM I DOING...?

BAMBOO BLADE

バンブーブレード

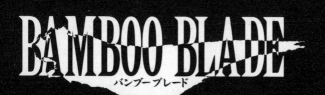

BAMBOO BLADE
バンブーブレード

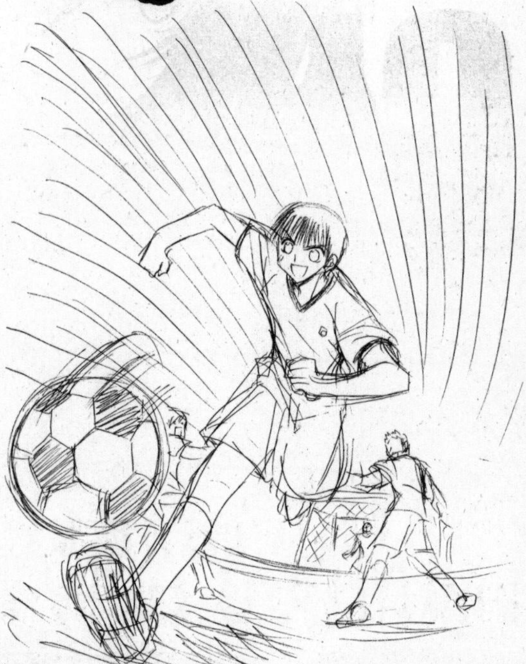

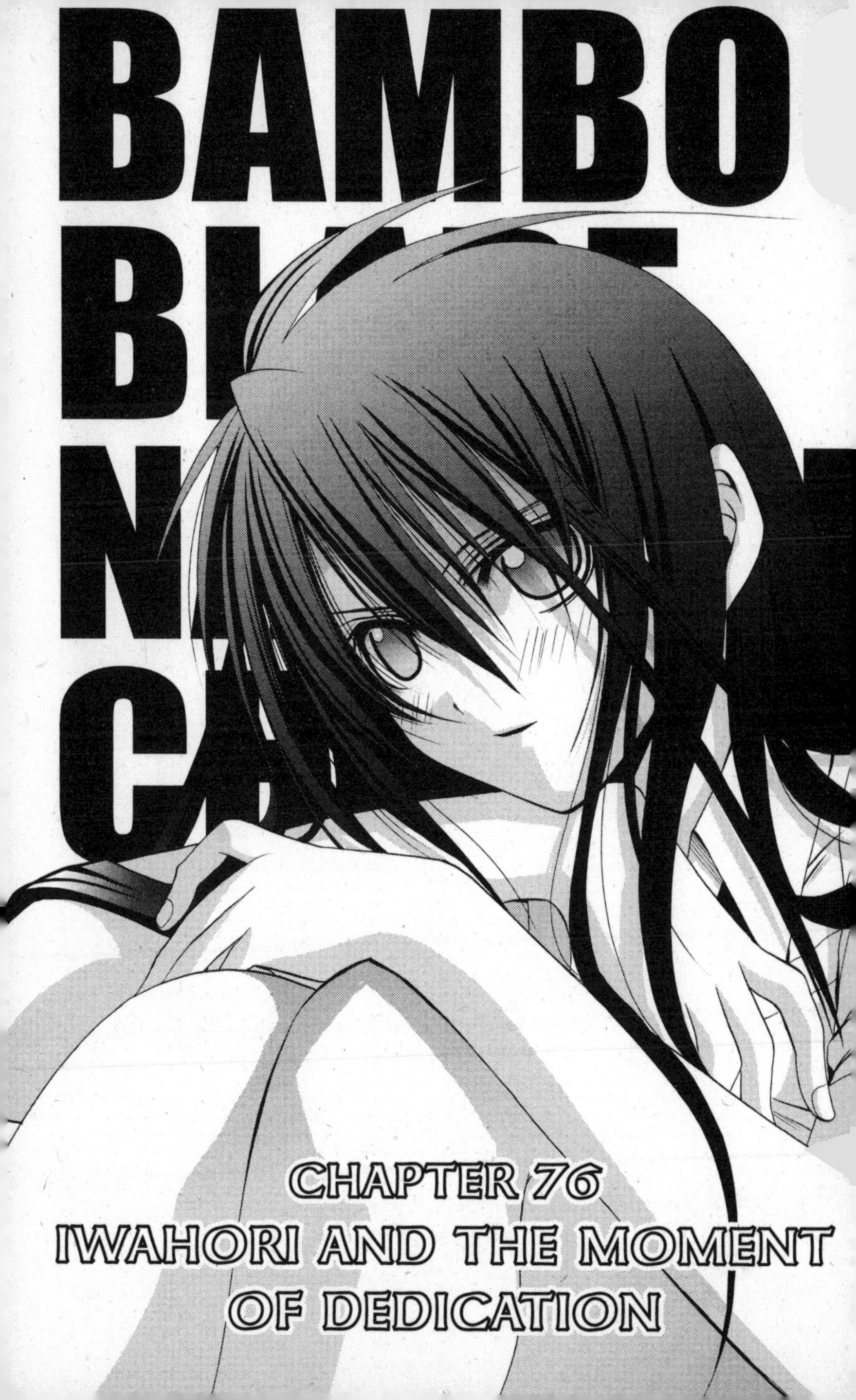
BAMBO
CHAPTER 76
IWAHORI AND THE MOMENT OF DEDICATION

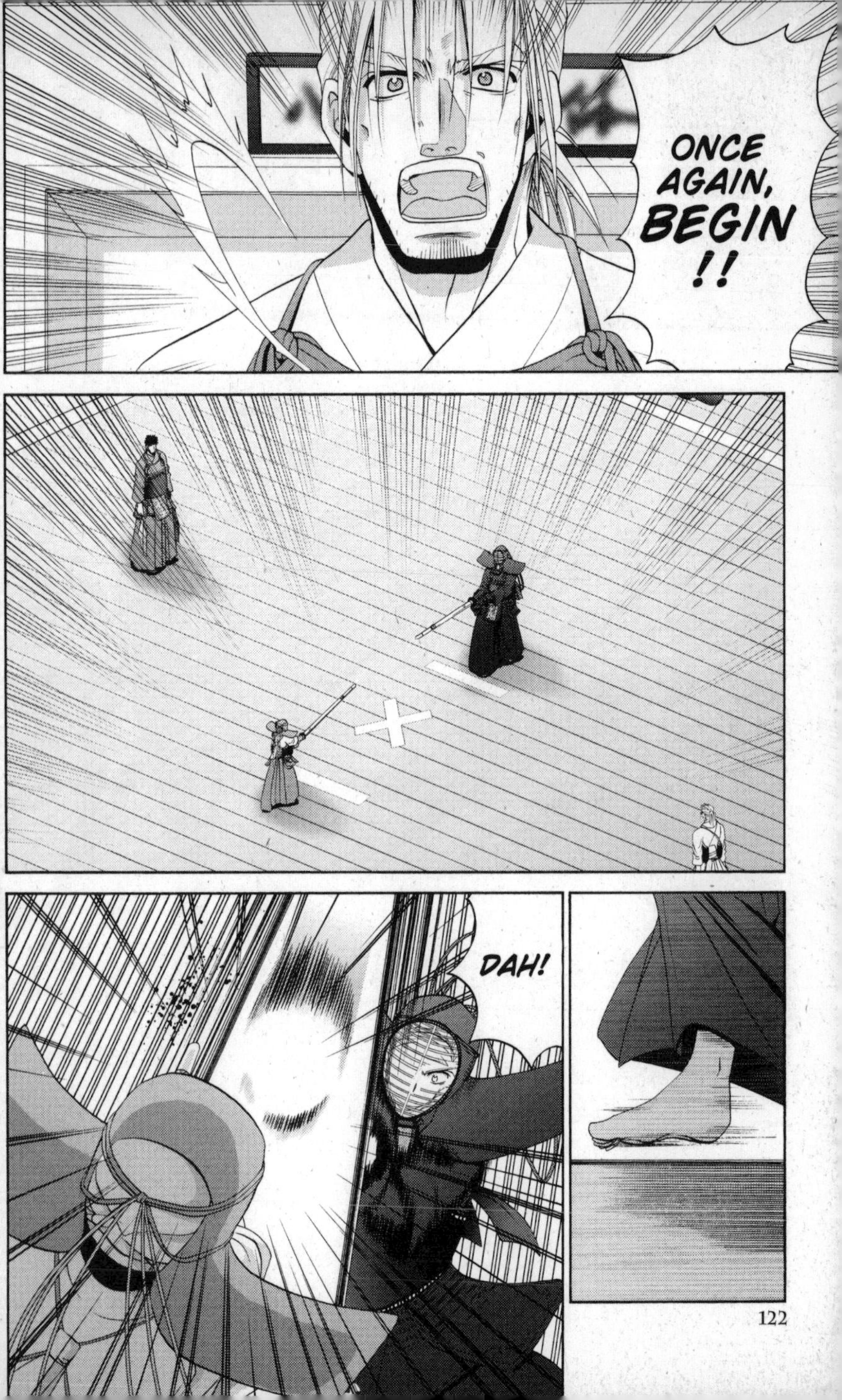
ONCE AGAIN, BEGIN !!
DAH!

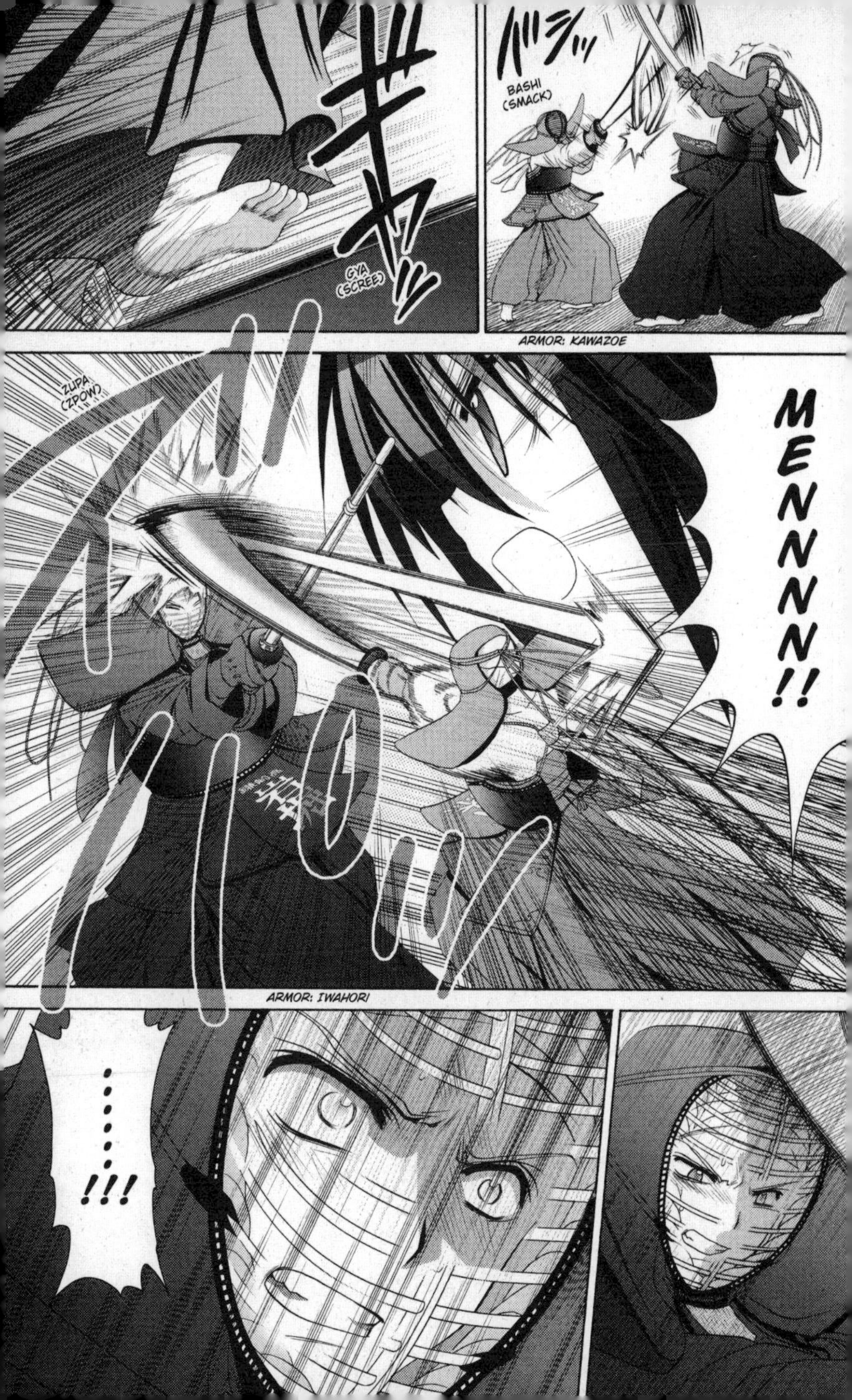

バシッ
BASHI (SMACK)
ARMOR: KAWAZOE
ギャッ
GYA (SCREE)
ZUPA (ZPOW)
MENNNNN!!
ARMOR: IWAHORI
......!!!

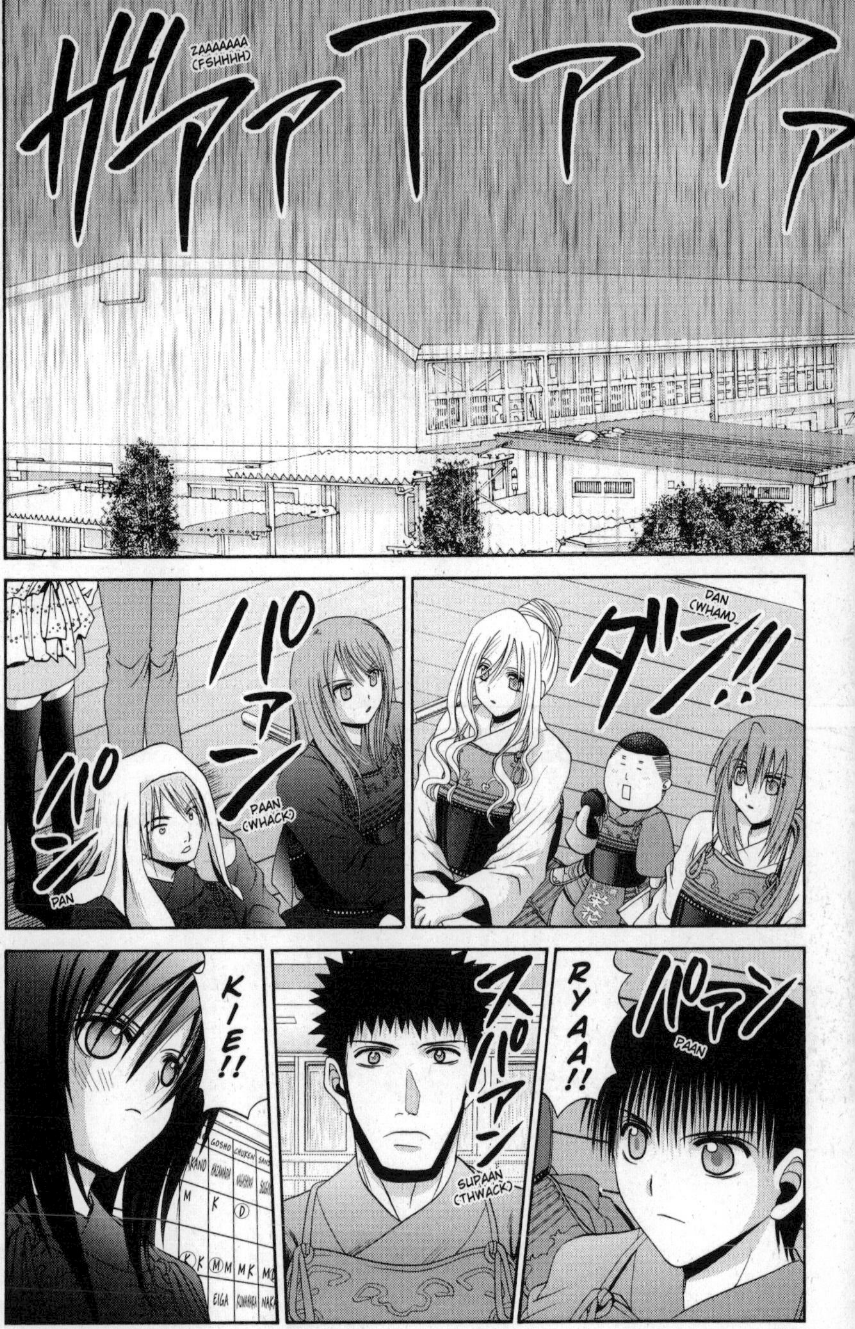
ザアアアアア
ZAAAAAAA (FSHHHH)
ダン!!
DAN (WHAM)
パアン
PAAN (WHACK)
パン
PAN
パァン
PAAN
RYAAA!!
スパァン
SUPAAN (THWACK)
KIE!!
GOSHO
CHUKEN
EIGA

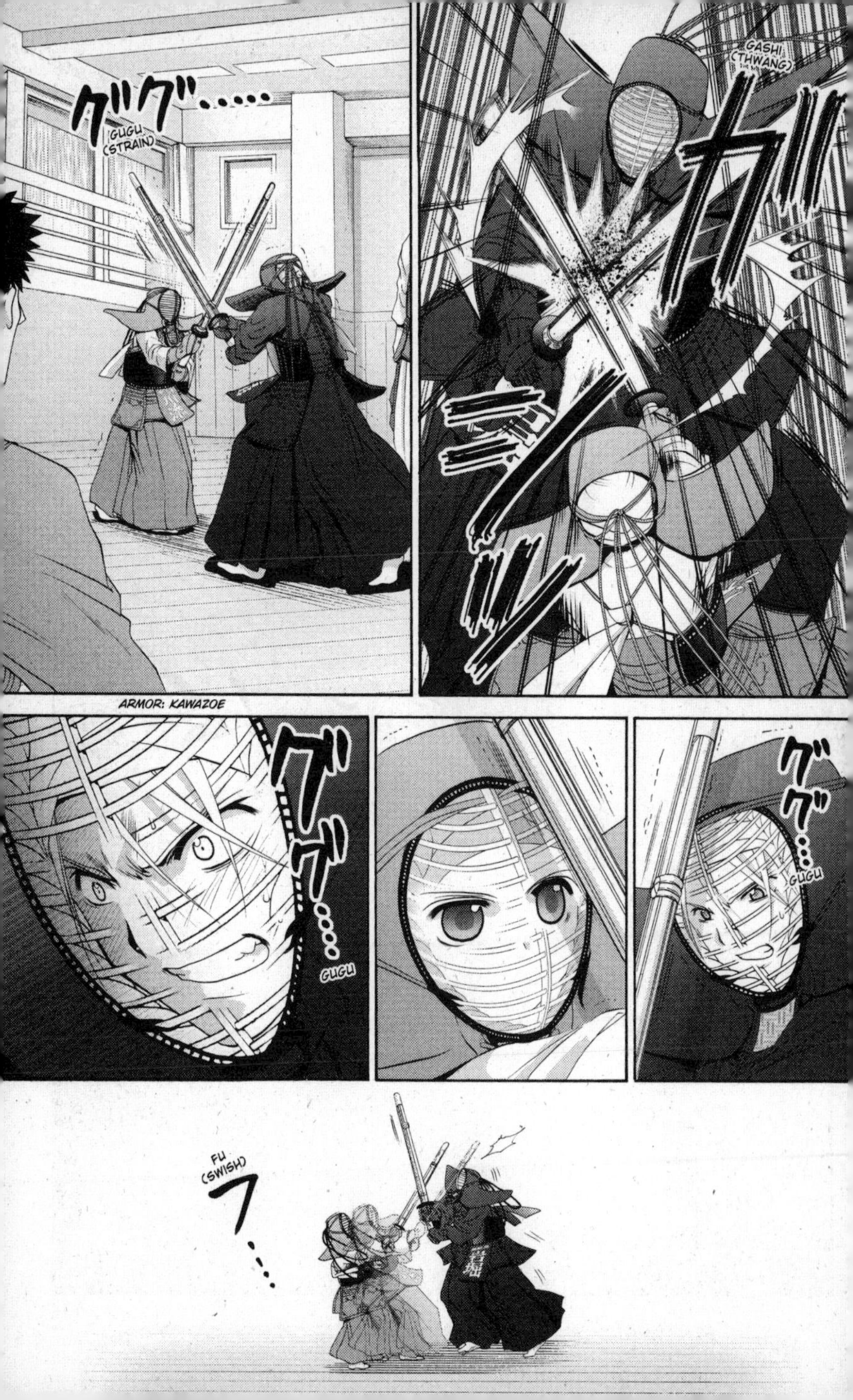
GASHI (THWANG)
GUGU (STRAIN)
ARMOR: KAWAZOE
GUGU
GUGU
FU (SWISH)

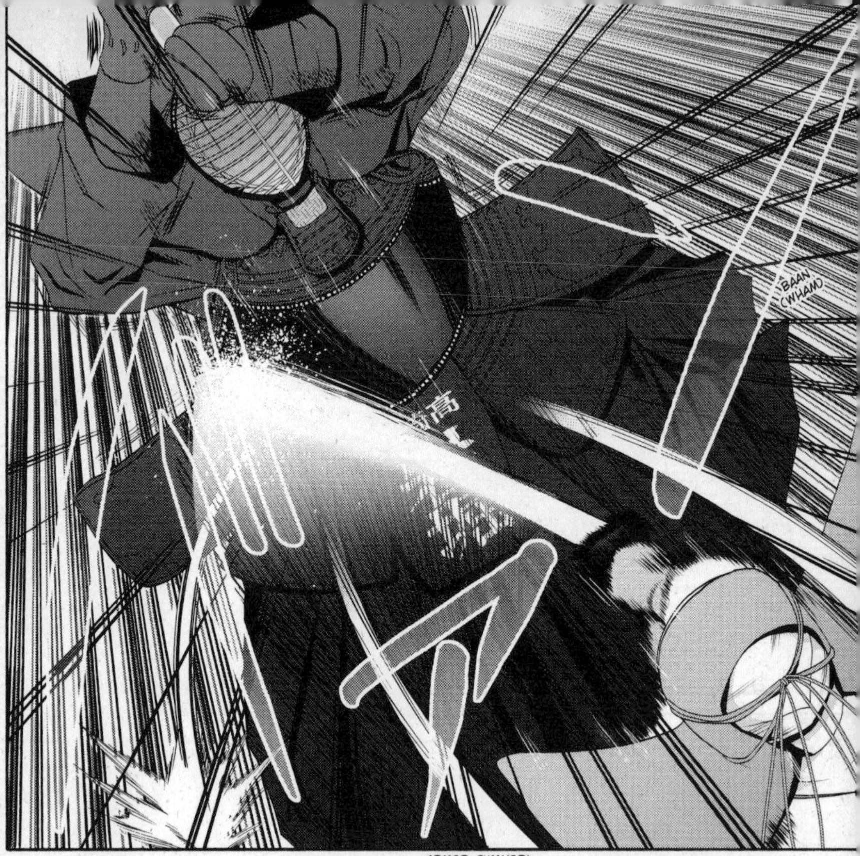
BAAN (WHAM)
ARMOR: IWAHORI

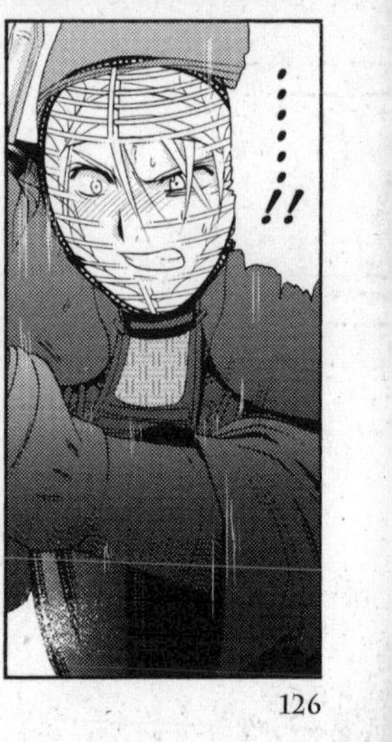
......!!

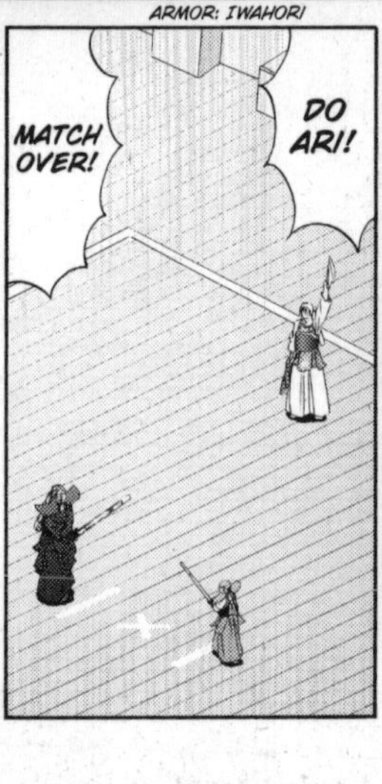
DO ARI!
MATCH OVER!

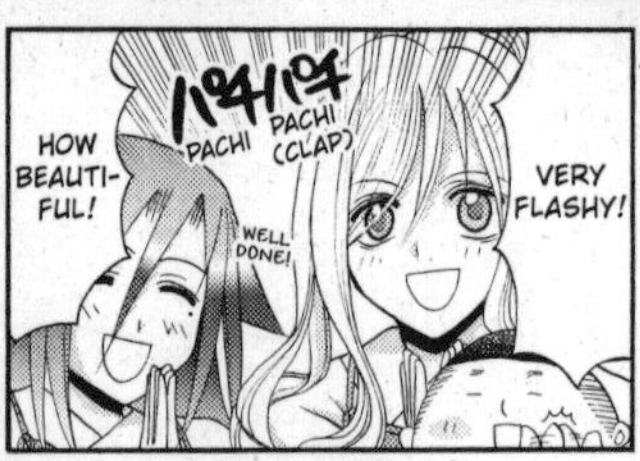
VERY FLASHY!
パチパチ PACHI PACHI (CLAP)
WELL DONE!
HOW BEAUTIFUL!

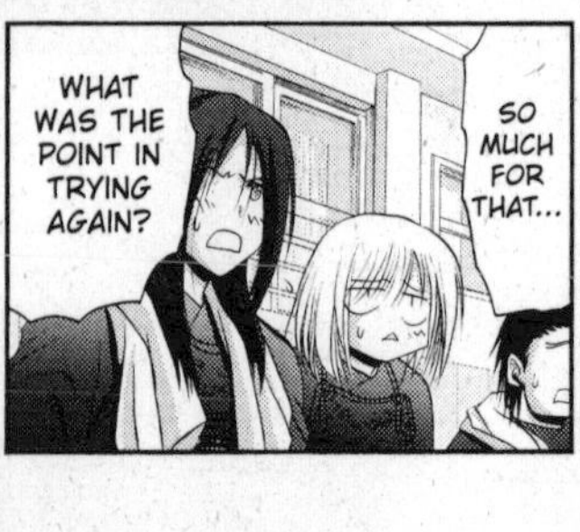
SO MUCH FOR THAT...
WHAT WAS THE POINT IN TRYING AGAIN?

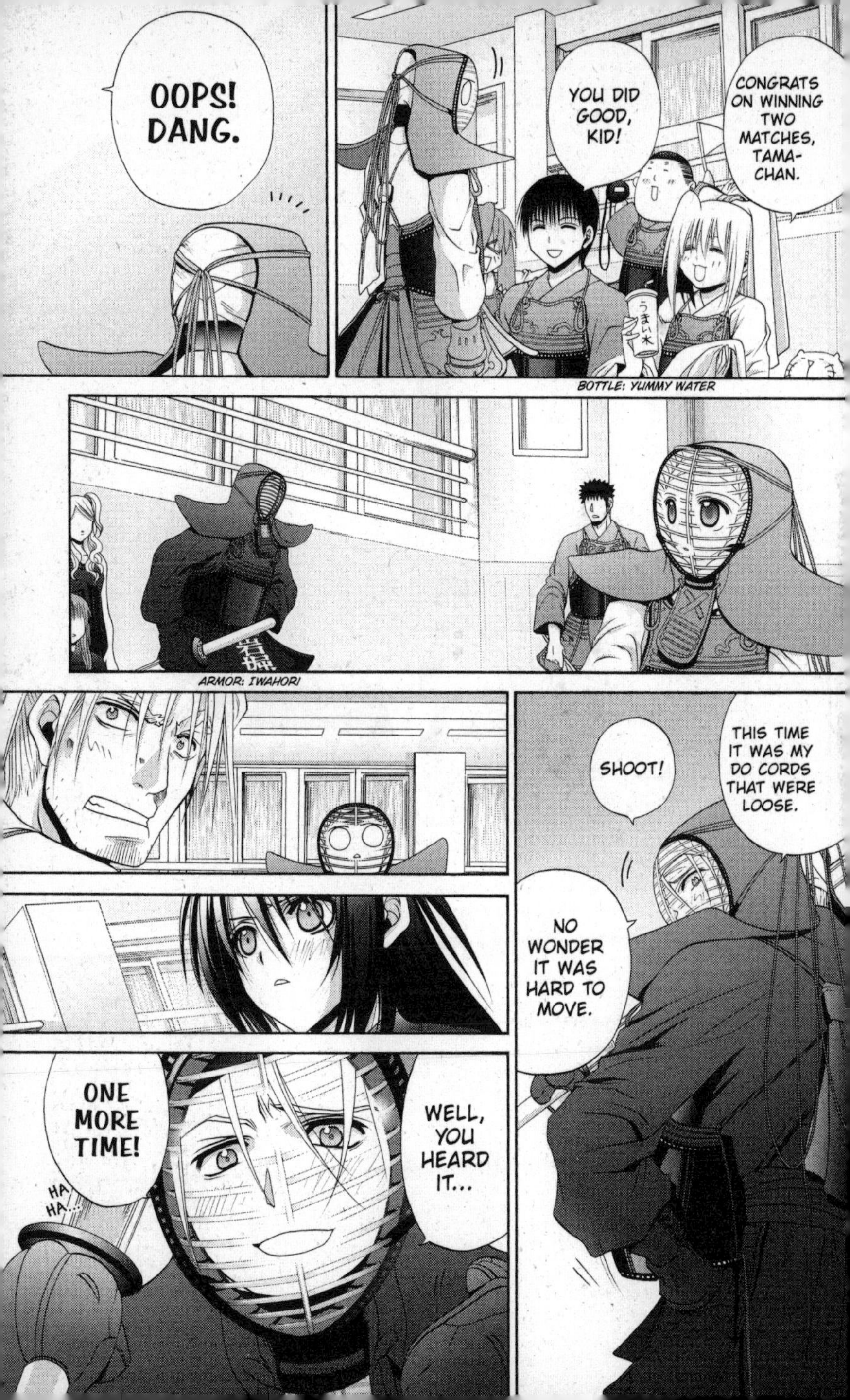
CONGRATS ON WINNING TWO MATCHES, TAMA-CHAN.
YOU DID GOOD, KID!
OOPS! DANG.
BOTTLE: YUMMY WATER
ARMOR: IWAHORI
THIS TIME IT WAS MY DO CORDS THAT WERE LOOSE.
SHOOT!
NO WONDER IT WAS HARD TO MOVE.
WELL, YOU HEARD IT...
ONE MORE TIME!
HA HA...

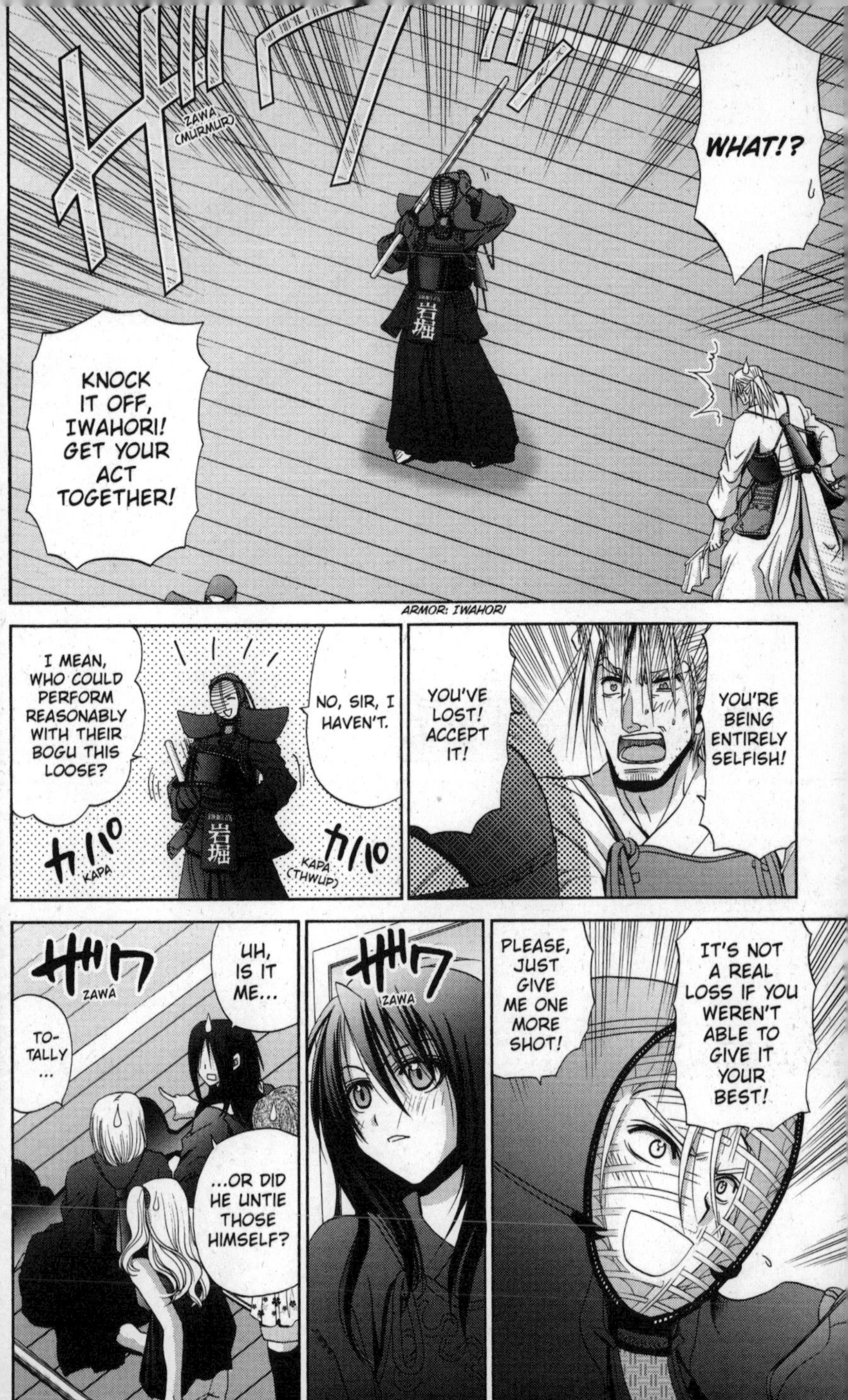
WHAT!?
ZAWA (MURMUR)
KNOCK IT OFF, IWAHORI! GET YOUR ACT TOGETHER!
ARMOR: IWAHORI
YOU'RE BEING ENTIRELY SELFISH!
YOU'VE LOST! ACCEPT IT!
NO, SIR, I HAVEN'T.
KAPA (THWUP)
I MEAN, WHO COULD PERFORM REASONABLY WITH THEIR BOGU THIS LOOSE?
KAPA
IT'S NOT A REAL LOSS IF YOU WEREN'T ABLE TO GIVE IT YOUR BEST!
PLEASE, JUST GIVE ME ONE MORE SHOT!
ZAWA
UH, IS IT ME...
ZAWA
TO-TALLY...
...OR DID HE UNTIE THOSE HIMSELF?

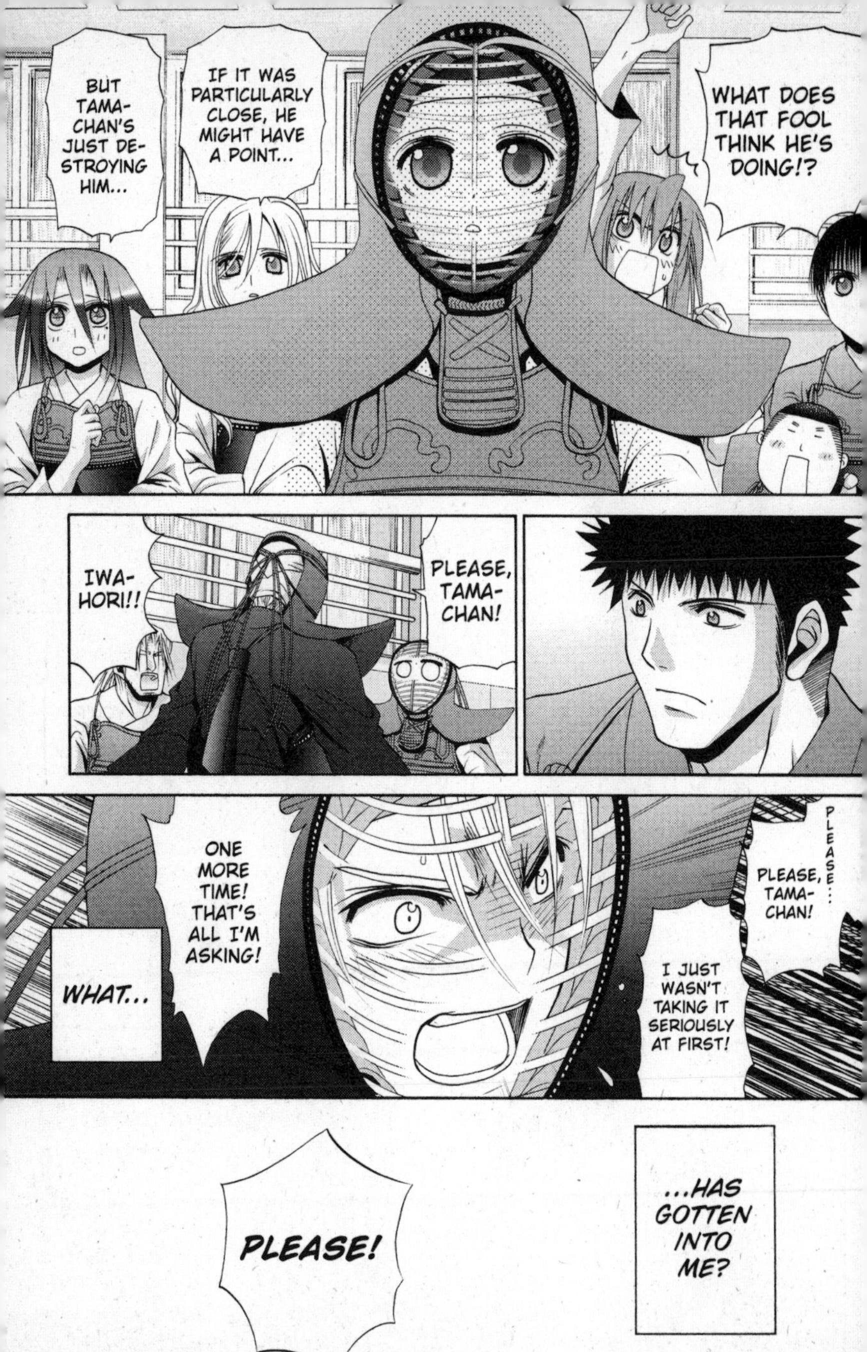
WHAT DOES THAT FOOL THINK HE'S DOING!?
IF IT WAS PARTICULARLY CLOSE, HE MIGHT HAVE A POINT...
BUT TAMA-CHAN'S JUST DE-STROYING HIM...
PLEASE, TAMA-CHAN!
IWA-HORI!!
PLEASE...
PLEASE, TAMA-CHAN!
I JUST WASN'T TAKING IT SERIOUSLY AT FIRST!
ONE MORE TIME! THAT'S ALL I'M ASKING!
WHAT...
...HAS GOTTEN INTO ME?
PLEASE!

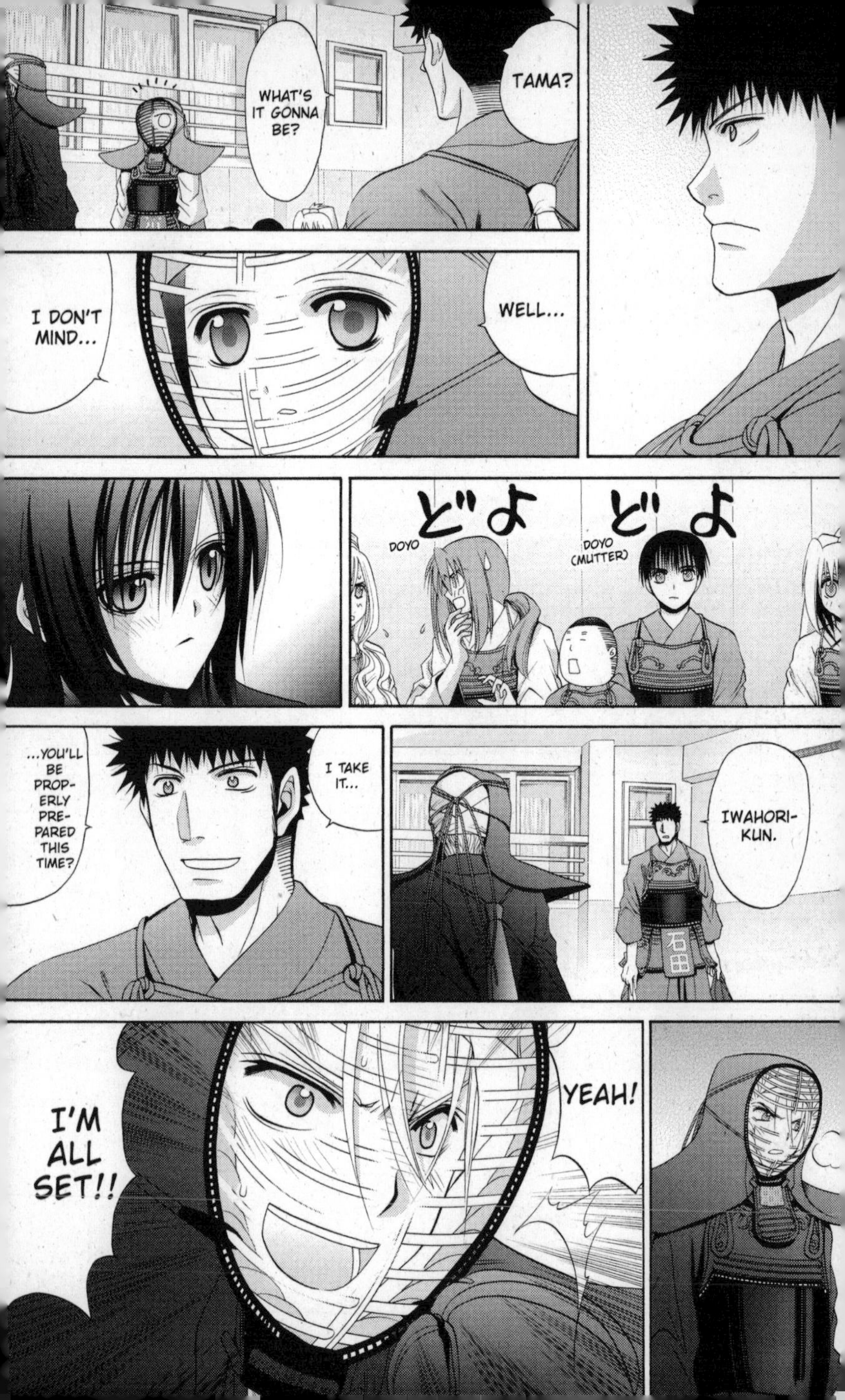
TAMA?
WHAT'S IT GONNA BE?
WELL...
I DON'T MIND...
どよ どよ
DOYO (MUTTER)
DOYO
IWAHORI-KUN.
I TAKE IT...
...YOU'LL BE PROPERLY PREPARED THIS TIME?
YEAH!
I'M ALL SET!!

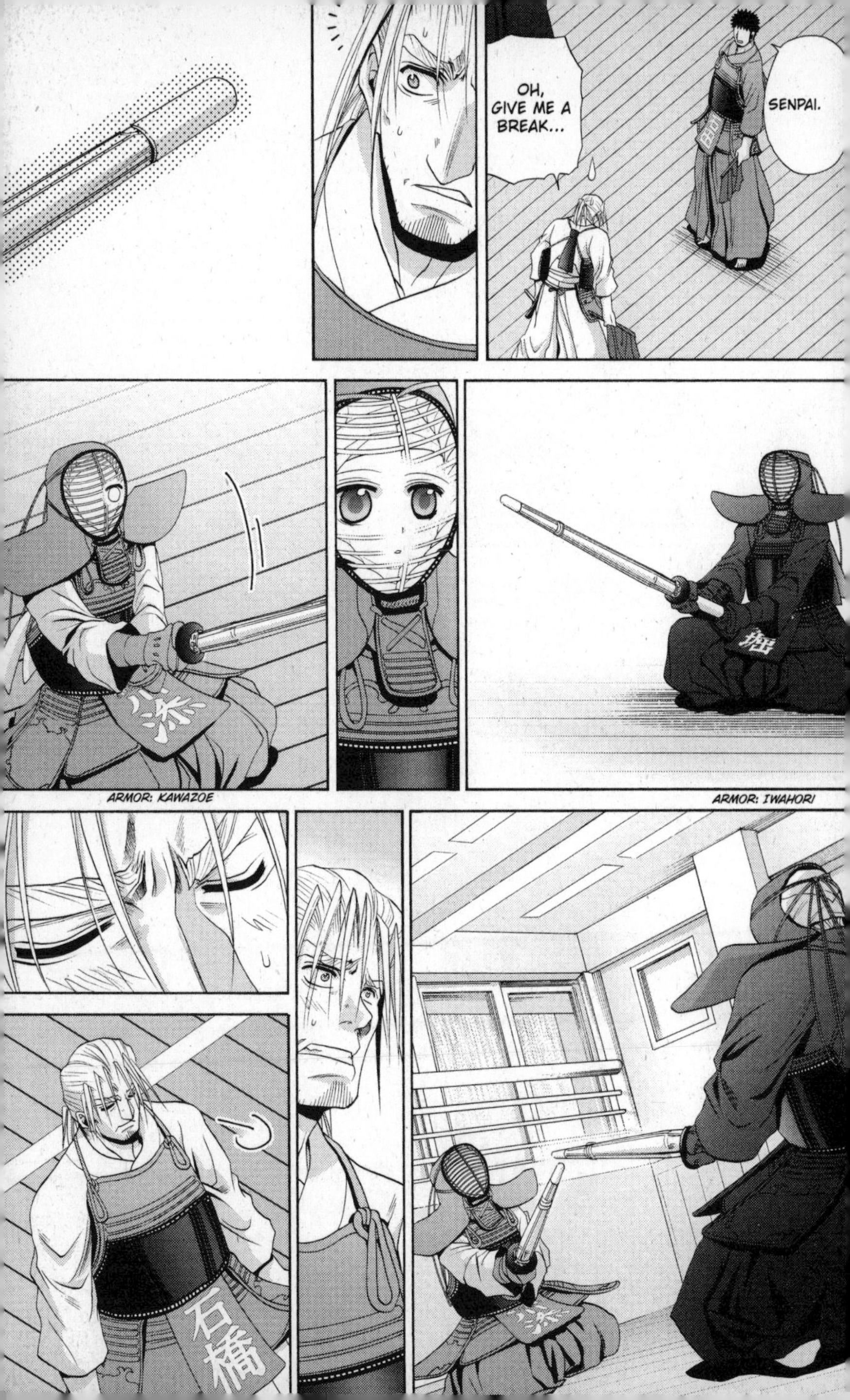
SENPAI.
OH, GIVE ME A BREAK...
ARMOR: IWAHORI
ARMOR: KAWAZOE
石橋

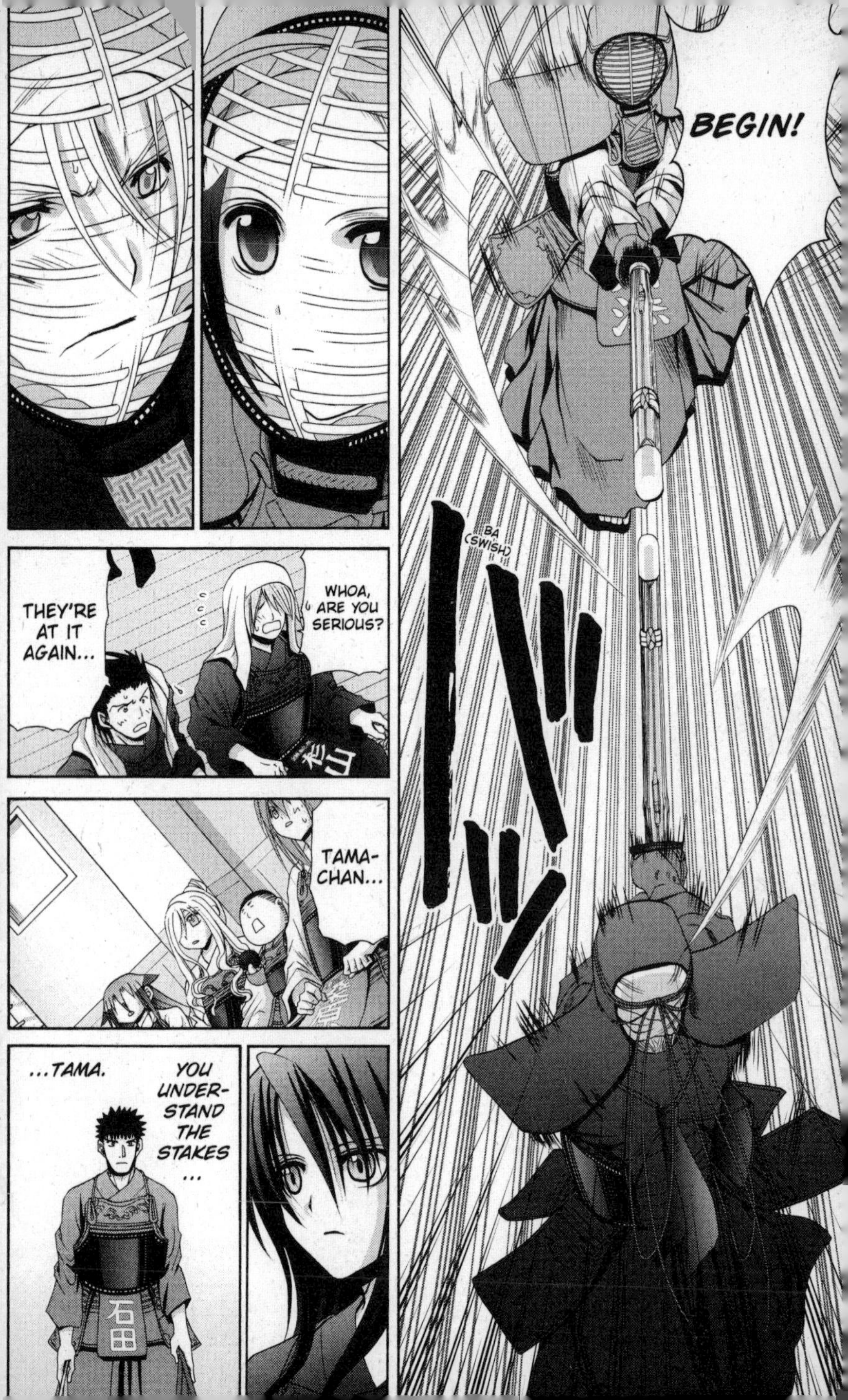
BEGIN!
BA (SWISH)
ドッ
WHOA, ARE YOU SERIOUS?
THEY'RE AT IT AGAIN...
TAMA-CHAN...
YOU UNDER-STAND THE STAKES ...
...TAMA.

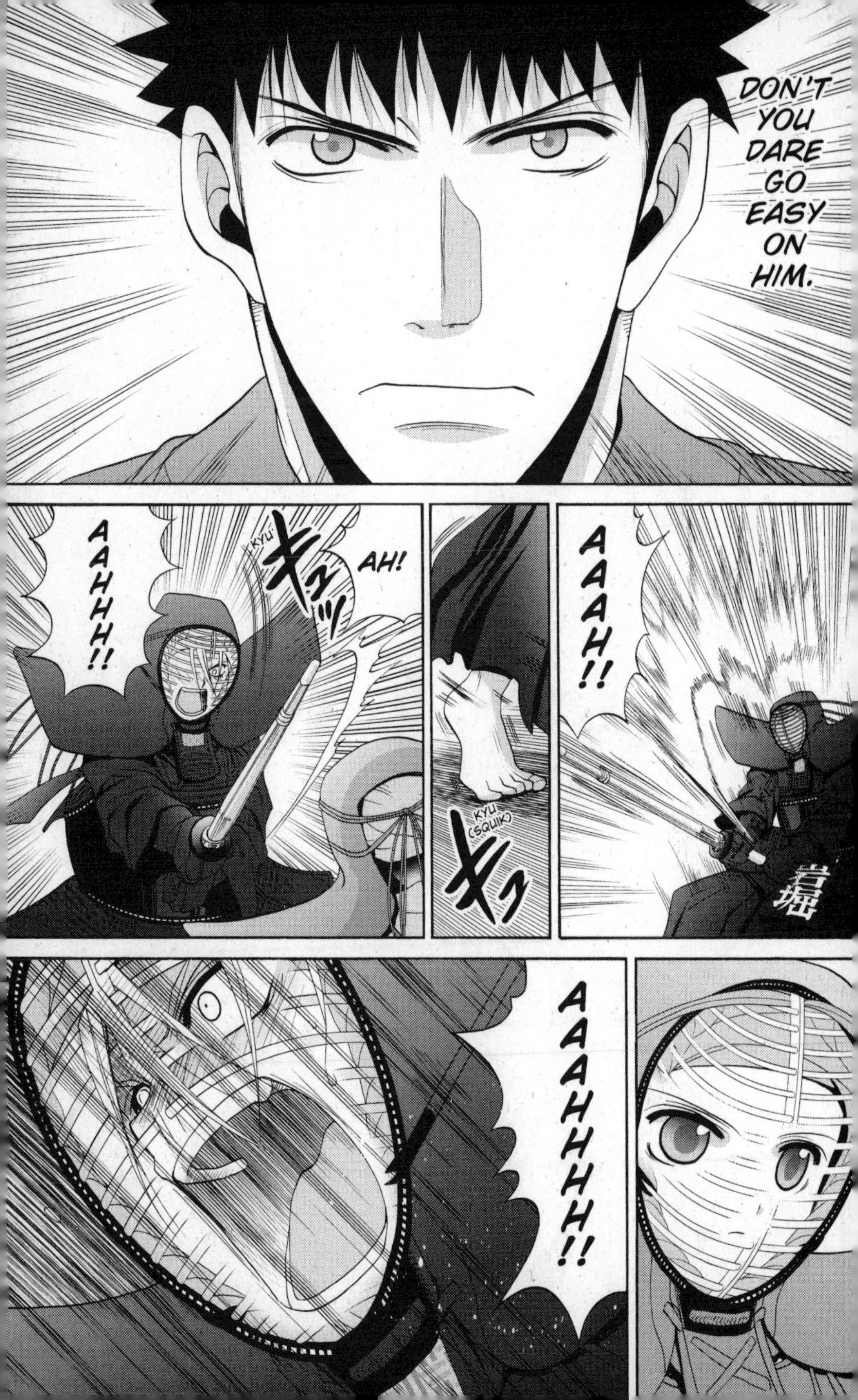
DON'T YOU DARE GO EASY ON HIM.
AAAAH!!
岩堀
KYU (SQUIK)
キュ
KYU
キュッ
AH!
AAHHH!!
AAAAHHHHH!!

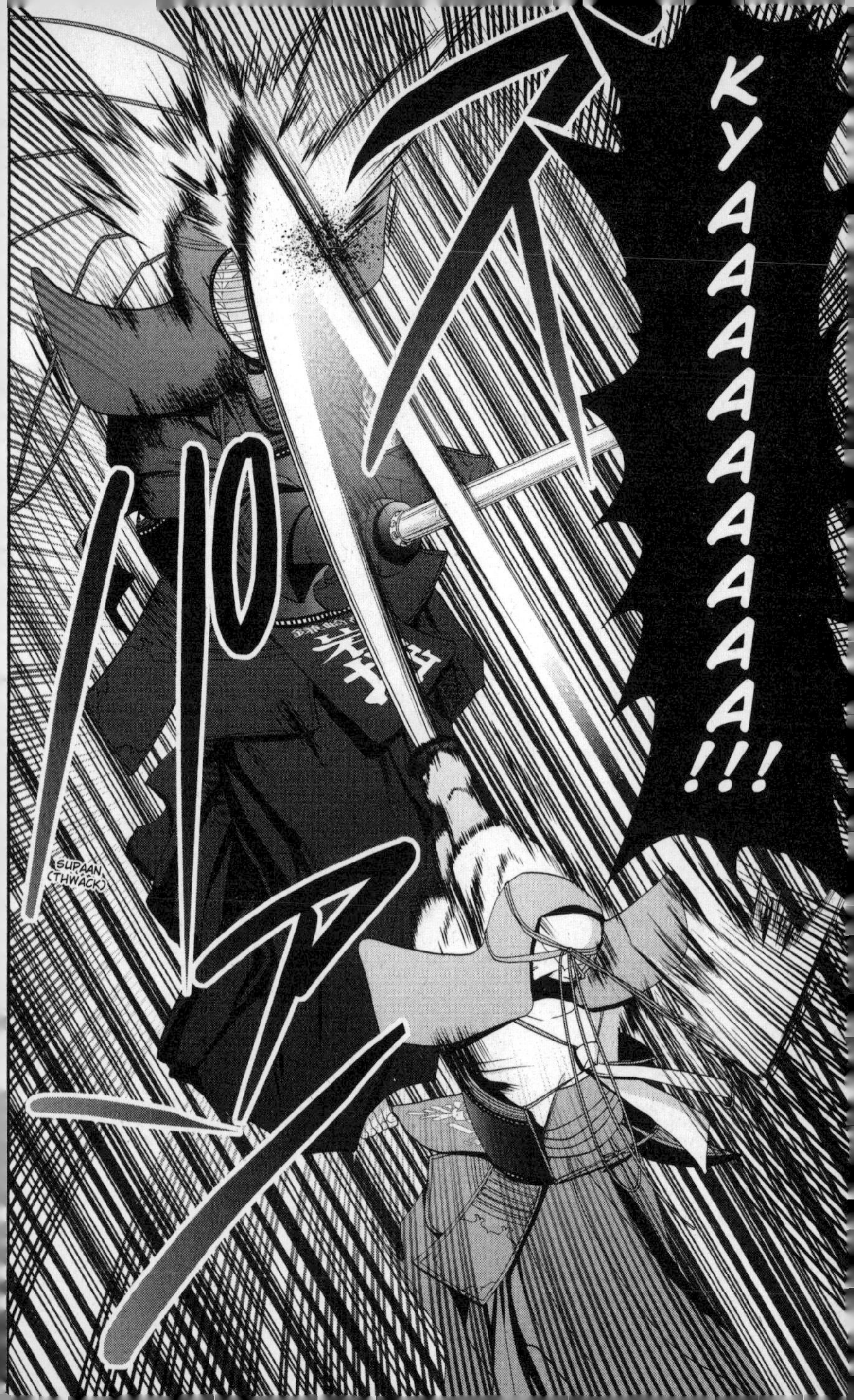
KYAAAAAAAAAAA!!!
SUPAAN (THWACK)

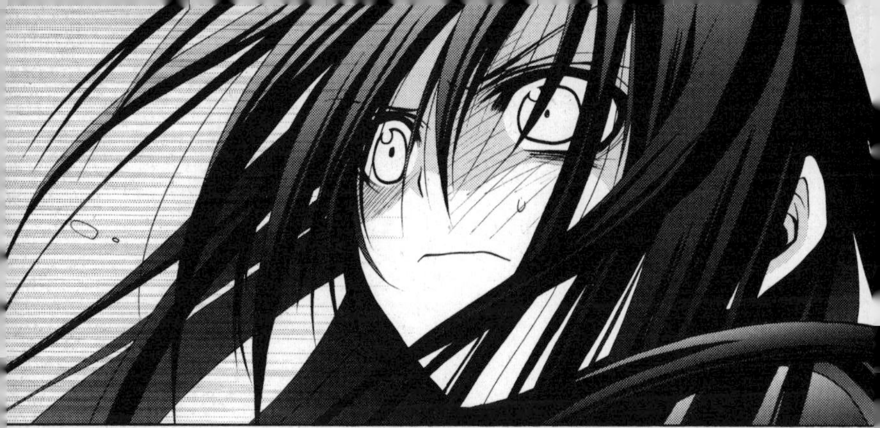

ARMOR: (BELOW) KAWAZOE, (RIGHT) IWAHORI

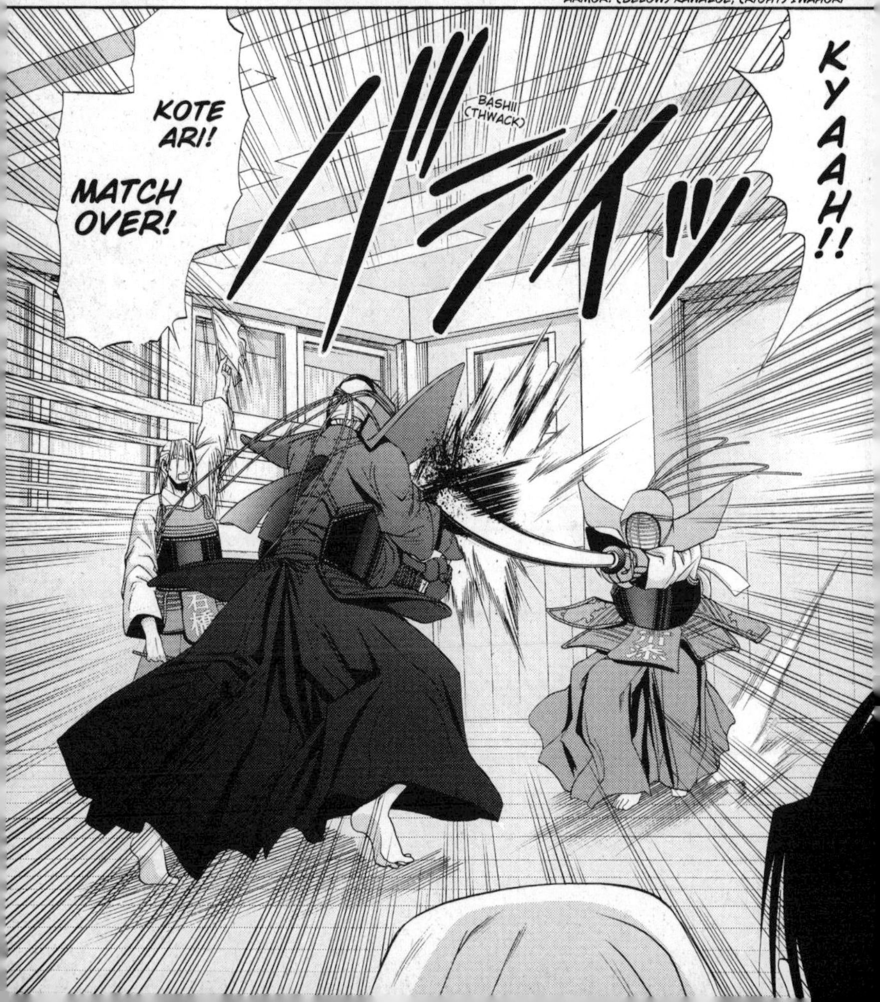
KYAAAH!!
BASHII (THWACK)
KOTE ARI!
MATCH OVER!

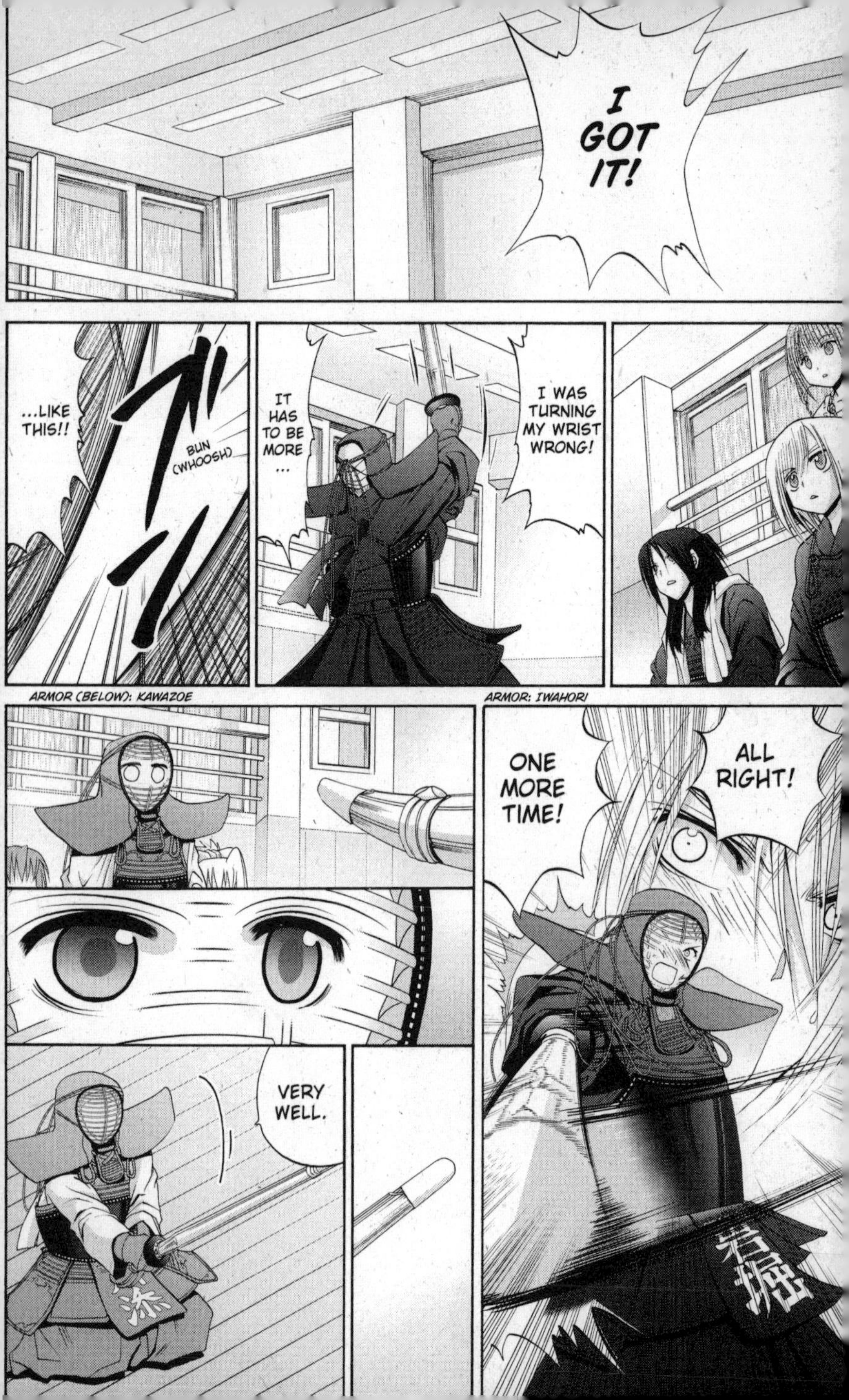
I GOT IT!
I WAS TURNING MY WRIST WRONG!
IT HAS TO BE MORE ...
...LIKE THIS!!
BUN (WHOOSH)
ARMOR: IWAHORI
ARMOR (BELOW): KAWAZOE
ALL RIGHT!
ONE MORE TIME!
VERY WELL.

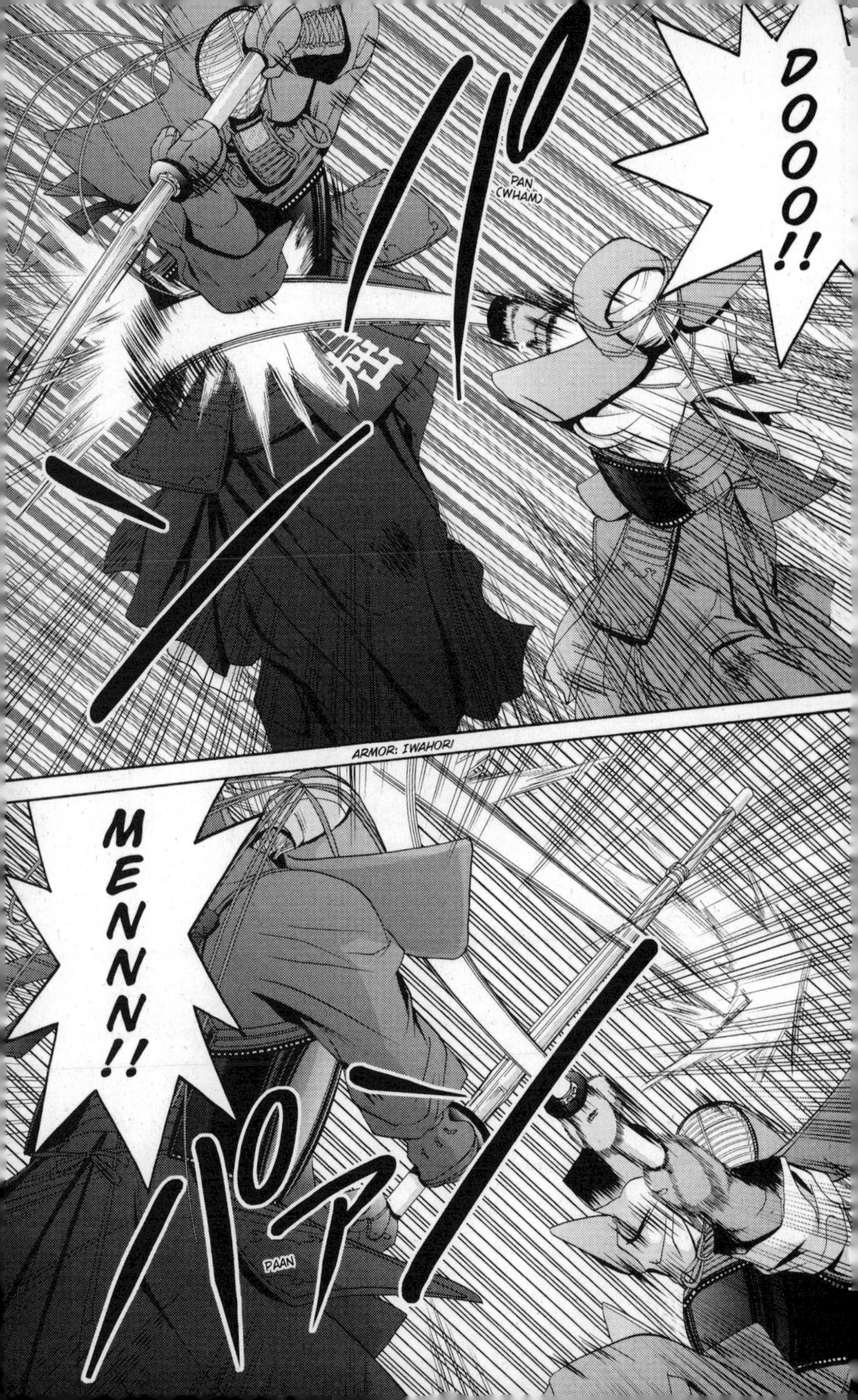
DOOOOO!!
PAN (WHAM)
ARMOR: IWAHORI
MENNNN!!
PAAN

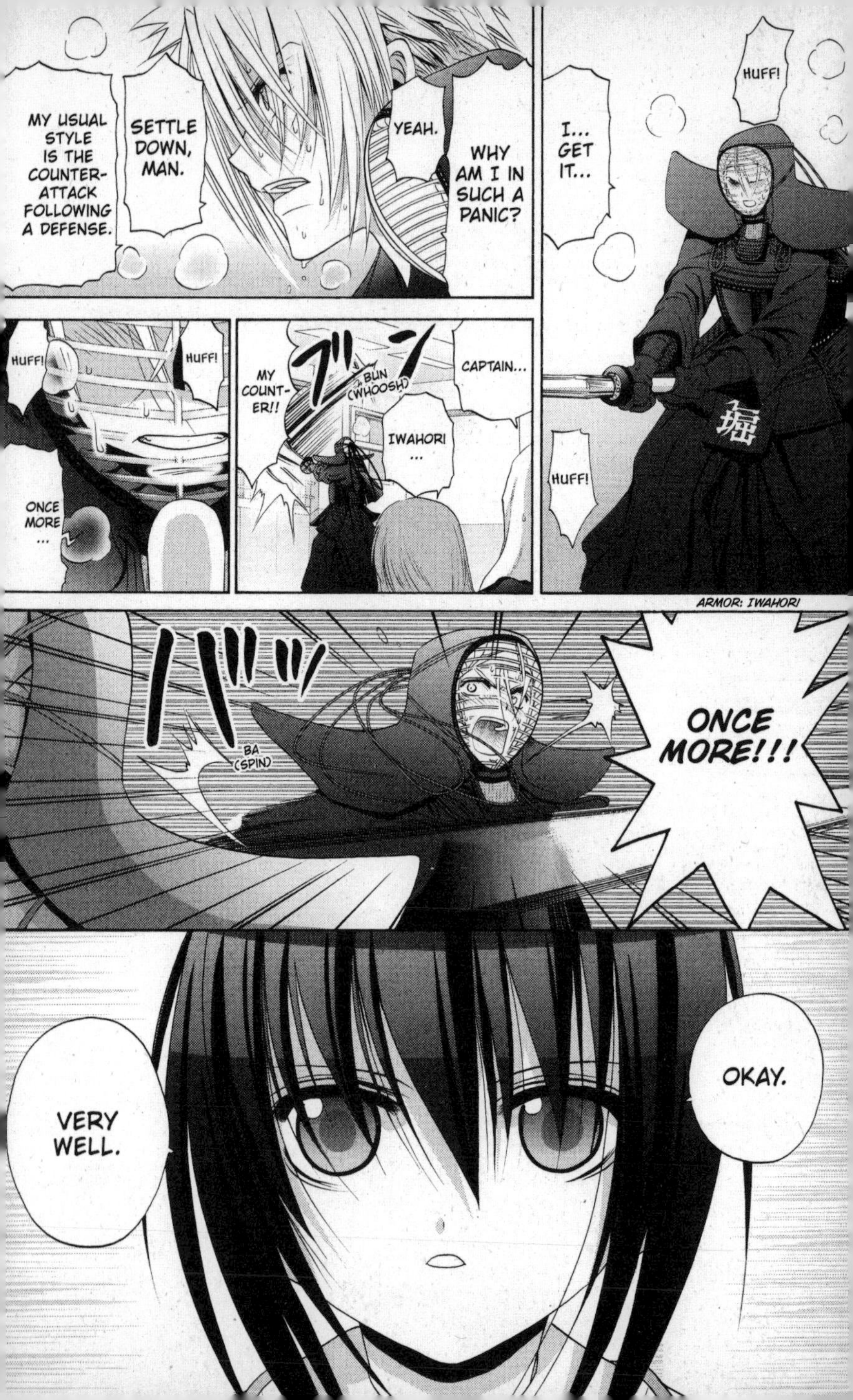
HUFF!
I... GET IT...
堀
HUFF!
WHY AM I IN SUCH A PANIC?
YEAH.
SETTLE DOWN, MAN.
MY USUAL STYLE IS THE COUNTER-ATTACK FOLLOWING A DEFENSE.
CAPTAIN...
MY COUNTER!!
BUN (WHOOSH)
IWAHORI ...
HUFF!
HUFF!
ONCE MORE ...
ARMOR: IWAHORI
ONCE MORE!!!
BA (SPIN)
OKAY.
VERY WELL.

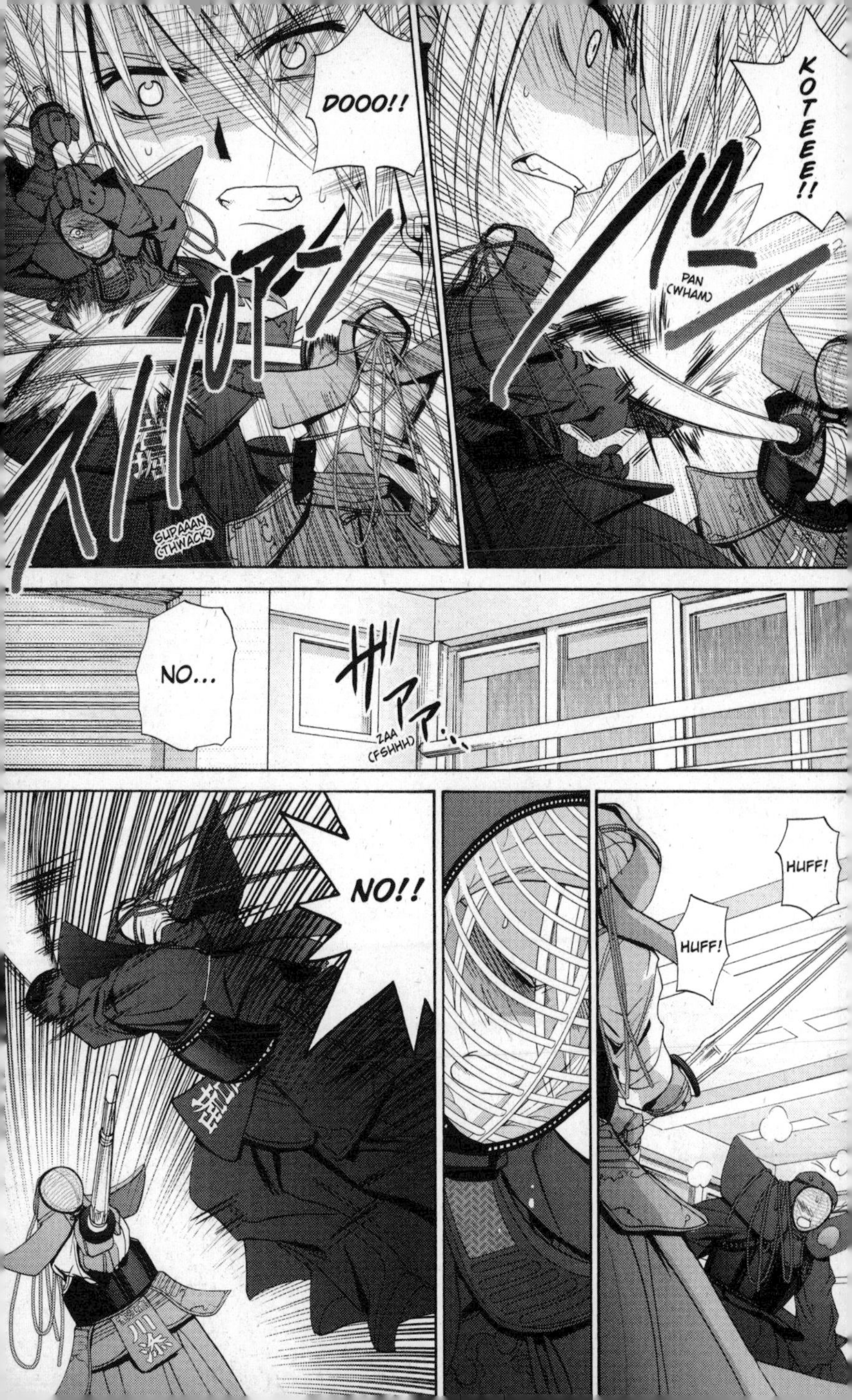
KOTEEEE!!
PAN (WHAM)
DOOO!!
SUPAAAN (THWACK)
NO...
ZAA (FSHHH)
HUFF!
HUFF!
NO!!

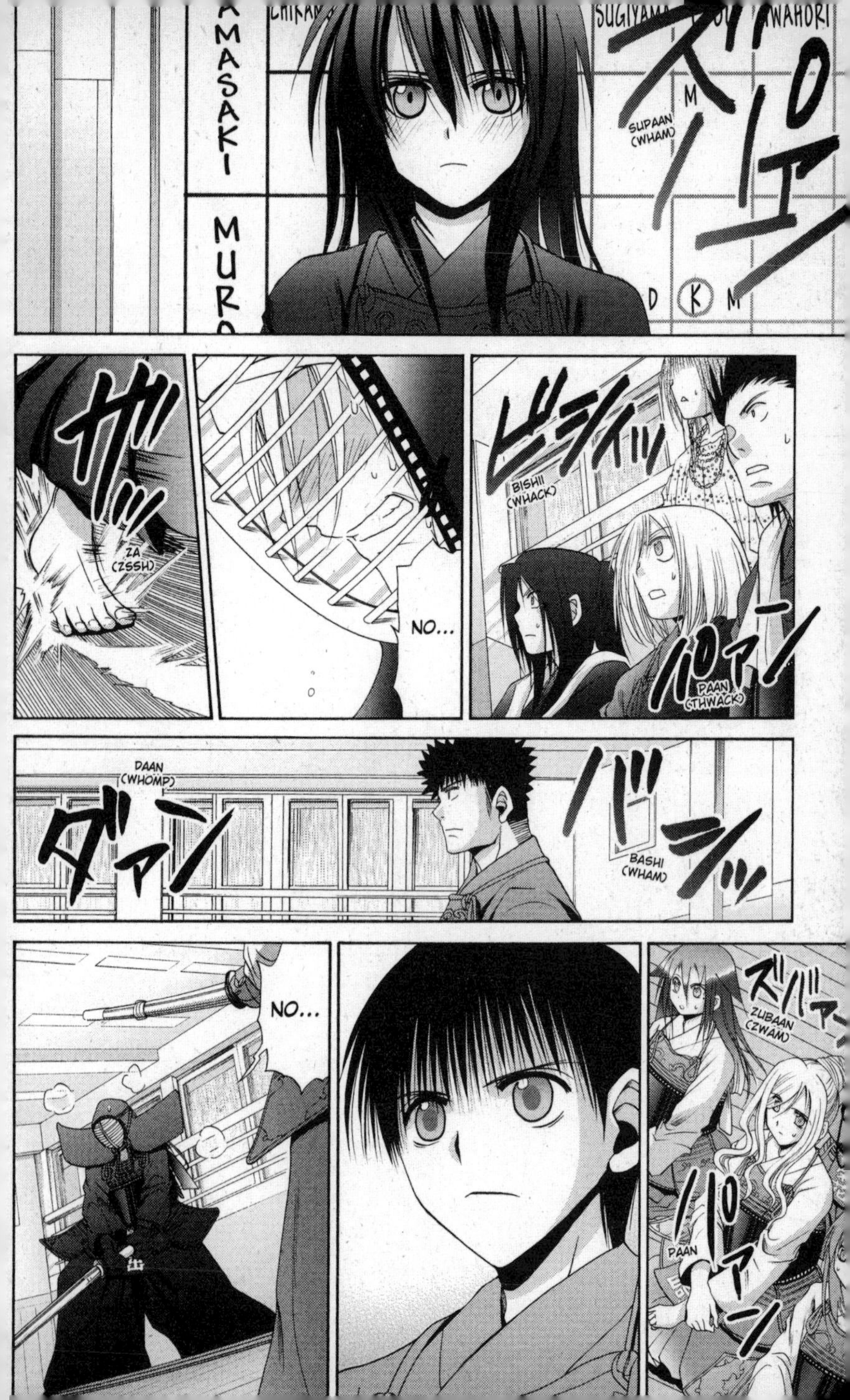
SUGIYAMA
SUPAAN (WHAM)
MURO
BISHII (WHACK)
PAAN (THWACK)
NO...
ZA (ZSSH)
BASHI (WHAM)
DAAN (WHOMP)
ZUBAAN (ZWAM)
PAAN
NO...

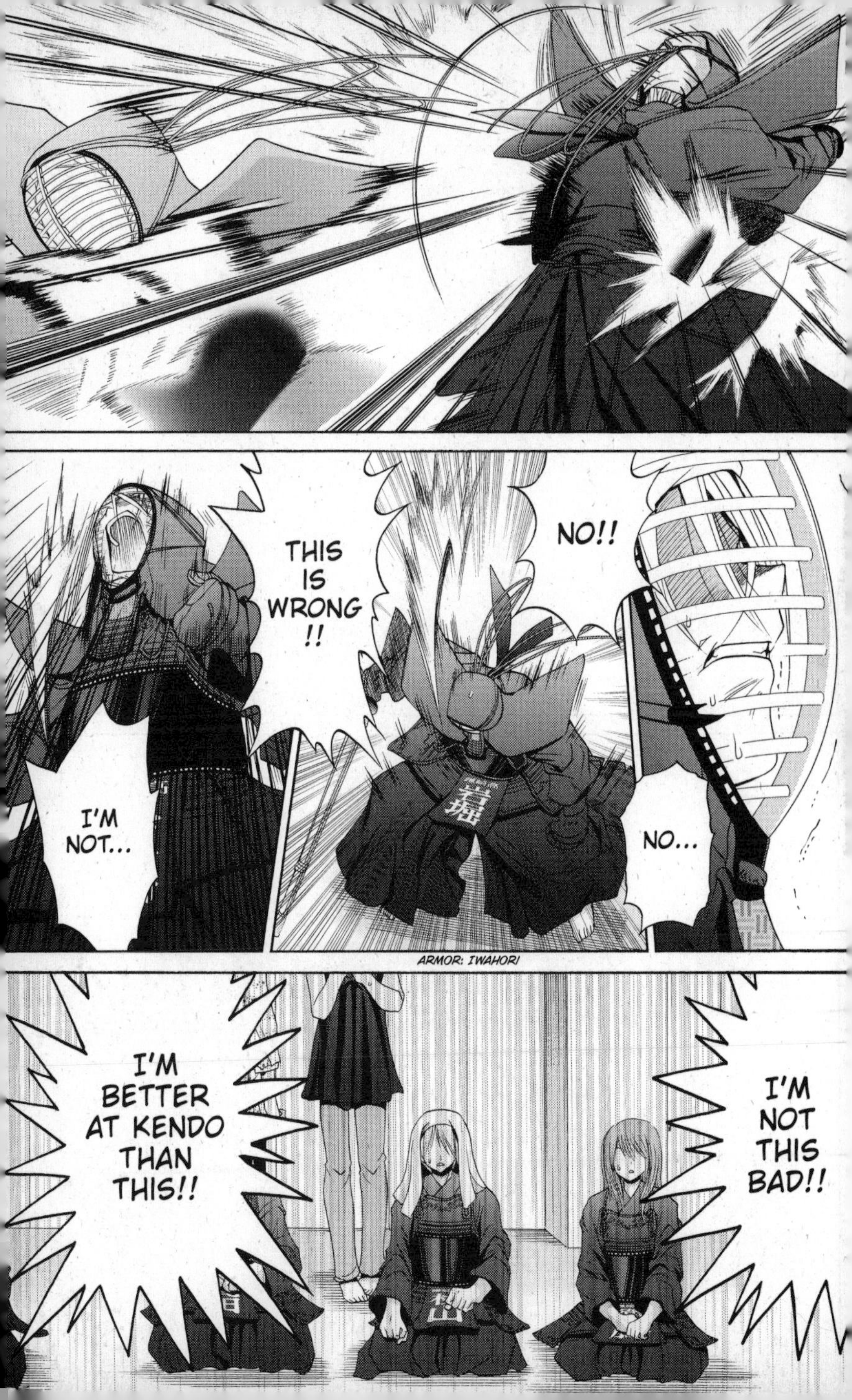
NO!!
NO...
THIS IS WRONG!!
I'M NOT...
ARMOR: IWAHORI
I'M NOT THIS BAD!!
I'M BETTER AT KENDO THAN THIS!!

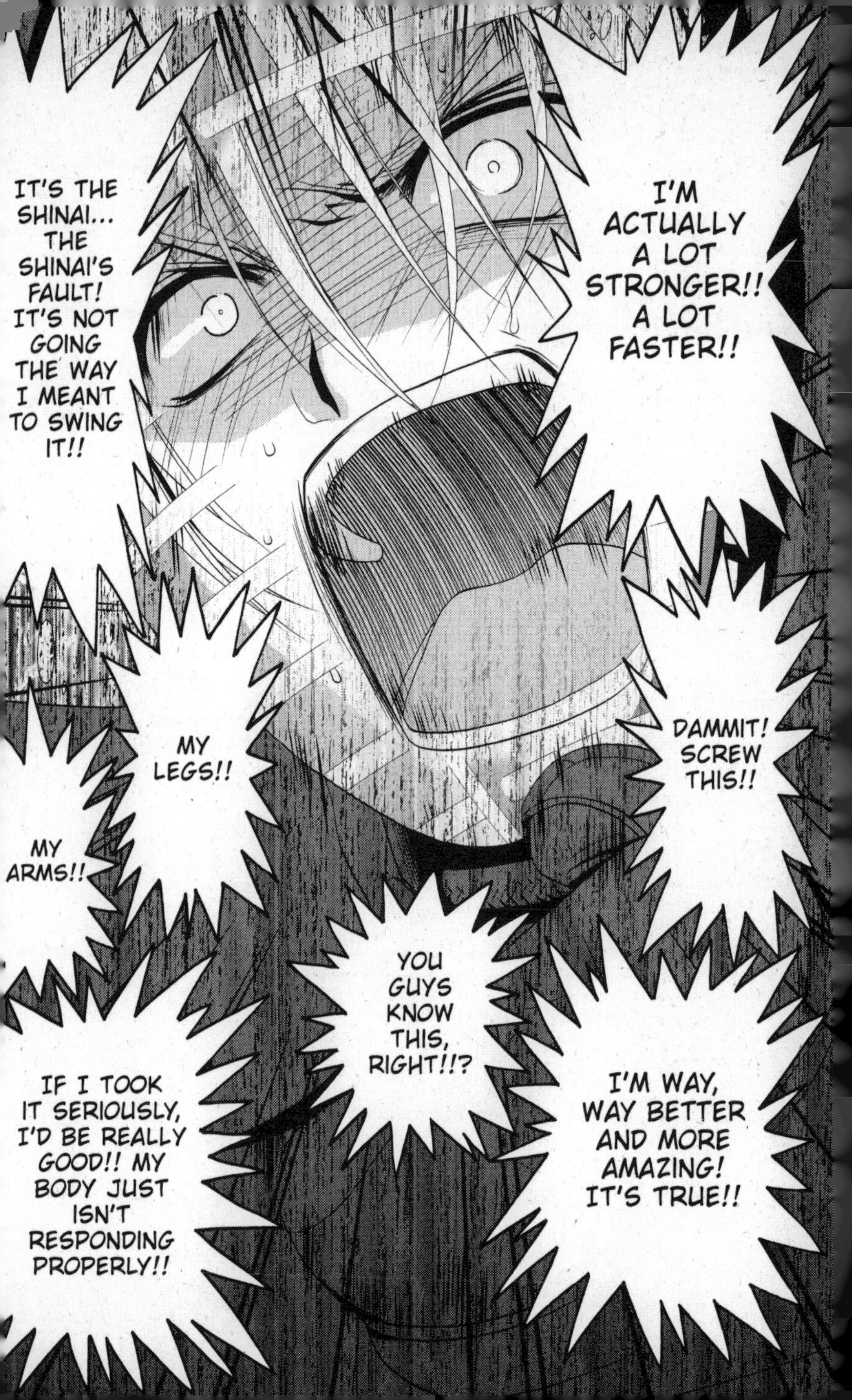
I'M ACTUALLY A LOT STRONGER!! A LOT FASTER!!
IT'S THE SHINAI... THE SHINAI'S FAULT! IT'S NOT GOING THE WAY I MEANT TO SWING IT!!
DAMMIT! SCREW THIS!!
MY LEGS!!
MY ARMS!!
YOU GUYS KNOW THIS, RIGHT!!?
I'M WAY, WAY BETTER AND MORE AMAZING! IT'S TRUE!!
IF I TOOK IT SERIOUSLY, I'D BE REALLY GOOD!! MY BODY JUST ISN'T RESPONDING PROPERLY!!

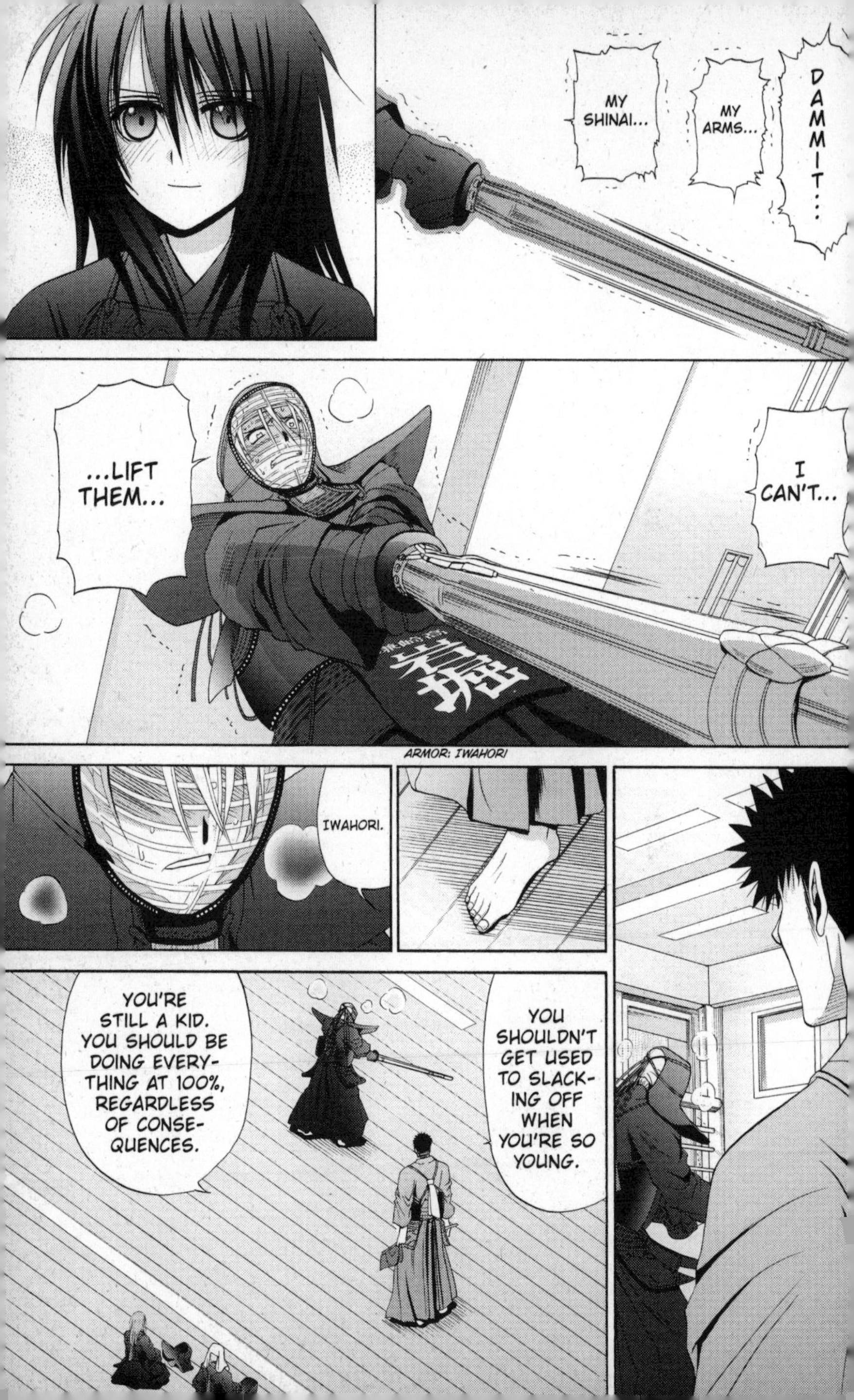
DAMMIT...
MY ARMS...
MY SHINAI...
I CAN'T...
...LIFT THEM...
ARMOR: IWAHORI
IWAHORI.
YOU SHOULDN'T GET USED TO SLACKING OFF WHEN YOU'RE SO YOUNG.
YOU'RE STILL A KID. YOU SHOULD BE DOING EVERYTHING AT 100%, REGARDLESS OF CONSEQUENCES.

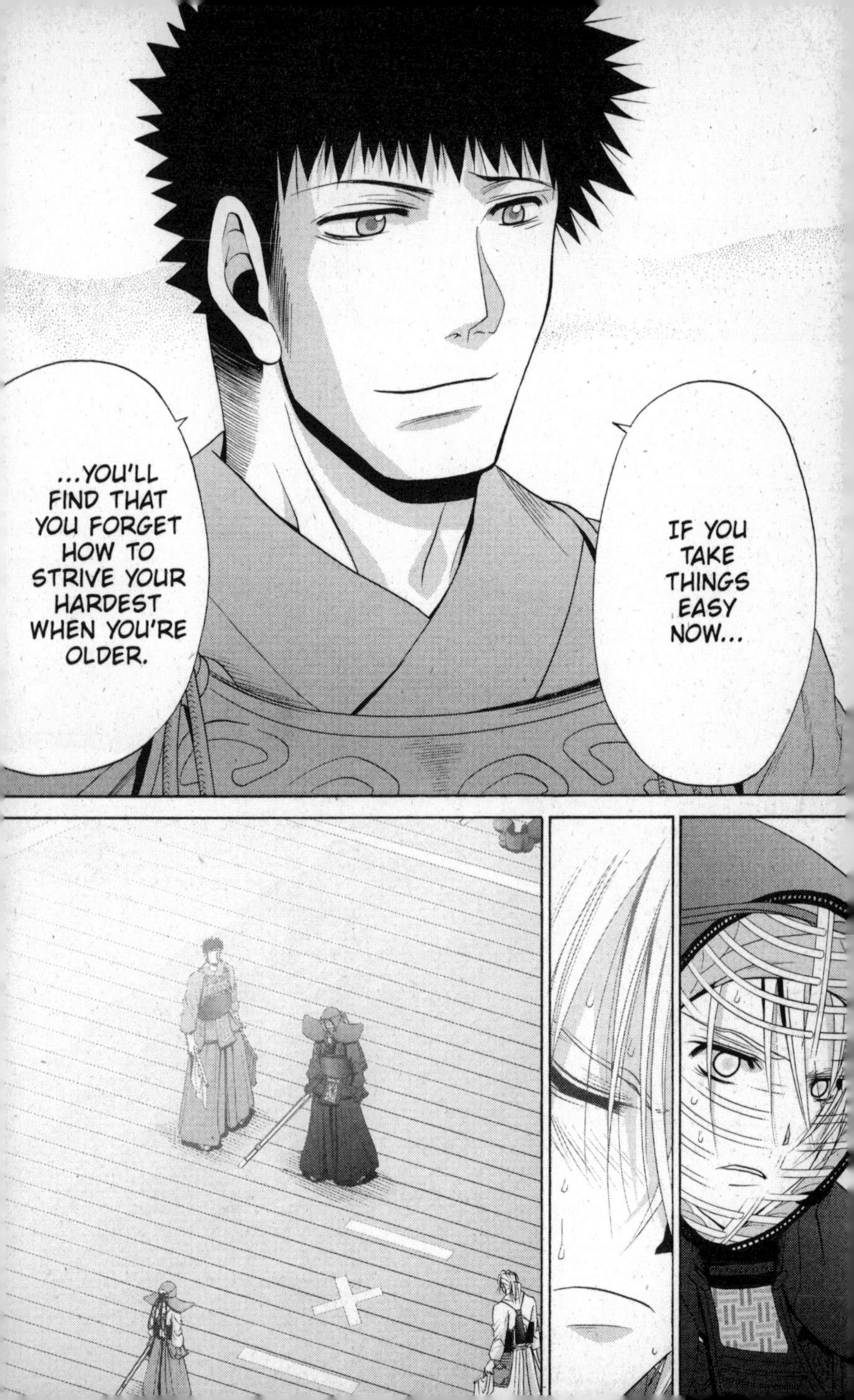
IF YOU TAKE THINGS EASY NOW...
...YOU'LL FIND THAT YOU FORGET HOW TO STRIVE YOUR HARDEST WHEN YOU'RE OLDER.

BAMBOO BLADE

バンブーブレード

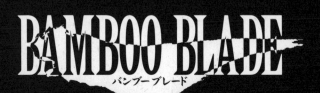

BAMBOO BLADE

バンブーブレード

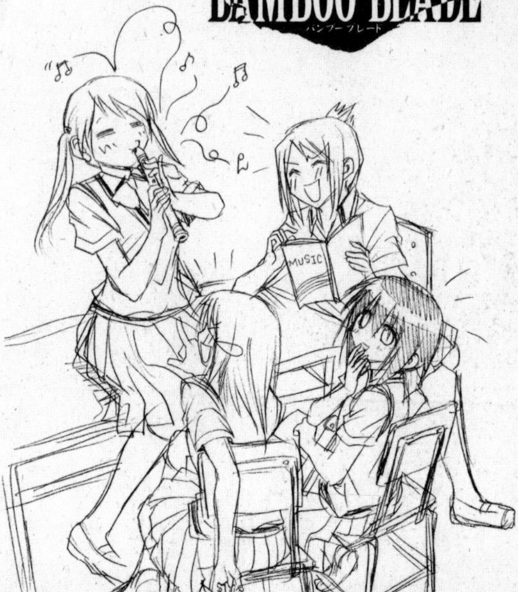
MUSIC

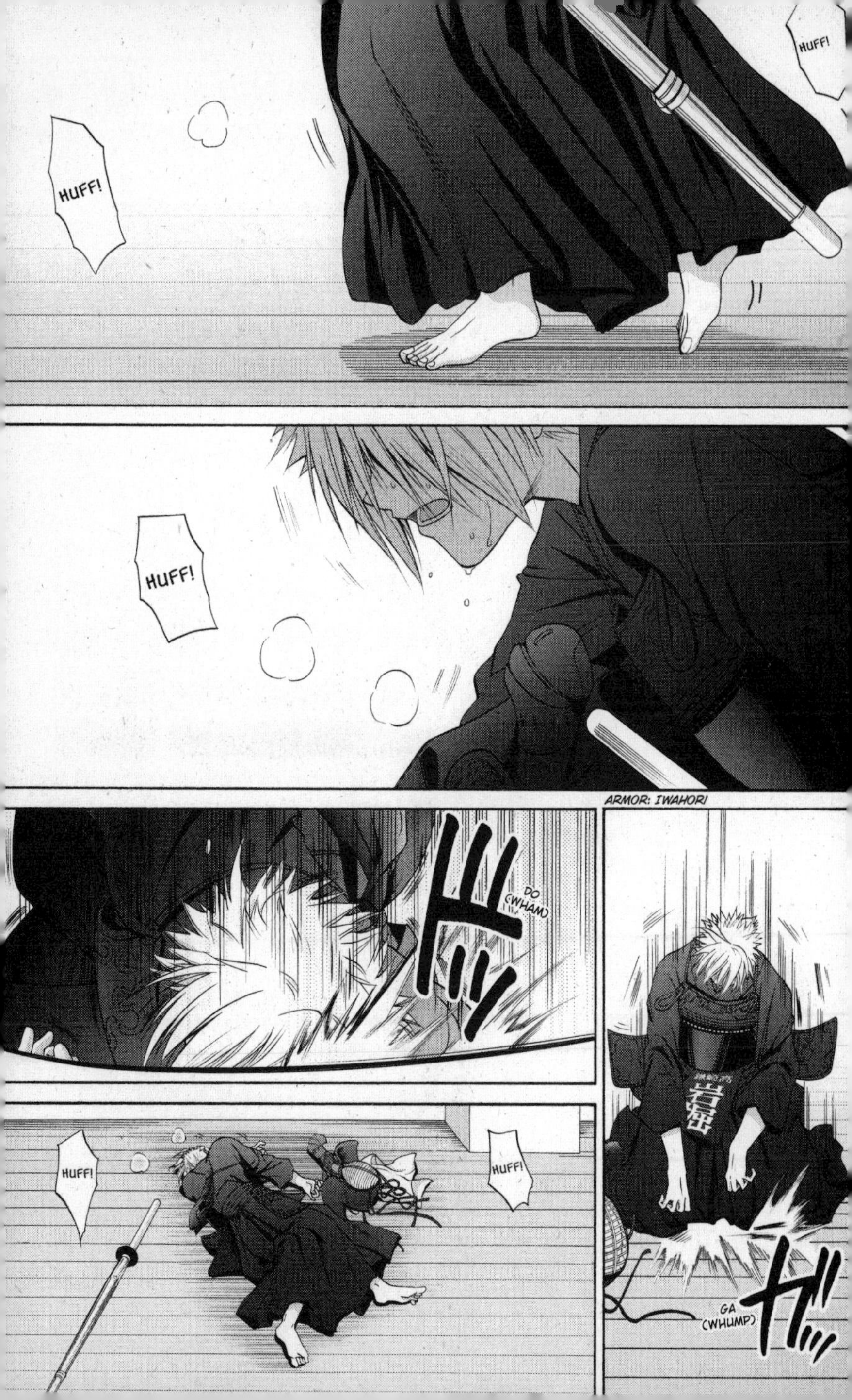
HUFF!
HUFF!
HUFF!
ARMOR: IWAHORI
GA (WHUMP)
DO (WHAM)
HUFF!
HUFF!

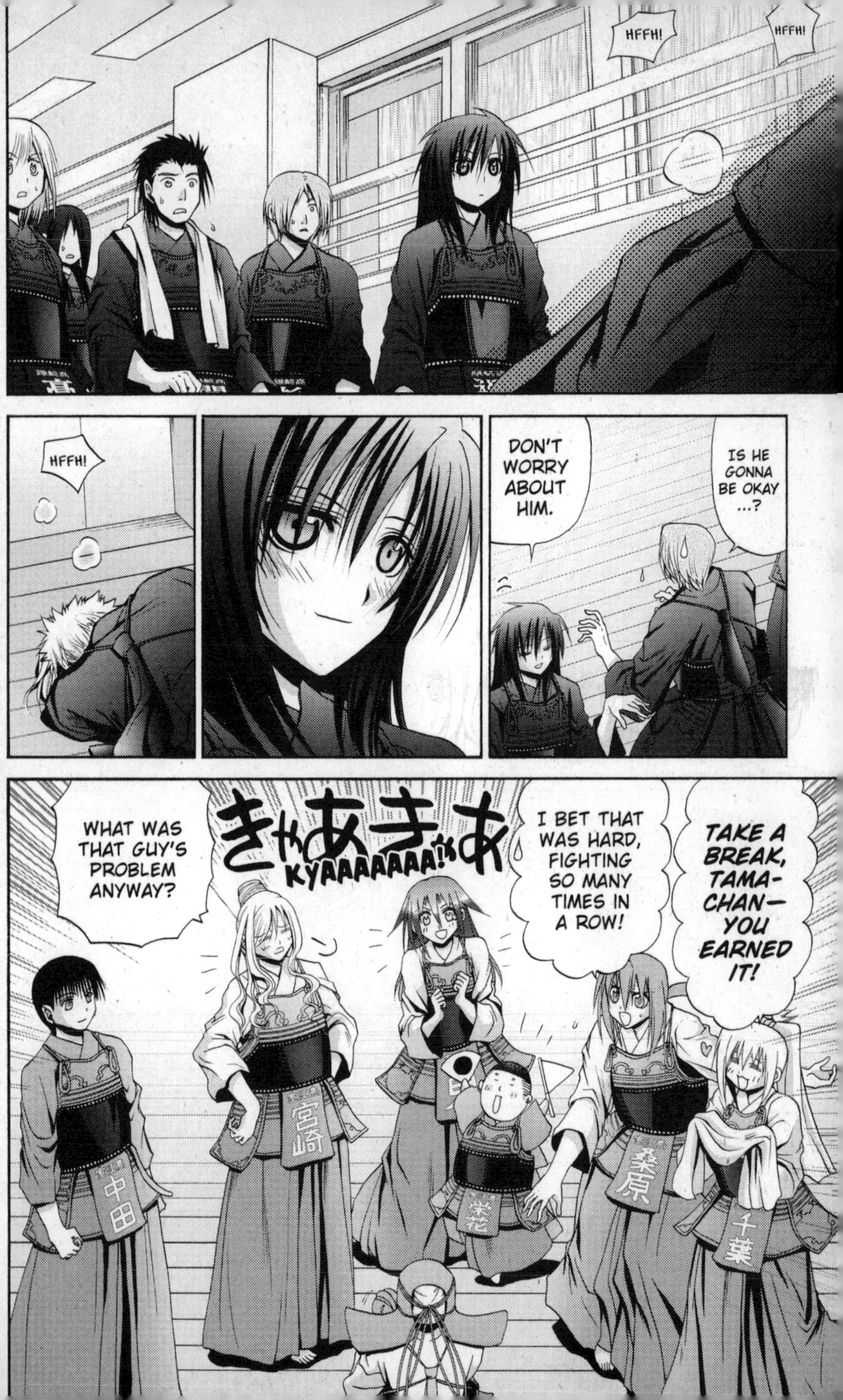
HFFH!
HFFH!
IS HE GONNA BE OKAY ...?
DON'T WORRY ABOUT HIM.
HFFH!
TAKE A BREAK, TAMA-CHAN—YOU EARNED IT!
I BET THAT WAS HARD, FIGHTING SO MANY TIMES IN A ROW!
きゃあきゃあ
KYAAAAAAA!!
WHAT WAS THAT GUY'S PROBLEM ANYWAY?
千葉
桑原
宮崎
中田

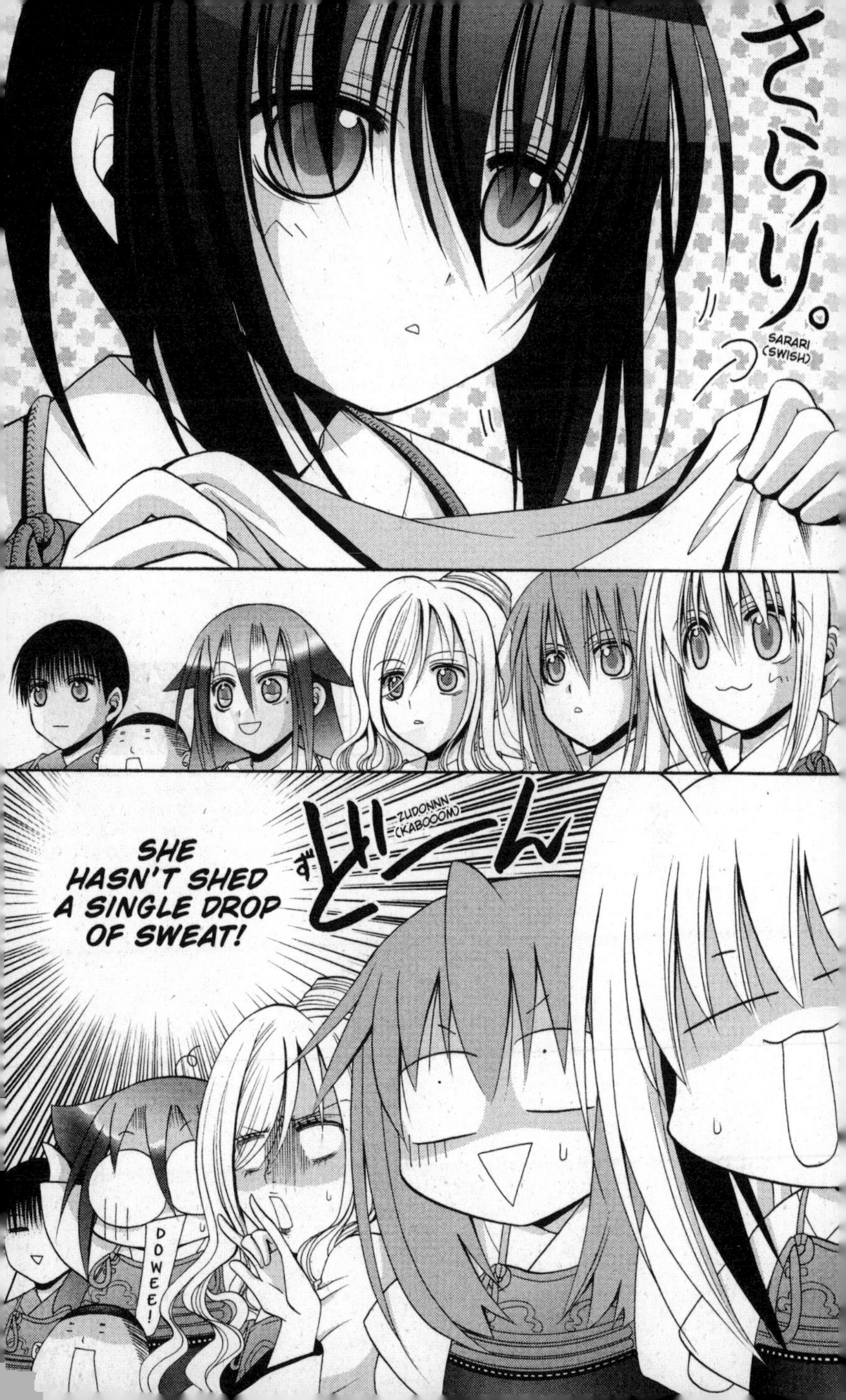
さらり。
SARARI (SWISH)
ずどーん
ZUDONNN (KABOOOM)
SHE HASN'T SHED A SINGLE DROP OF SWEAT!
DOWEE!

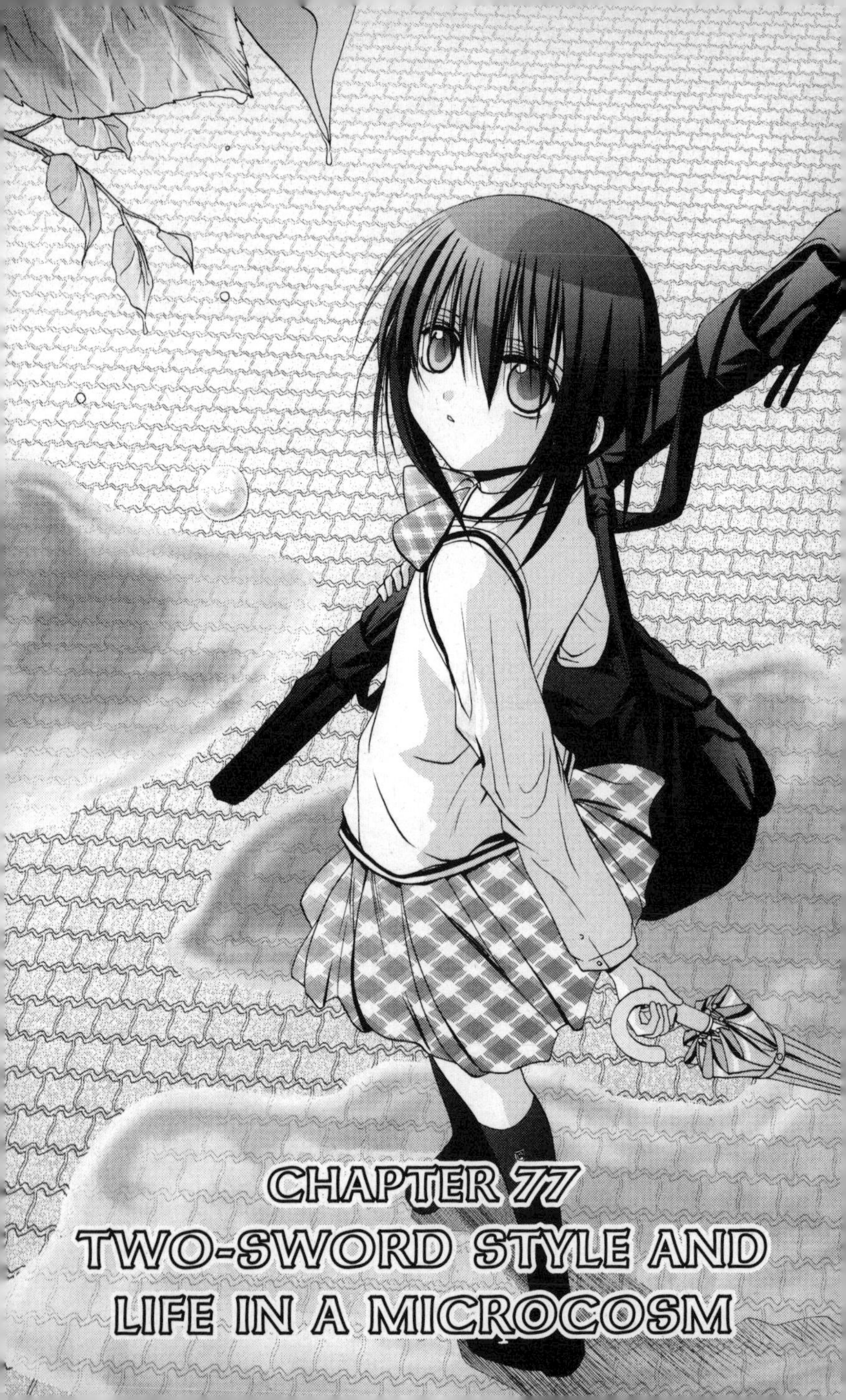
CHAPTER 77
TWO-SWORD STYLE AND
LIFE IN A MICROCOSM

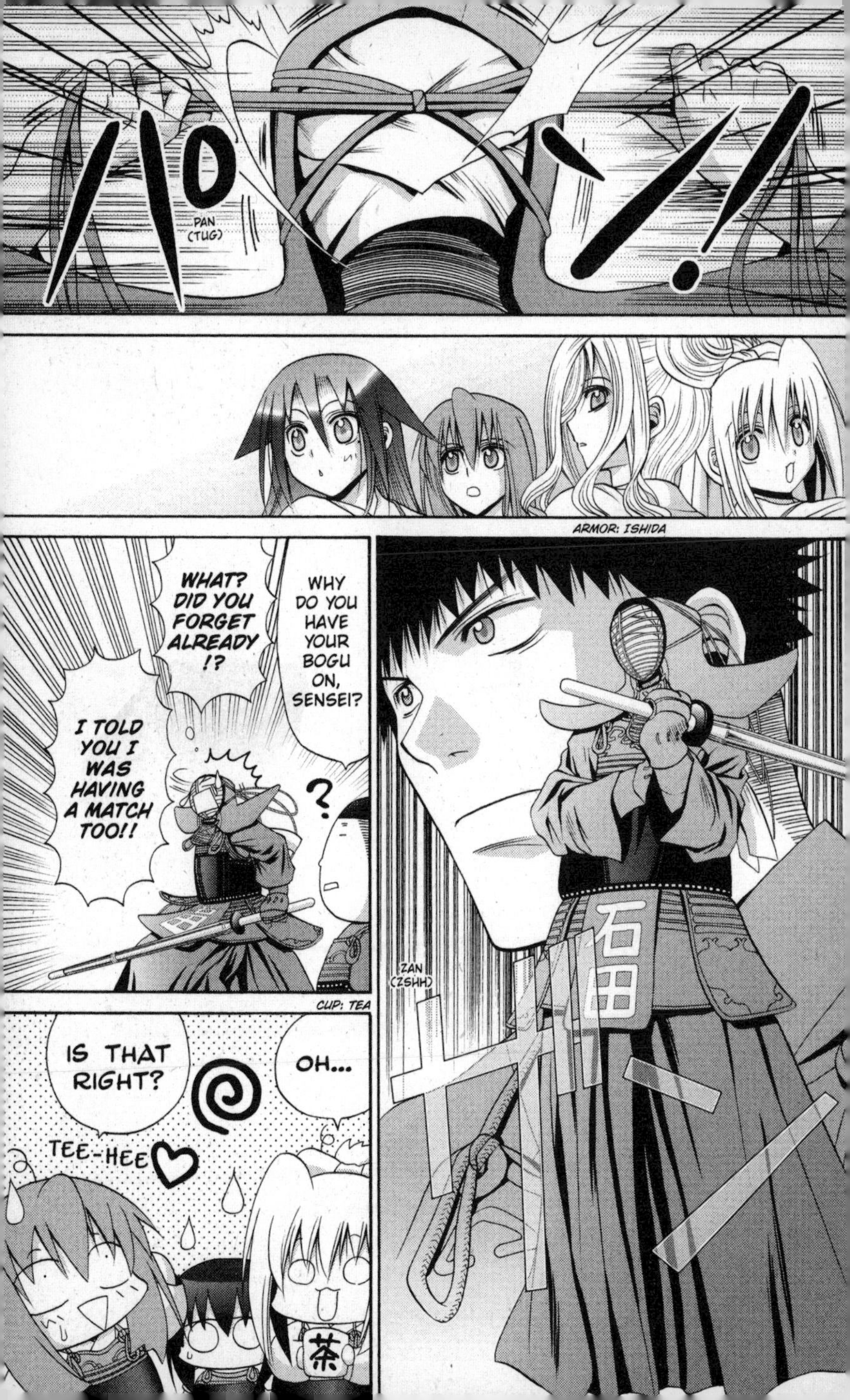
PAN (TUG)
ARMOR: ISHIDA
ZAN (ZSHH)
WHY DO YOU HAVE YOUR BOGU ON, SENSEI?
WHAT? DID YOU FORGET ALREADY!?
I TOLD YOU I WAS HAVING A MATCH TOO!!
CUP: TEA
OH...
IS THAT RIGHT?
TEE-HEE

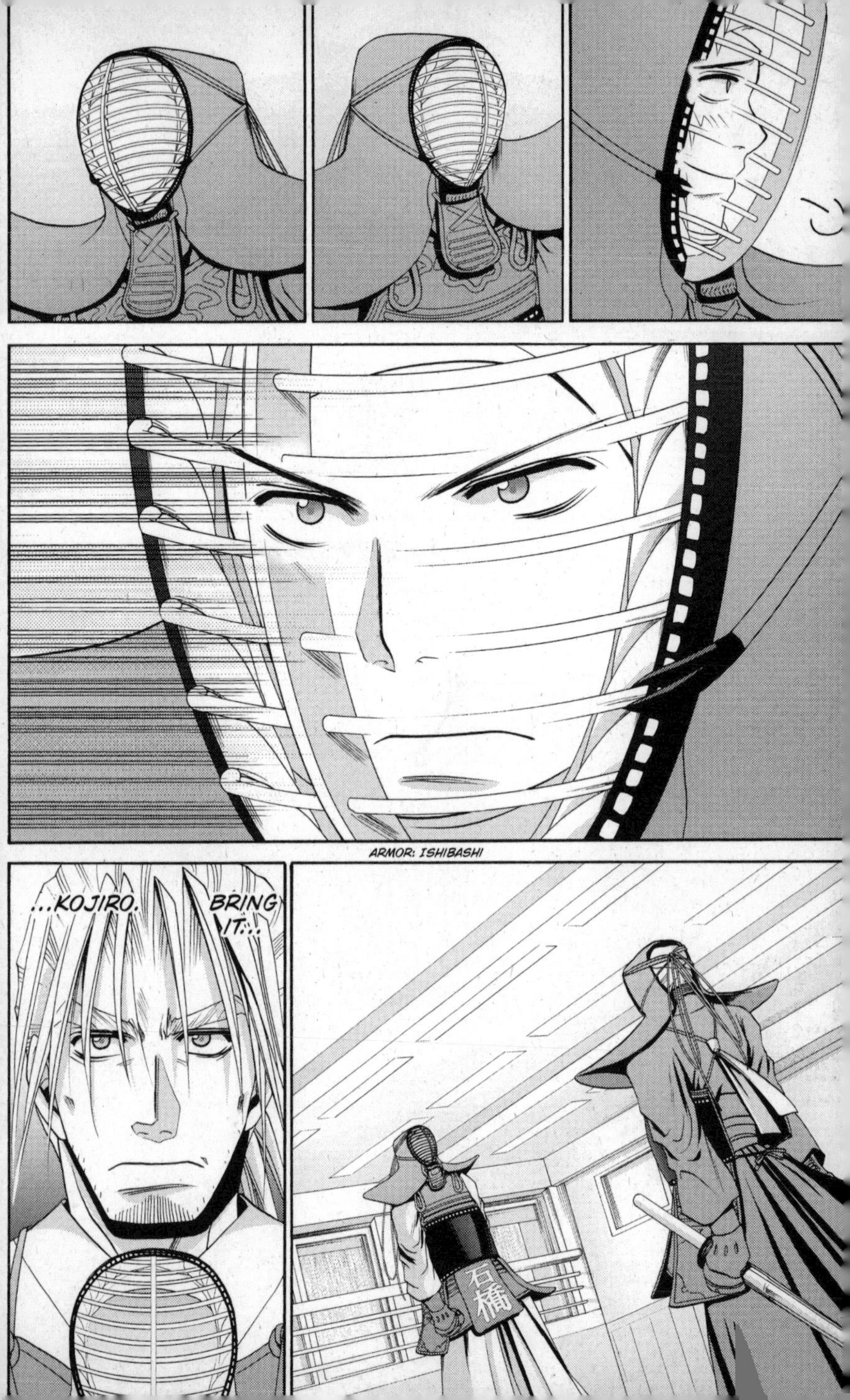
ARMOR: ISHIBASHI
石橋
BRING IT...
...KOJIRO.

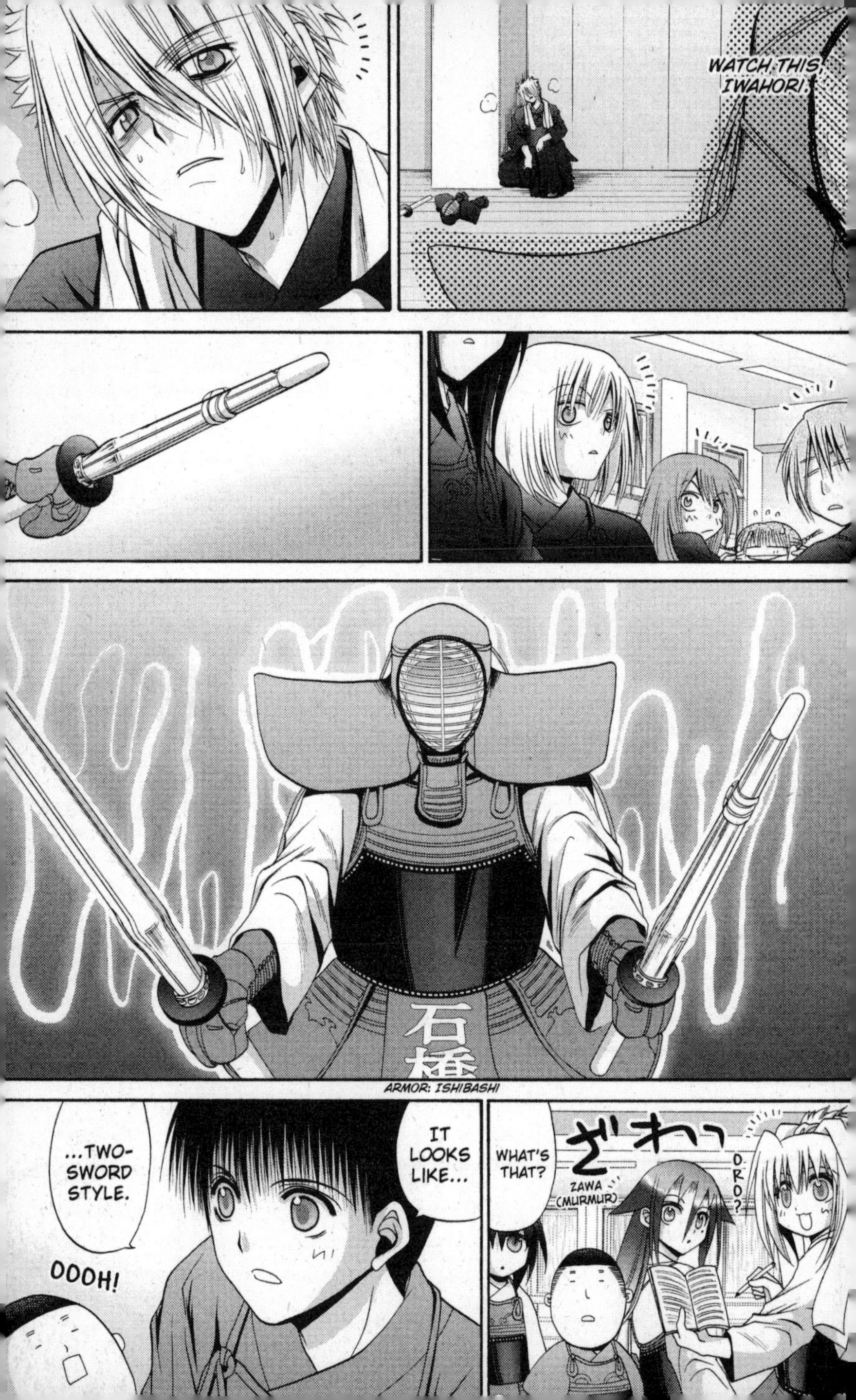
WATCH THIS, IWAHORI.
石橋
ARMOR: ISHIBASHI
ざわ
ORO?
WHAT'S THAT?
ZAWA (MURMUR)
IT LOOKS LIKE...
...TWO-SWORD STYLE.
OOOH!

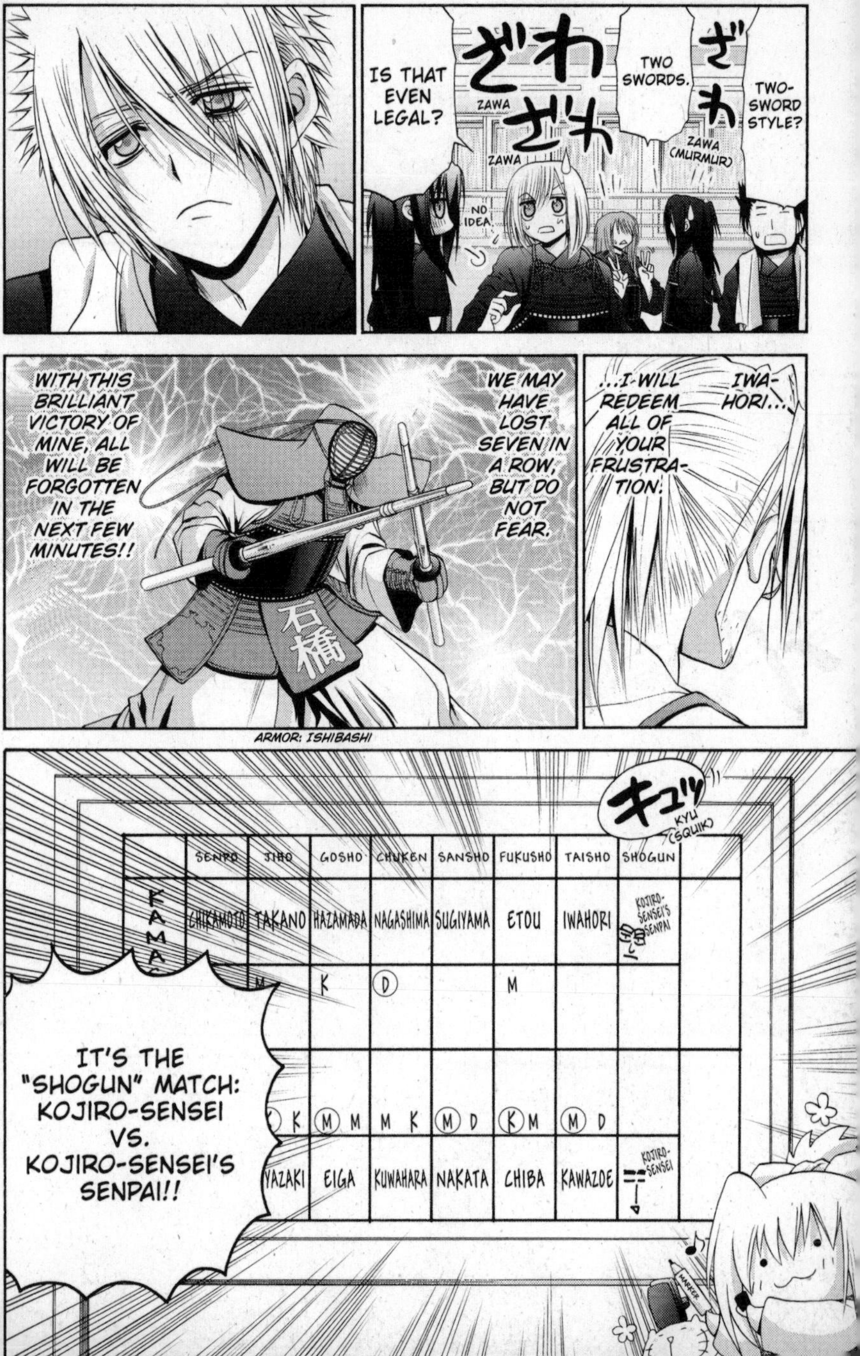
TWO-SWORD STYLE?
ざわ
ZAWA (MURMUR)
TWO SWORDS.
ざわ
ZAWA
ざわ
ZAWA
IS THAT EVEN LEGAL?
NO IDEA.
IWAHORI...
...I WILL REDEEM ALL OF YOUR FRUSTRATION.
WE MAY HAVE LOST SEVEN IN A ROW, BUT DO NOT FEAR.
WITH THIS BRILLIANT VICTORY OF MINE, ALL WILL BE FORGOTTEN IN THE NEXT FEW MINUTES!!
石橋
ARMOR: ISHIBASHI
キュッ
KYU (SQUIK)
SENPO JIHO GOSHO CHUKEN SANSHO FUKUSHO TAISHO SHOGUN
CHIKAMOTO TAKANO HAZAMADA NAGASHIMA SUGIYAMA ETOU IWAHORI KOJIRO-SENSEI'S SENPAI
YAZAKI EIGA KUWAHARA NAKATA CHIBA KAWAZOE KOJIRO-SENSEI
IT'S THE "SHOGUN" MATCH: KOJIRO-SENSEI VS. KOJIRO-SENSEI'S SENPAI!!
MARKER

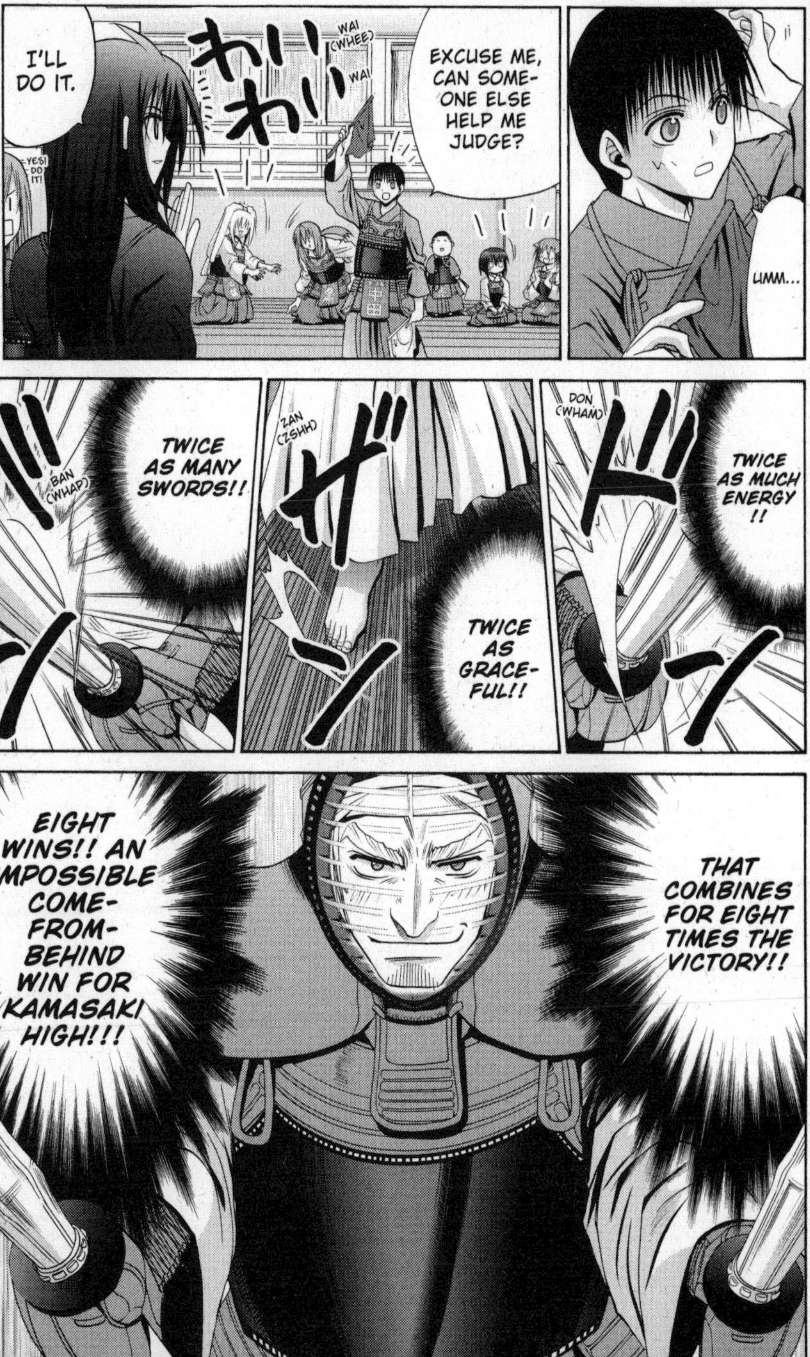

UMM...
EXCUSE ME, CAN SOME-ONE ELSE HELP ME JUDGE?
わいわい
WAI (WHEE)
WAI
YES! DO IT!
I'LL DO IT.
ドン
DON (WHAM)
TWICE AS MUCH ENERGY!!
ザン
ZAN (ZSHH)
TWICE AS GRACEFUL!!
バン
BAN (WHAP)
TWICE AS MANY SWORDS!!
THAT COMBINES FOR EIGHT TIMES THE VICTORY!!
EIGHT WINS!! AN IMPOSSIBLE COME-FROM-BEHIND WIN FOR KAMASAKI HIGH!!!

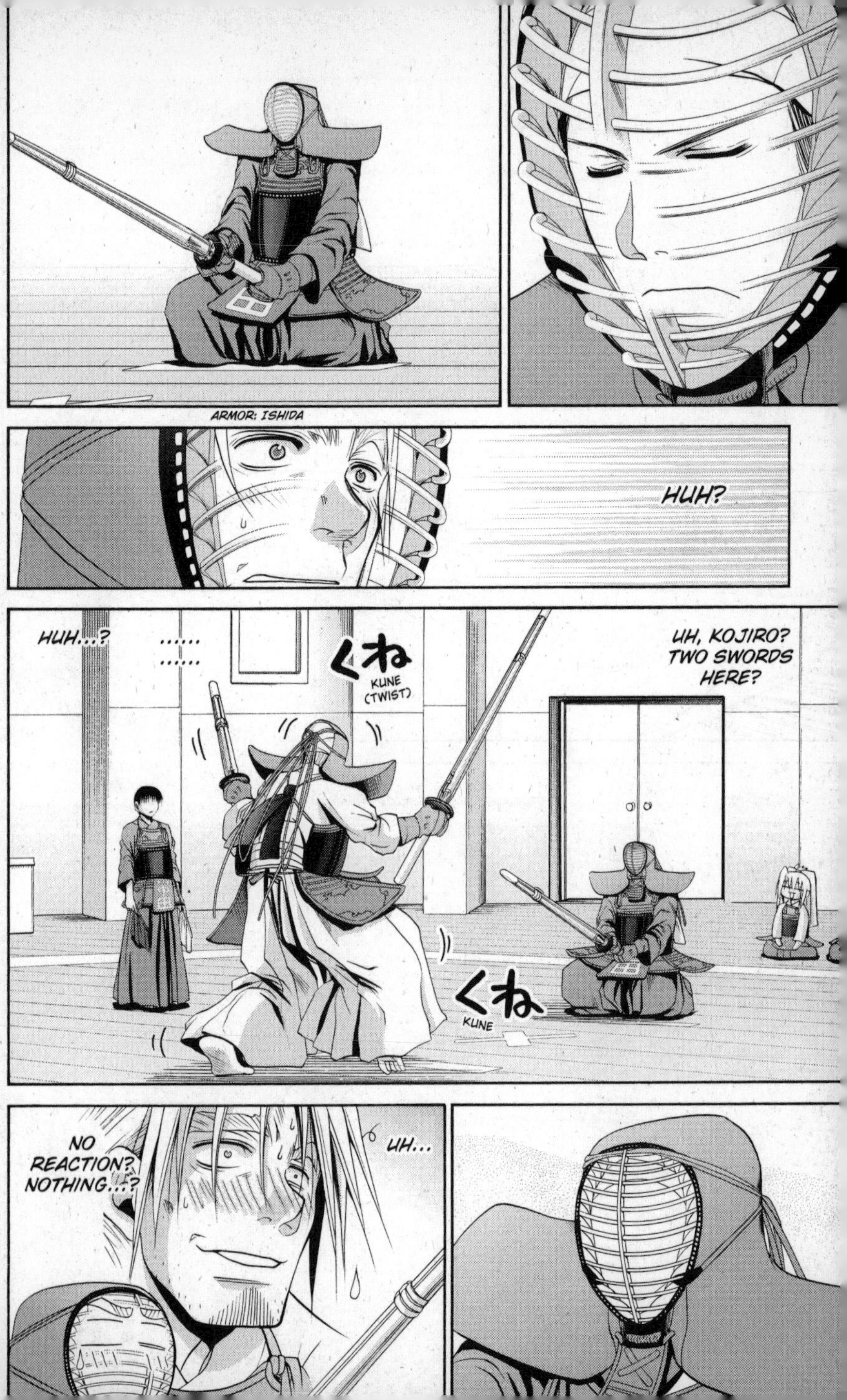
ARMOR: ISHIDA
HUH?
UH, KOJIRO? TWO SWORDS HERE?
くね
KUNE (TWIST)
......
......
HUH...?
くね
KUNE
UH...
NO REACTION? NOTHING...?

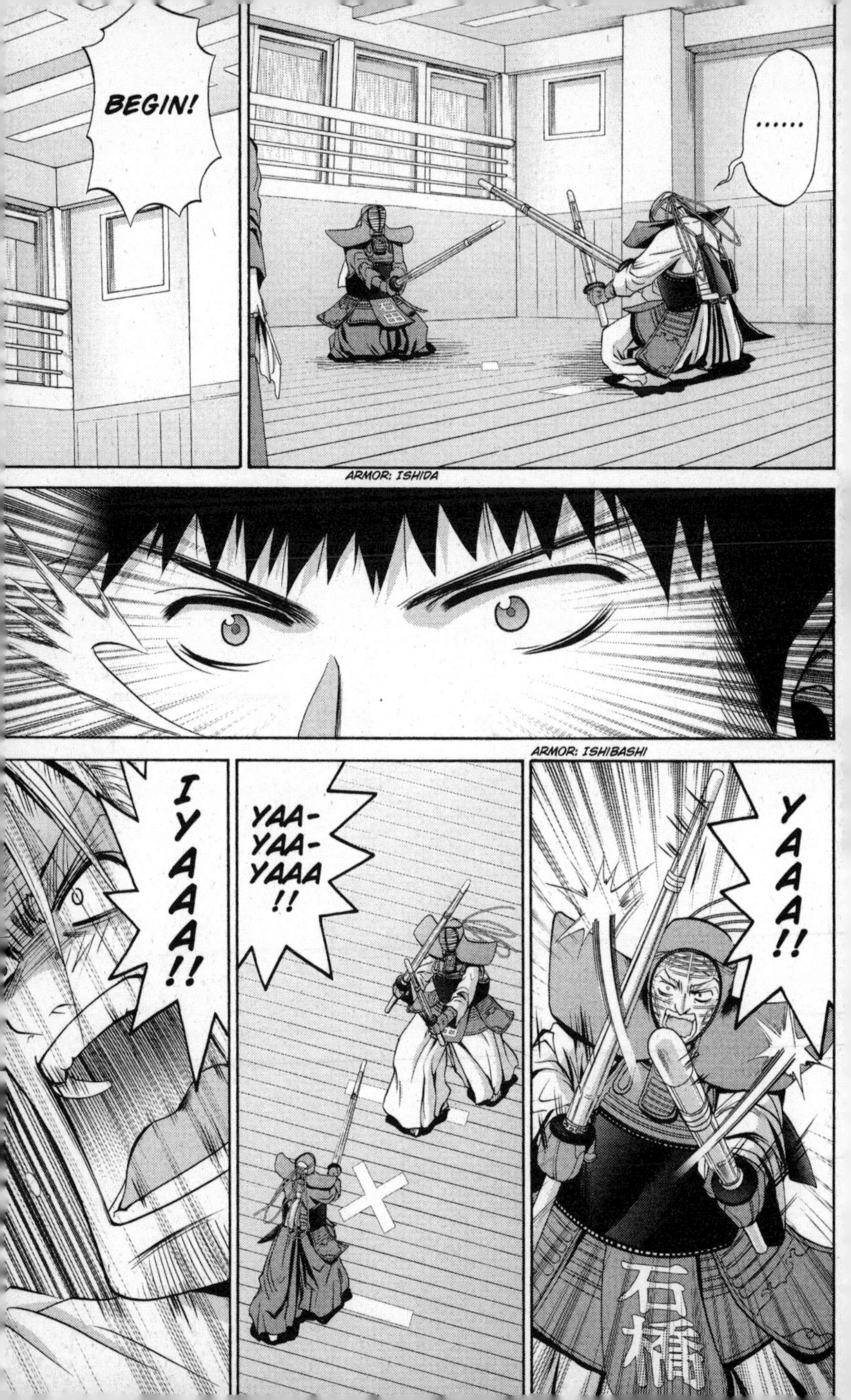
......
BEGIN!
ARMOR: ISHIDA
ARMOR: ISHIBASHI
YAAAA!!
YAA-YAA-YAAA!!
IYAAAA!!

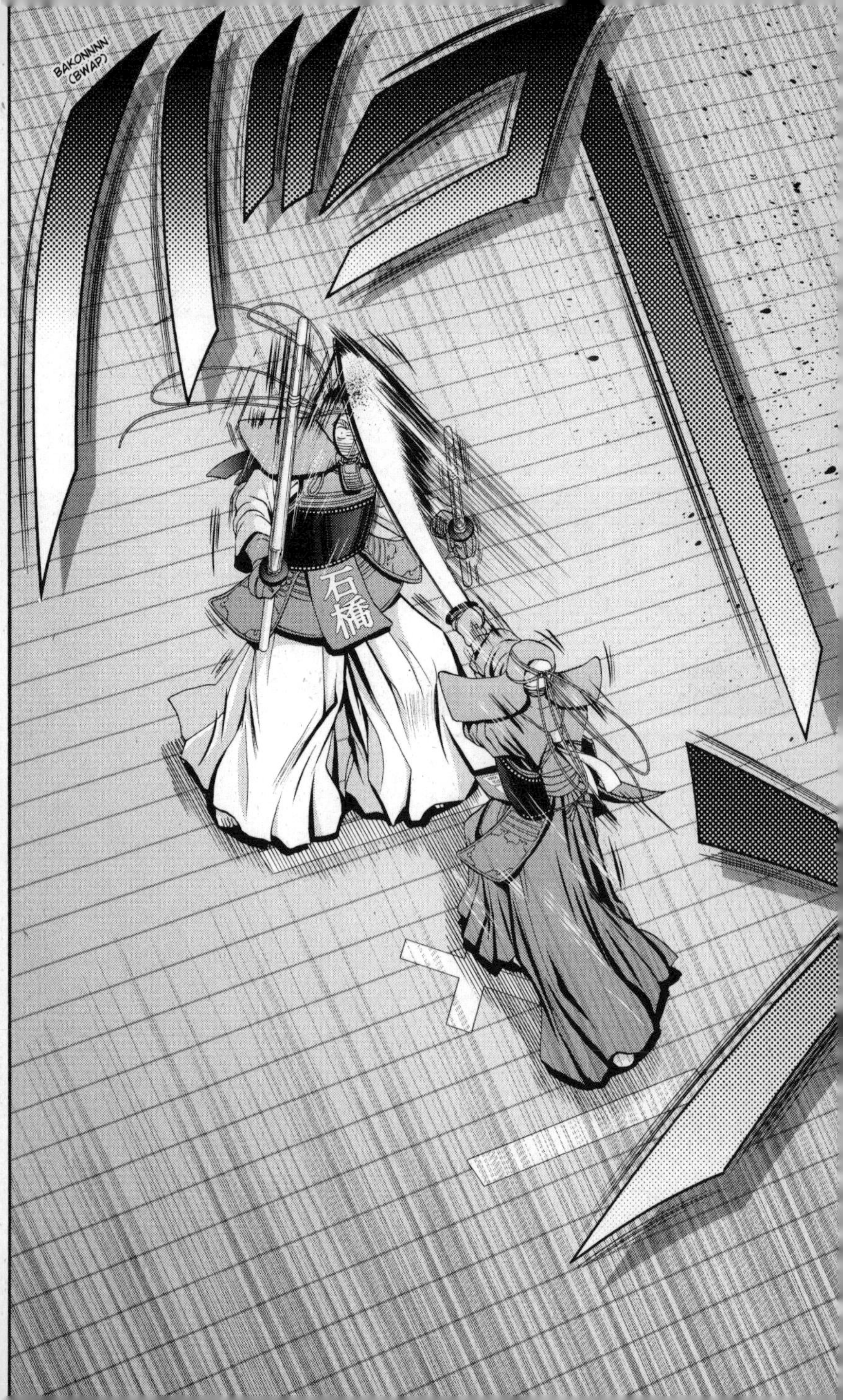
BAKONNNN
(BWAP)
石橋

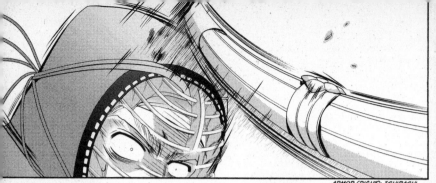

ARMOR (RIGHT): ISHIBASHI

UH...

HUH....?

MEN ARI!!

ARMOR: ISHIDA

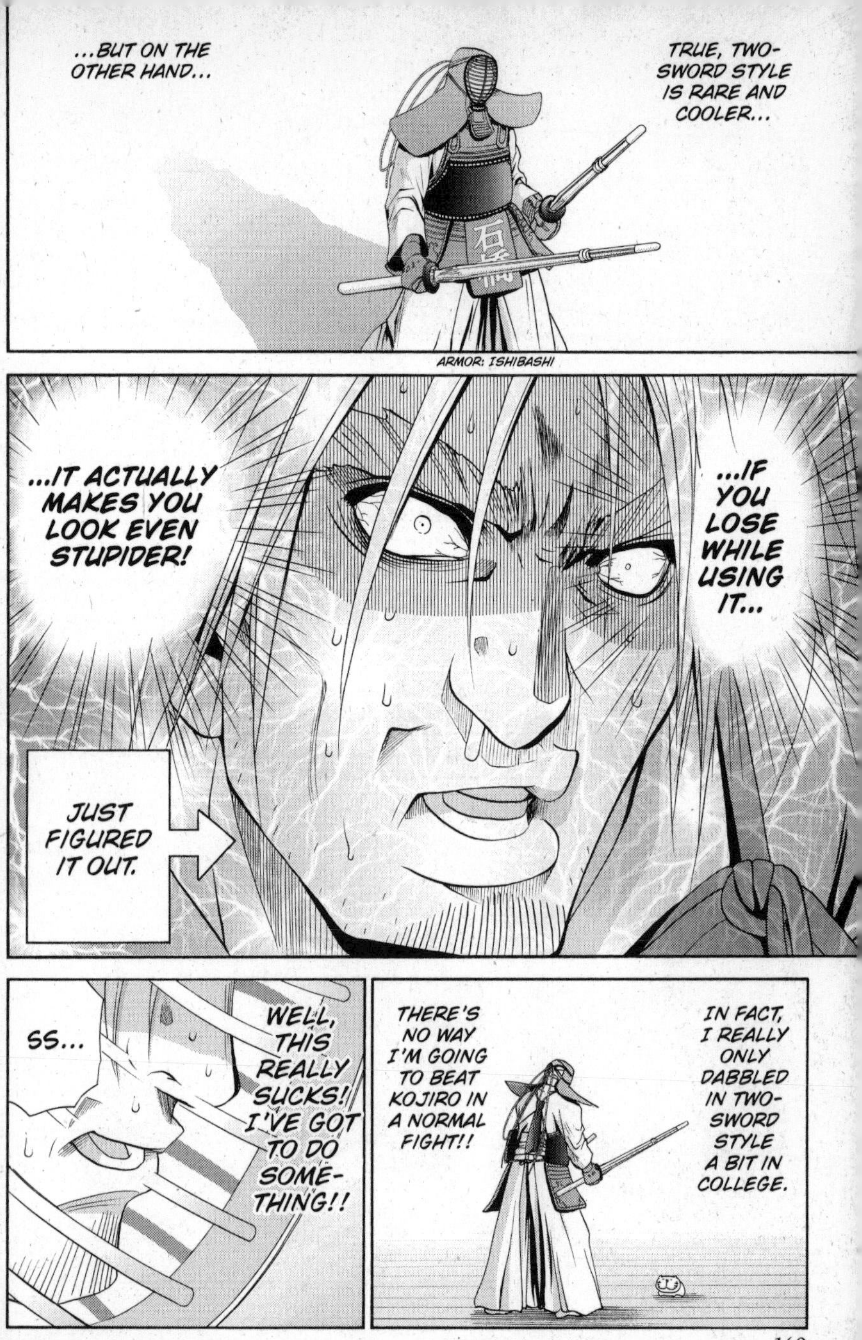
TRUE, TWO-SWORD STYLE IS RARE AND COOLER...
...BUT ON THE OTHER HAND...
ARMOR: ISHIBASHI
...IF YOU LOSE WHILE USING IT...
...IT ACTUALLY MAKES YOU LOOK EVEN STUPIDER!
JUST FIGURED IT OUT.
IN FACT, I REALLY ONLY DABBLED IN TWO-SWORD STYLE A BIT IN COLLEGE.
THERE'S NO WAY I'M GOING TO BEAT KOJIRO IN A NORMAL FIGHT!!
WELL, THIS REALLY SUCKS! I'VE GOT TO DO SOMETHING!!
SS...

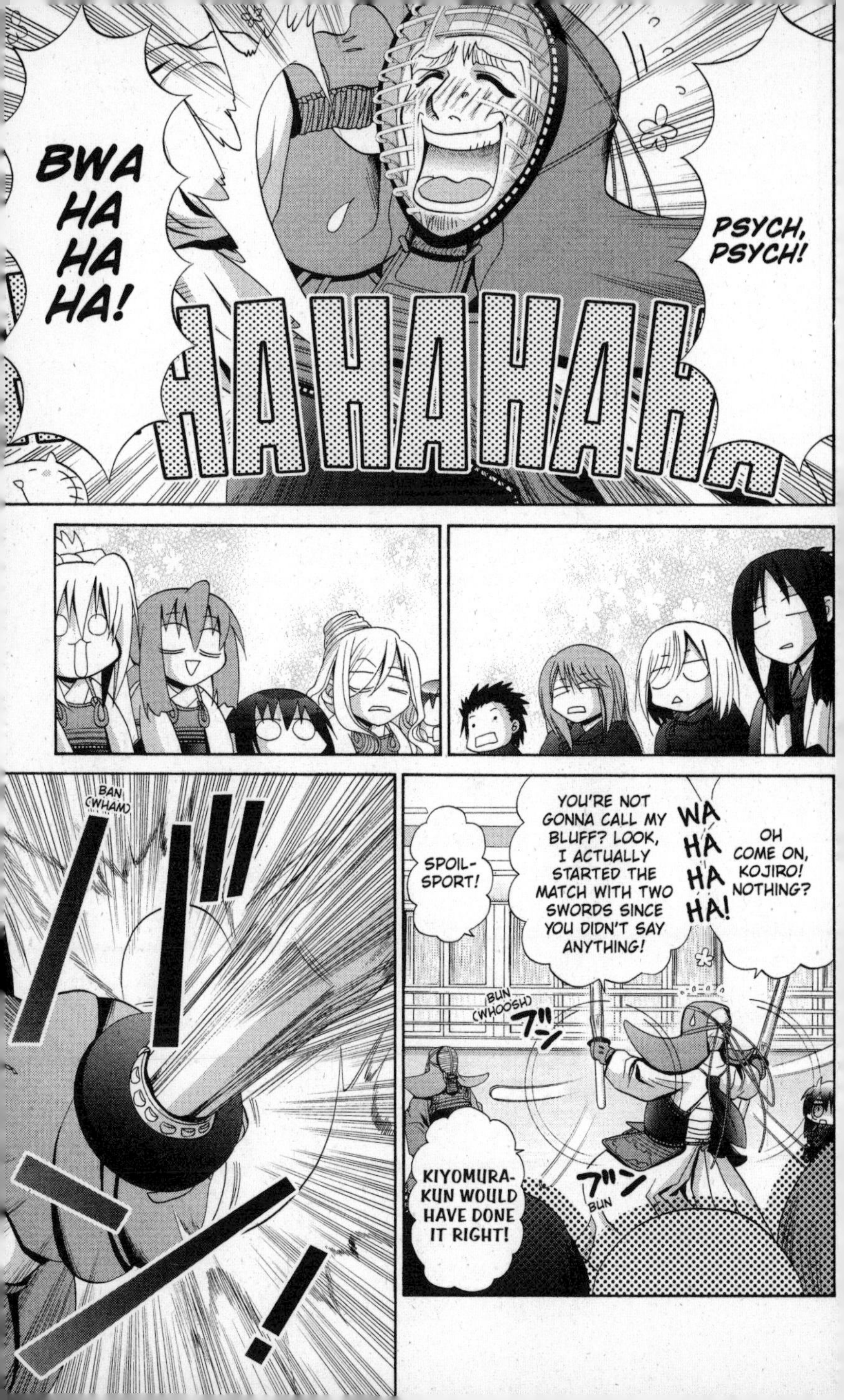
PSYCH, PSYCH!
BWA HA HA HA!
OH COME ON, KOJIRO! NOTHING?
WA HA HA HA HA!
YOU'RE NOT GONNA CALL MY BLUFF? LOOK, I ACTUALLY STARTED THE MATCH WITH TWO SWORDS SINCE YOU DIDN'T SAY ANYTHING!
SPOIL-SPORT!
BUN (WHOOSH)
BUN
KIYOMURA-KUN WOULD HAVE DONE IT RIGHT!
BAN (WHAM)

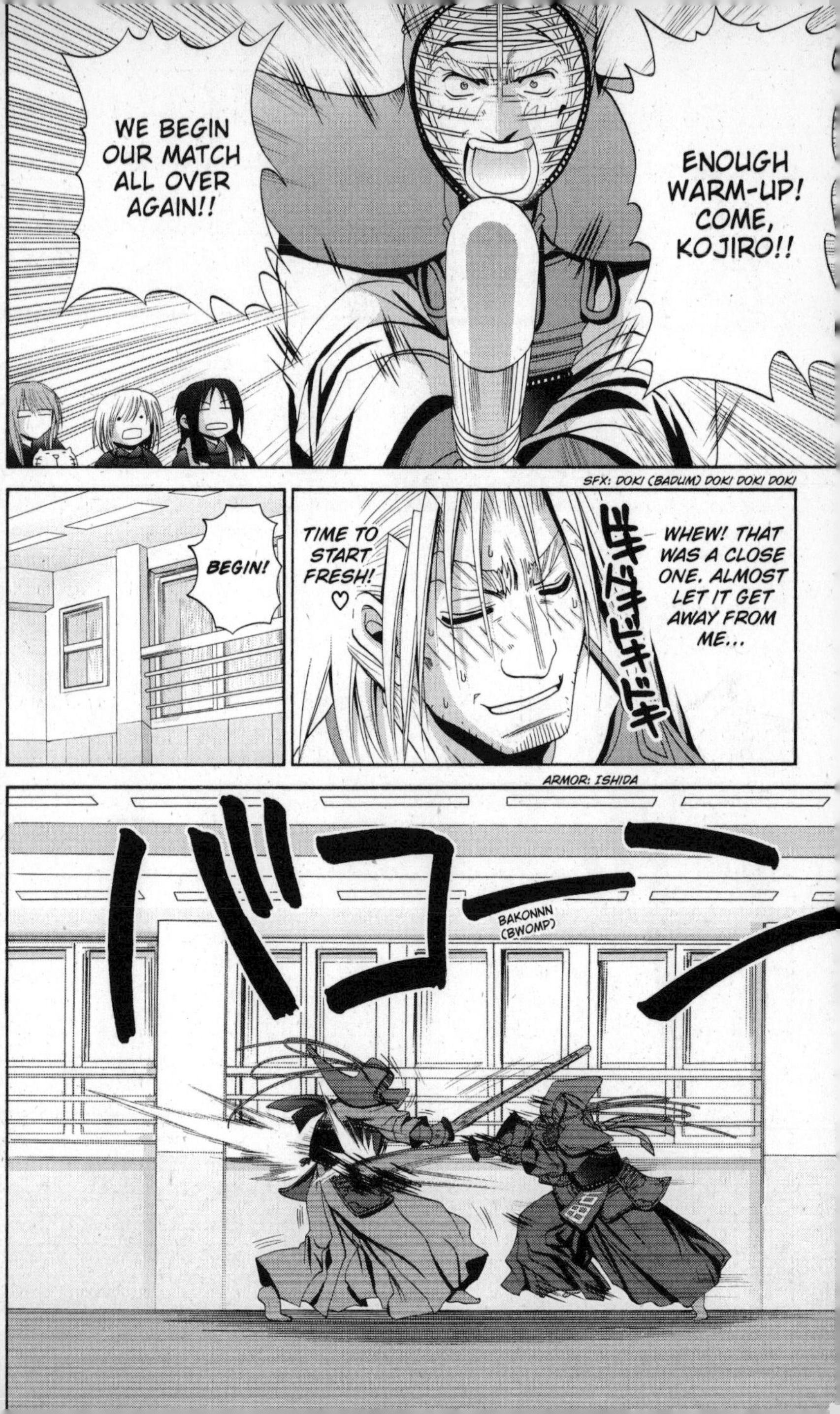
ENOUGH WARM-UP! COME, KOJIRO!!
WE BEGIN OUR MATCH ALL OVER AGAIN!!
SFX: DOKI (BADUM) DOKI DOKI DOKI
WHEW! THAT WAS A CLOSE ONE. ALMOST LET IT GET AWAY FROM ME...
TIME TO START FRESH! ♡
BEGIN!
ARMOR: ISHIDA
バコーン
BAKONNN (BWOMP)

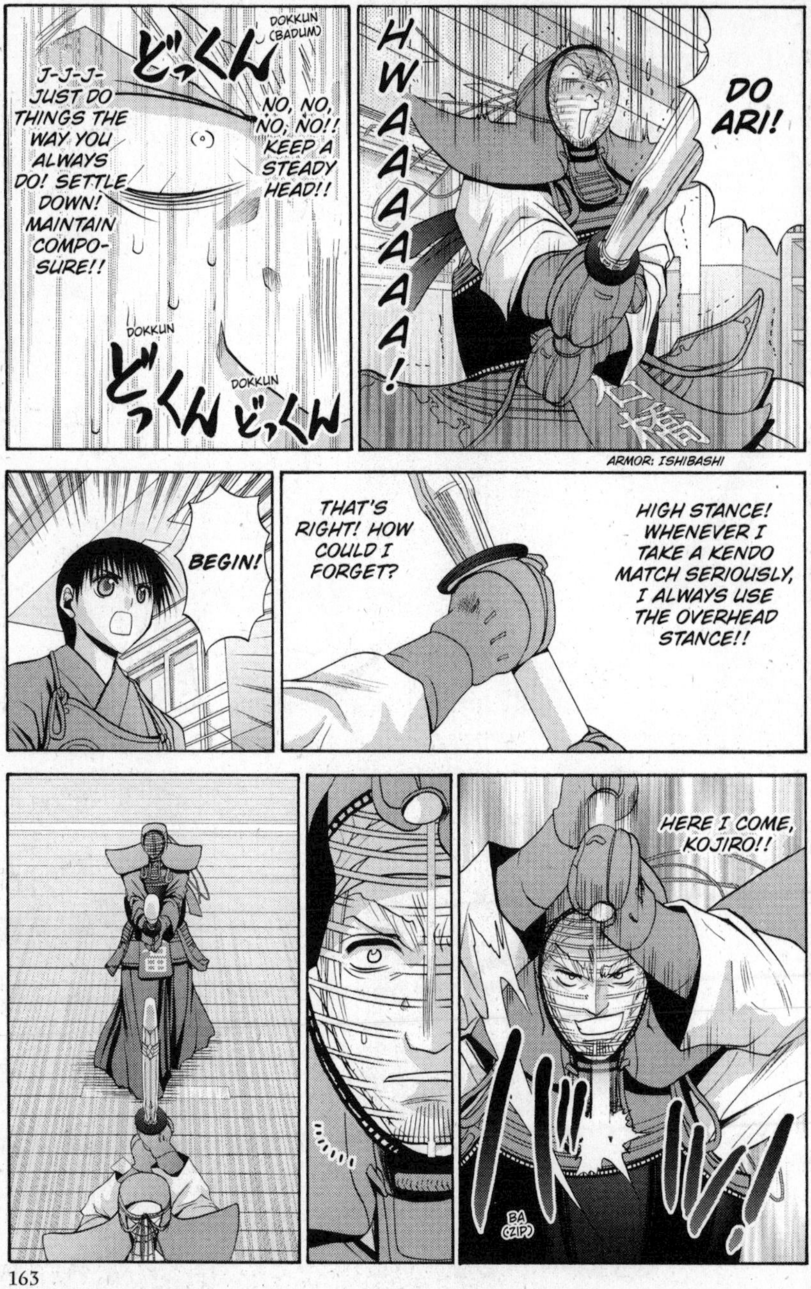
HWAAAAAAAA!
DO ARI!
ARMOR: ISHIBASHI
DOKKUN (BADUM)
どっくん
J-J-J-JUST DO THINGS THE WAY YOU ALWAYS DO! SETTLE DOWN! MAINTAIN COMPO-SURE!!
NO, NO, NO, NO!! KEEP A STEADY HEAD!!
DOKKUN
どっくん
DOKKUN
どっくん
HIGH STANCE! WHENEVER I TAKE A KENDO MATCH SERIOUSLY, I ALWAYS USE THE OVERHEAD STANCE!!
THAT'S RIGHT! HOW COULD I FORGET?
BEGIN!
HERE I COME, KOJIRO!!
BA (ZIP)
......

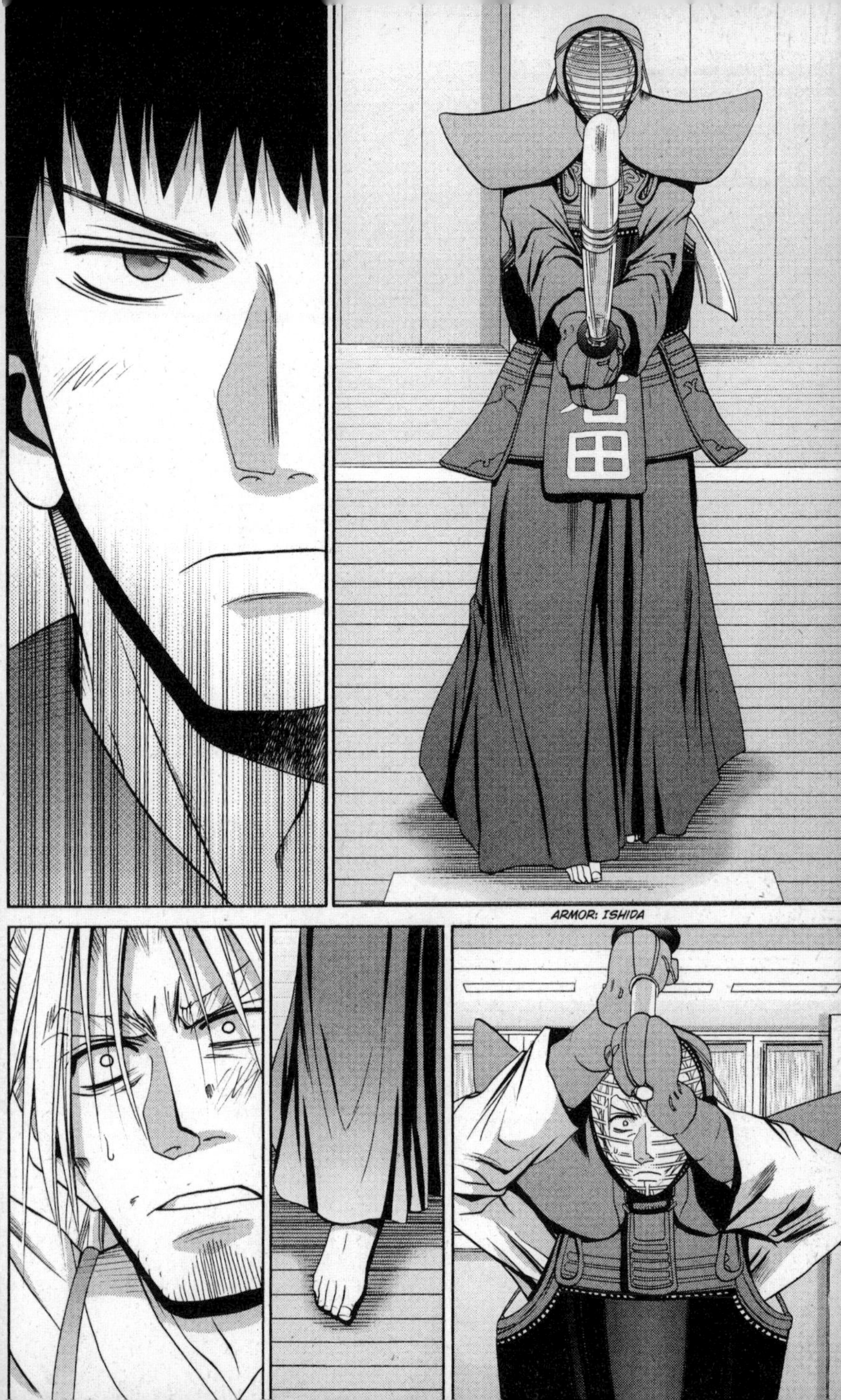
ARMOR: ISHIDA

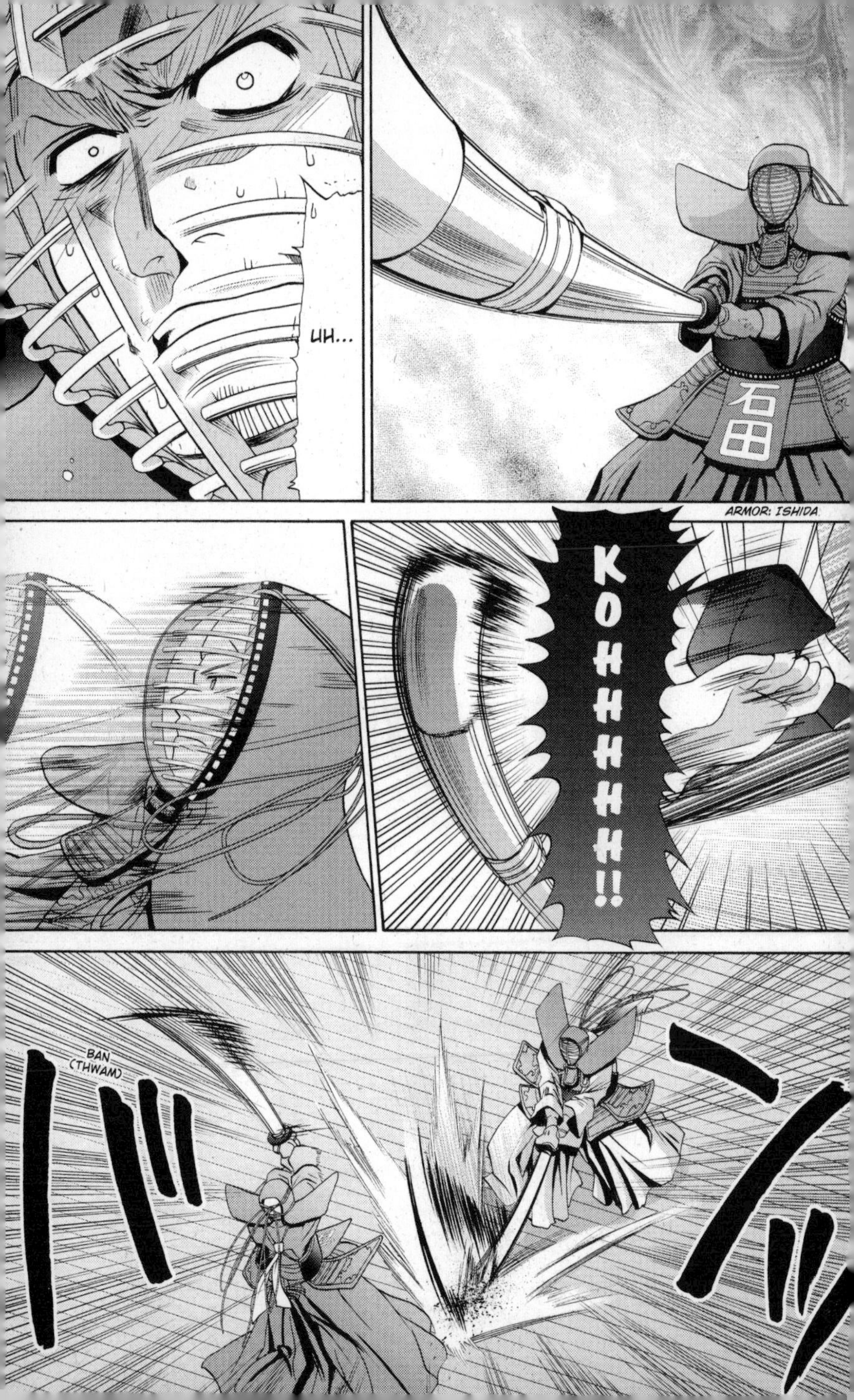
石田
ARMOR: ISHIDA
UH...
KOHHHHHH!!
BAN
(THWAM)

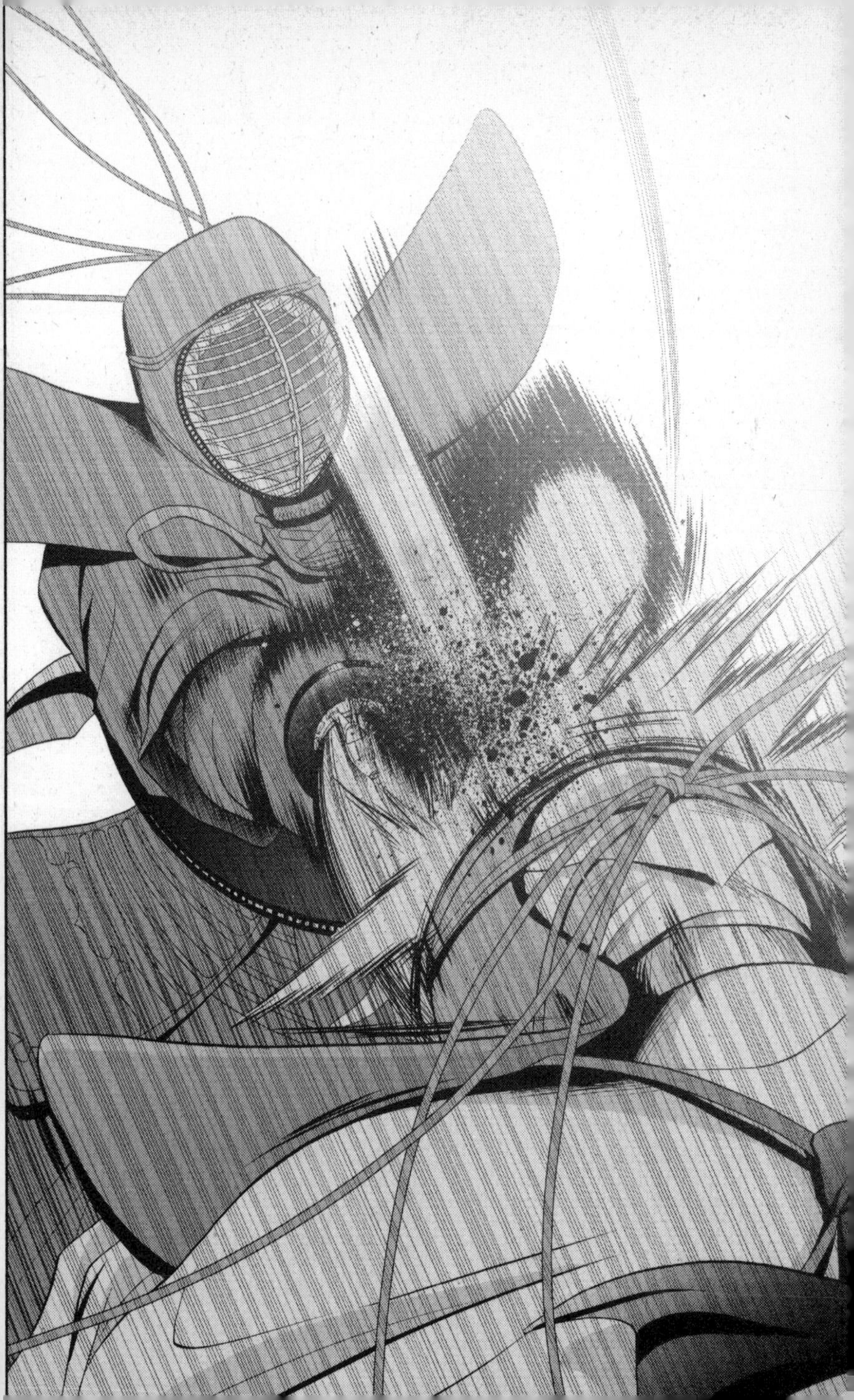

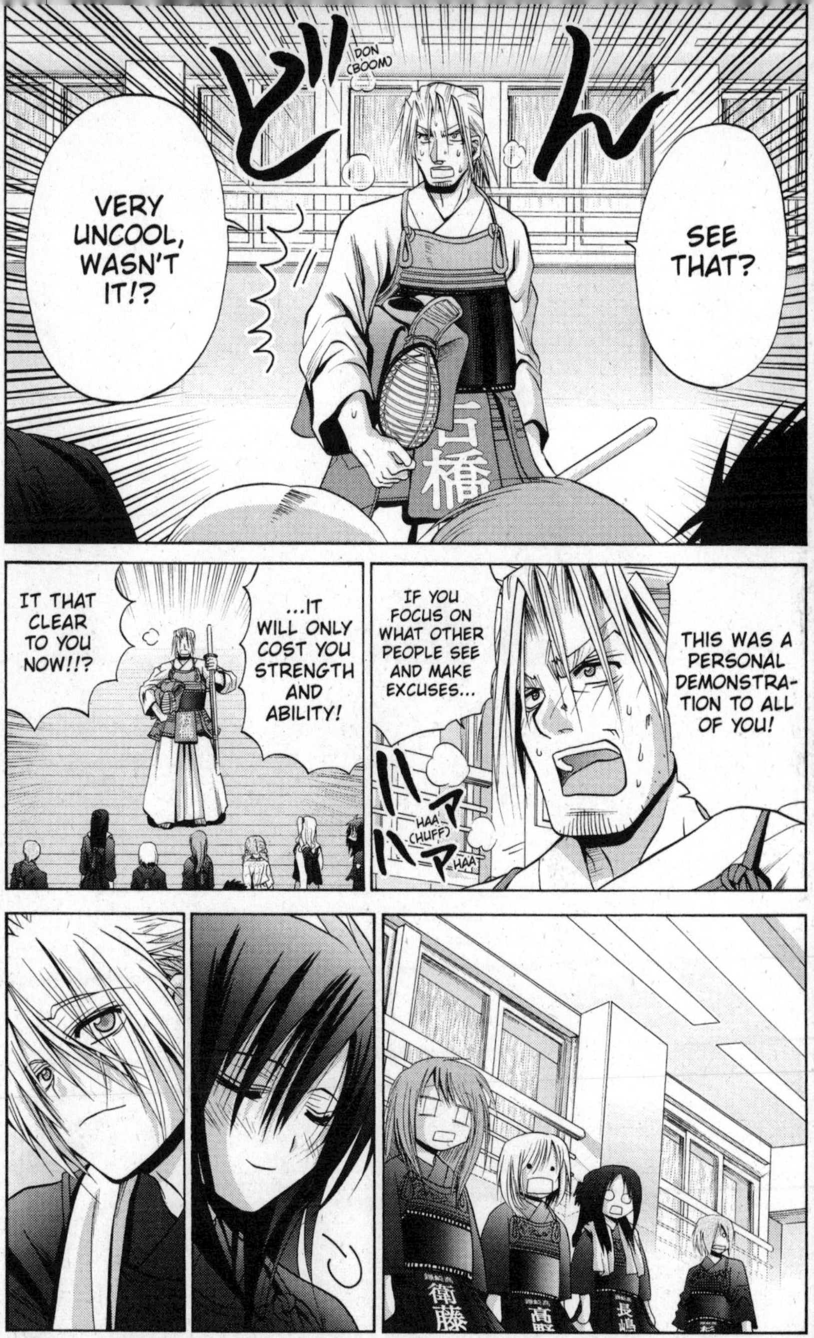
DON (BOOM)
SEE THAT?
VERY UNCOOL, WASN'T IT!?
THIS WAS A PERSONAL DEMONSTRATION TO ALL OF YOU!
IF YOU FOCUS ON WHAT OTHER PEOPLE SEE AND MAKE EXCUSES...
HAA (CHUFF) HAA
...IT WILL ONLY COST YOU STRENGTH AND ABILITY!
IT THAT CLEAR TO YOU NOW!!?

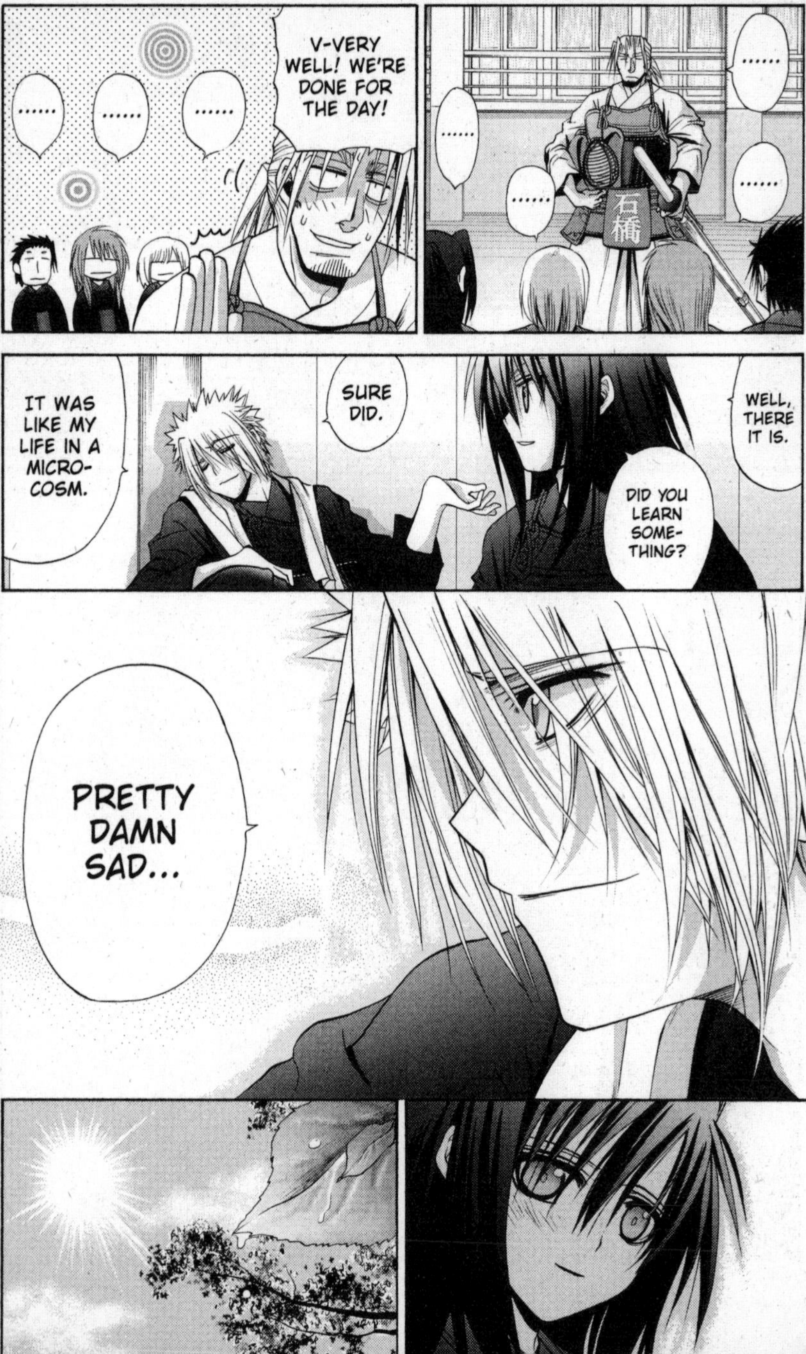
......
......
石橋
......
......
......
V-VERY WELL! WE'RE DONE FOR THE DAY!
......
......
......
WELL, THERE IT IS.
DID YOU LEARN SOMETHING?
SURE DID.
IT WAS LIKE MY LIFE IN A MICROCOSM.
PRETTY DAMN SAD...

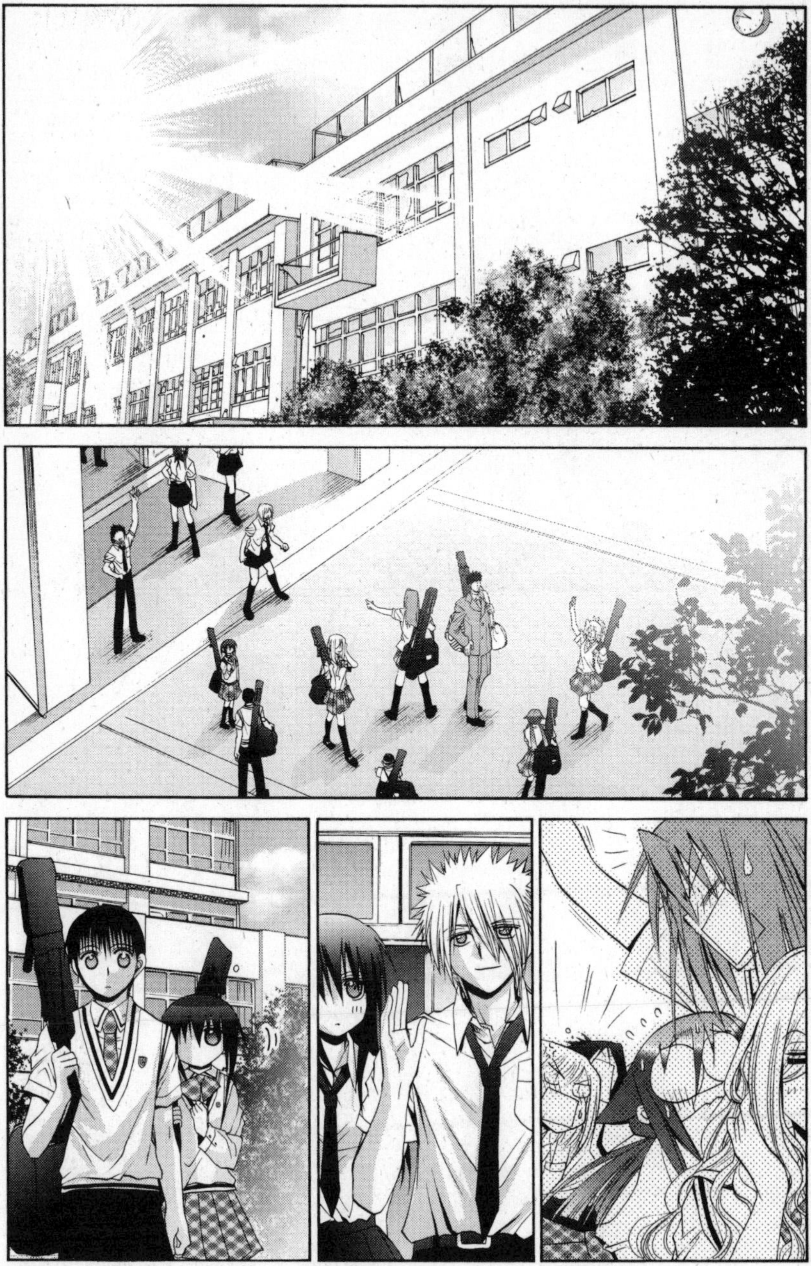

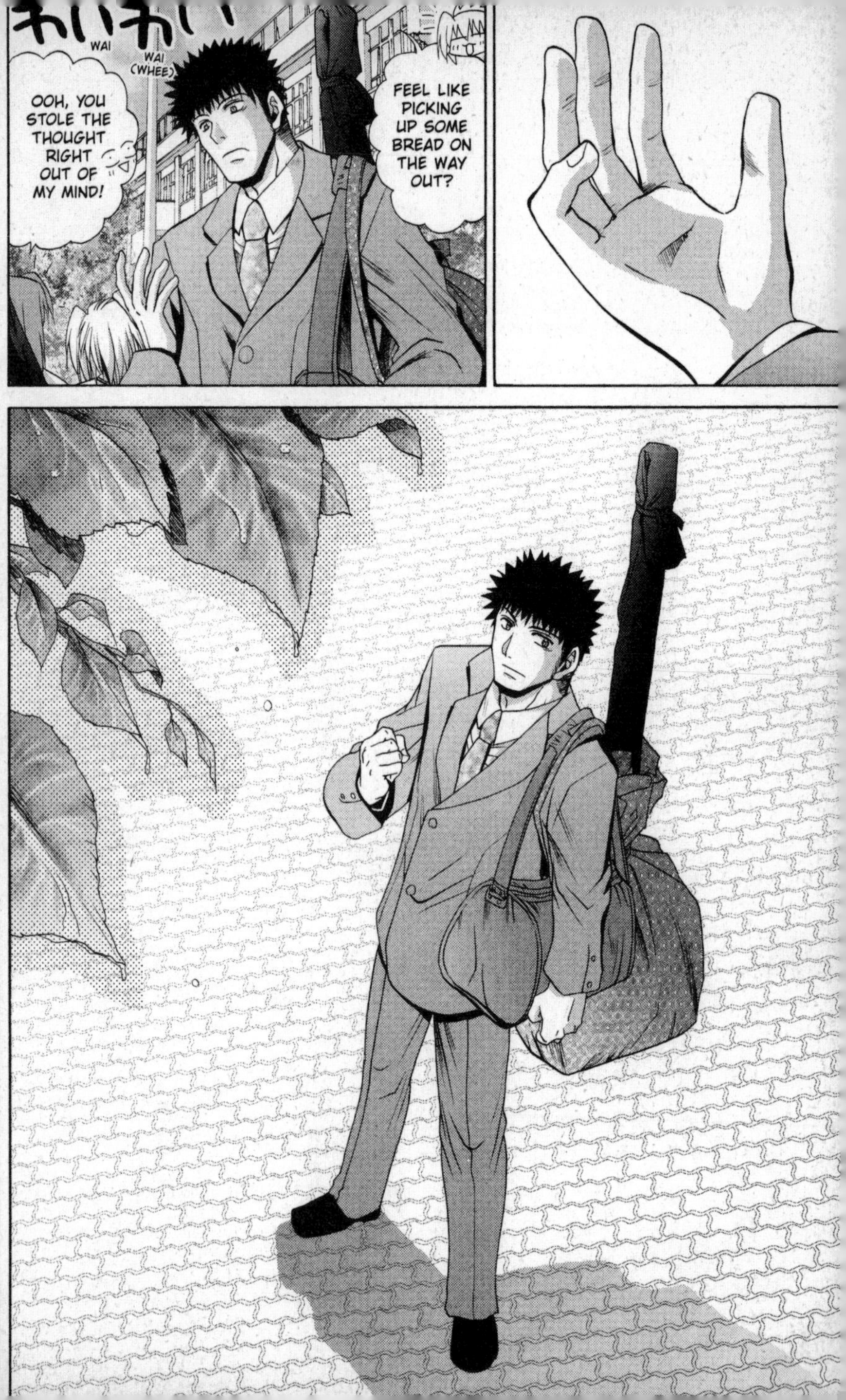
FEEL LIKE PICKING UP SOME BREAD ON THE WAY OUT?
わいわい
WAI WAI (WHEE)
OOH, YOU STOLE THE THOUGHT RIGHT OUT OF MY MIND!

BAMBOO BLADE

バンブーブレード

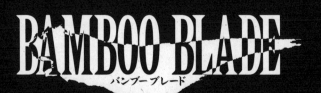

BAMBOO BLADE
バンブーブレード

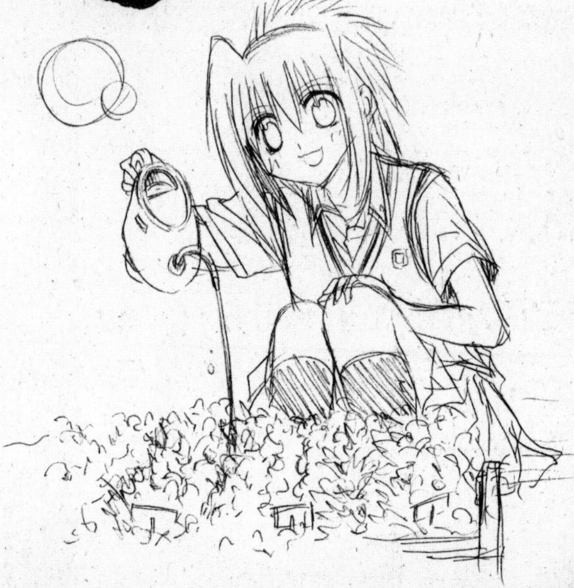

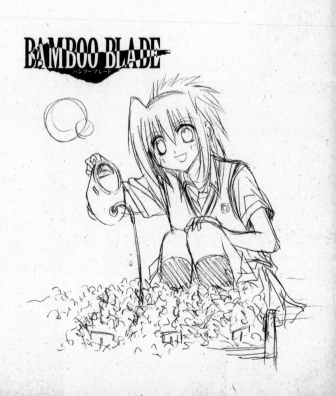

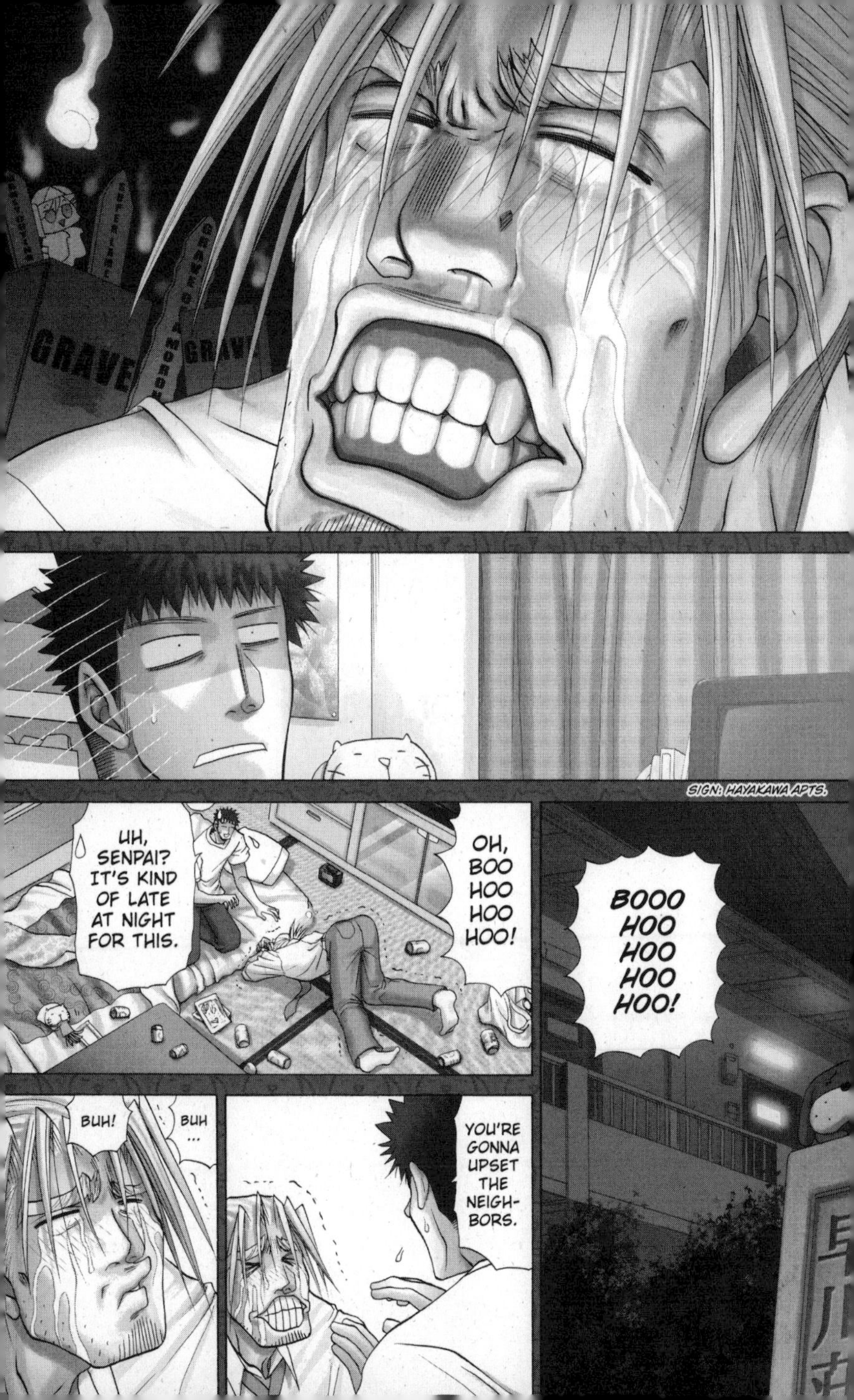
GRAVE OF A MORON
GRAVE
SIGN: HAYAKAWA APTS.
BOOO HOO HOO HOO HOO!
OH, BOO HOO HOO HOO!
UH, SENPAI? IT'S KIND OF LATE AT NIGHT FOR THIS.
YOU'RE GONNA UPSET THE NEIGH-BORS.
BUH ...
BUH!

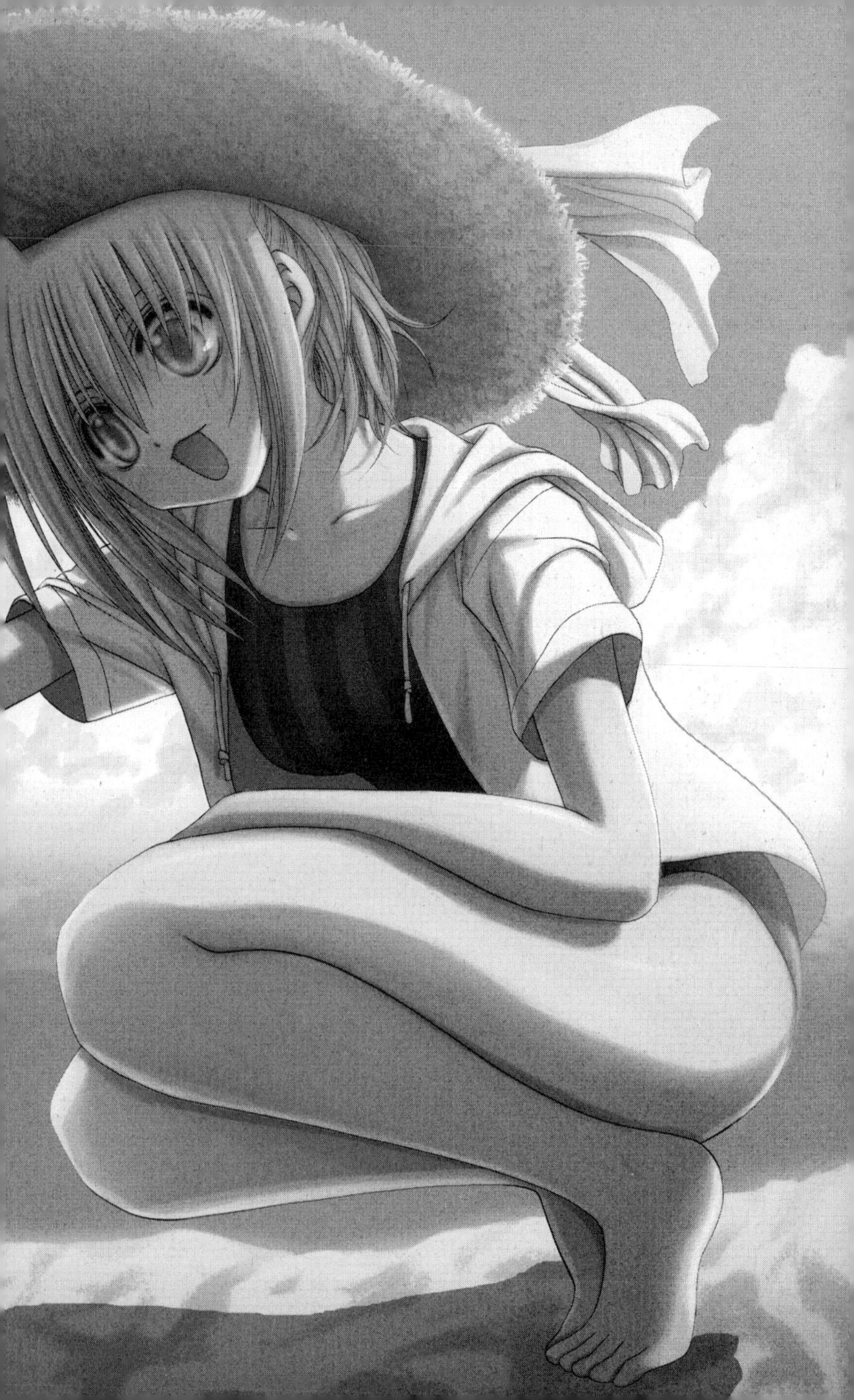

CHAPTER 77
THE MAN WHO CRIES AND THE MAN WHO LEAVES

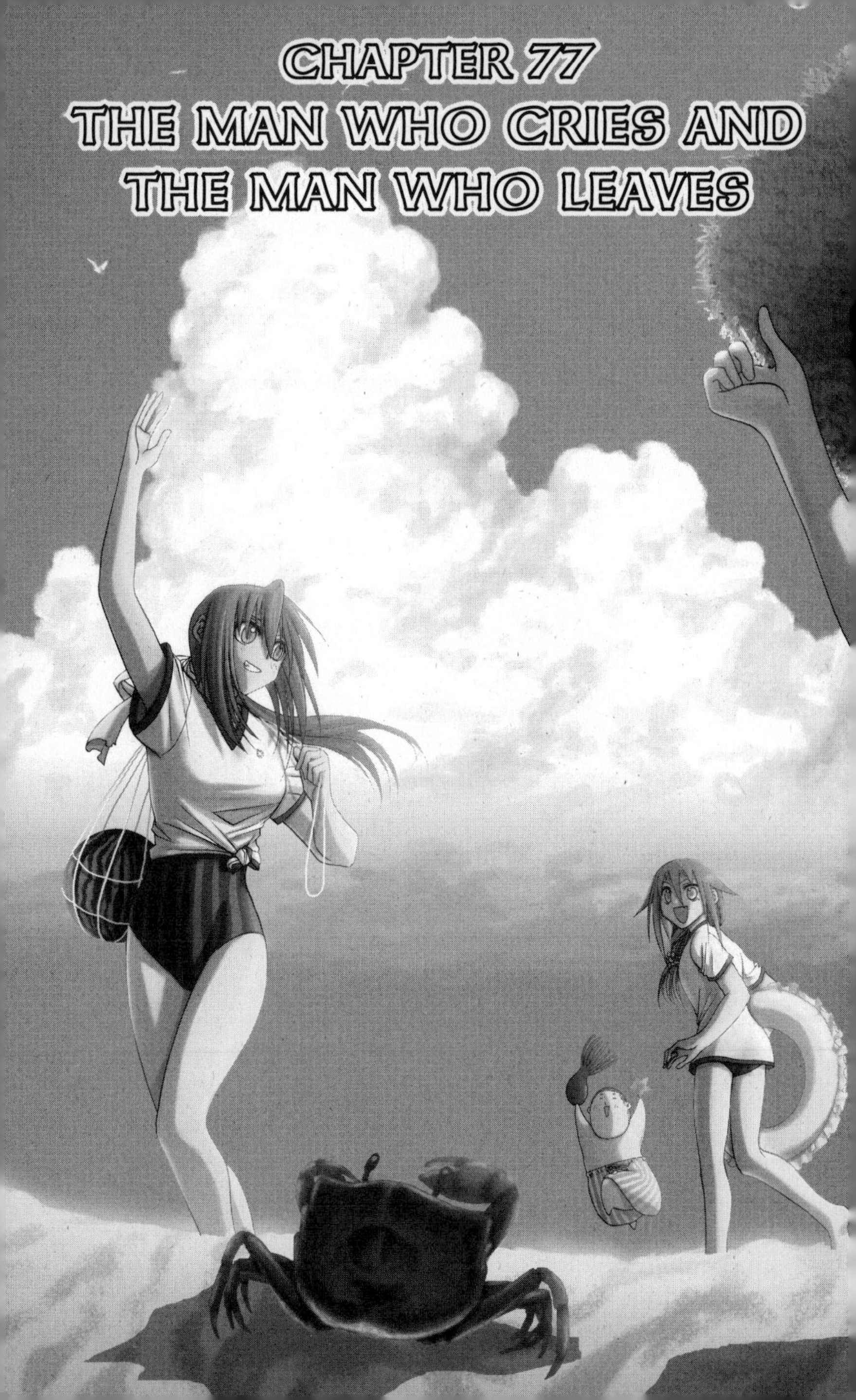

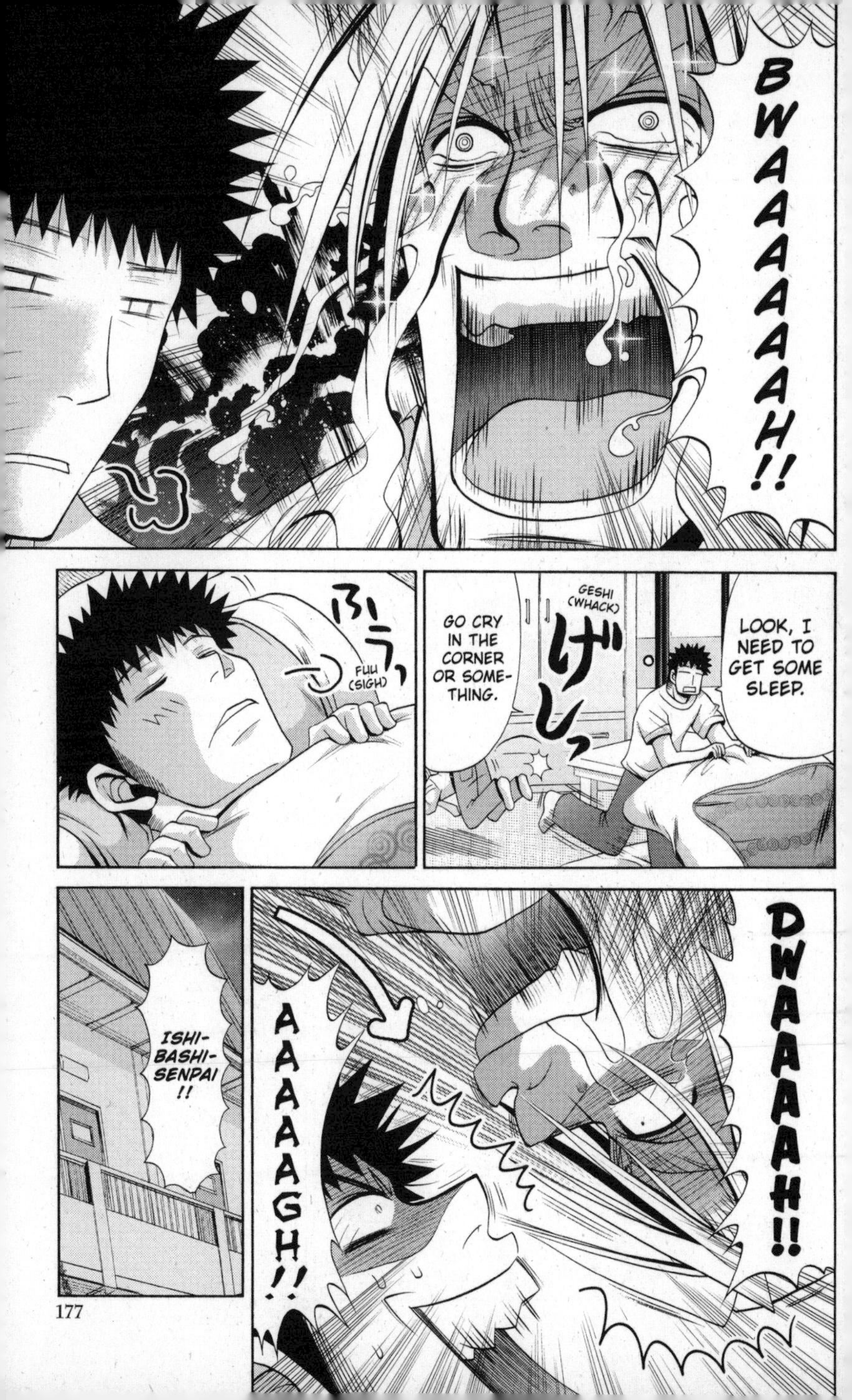
BWAAAAAAAAH!!
LOOK, I NEED TO GET SOME SLEEP.
GESHI (WHACK)
げしっ
GO CRY IN THE CORNER OR SOME-THING.
ふうっ
FUU (SIGH)
DWAAAAAAH!!
AAAAAAGH!!
ISHI-BASHI-SENPAI!!

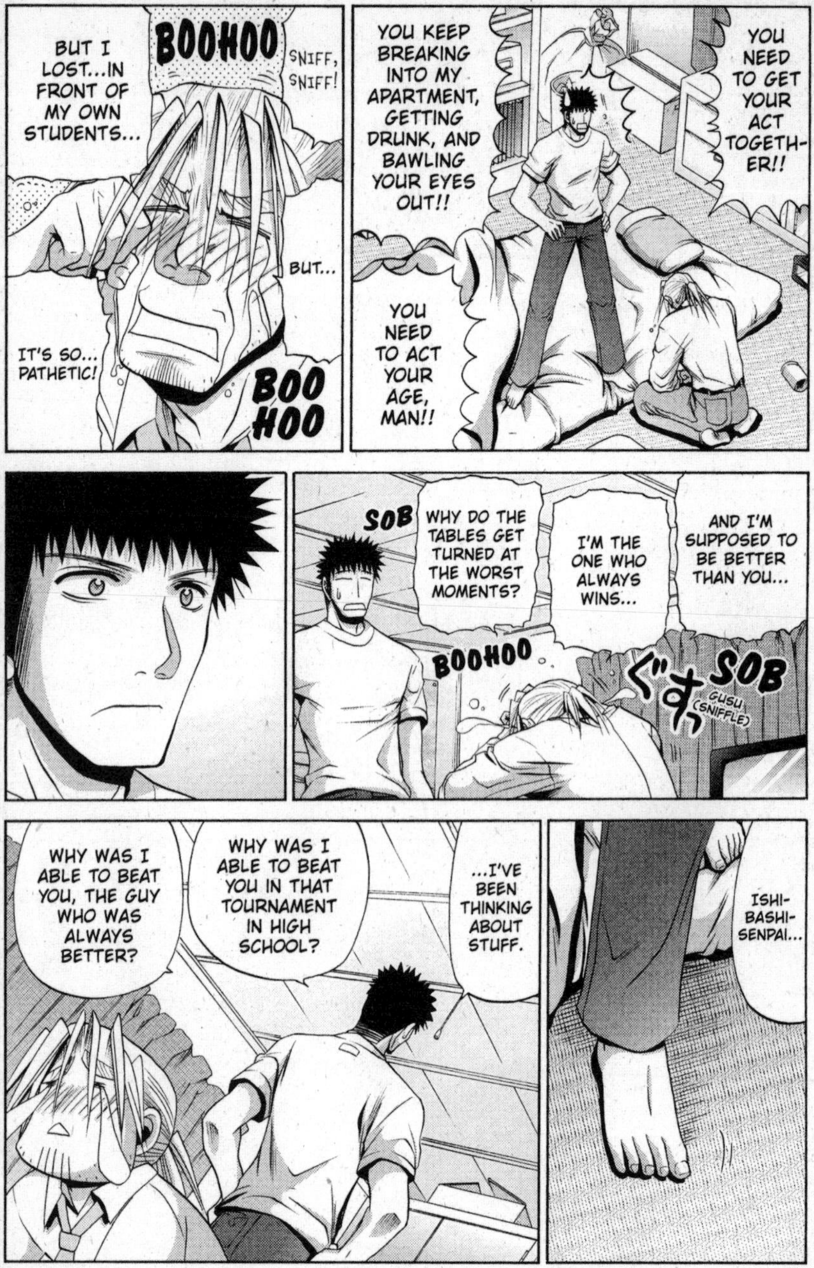
YOU NEED TO GET YOUR ACT TOGETHER!!
YOU KEEP BREAKING INTO MY APARTMENT, GETTING DRUNK, AND BAWLING YOUR EYES OUT!!
YOU NEED TO ACT YOUR AGE, MAN!!
BOOHOO
SNIFF, SNIFF!
BUT I LOST...IN FRONT OF MY OWN STUDENTS...
BUT...
IT'S SO... PATHETIC!
BOO HOO
AND I'M SUPPOSED TO BE BETTER THAN YOU...
I'M THE ONE WHO ALWAYS WINS...
WHY DO THE TABLES GET TURNED AT THE WORST MOMENTS?
SOB
BOOHOO
ぐすっ GUSU (SNIFFLE)
SOB
ISHIBASHI-SENPAI...
...I'VE BEEN THINKING ABOUT STUFF.
WHY WAS I ABLE TO BEAT YOU IN THAT TOURNAMENT IN HIGH SCHOOL?
WHY WAS I ABLE TO BEAT YOU, THE GUY WHO WAS ALWAYS BETTER?

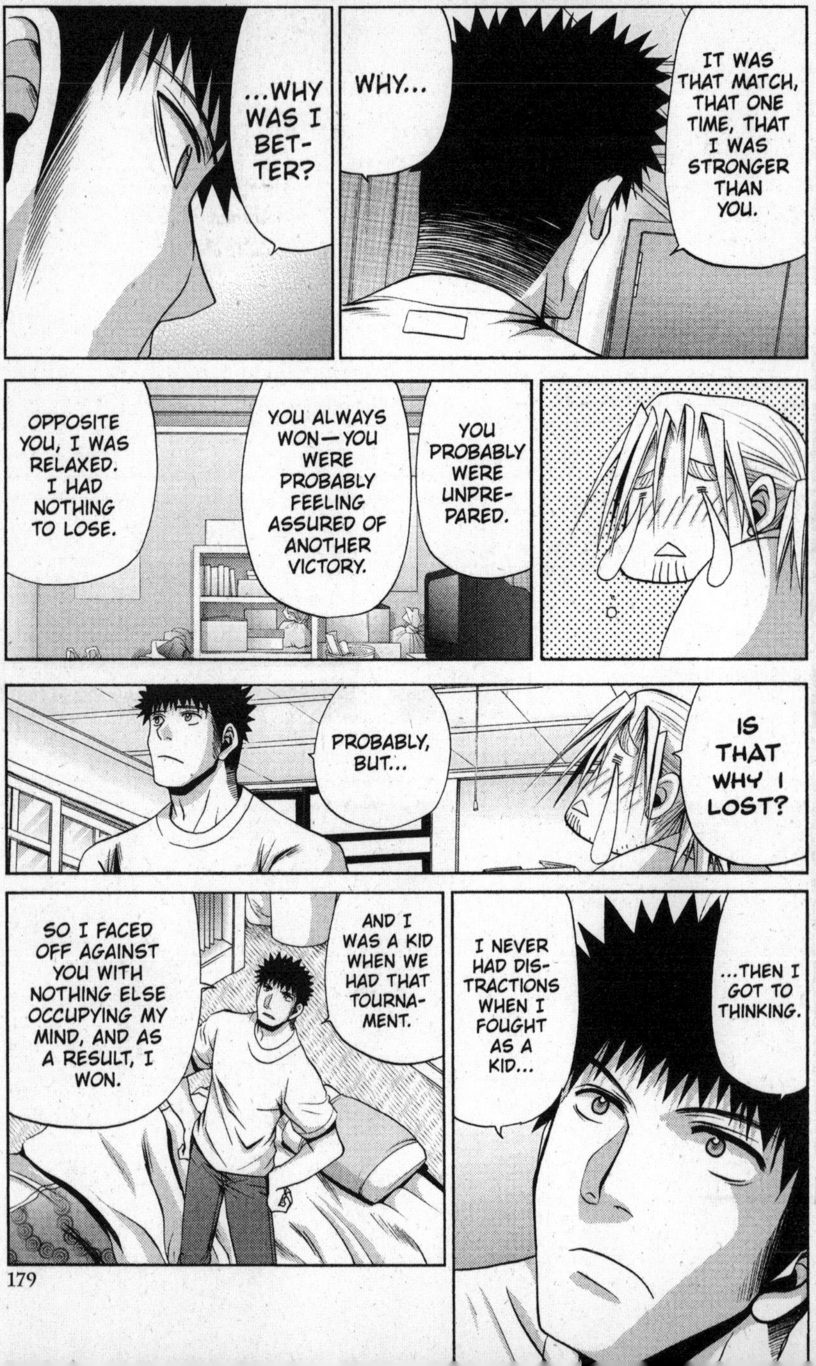
IT WAS THAT MATCH, THAT ONE TIME, THAT I WAS STRONGER THAN YOU.
WHY...
...WHY WAS I BETTER?
YOU PROBABLY WERE UNPREPARED.
YOU ALWAYS WON—YOU WERE PROBABLY FEELING ASSURED OF ANOTHER VICTORY.
OPPOSITE YOU, I WAS RELAXED. I HAD NOTHING TO LOSE.
IS THAT WHY I LOST?
PROBABLY, BUT...
...THEN I GOT TO THINKING.
I NEVER HAD DISTRACTIONS WHEN I FOUGHT AS A KID...
AND I WAS A KID WHEN WE HAD THAT TOURNAMENT.
SO I FACED OFF AGAINST YOU WITH NOTHING ELSE OCCUPYING MY MIND, AND AS A RESULT, I WON.

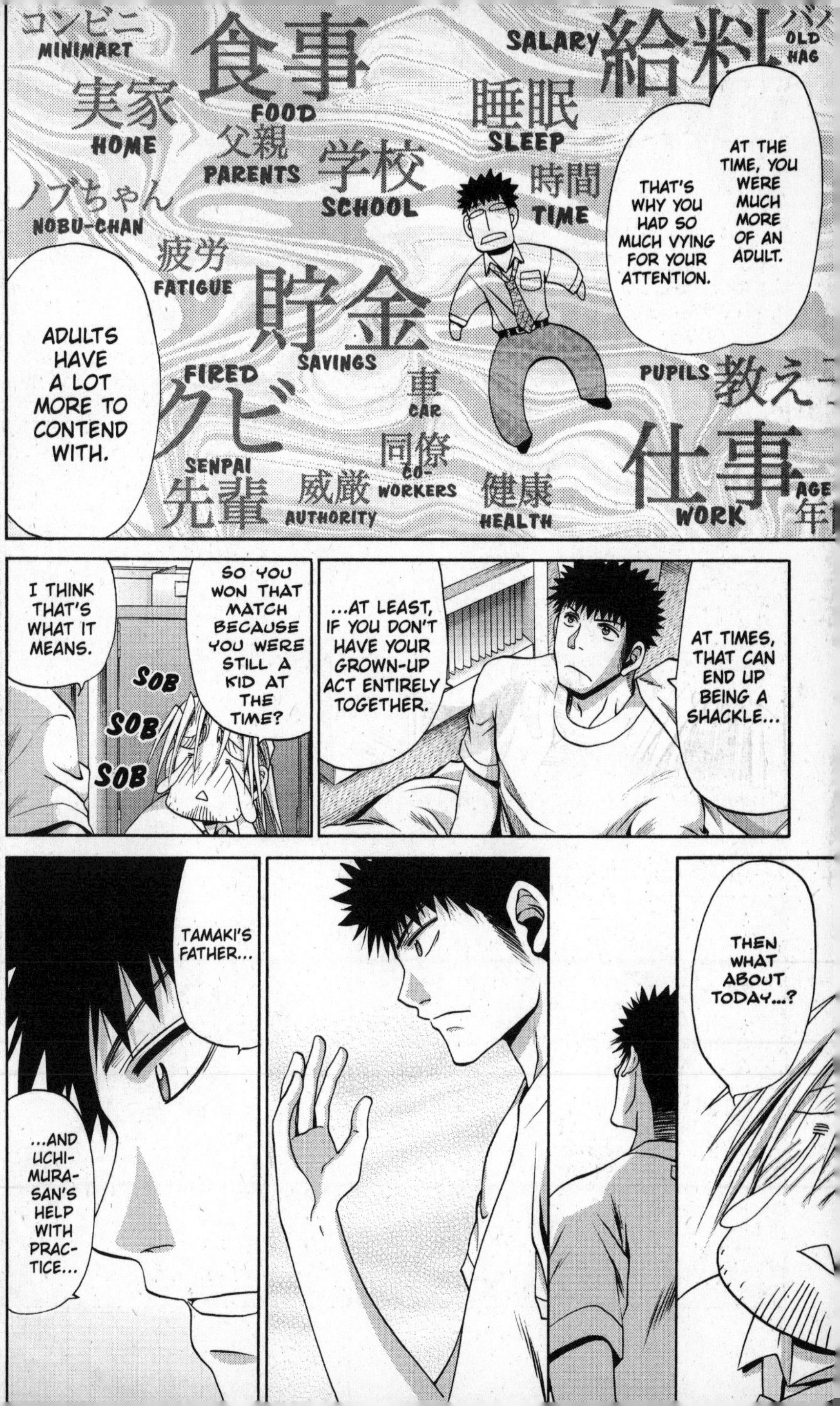
AT THE TIME, YOU WERE MUCH MORE OF AN ADULT.
THAT'S WHY YOU HAD SO MUCH VYING FOR YOUR ATTENTION.
OLD HAG
給料 SALARY
睡眠 SLEEP
時間 TIME
食事 FOOD
学校 SCHOOL
父親 PARENTS
コンビニ MINIMART
実家 HOME
ノブちゃん NOBU-CHAN
疲労 FATIGUE
貯金 SAVINGS
PUPILS
AGE
仕事 WORK
車 CAR
同僚 CO-WORKERS
健康 HEALTH
威厳 AUTHORITY
クビ FIRED
先輩 SENPAI
ADULTS HAVE A LOT MORE TO CONTEND WITH.
AT TIMES, THAT CAN END UP BEING A SHACKLE...
...AT LEAST, IF YOU DON'T HAVE YOUR GROWN-UP ACT ENTIRELY TOGETHER.
SO YOU WON THAT MATCH BECAUSE YOU WERE STILL A KID AT THE TIME?
SOB
SOB
SOB
I THINK THAT'S WHAT IT MEANS.
THEN WHAT ABOUT TODAY...?
TAMAKI'S FATHER...
...AND UCHIMURA-SAN'S HELP WITH PRACTICE...

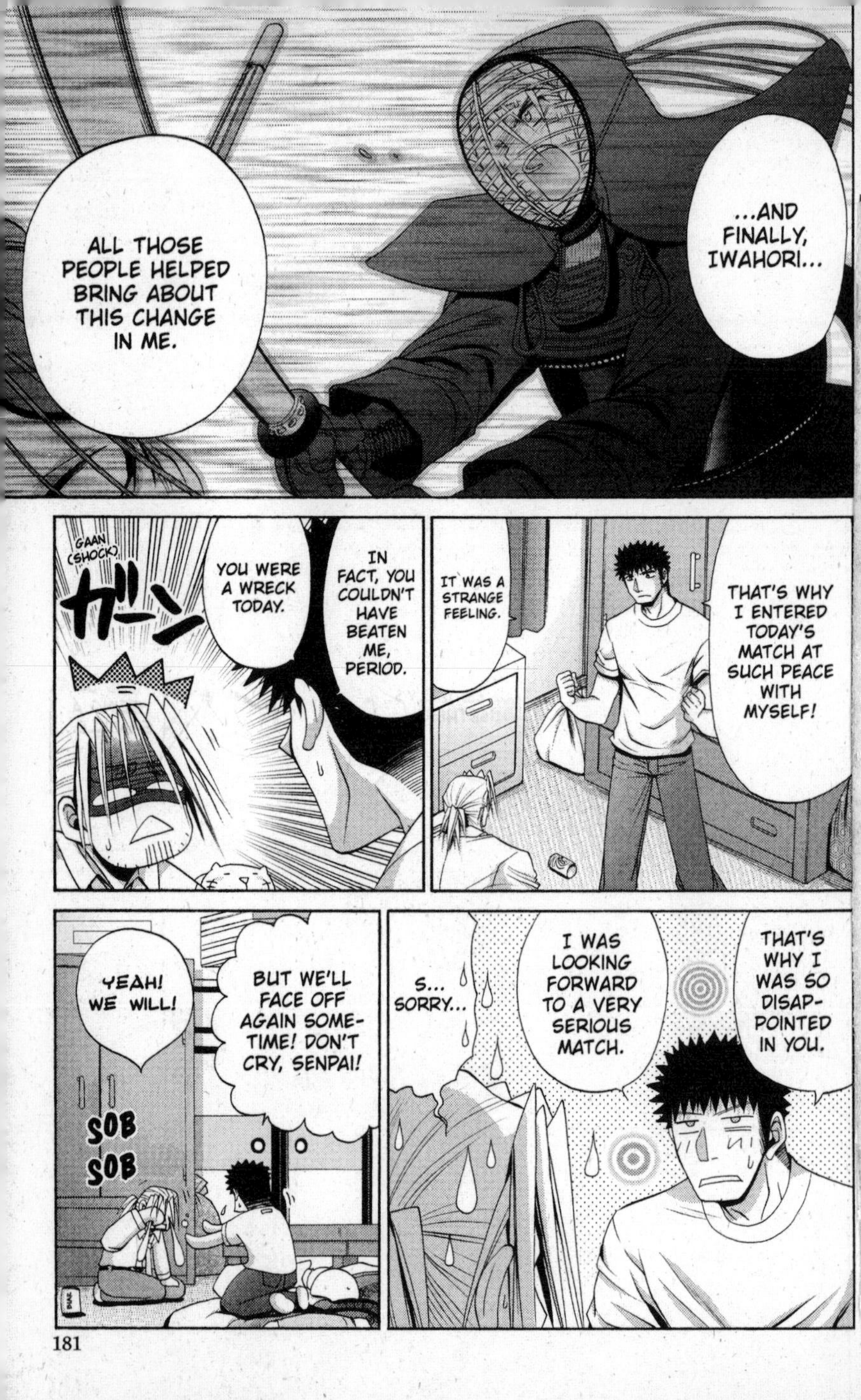
...AND FINALLY, IWAHORI...
ALL THOSE PEOPLE HELPED BRING ABOUT THIS CHANGE IN ME.
THAT'S WHY I ENTERED TODAY'S MATCH AT SUCH PEACE WITH MYSELF!
IT WAS A STRANGE FEELING.
IN FACT, YOU COULDN'T HAVE BEATEN ME, PERIOD.
YOU WERE A WRECK TODAY.
GAAN (SHOCK)
ガーン
THAT'S WHY I WAS SO DISAP-POINTED IN YOU.
I WAS LOOKING FORWARD TO A VERY SERIOUS MATCH.
S... SORRY...
BUT WE'LL FACE OFF AGAIN SOME-TIME! DON'T CRY, SENPAI!
YEAH! WE WILL!
SOB SOB

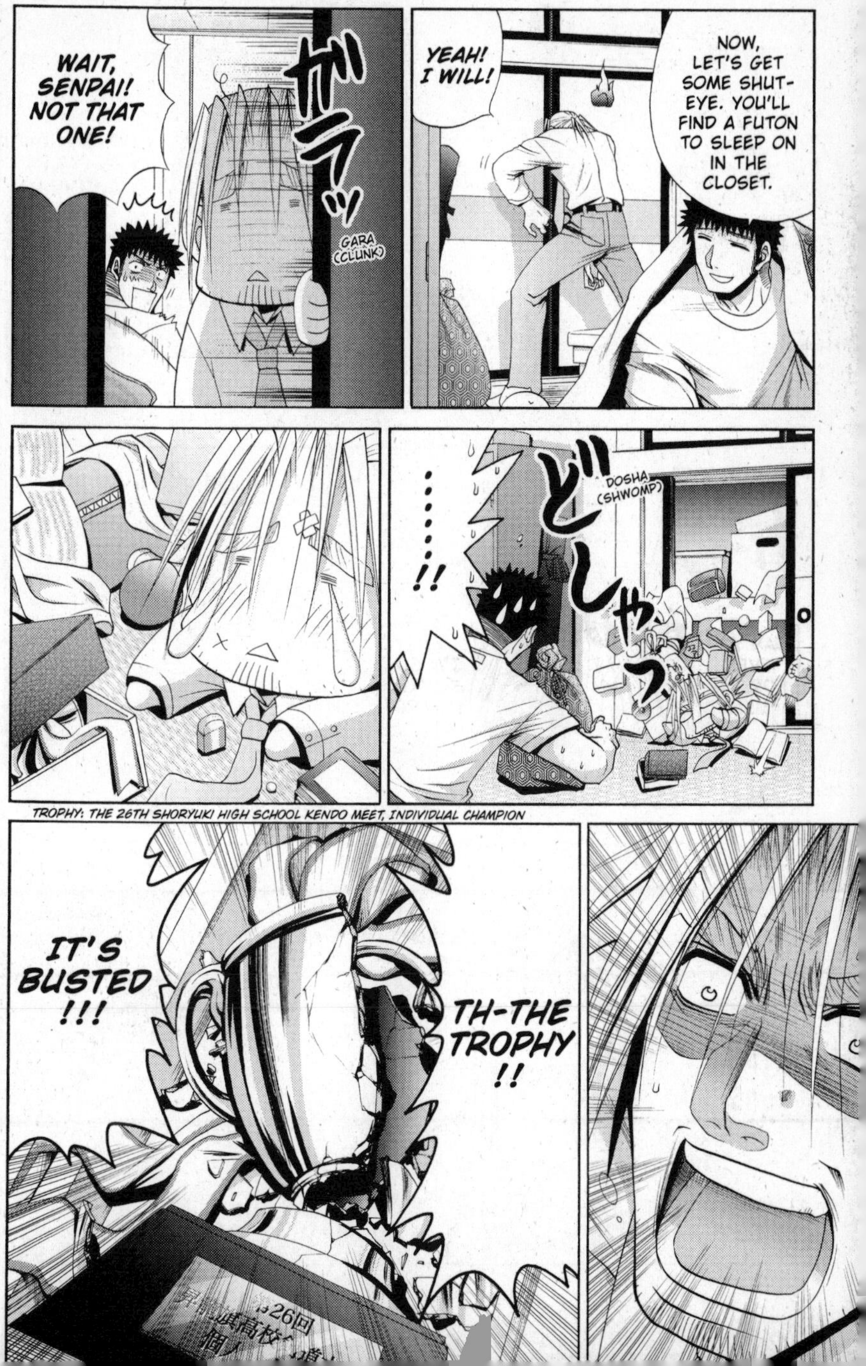
NOW, LET'S GET SOME SHUT-EYE. YOU'LL FIND A FUTON TO SLEEP ON IN THE CLOSET.
YEAH! I WILL!
ガラッ
GARA (CLUNK)
WAIT, SENPAI! NOT THAT ONE!
どしゃっ
DOSHA (SHWOMP)
......!!
TROPHY: THE 26TH SHORYUKI HIGH SCHOOL KENDO MEET, INDIVIDUAL CHAMPION
TH-THE TROPHY!!
IT'S BUSTED!!!

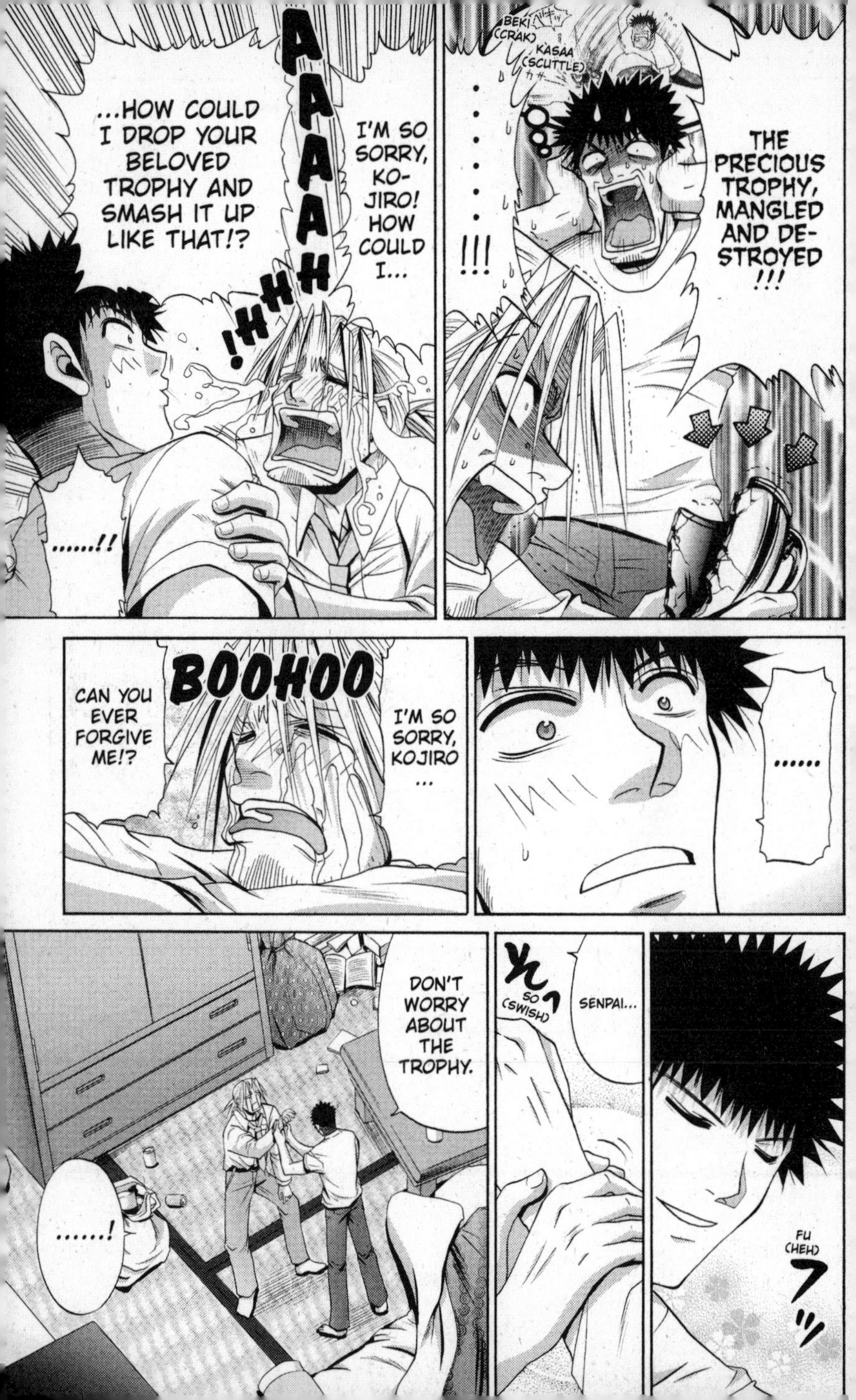

BEKI (CRAK)
KASAA (SCUTTLE)
THE PRECIOUS TROPHY, MANGLED AND DE-STROYED!!!
......!!!
AAAAHHH!
I'M SO SORRY, KO-JIRO! HOW COULD I...
...HOW COULD I DROP YOUR BELOVED TROPHY AND SMASH IT UP LIKE THAT!?
......!!
......
I'M SO SORRY, KOJIRO...
BOOHOO
CAN YOU EVER FORGIVE ME!?
FU (HEH)
SENPAI...
SO (SWISH)
DON'T WORRY ABOUT THE TROPHY.
......!

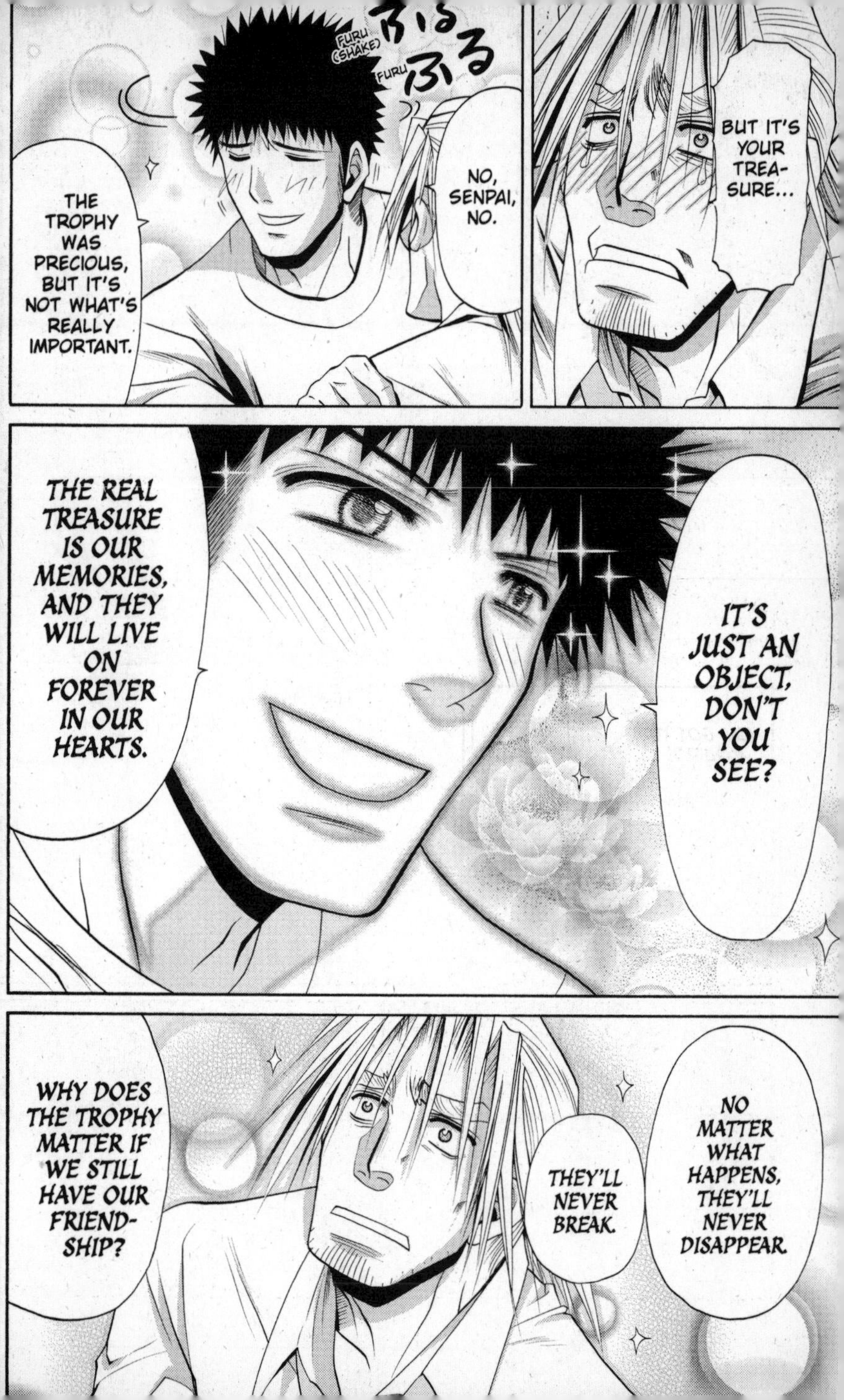
BUT IT'S YOUR TREA-SURE...
NO, SENPAI, NO.
FURU (SHAKE) ふる
FURU ふる
THE TROPHY WAS PRECIOUS, BUT IT'S NOT WHAT'S REALLY IMPORTANT.
IT'S JUST AN OBJECT, DON'T YOU SEE?
THE REAL TREASURE IS OUR MEMORIES, AND THEY WILL LIVE ON FOREVER IN OUR HEARTS.
NO MATTER WHAT HAPPENS, THEY'LL NEVER DISAPPEAR.
THEY'LL NEVER BREAK.
WHY DOES THE TROPHY MATTER IF WE STILL HAVE OUR FRIEND-SHIP?

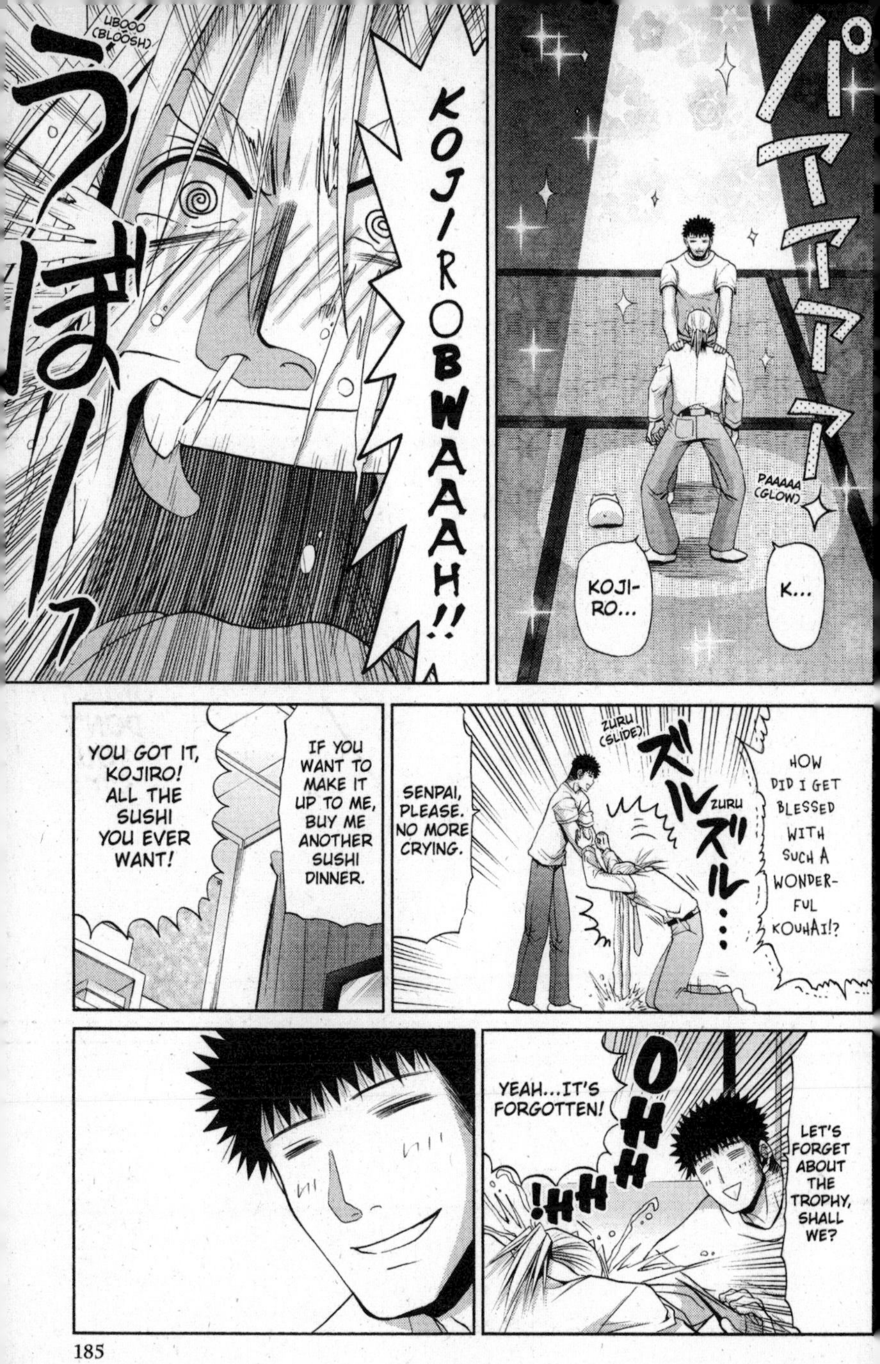
パアアアアア
PAAAAA (GLOW)
K...
KOJI-RO...
UBOOO (BLOOSH)
うぼーっ
KOJIRO BWAAAH!!
HOW DID I GET BLESSED WITH SUCH A WONDERFUL KOUHAI!?
ZURU (SLIDE)
ズルズル...
SENPAI, PLEASE. NO MORE CRYING.
IF YOU WANT TO MAKE IT UP TO ME, BUY ME ANOTHER SUSHI DINNER.
YOU GOT IT, KOJIRO! ALL THE SUSHI YOU EVER WANT!
LET'S FORGET ABOUT THE TROPHY, SHALL WE?
OHHHH!!
YEAH...IT'S FORGOTTEN!

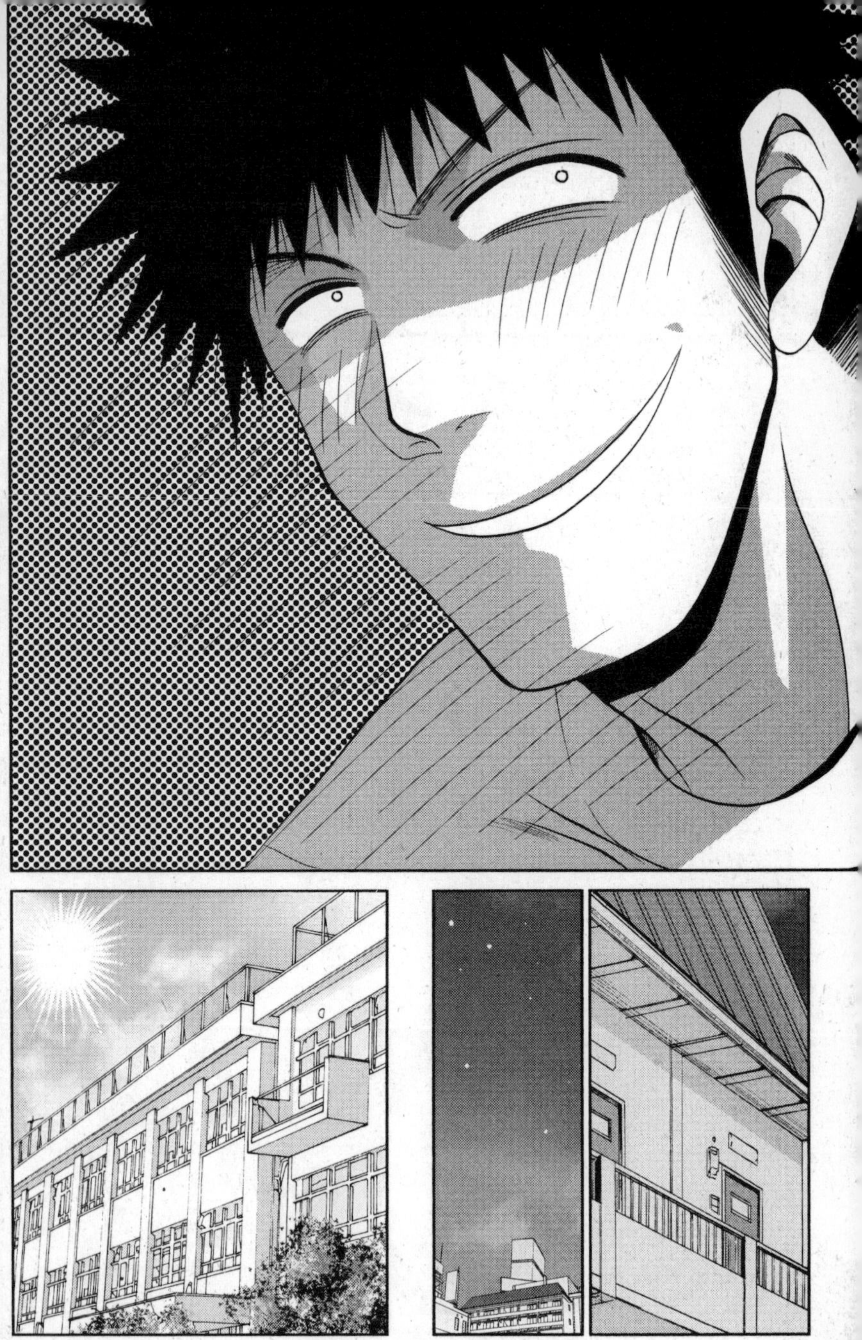

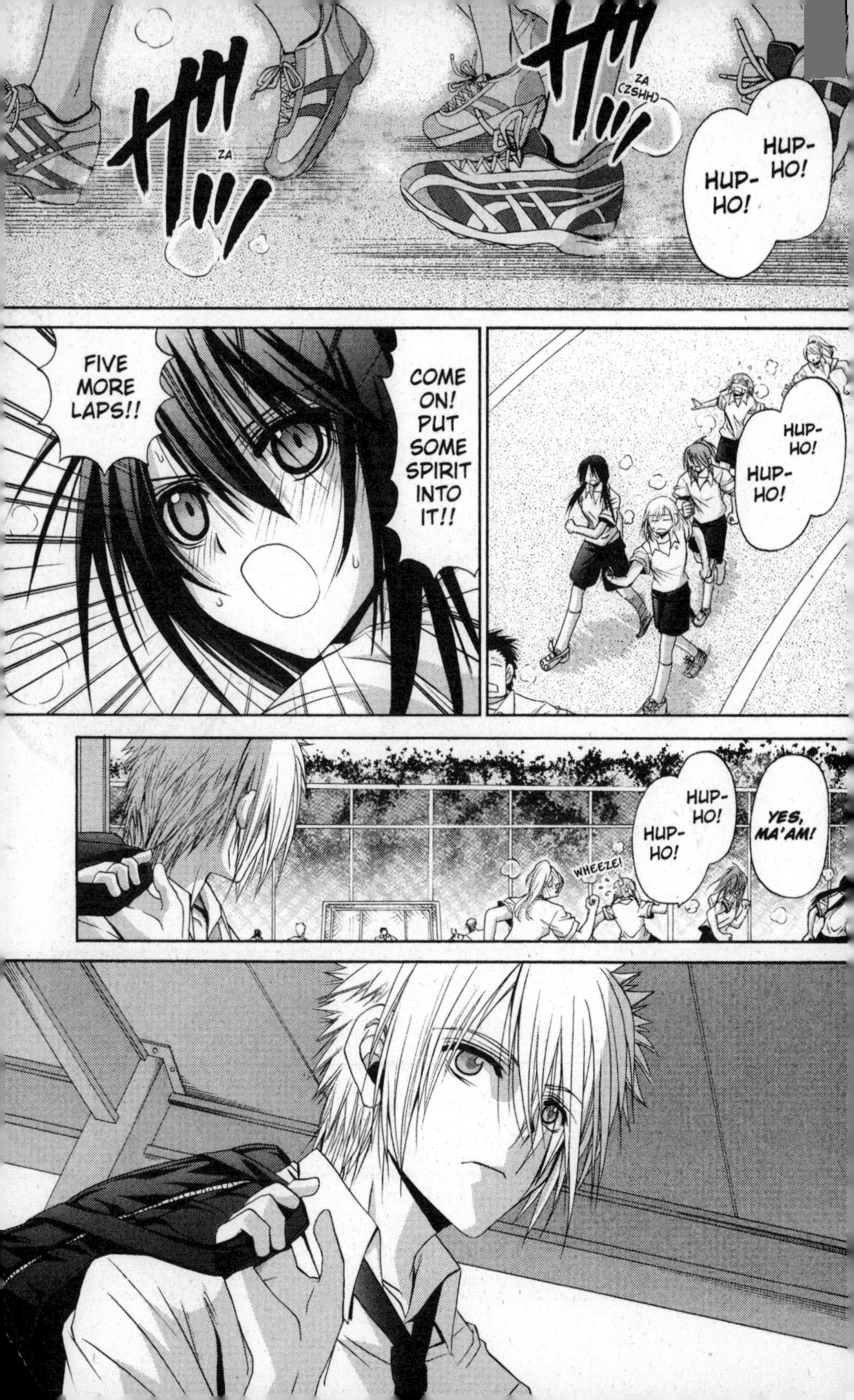
HUP-HO! HUP-HO!
ZA (ZSHH)
ZA
HUP-HO! HUP-HO!
COME ON! PUT SOME SPIRIT INTO IT!!
FIVE MORE LAPS!!
YES, MA'AM!
HUP-HO! HUP-HO!
WHEEZE!

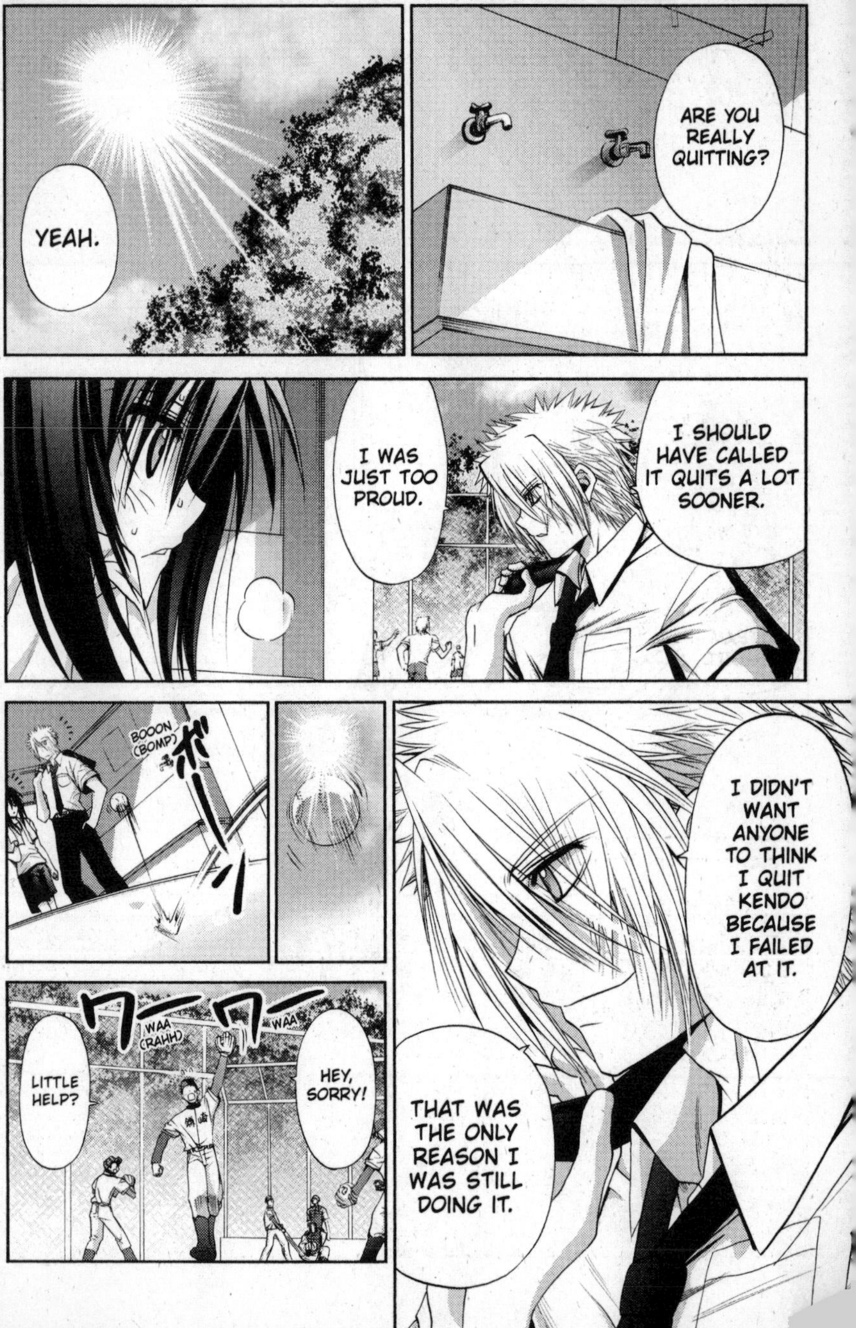
ARE YOU REALLY QUITTING?
YEAH.
I SHOULD HAVE CALLED IT QUITS A LOT SOONER.
I WAS JUST TOO PROUD.
I DIDN'T WANT ANYONE TO THINK I QUIT KENDO BECAUSE I FAILED AT IT.
THAT WAS THE ONLY REASON I WAS STILL DOING IT.
BOOON (BOMP)
WAA
WAA (RAHH)
HEY, SORRY!
LITTLE HELP?

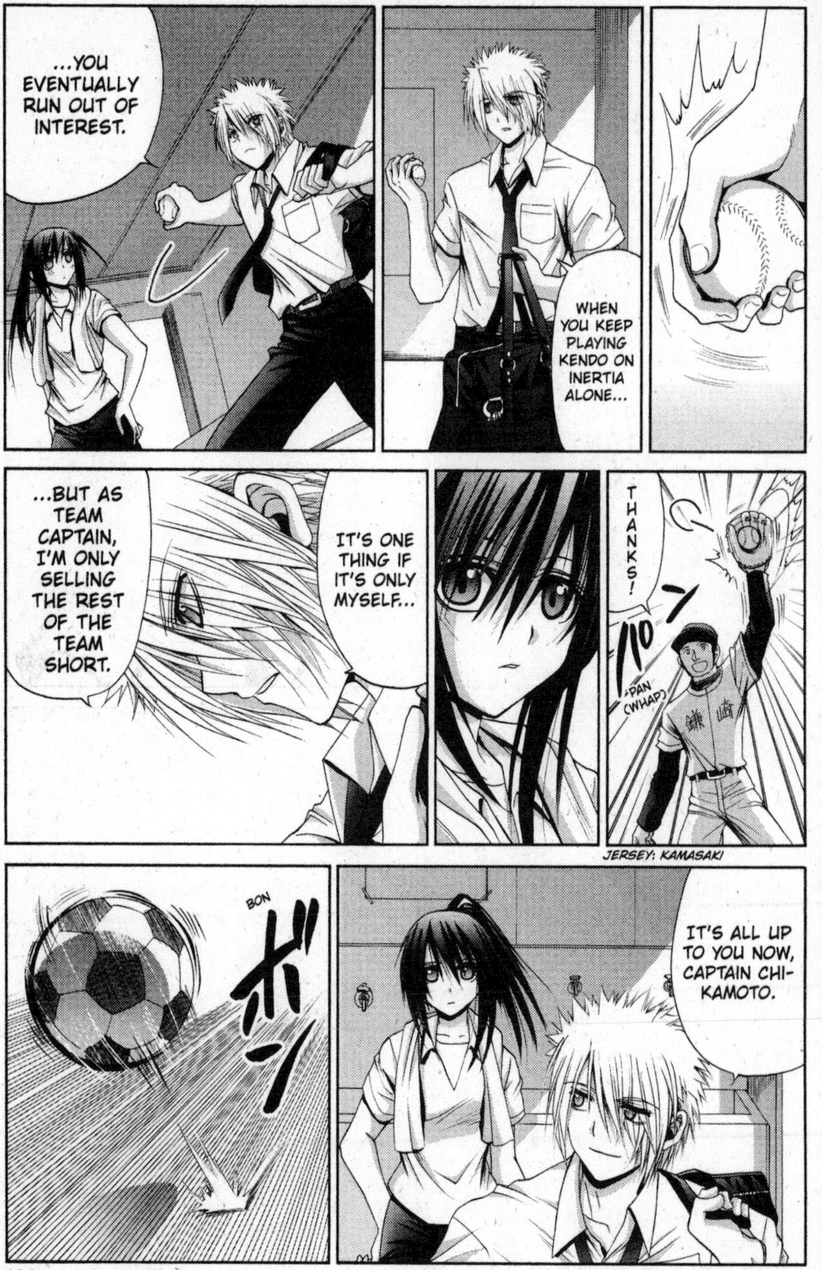
WHEN YOU KEEP PLAYING KENDO ON INERTIA ALONE...
...YOU EVENTUALLY RUN OUT OF INTEREST.
THANKS!
PAN (WHAP)
JERSEY: KAMASAKI
IT'S ONE THING IF IT'S ONLY MYSELF...
...BUT AS TEAM CAPTAIN, I'M ONLY SELLING THE REST OF THE TEAM SHORT.
IT'S ALL UP TO YOU NOW, CAPTAIN CHI-KAMOTO.
BON

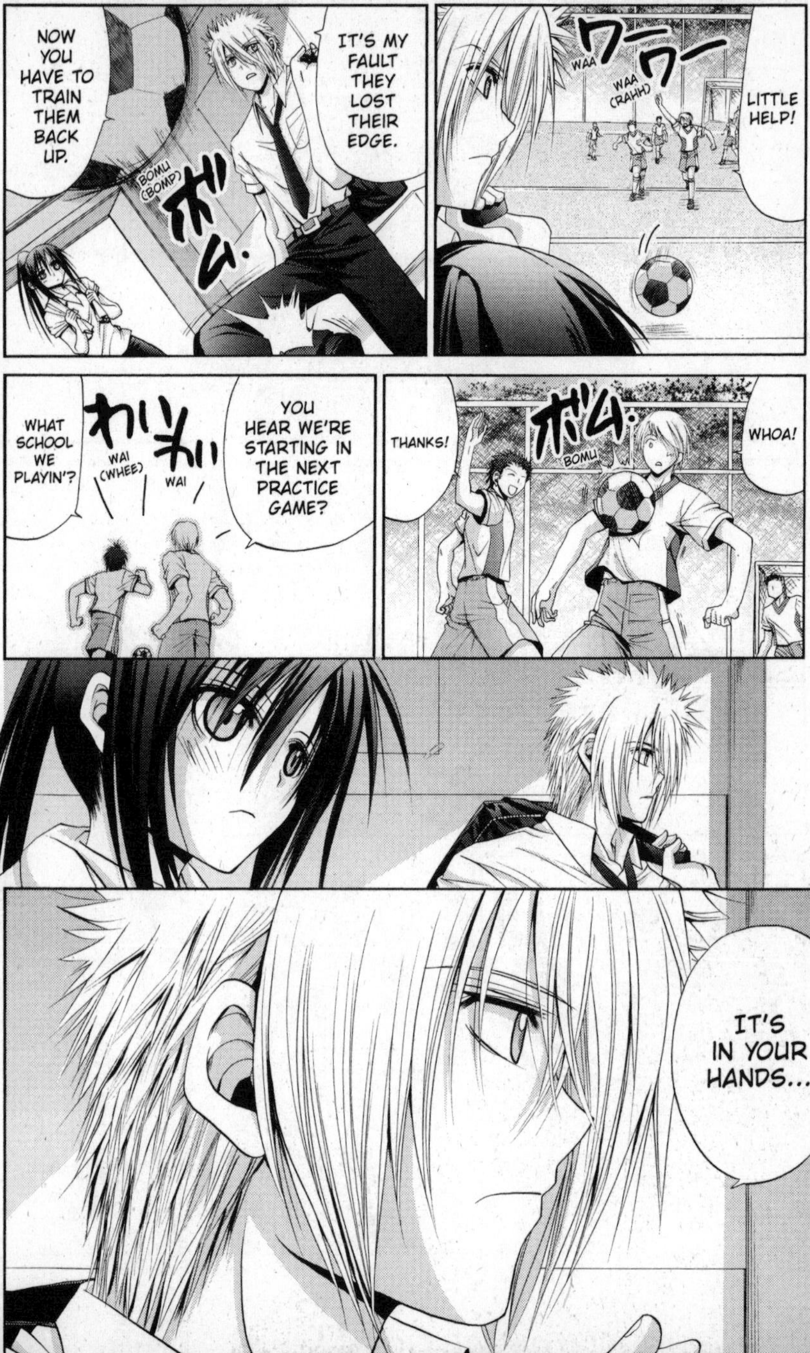
ワー
WAA
ワー
WAA (RAHH)
LITTLE HELP!
IT'S MY FAULT THEY LOST THEIR EDGE.
NOW YOU HAVE TO TRAIN THEM BACK UP.
ボム
BOMU (BOMP)
WHOA!
ボム
BOMU
THANKS!
YOU HEAR WE'RE STARTING IN THE NEXT PRACTICE GAME?
わいわい
WAI (WHEE)
WAI
WHAT SCHOOL WE PLAYIN'?
IT'S IN YOUR HANDS...

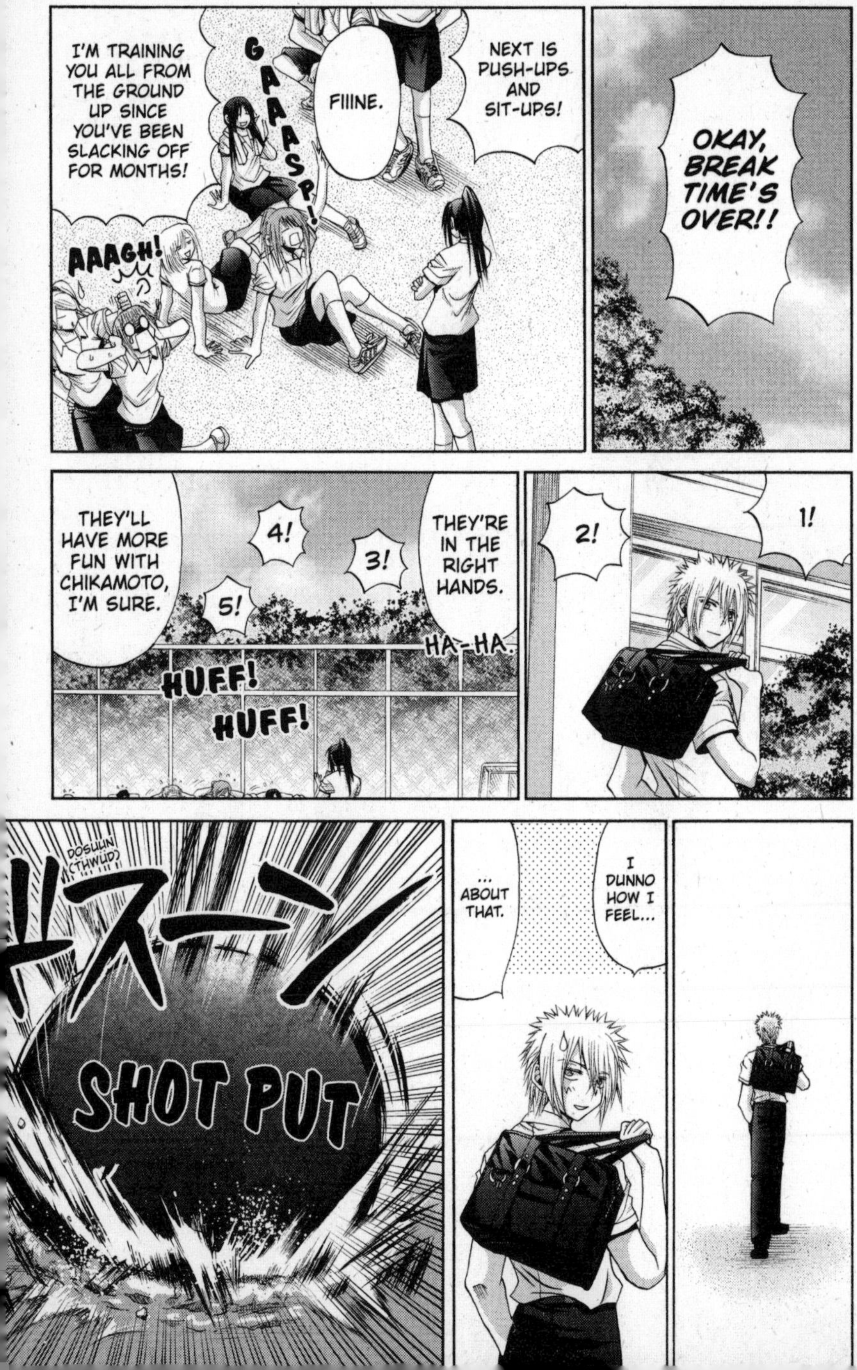
OKAY, BREAK TIME'S OVER!!
NEXT IS PUSH-UPS AND SIT-UPS!
FIIINE.
GAAASP!
I'M TRAINING YOU ALL FROM THE GROUND UP SINCE YOU'VE BEEN SLACKING OFF FOR MONTHS!
AAAGH!
1!
2!
THEY'RE IN THE RIGHT HANDS.
HA-HA.
3!
4!
5!
THEY'LL HAVE MORE FUN WITH CHIKAMOTO, I'M SURE.
HUFF!
HUFF!
I DUNNO HOW I FEEL...
... ABOUT THAT.
DOSUUN (THWUD)
SHOT PUT

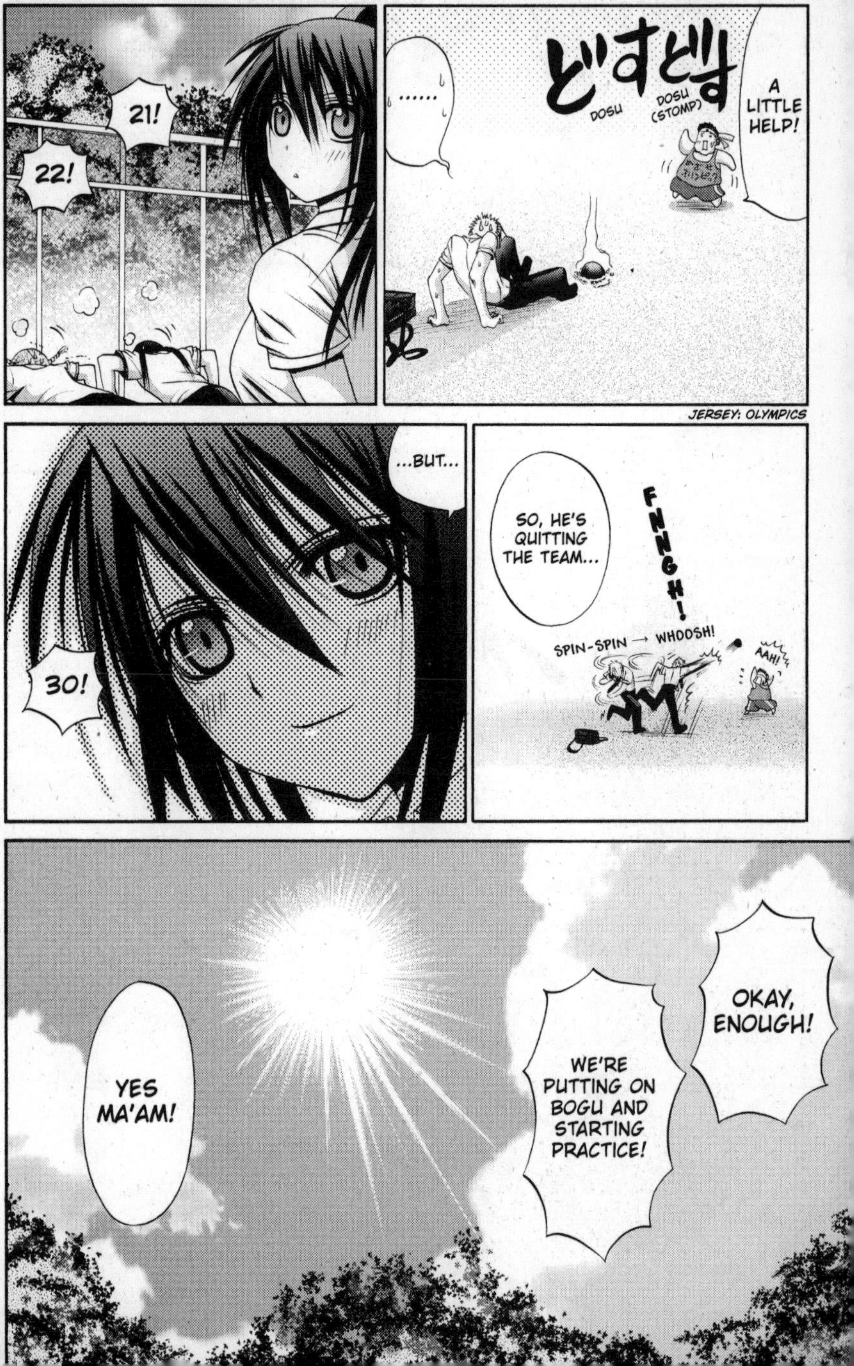

A LITTLE HELP!
どすどす
DOSU DOSU (STOMP)
......
21!
22!
JERSEY: OLYMPICS
SO, HE'S QUITTING THE TEAM...
FNNGH!
SPIN-SPIN → WHOOSH!
AAH!
...BUT...
30!
OKAY, ENOUGH!
WE'RE PUTTING ON BOGU AND STARTING PRACTICE!
YES MA'AM!

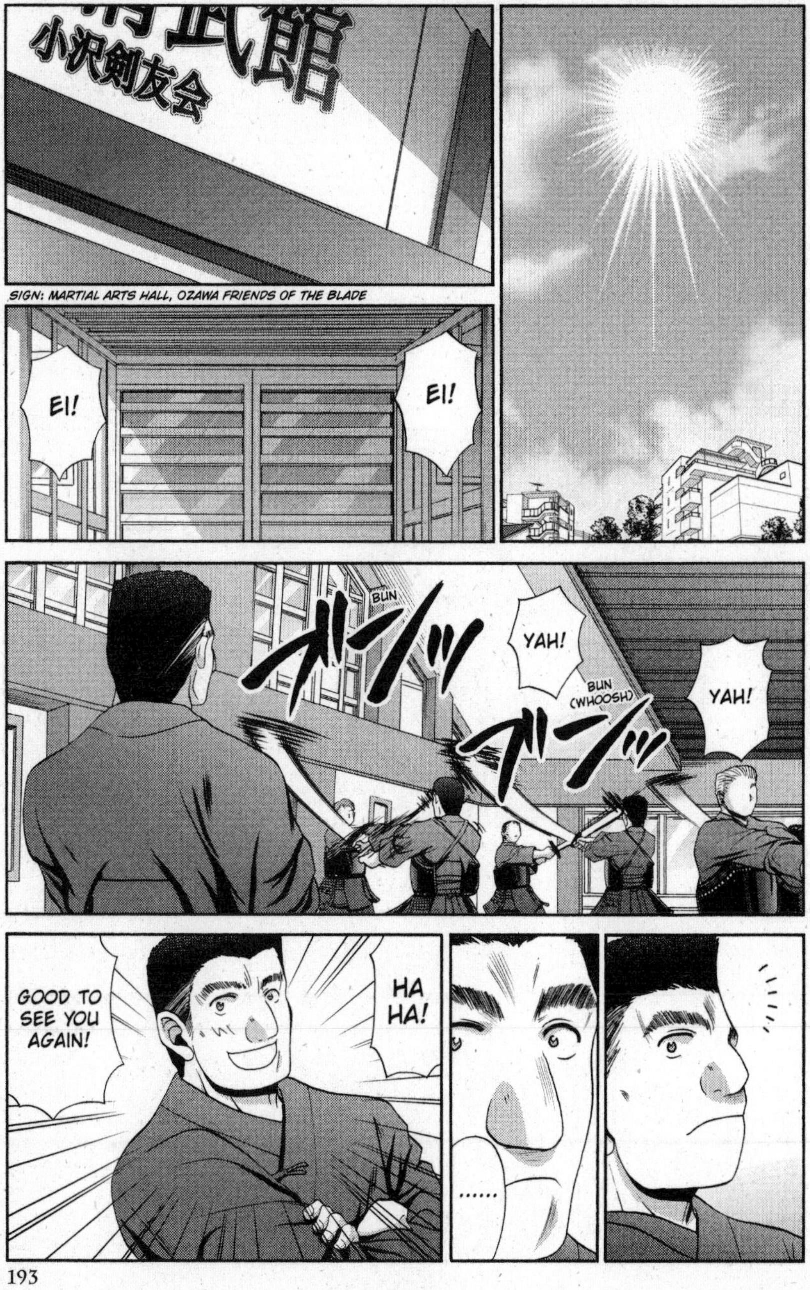
小沢剣友会
SIGN: MARTIAL ARTS HALL, OZAWA FRIENDS OF THE BLADE
EI!
EI!
YAH!
BUN (WHOOSH)
YAH!
BUN
......
HA HA!
GOOD TO SEE YOU AGAIN!

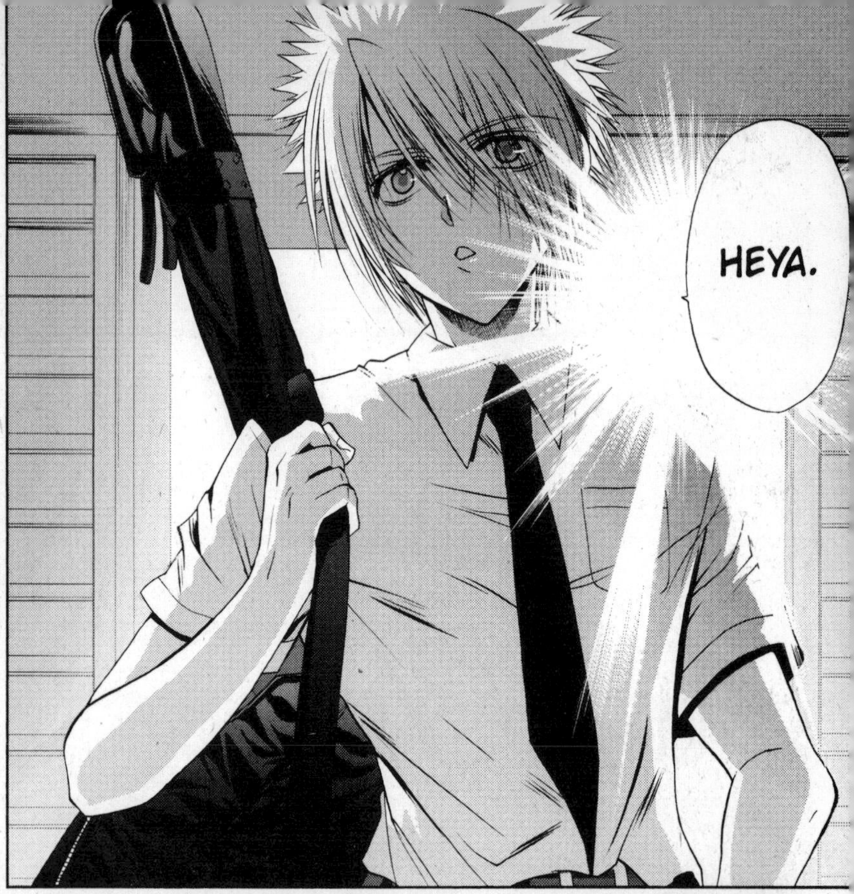
HEYA.
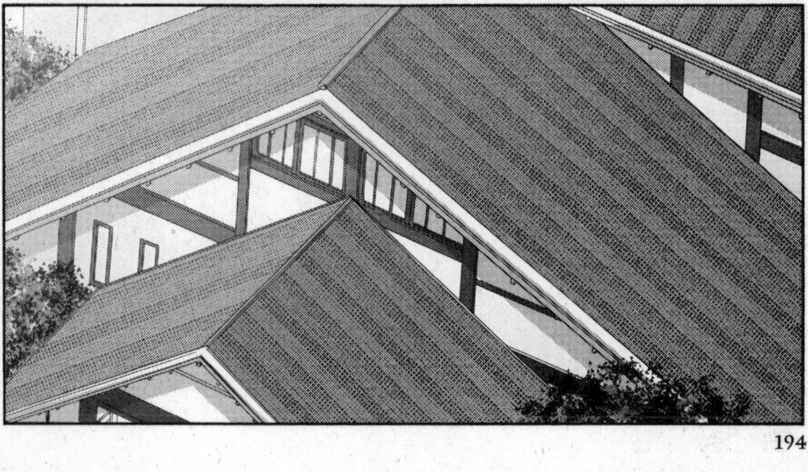

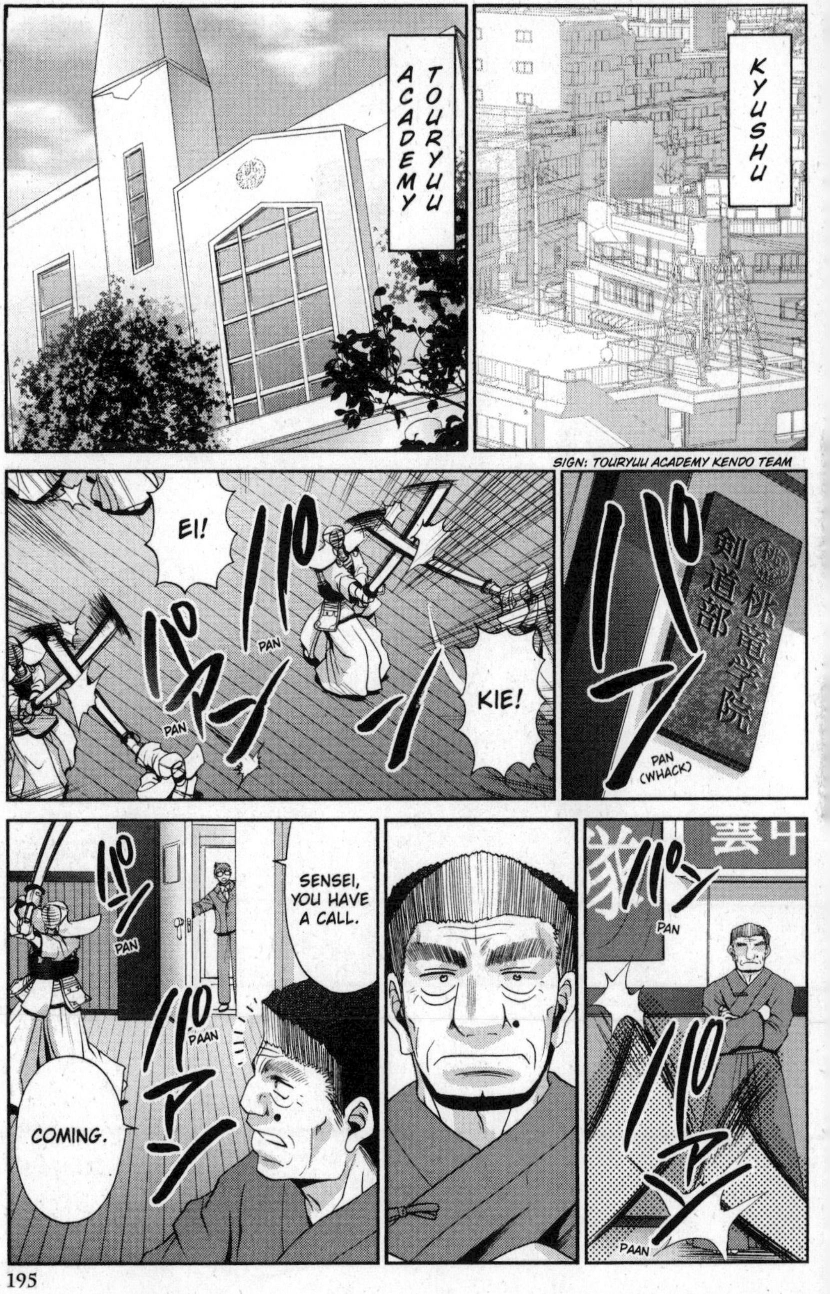
KYUSHU
TOURYUU ACADEMY
SIGN: TOURYUU ACADEMY KENDO TEAM
桃竜学院
剣道部
PAN (WHACK)
EI!
KIE!
PAN
PAN
PAN
PAAN
SENSEI, YOU HAVE A CALL.
PAN
PAAN
COMING.

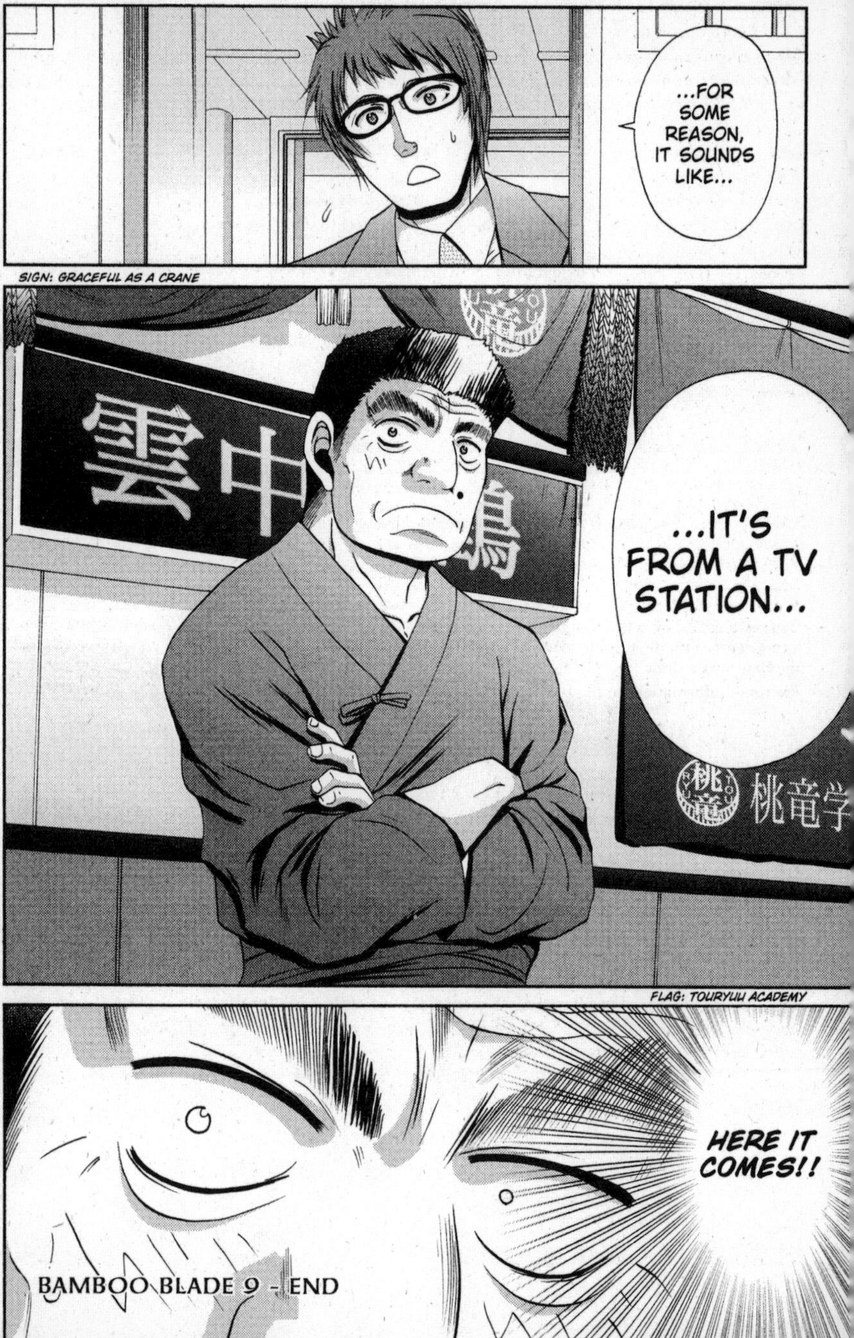
...FOR SOME REASON, IT SOUNDS LIKE...
SIGN: GRACEFUL AS A CRANE
...IT'S FROM A TV STATION...
FLAG: TOURYUU ACADEMY
HERE IT COMES!!
BAMBOO BLADE 9 - END

TRANSLATION NOTES

Common Honorifics

No honorific: Indicates familiarity or closeness; if used without permission or reason, addressing someone in this manner would constitute an insult.

-san: The Japanese equivalent of Mr./Mrs./Miss. If a situation calls for politeness, this is the fail-safe honorific.

-sama: Conveys great respect; may also indicate that the social status of the speaker is lower than that of the addressee.

-kun: Used most often when referring to boys, this indicates affection or familiarity. Occasionally used by older men among their peers, but it may also be used by anyone referring to a person of lower standing.

-chan: An affectionate honorific indicating familiarity used mostly in reference to girls; also used in reference to cute persons or animals of either gender.

-senpai: Used as a suffix or alone to address one's upperclassmen.

kouhai: The opposite of *senpai*, used to address younger schoolmates or team members.

-sensei: A respectful term for teachers, artists, or high-level professionals.

-dono: A polite, formal honorific used to show respect. Uncommon in modern Japanese.

General Notes

Armor: The guards, or *bogu*, worn in kendo all have their own names: The *men* is the helmet and face mask, the *do* is the breastplate, *tare* refers to the hanging plates worn like a belt, and the *kote* are the gauntlets that protect the hands.

Senpo, Jiho, Chuken, Fukusho, Taisho: These are the five ranks that make up a kendo team and determine the order in which the players appear.

Ari: When a point has been scored, the judge will call out the area struck (*men, kote, do*, etc.) and then "*ari*," signifying that a point has been scored in the area named.

Shobu ari: The judge calls "*shobu ari*" when the match is over and one combatant has won.

Scoreboard: The letters indicate on which part of the armor the point was scored. The circled letter denotes the first point scored. "F" stands for "foul," and an "X" across the center line means the bout was a draw.

For more information on the formal rules and workings of kendo, see Volume 2 pages 152-154!

Page 3

Ranks: While *taisho* and *fukusho* mean "great general" and "vice general" respectively, *sansho* means "third general" and *gosho* means "fifth general." Using this numerical pattern, you could theoretically have any number of players in a team, as seen in Satori's list of "25-*sho*, 26-*sho*, etc."

Page 161

Kiyomura-kun: The titular character from *Bamboo Blade* writer Masahiro Totsuka's comedy manga *Kiyomura-kun to Sugi Kouji-kun*.

Page 201

Hachiko: The famous Akita who returned to Shibuya Station at the same time every day to wait for his master, even after the man's death. This display of loyalty struck a chord with the Japanese public, and the statue of Hachiko is a recognizable landmark at one of the five entrances to Shibuya Station.

BAMBOO BLADE
バンブーブレード

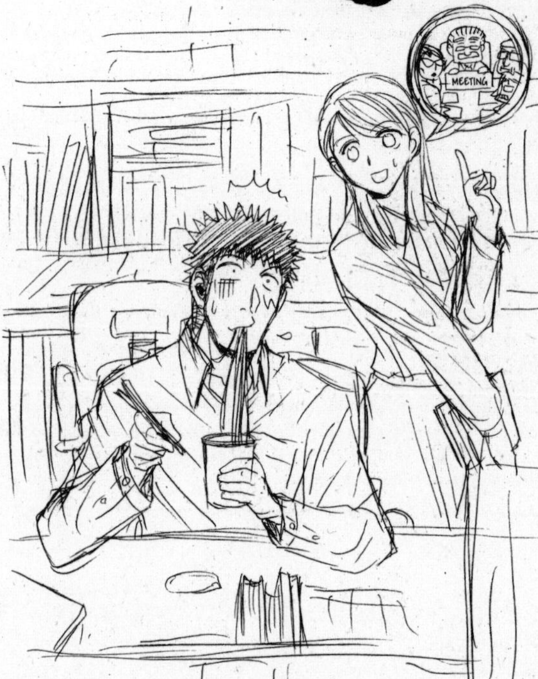
MEETING

OMAKE MANGA THEATER 1

THE KENDO TEAM AND THE SEASON OF HELL

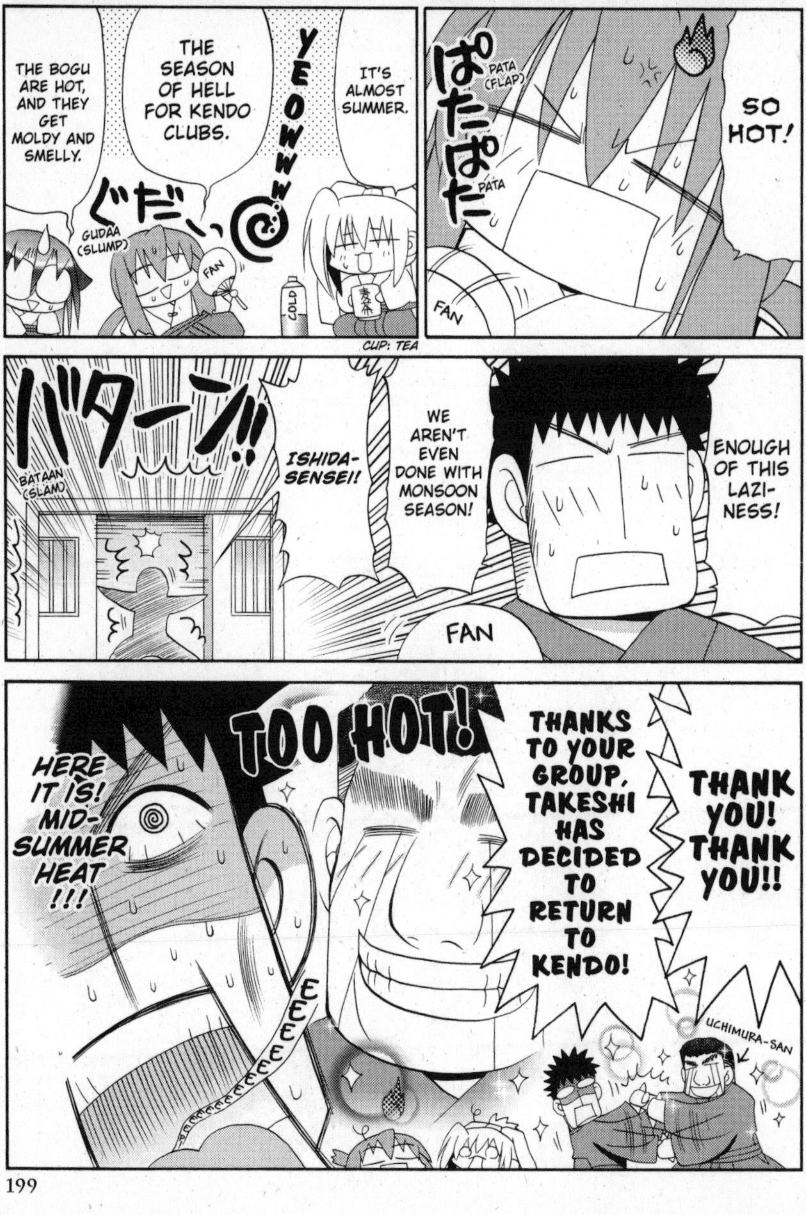
ぱたぱた
PATA (FLAP) PATA
SO HOT!
FAN
IT'S ALMOST SUMMER.
YEOWWWW
THE SEASON OF HELL FOR KENDO CLUBS.
THE BOGU ARE HOT, AND THEY GET MOLDY AND SMELLY.
ぐだ〜
GUDAA (SLUMP)
FAN
COLD
CUP: TEA
ENOUGH OF THIS LAZINESS!
WE AREN'T EVEN DONE WITH MONSOON SEASON!
ISHIDA-SENSEI!!
バターン!!
BATAAN (SLAM)
FAN
THANK YOU! THANK YOU!!
THANKS TO YOUR GROUP, TAKESHI HAS DECIDED TO RETURN TO KENDO!
TOO HOT!
HERE IT IS! MID-SUMMER HEAT!!!
EEEEEEEEEEEEEE
UCHIMURA-SAN

OMAKE MANGA THEATER ❷

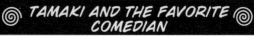

TAMAKI AND THE FAVORITE COMEDIAN

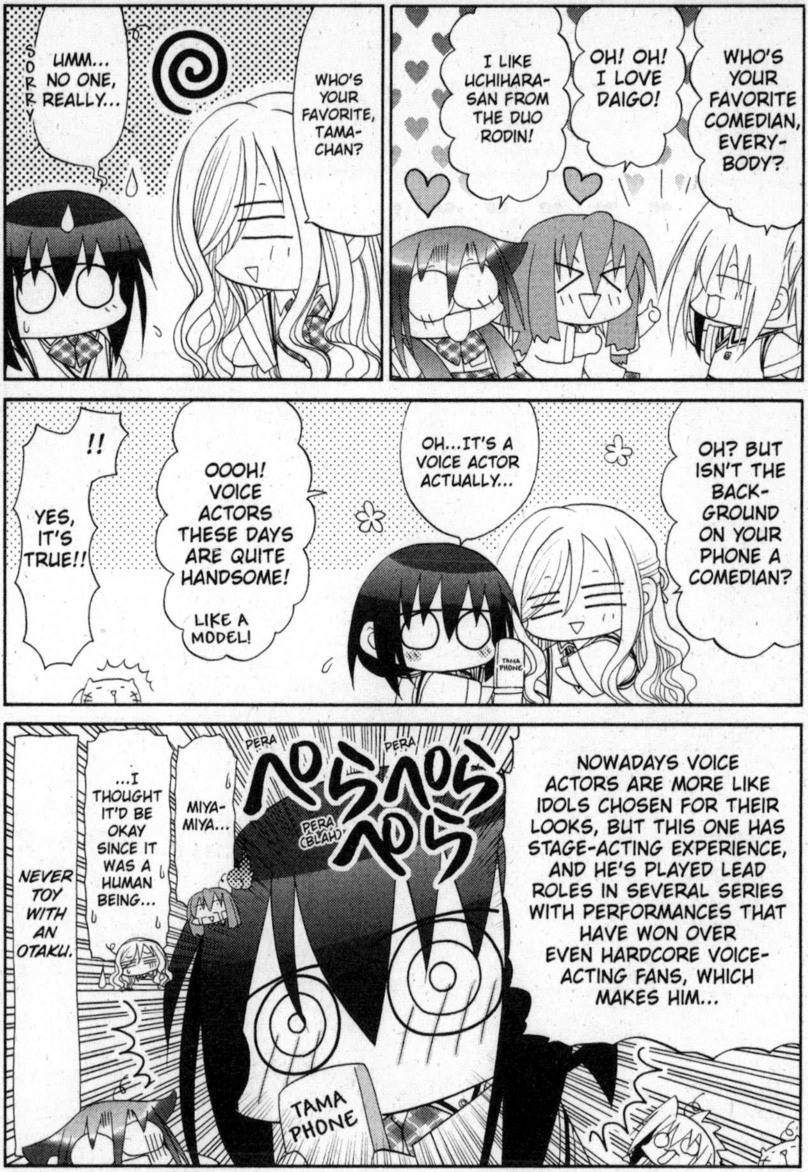

WHO'S YOUR FAVORITE COMEDIAN, EVERYBODY?
OH! OH! I LOVE DAIGO!
I LIKE UCHIHARA-SAN FROM THE DUO RODIN!
WHO'S YOUR FAVORITE, TAMA-CHAN?
UMM... NO ONE, REALLY...
SORRY
OH? BUT ISN'T THE BACK-GROUND ON YOUR PHONE A COMEDIAN?
OH...IT'S A VOICE ACTOR ACTUALLY...
TAMA PHONE
OOOH! VOICE ACTORS THESE DAYS ARE QUITE HANDSOME!
LIKE A MODEL!
!!
YES, IT'S TRUE!!
NOWADAYS VOICE ACTORS ARE MORE LIKE IDOLS CHOSEN FOR THEIR LOOKS, BUT THIS ONE HAS STAGE-ACTING EXPERIENCE, AND HE'S PLAYED LEAD ROLES IN SEVERAL SERIES WITH PERFORMANCES THAT HAVE WON OVER EVEN HARDCORE VOICE-ACTING FANS, WHICH MAKES HIM...
ぺらぺらぺら
PERA PERA
PERA (BLAH)
TAMA PHONE
MIYA-MIYA...
...I THOUGHT IT'D BE OKAY SINCE IT WAS A HUMAN BEING...
NEVER TOY WITH AN OTAKU.

OMAKE MANGA THEATER 3

MUROE MEMBERS AND THEIR BIRD MODELS

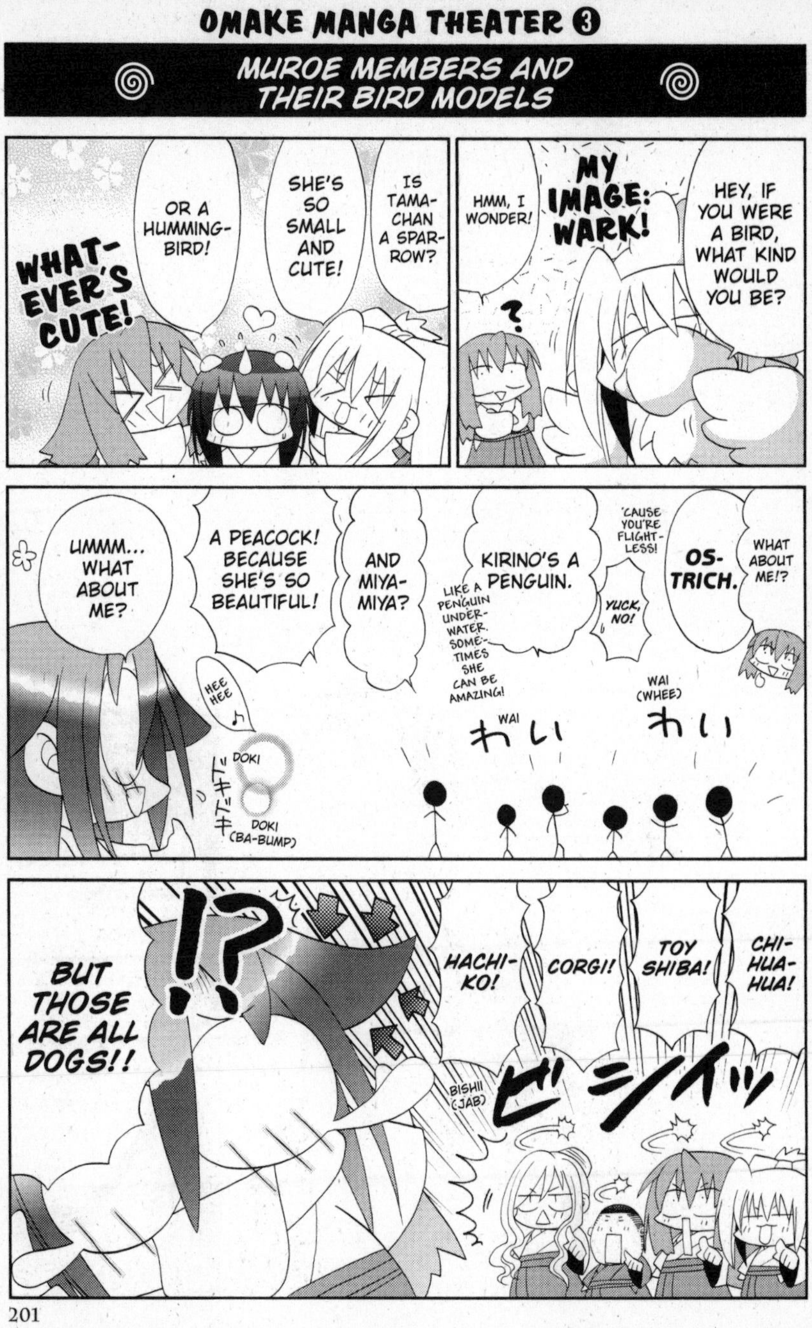
HEY, IF YOU WERE A BIRD, WHAT KIND WOULD YOU BE?
MY IMAGE: WARK!
HMM, I WONDER!
?
IS TAMA-CHAN A SPARROW?
SHE'S SO SMALL AND CUTE!
OR A HUMMING-BIRD!
WHAT-EVER'S CUTE!
WHAT ABOUT ME!?
OS-TRICH.
'CAUSE YOU'RE FLIGHT-LESS!
YUCK, NO!
KIRINO'S A PENGUIN.
LIKE A PENGUIN UNDER-WATER. SOME-TIMES SHE CAN BE AMAZING!
AND MIYA-MIYA?
A PEACOCK! BECAUSE SHE'S SO BEAUTIFUL!
わい
WAI (WHEE)
わい
WAI
HEE HEE ♪
UMMM... WHAT ABOUT ME?
ドキドキ
DOKI
DOKI (BA-BUMP)
CHI-HUA-HUA!
TOY SHIBA!
CORGI!
HACHI-KO!
ビシイッ
BISHII (JAB)
!?
BUT THOSE ARE ALL DOGS!!

AFTERWORD

AS YOU SAW FROM READING THIS VOLUME, THE CONCEPT IS DIFFERENT FROM THE USUAL *BAMBOO BLADE* THIS TIME AROUND.

THIS IS THE STORY OF A GROUP OF GIRLS AND THE MAN WHO TEACHES THEM, SO I'VE TENDED TO IGNORE STORIES ABOUT THE BOYS. I THINK THIS IS PRETTY OBVIOUS IF YOU LOOK AT THE WAY I'VE TREATED YUJI, DAN, TOYAMA, AND IWASA.

I'VE DRAWN PLENTY OF BOYS IN MY OTHER SERIES, ESPECIALLY IN *MATERIAL PUZZLE*, SO I DON'T USUALLY FEEL THE NEED TO INCLUDE THEM HERE.

BUT I REALLY WANTED TO COVER IWAHORI'S STORY, SO I SWITCHED UP MY USUAL CONCEIT THIS ONE TIME. SORRY FOLKS—I WON'T DO IT AGAIN.

HOWEVER, TRYING THIS EXPERIMENT MADE ME WANT TO DO MORE STORIES ABOUT BOYS PRACTICING KENDO, SO I'M GOING TO TRY TWEAKING A FEW MORE IDEAS. IT WOULD BE NICE IF I COULD START A SIDE STORY TO *BAMBOO BLADE*. A SPIN-OFF, SO TO SPEAK. I'D PROBABLY WANT TO MAKE THEM YOUNGER—MIDDLE SCHOOL AGE—AND RUN IT IN A SHOUNEN MAGAZINE.

IN OTHER WORDS, GIVE ME MORE WORK.

SO, STARTING NEXT VOLUME, WE'LL BE TACKLING THE CONFRONTATION WITH URA SAKAKI HEAD-ON. THERE WILL BE PLENTY OF NEW CHARACTERS. THIS WILL BE THE LARGEST PIECE OF THE STORY. HOPE YOU LIKE IT!

MASAHIRO TOTSUKA

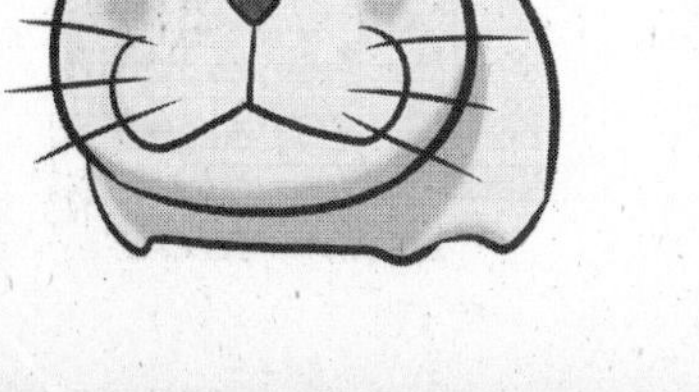

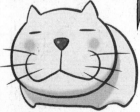

SYMBOL: CAGE

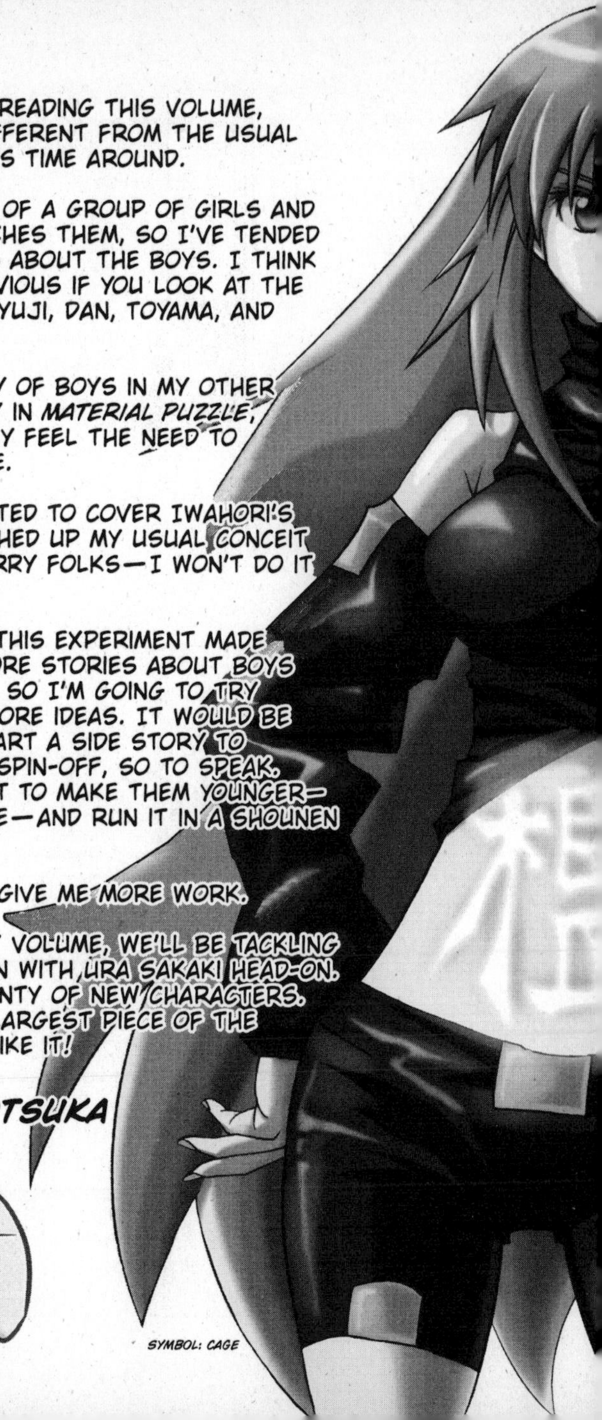

BACKSTAGE AFTERWORD

DRAWN BY ARTIST

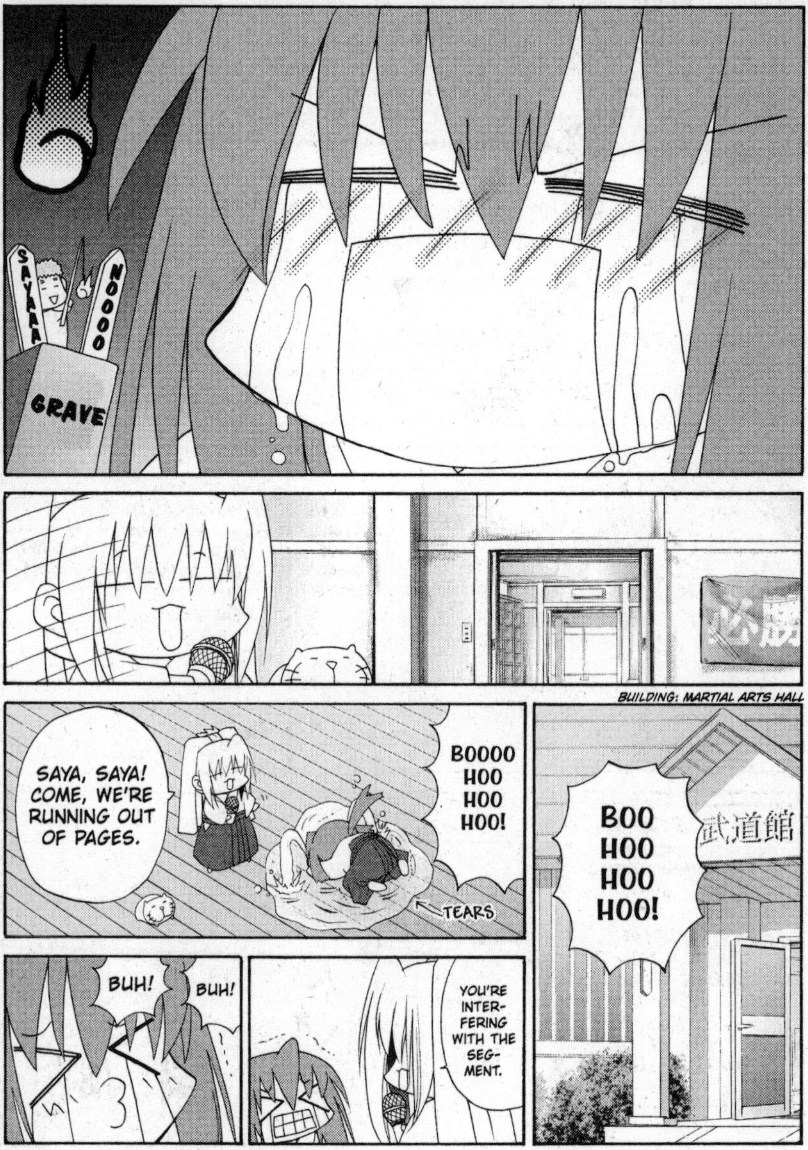
NOOOO
SAYAAA
GRAVE
BUILDING: MARTIAL ARTS HALL
武道館
BOO HOO HOO HOO!
BOOOO HOO HOO HOO!
SAYA, SAYA! COME, WE'RE RUNNING OUT OF PAGES.
TEARS
YOU'RE INTER-FERING WITH THE SEG-MENT.
BUH!
BUH!

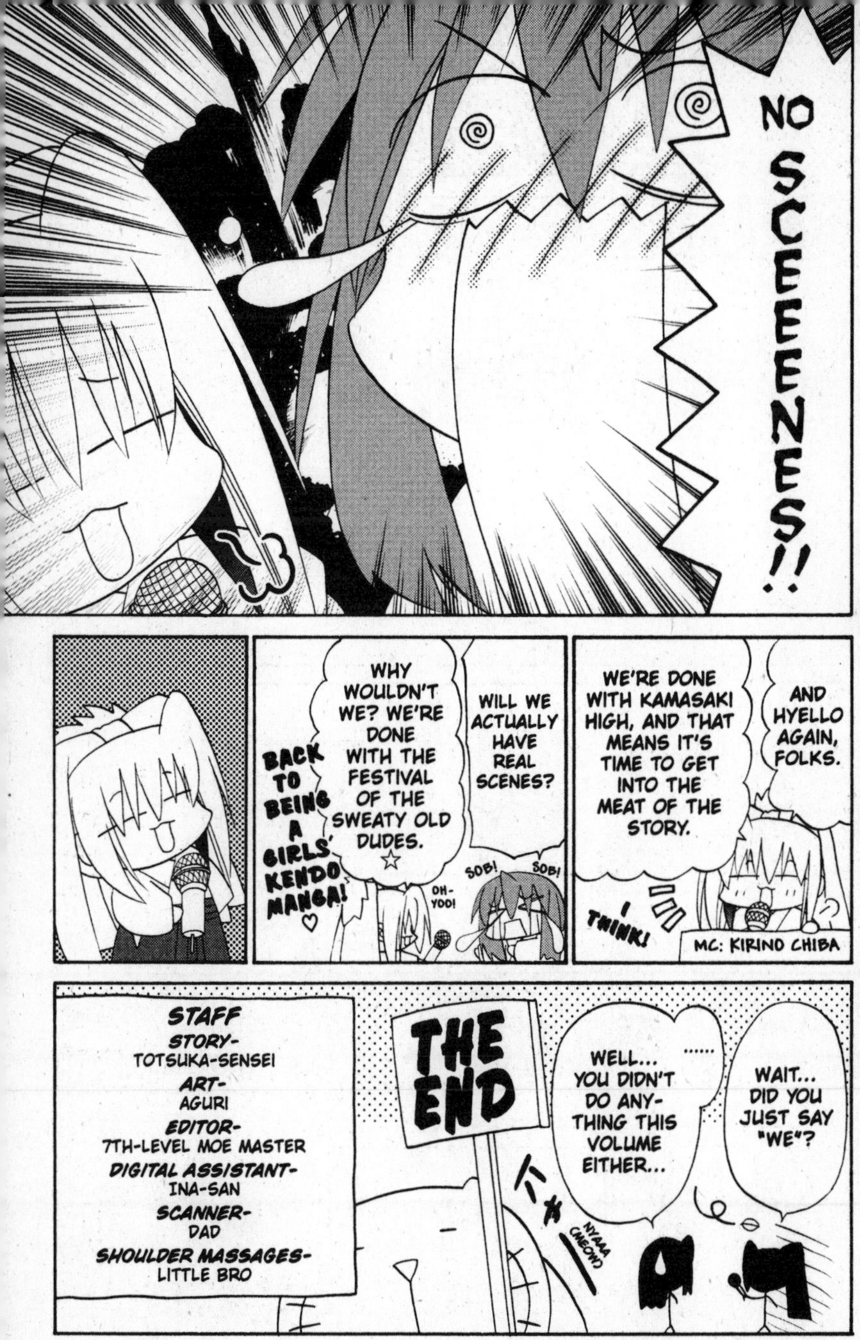
NO SCEEENES!!
AND HYELLO AGAIN, FOLKS.
WE'RE DONE WITH KAMASAKI HIGH, AND THAT MEANS IT'S TIME TO GET INTO THE MEAT OF THE STORY.
I THINK!
MC: KIRINO CHIBA
WILL WE ACTUALLY HAVE REAL SCENES?
WHY WOULDN'T WE? WE'RE DONE WITH THE FESTIVAL OF THE SWEATY OLD DUDES. ☆
BACK TO BEING A GIRLS' KENDO MANGA! ♡
SOB! SOB!
OH-YOO!
WAIT... DID YOU JUST SAY "WE"?
......
WELL... YOU DIDN'T DO ANYTHING THIS VOLUME EITHER...
THE END
NYAAA (MEOW)
STAFF
STORY-
TOTSUKA-SENSEI
ART-
AGURI
EDITOR-
7TH-LEVEL MOE MASTER
DIGITAL ASSISTANT-
INA-SAN
SCANNER-
DAD
SHOULDER MASSAGES-
LITTLE BRO

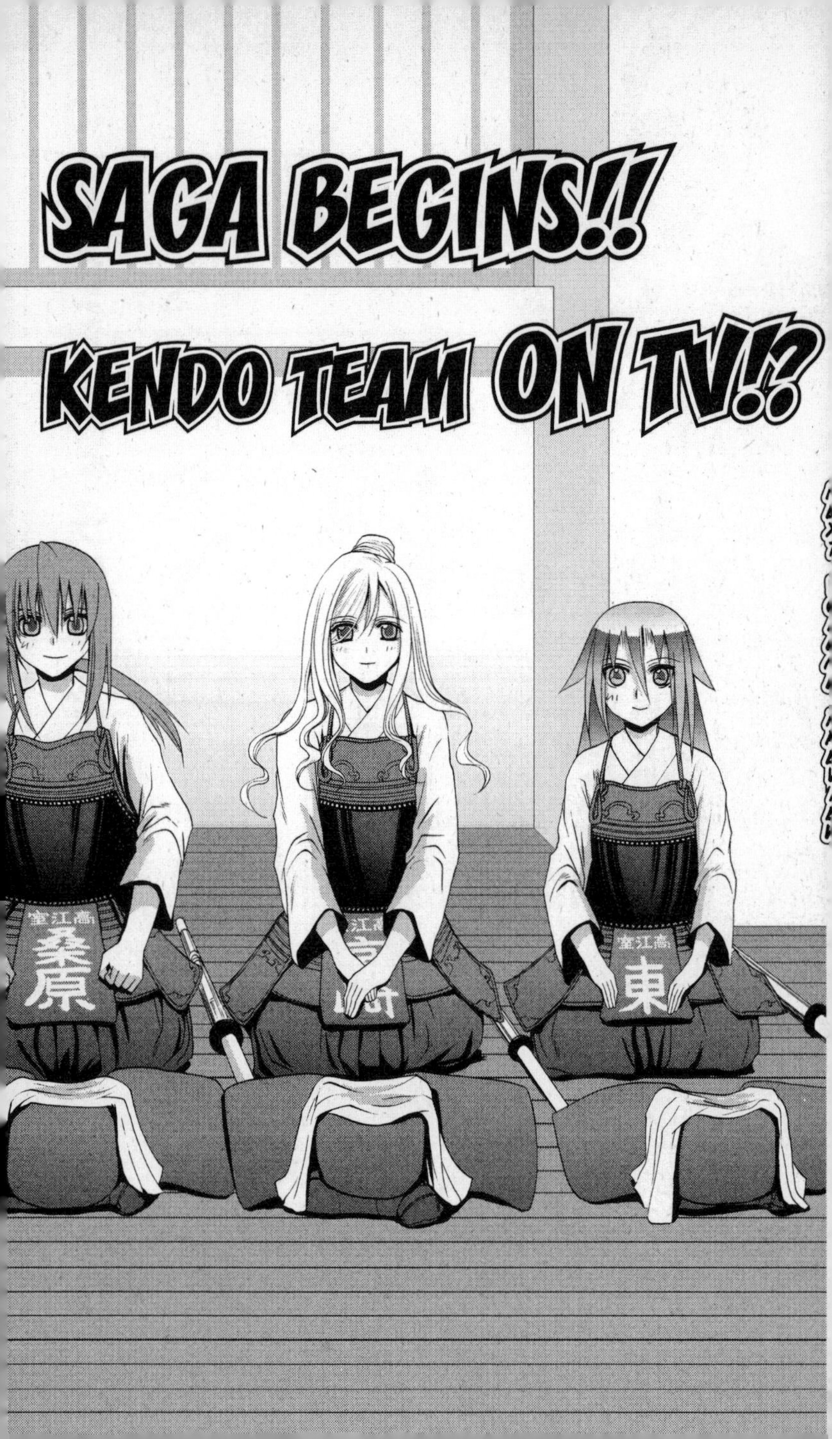
SAGA BEGINS!!
KENDO TEAM ON TV!?
室江高
桑原
室江高
東

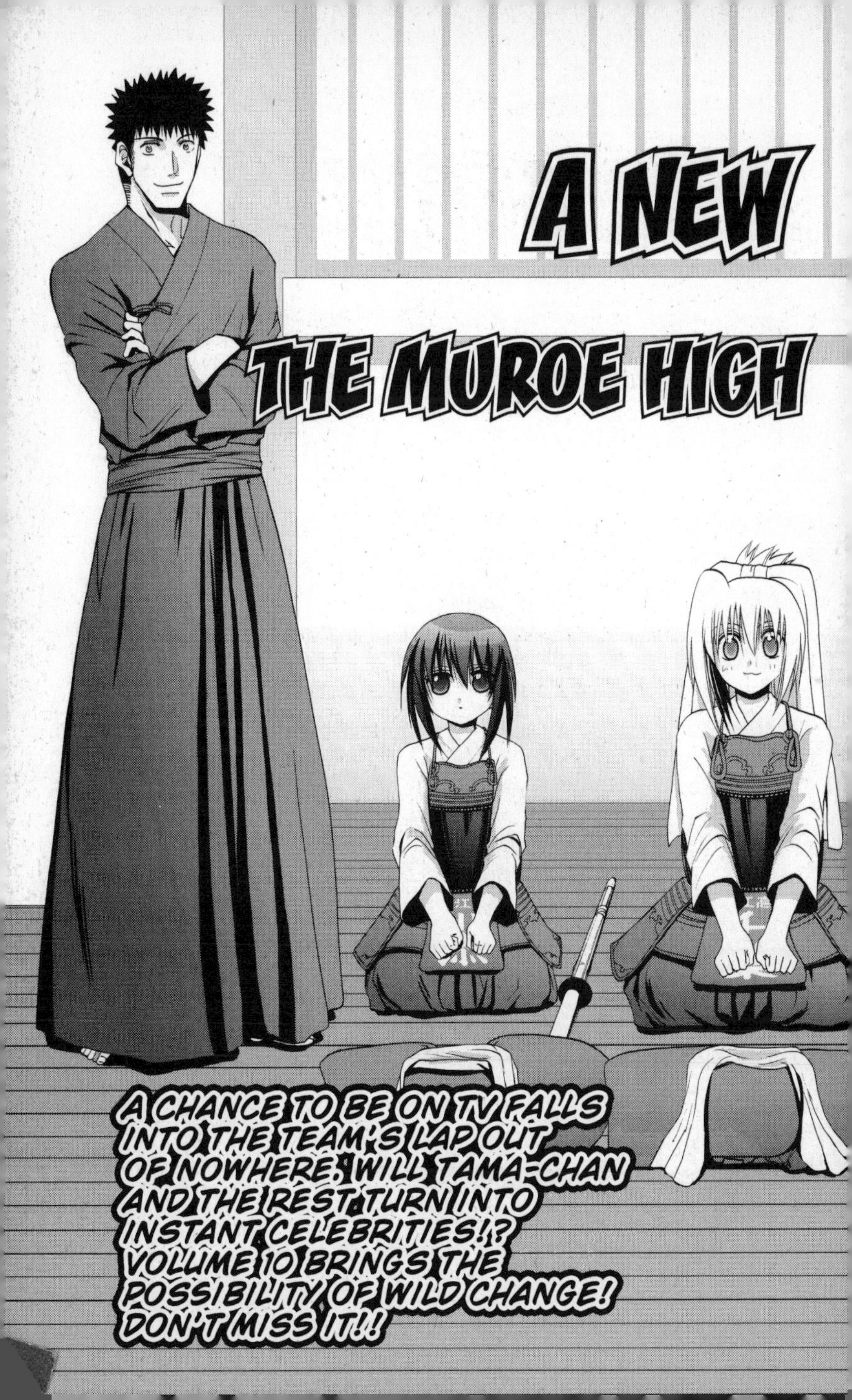
A NEW
THE MUROE HIGH
A CHANCE TO BE ON TV FALLS INTO THE TEAM'S LAP OUT OF NOWHERE. WILL TAMA-CHAN AND THE REST TURN INTO INSTANT CELEBRITIES!? VOLUME 10 BRINGS THE POSSIBILITY OF WILD CHANGE! DON'T MISS IT!!

BAMBOO BLADE ⑨

MASAHIRO TOTSUKA
AGURI IGARASHI

Translation: Stephen Paul

Lettering: Terri Delgado

Yen Press
Hachette Book Group
237 Park Avenue, New York, NY 10017

www.HachetteBookGroup.com
www.YenPress.com

Yen Press is an imprint of Hachette Book Group, Inc. The Yen Press name and logo are trademarks of Hachette Book Group, Inc.

First Yen Press Edition: June 2011

ISBN: 978-0-316-18410-6

10 9 8 7 6 5 4 3 2 1

BVG

Printed in the United States of America